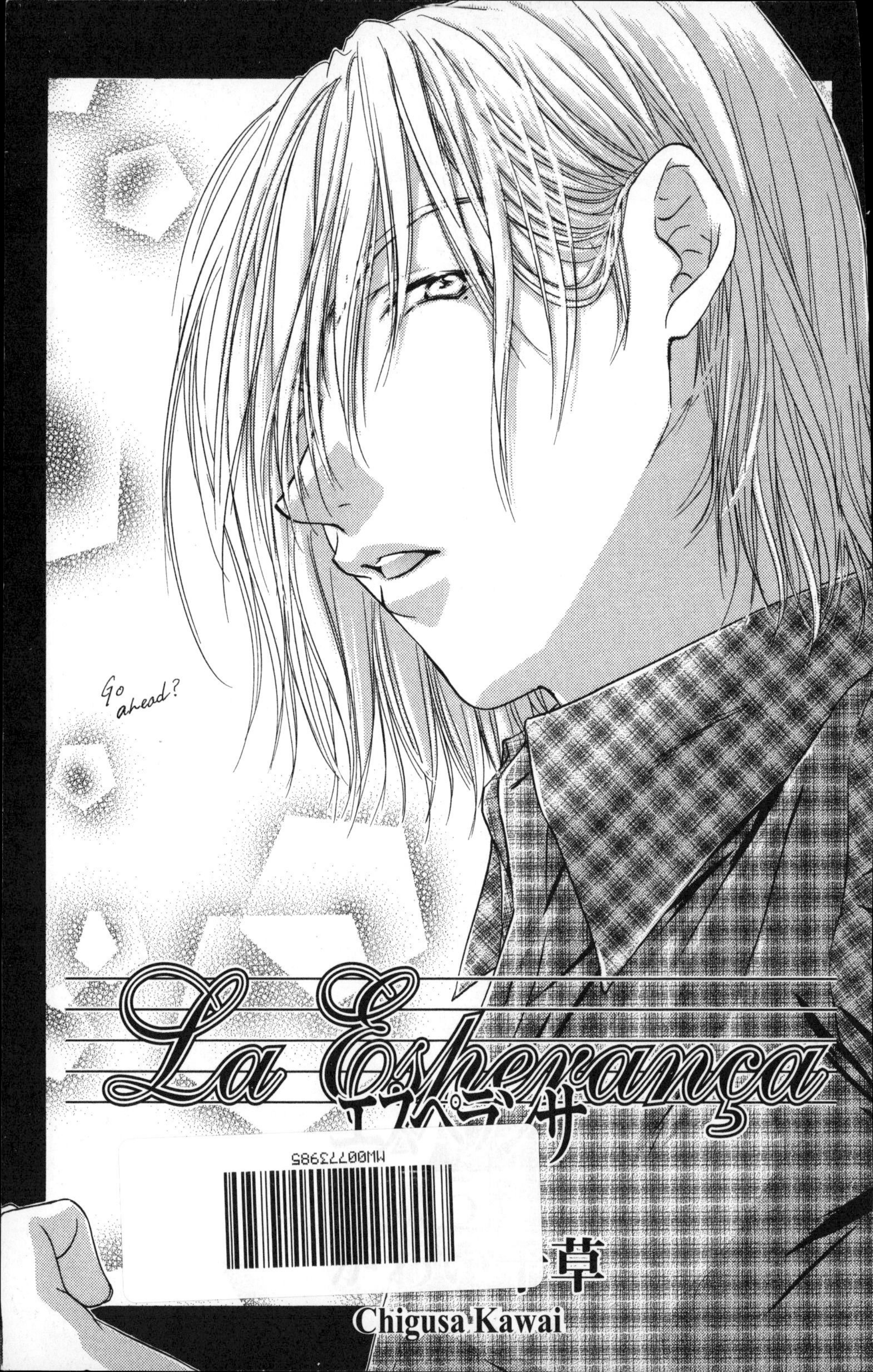
Go ahead?
La Esperança
Chigusa Kawai

La Esperança

5

Translation	Sachiko Sato
Lettering	Replibooks
Graphic Design	Fred Lui
Editing	Stephanie Donnelly
Editor in Chief	Fred Lui
Publisher	Hikaru Sasahara

English Edition Published by
DIGITAL MANGA PUBLISHING
A division of DIGITAL MANGA, Inc.
1487 W 178th Street, Suite 300
Gardena, CA 90248

www.dmpbooks.com

First Edition: November 2006
ISBN: 1-56970-929-7

1 3 5 7 9 10 8 6 4 2

Printed in China

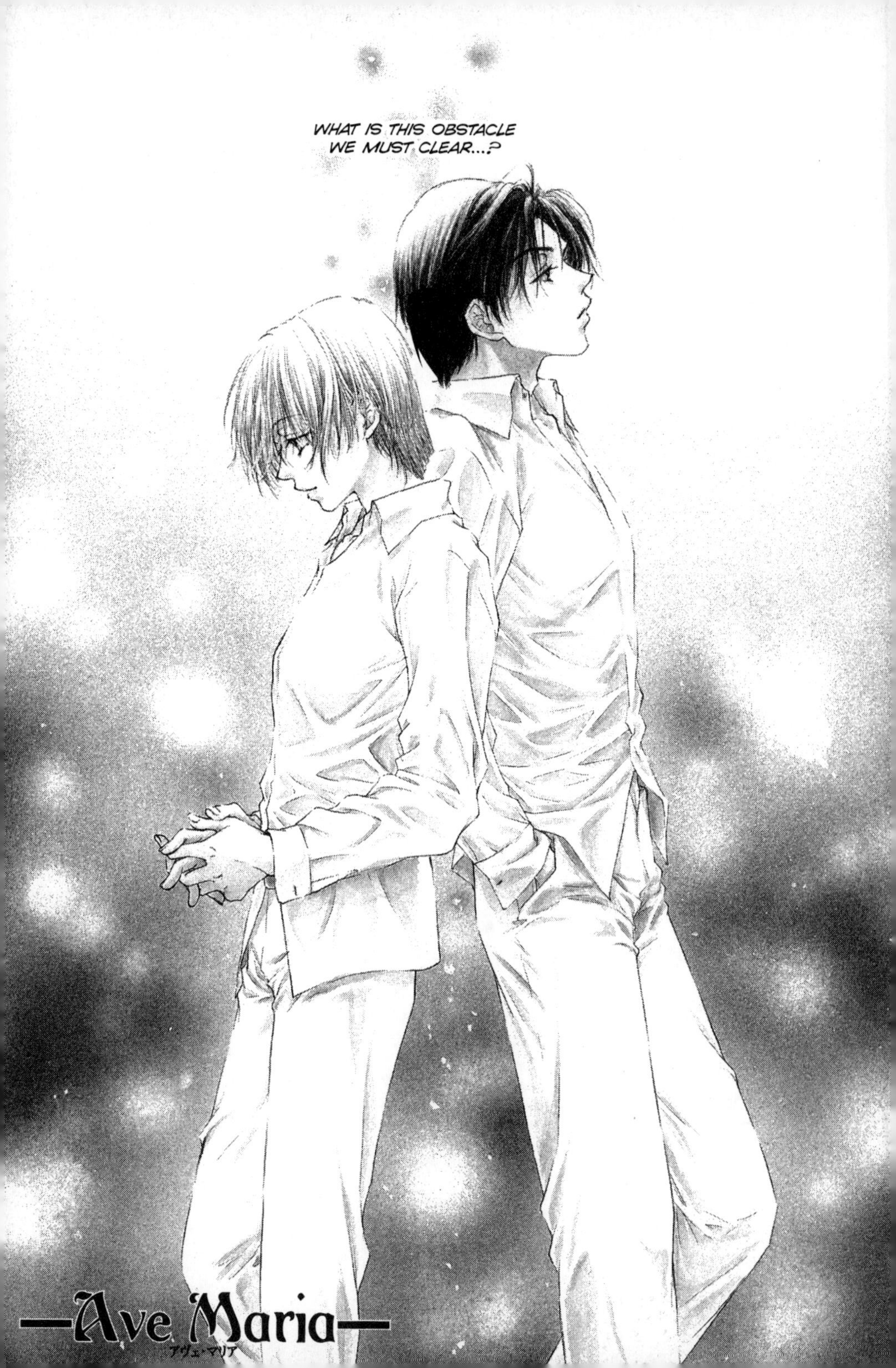
WHAT IS THIS OBSTACLE WE MUST CLEAR...?
—Ave Maria—
アヴェ・マリア

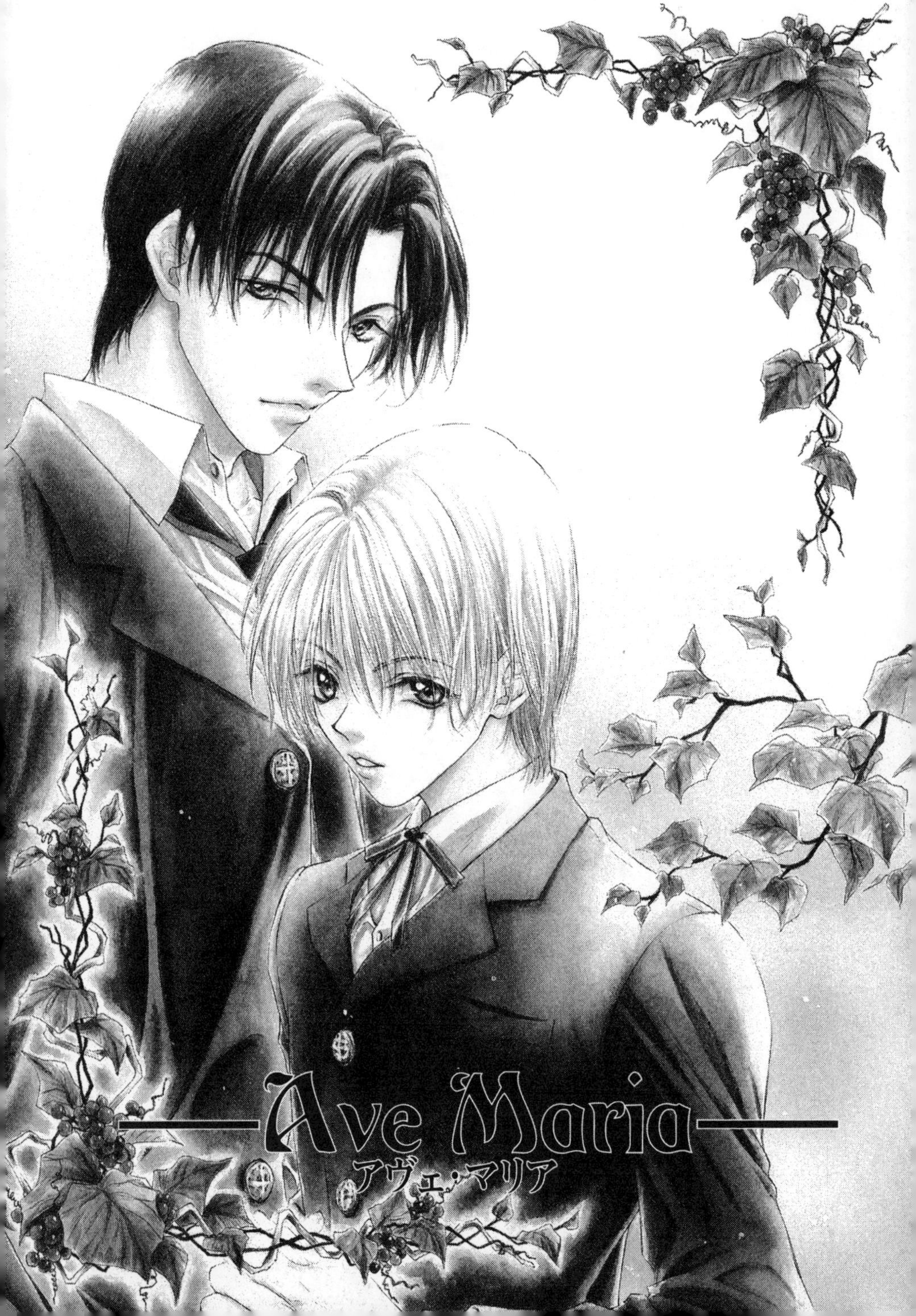
Ave Maria
アヴェ・マリア

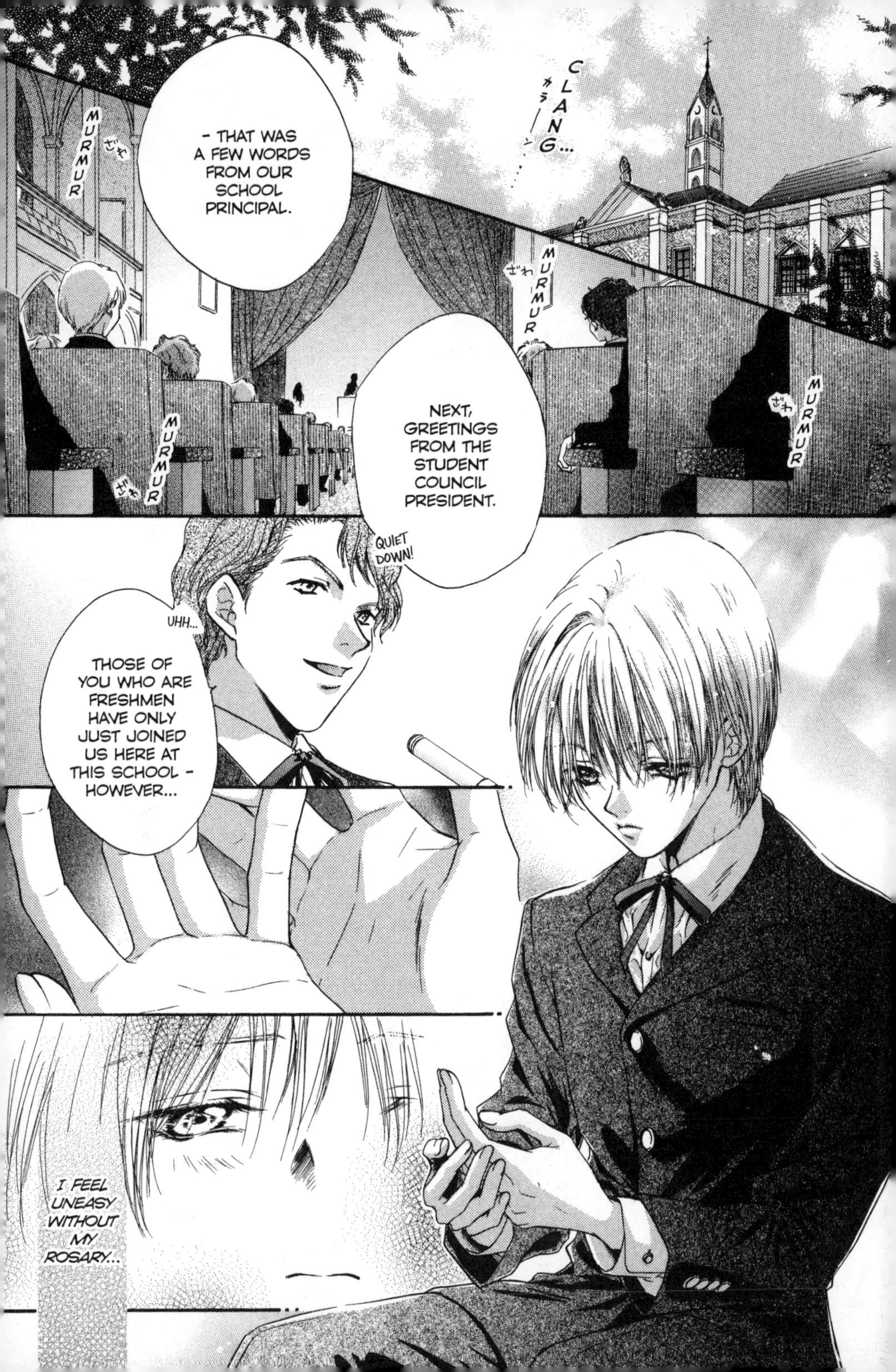

CLANG...
- THAT WAS A FEW WORDS FROM OUR SCHOOL PRINCIPAL.
MURMUR
MURMUR
MURMUR
MURMUR
NEXT, GREETINGS FROM THE STUDENT COUNCIL PRESIDENT.
QUIET DOWN!
UHH...
THOSE OF YOU WHO ARE FRESHMEN HAVE ONLY JUST JOINED US HERE AT THIS SCHOOL - HOWEVER...
I FEEL UNEASY WITHOUT MY ROSARY...

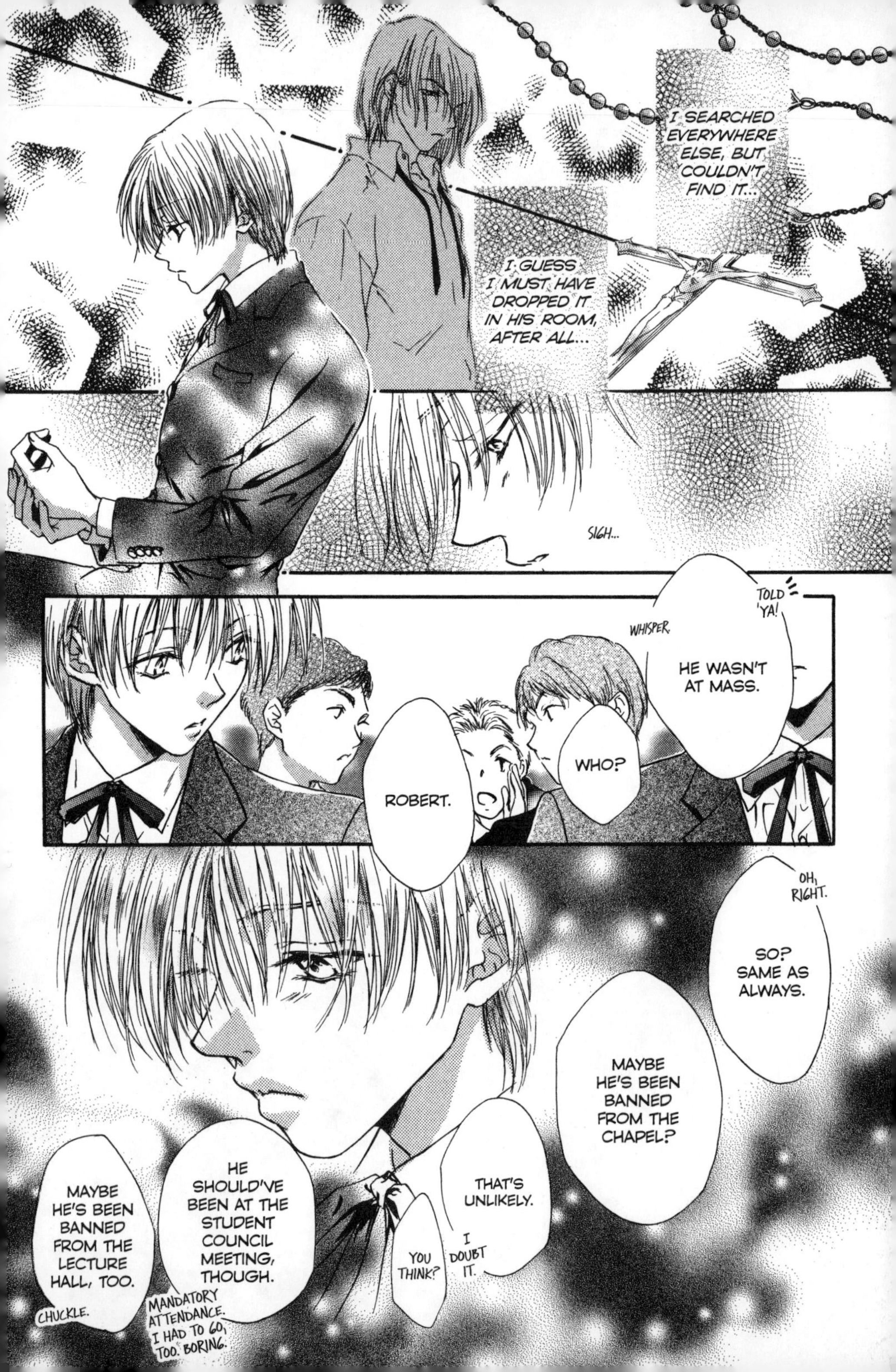
I SEARCHED EVERYWHERE ELSE, BUT COULDN'T FIND IT...
I GUESS I MUST HAVE DROPPED IT IN HIS ROOM, AFTER ALL...
SIGH...
TOLD 'YA!
WHISPER.
HE WASN'T AT MASS.
WHO?
ROBERT.
OH, RIGHT.
SO? SAME AS ALWAYS.
MAYBE HE'S BEEN BANNED FROM THE CHAPEL?
THAT'S UNLIKELY.
I DOUBT IT.
YOU THINK?
HE SHOULD'VE BEEN AT THE STUDENT COUNCIL MEETING, THOUGH.
MANDATORY ATTENDANCE. I HAD TO GO, TOO. BORING.
MAYBE HE'S BEEN BANNED FROM THE LECTURE HALL, TOO.
CHUCKLE.

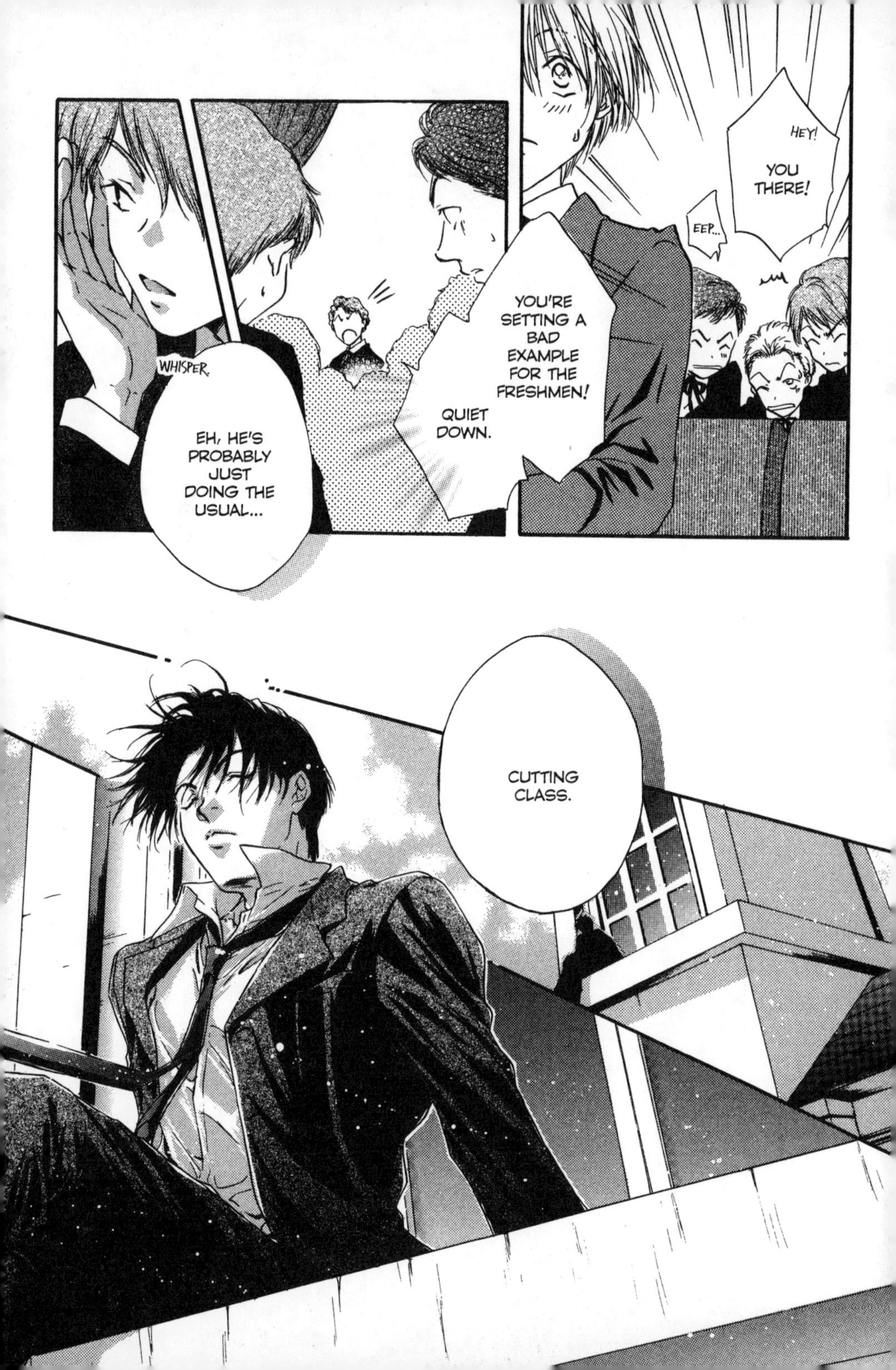
HEY!
YOU THERE!
EEP...
YOU'RE SETTING A BAD EXAMPLE FOR THE FRESHMEN!
QUIET DOWN.
WHISPER.
EH, HE'S PROBABLY JUST DOING THE USUAL...
CUTTING CLASS.

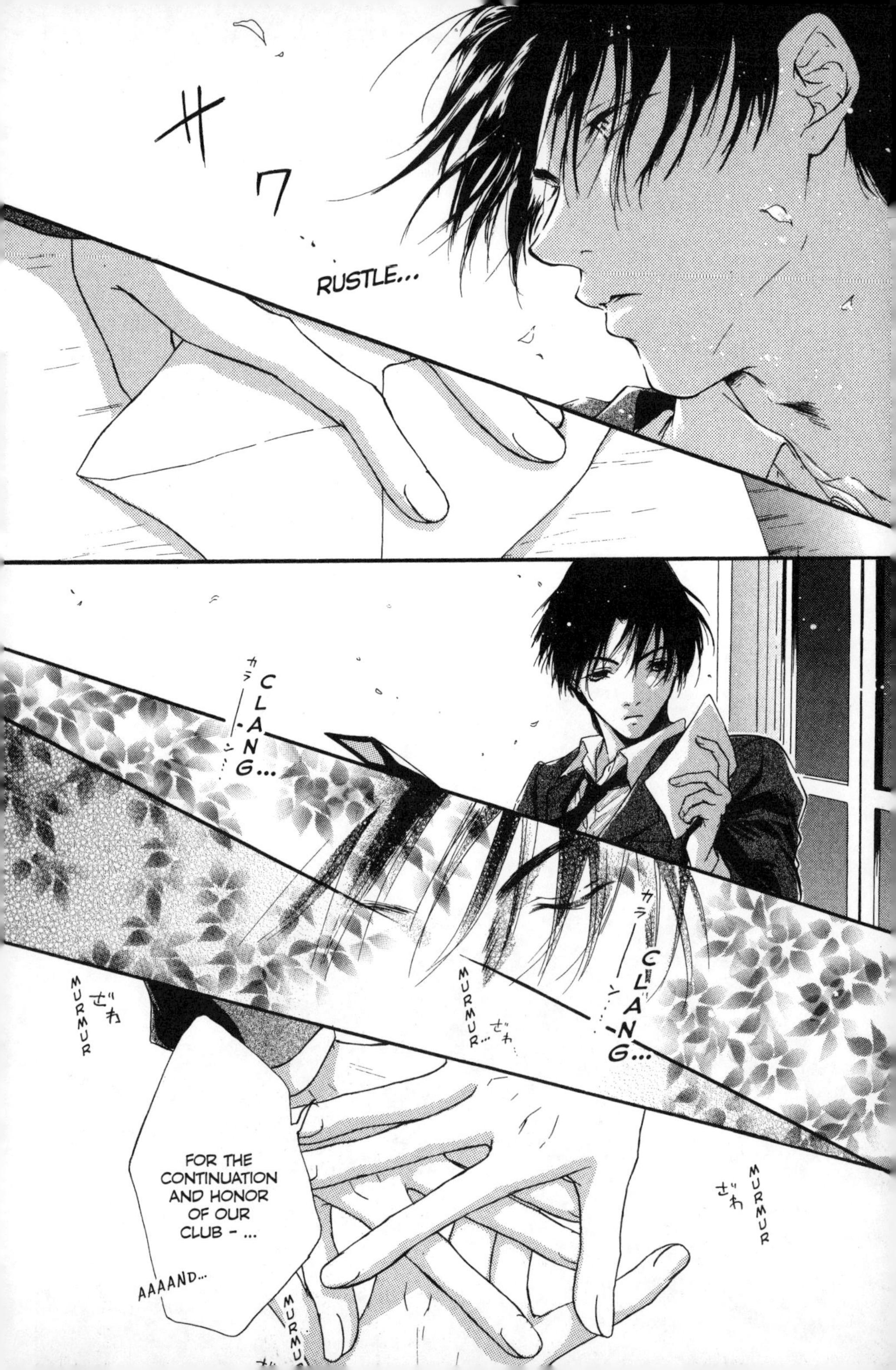

サワ
RUSTLE...
カラ
CLANG...
カラ
CLANG...
MURMUR... ざわ...
ざわ MURMUR
FOR THE CONTINUATION AND HONOR OF OUR CLUB - ...
AAAAND...
MURMUR ざわ

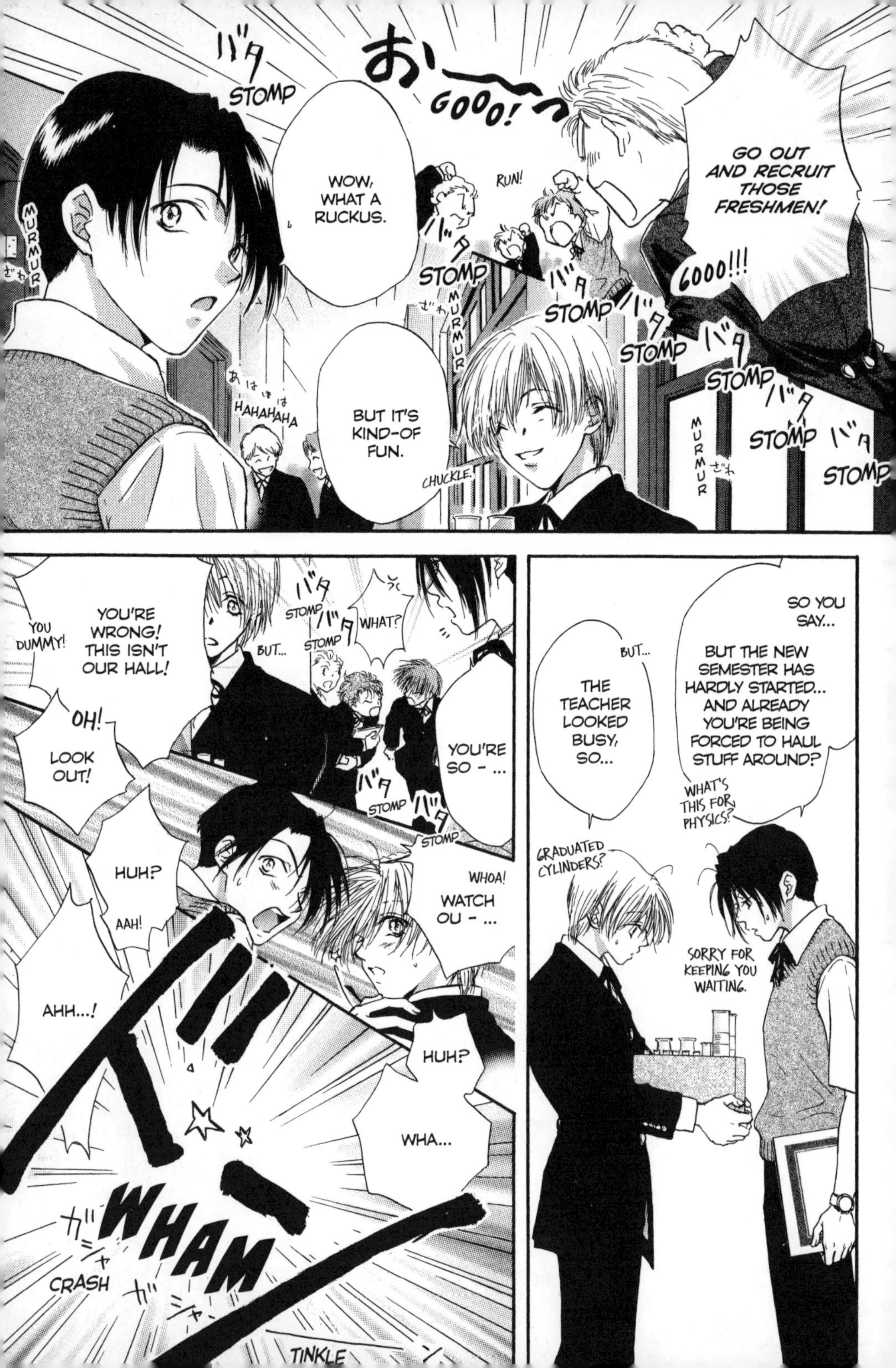

おー
GOOO!
GO OUT AND RECRUIT THOSE FRESHMEN!
GOOO!!!
STOMP
STOMP
STOMP
STOMP
STOMP
MURMUR
RUN!
STOMP
STOMP
WOW, WHAT A RUCKUS.
MURMUR
BUT IT'S KIND-OF FUN.
CHUCKLE.
HAHAHAHA
MURMUR
SO YOU SAY...
BUT THE NEW SEMESTER HAS HARDLY STARTED... AND ALREADY YOU'RE BEING FORCED TO HAUL STUFF AROUND?
BUT...
THE TEACHER LOOKED BUSY, SO...
WHAT'S THIS FOR, PHYSICS?
GRADUATED CYLINDERS?
SORRY FOR KEEPING YOU WAITING.
WHAT?
STOMP
STOMP
YOU'RE SO - ...
BUT...
YOU'RE WRONG! THIS ISN'T OUR HALL!
YOU DUMMY!
OH!
LOOK OUT!
STOMP
STOMP
WHOA!
WATCH OU - ...
HUH?
AAH!
AHH...!
HUH?
WHA...
WHAM
CRASH
TINKLE

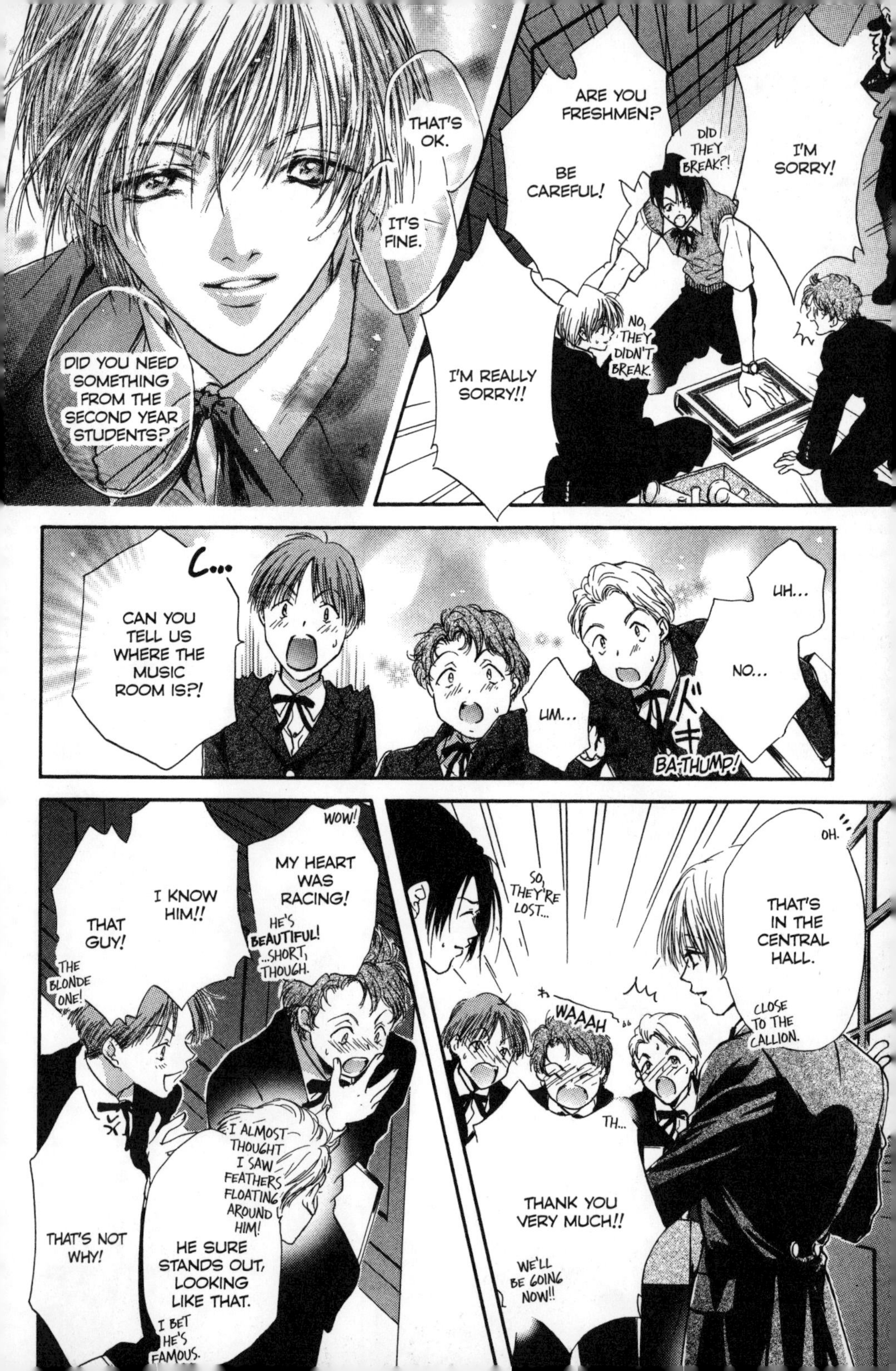

I'M SORRY!
DID THEY BREAK?!
ARE YOU FRESHMEN?
BE CAREFUL!
NO, THEY DIDN'T BREAK.
I'M REALLY SORRY!!
THAT'S OK.
IT'S FINE.
DID YOU NEED SOMETHING FROM THE SECOND YEAR STUDENTS?
UH...
NO...
BA-THUMP!
UM...
C...
CAN YOU TELL US WHERE THE MUSIC ROOM IS?!
OH.
THAT'S IN THE CENTRAL HALL.
CLOSE TO THE CALLION.
SO, THEY'RE LOST...
WAAAH
TH...
THANK YOU VERY MUCH!!
WE'LL BE GOING NOW!!
WOW!
MY HEART WAS RACING!
HE'S BEAUTIFUL! ...SHORT, THOUGH.
I KNOW HIM!!
THAT GUY!
THE BLONDE ONE!
I ALMOST THOUGHT I SAW FEATHERS FLOATING AROUND HIM!
HE SURE STANDS OUT, LOOKING LIKE THAT.
THAT'S NOT WHY!
I BET HE'S FAMOUS.

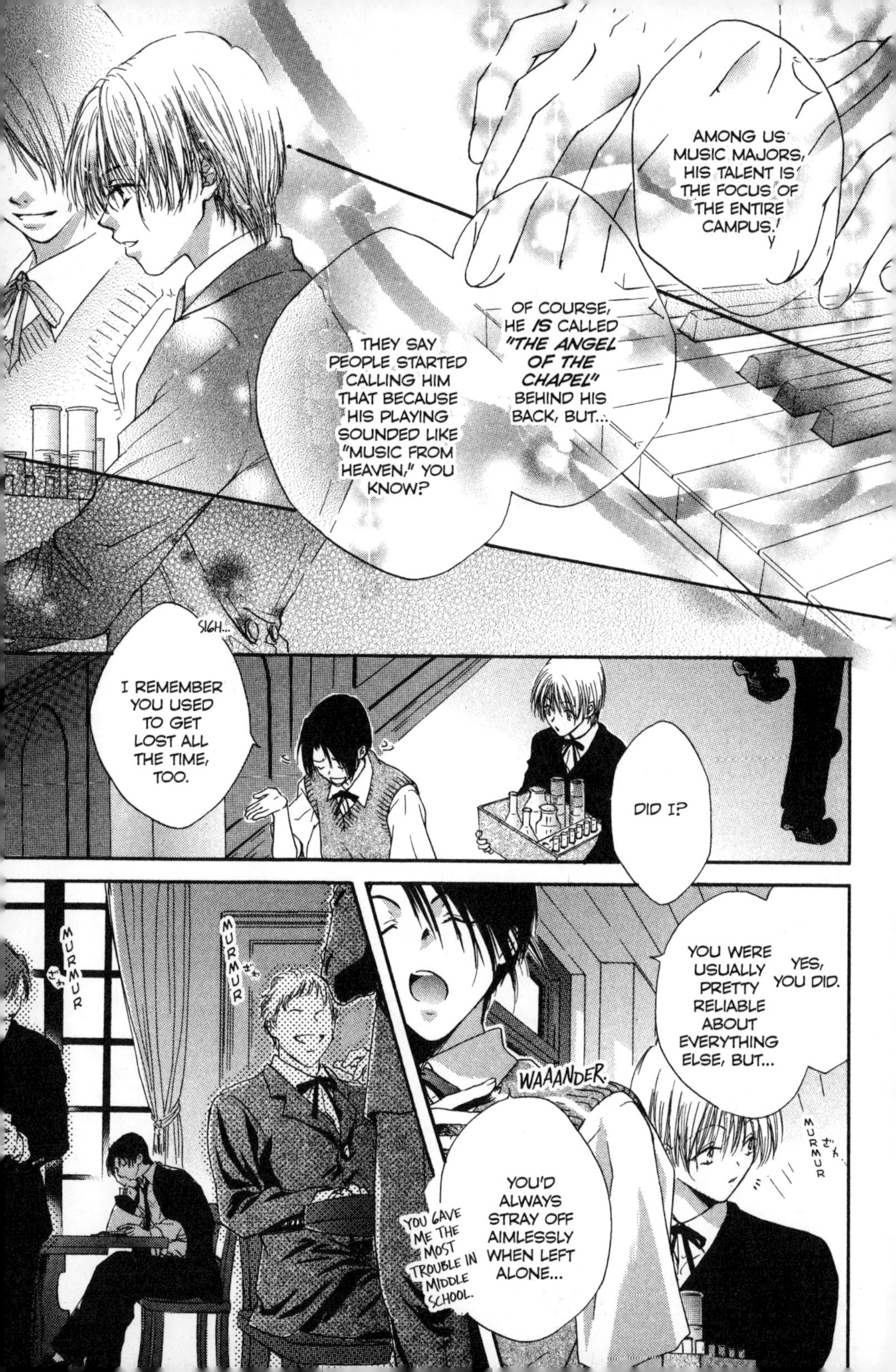
AMONG US MUSIC MAJORS, HIS TALENT IS THE FOCUS OF THE ENTIRE CAMPUS.
OF COURSE, HE *IS* CALLED **"THE ANGEL OF THE CHAPEL"** BEHIND HIS BACK, BUT...
THEY SAY PEOPLE STARTED CALLING HIM THAT BECAUSE HIS PLAYING SOUNDED LIKE "MUSIC FROM HEAVEN," YOU KNOW?
SIGH...
I REMEMBER YOU USED TO GET LOST ALL THE TIME, TOO.
DID I?
YES, YOU DID.
YOU WERE USUALLY PRETTY RELIABLE ABOUT EVERYTHING ELSE, BUT...
WAAANDER.
MURMUR
YOU'D ALWAYS STRAY OFF AIMLESSLY WHEN LEFT ALONE...
YOU GAVE ME THE MOST TROUBLE IN MIDDLE SCHOOL.
MURMUR
MURMUR

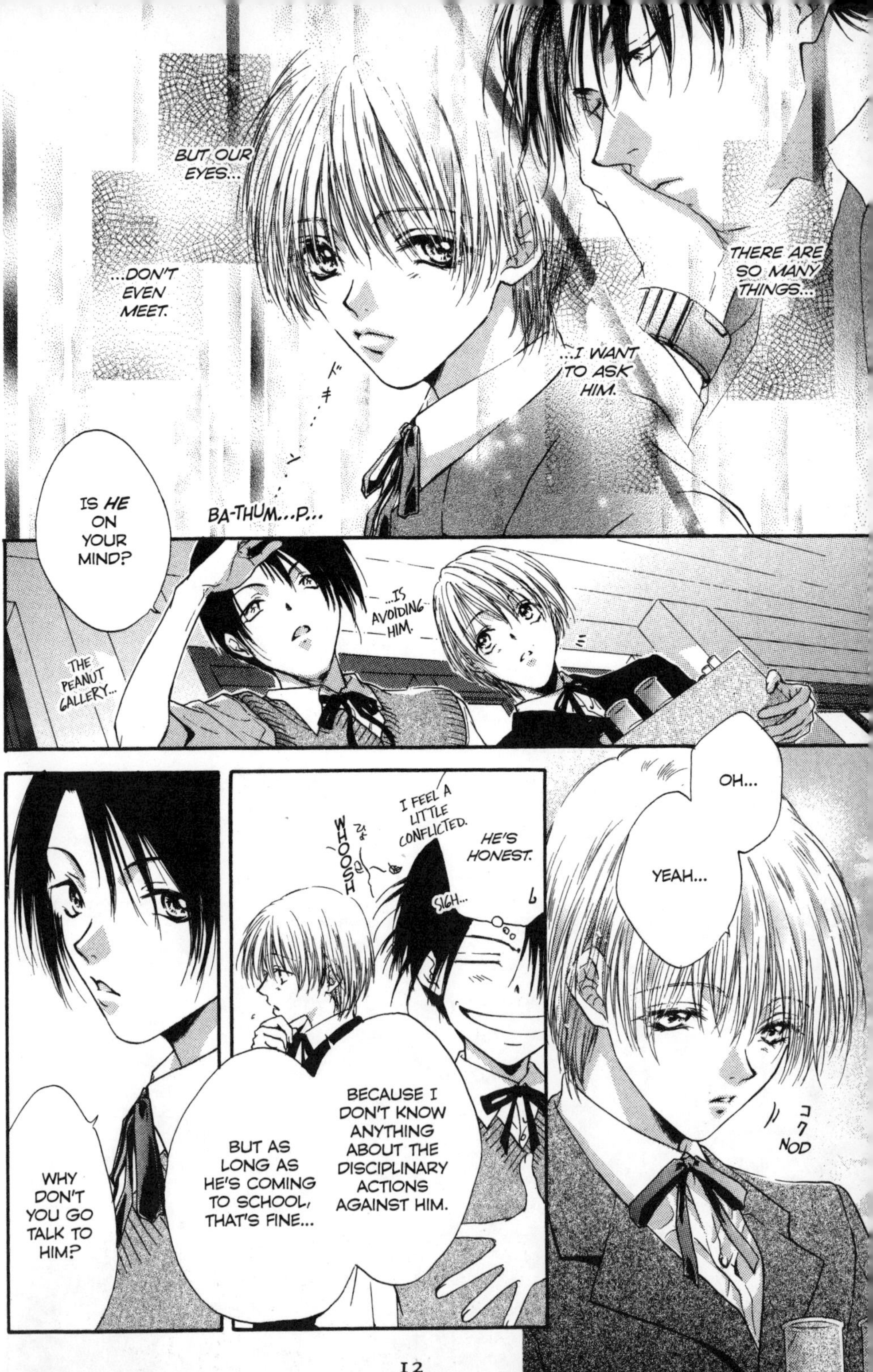
THERE ARE SO MANY THINGS...
...I WANT TO ASK HIM.
BUT OUR EYES...
...DON'T EVEN MEET.
BA-THUM...P...
IS HE ON YOUR MIND?
...IS AVOIDING HIM.
THE PEANUT GALLERY...
OH...
YEAH...
NOD
HE'S HONEST.
I FEEL A LITTLE CONFLICTED.
SIGH...
WHOOSH
BECAUSE I DON'T KNOW ANYTHING ABOUT THE DISCIPLINARY ACTIONS AGAINST HIM.
BUT AS LONG AS HE'S COMING TO SCHOOL, THAT'S FINE...
WHY DON'T YOU GO TALK TO HIM?

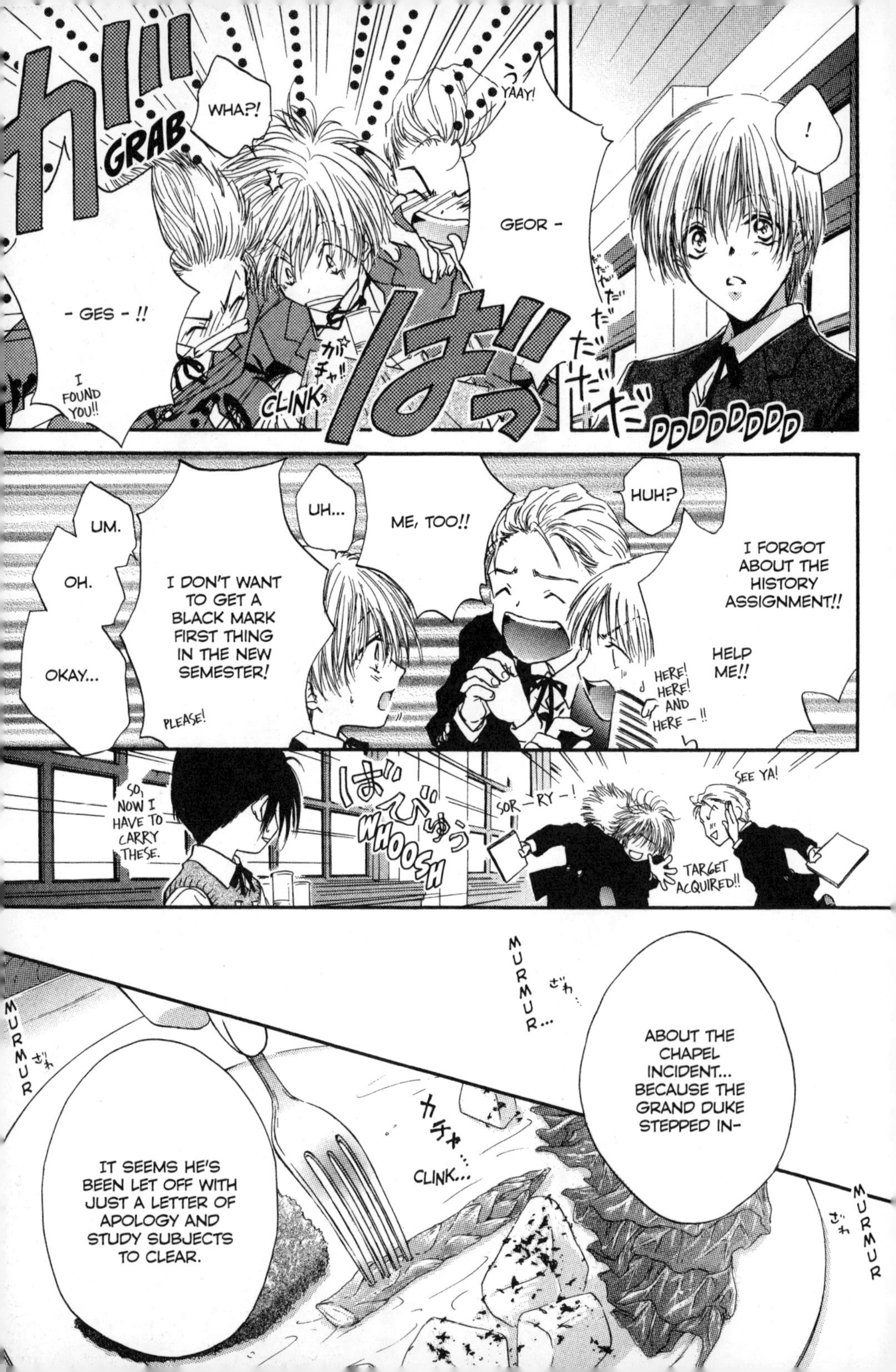
!
GEOR –
YAAY!
WHA?!
GRAB
– GES – !!
CLINK
ばっ
だだだ
DDDDDDDD
I FOUND YOU!!
I FORGOT ABOUT THE HISTORY ASSIGNMENT!!
HELP ME!!
HUH?
HERE! HERE! AND HERE – !!
ME, TOO!!
UH...
I DON'T WANT TO GET A BLACK MARK FIRST THING IN THE NEW SEMESTER!
PLEASE!
UM.
OH.
OKAY...
SEE YA!
TARGET ACQUIRED!!
SOR – RY – !
WHOOSH
SO, NOW I HAVE TO CARRY THESE.
MURMUR
MURMUR...
ABOUT THE CHAPEL INCIDENT... BECAUSE THE GRAND DUKE STEPPED IN–
CLINK...
IT SEEMS HE'S BEEN LET OFF WITH JUST A LETTER OF APOLOGY AND STUDY SUBJECTS TO CLEAR.
MURMUR

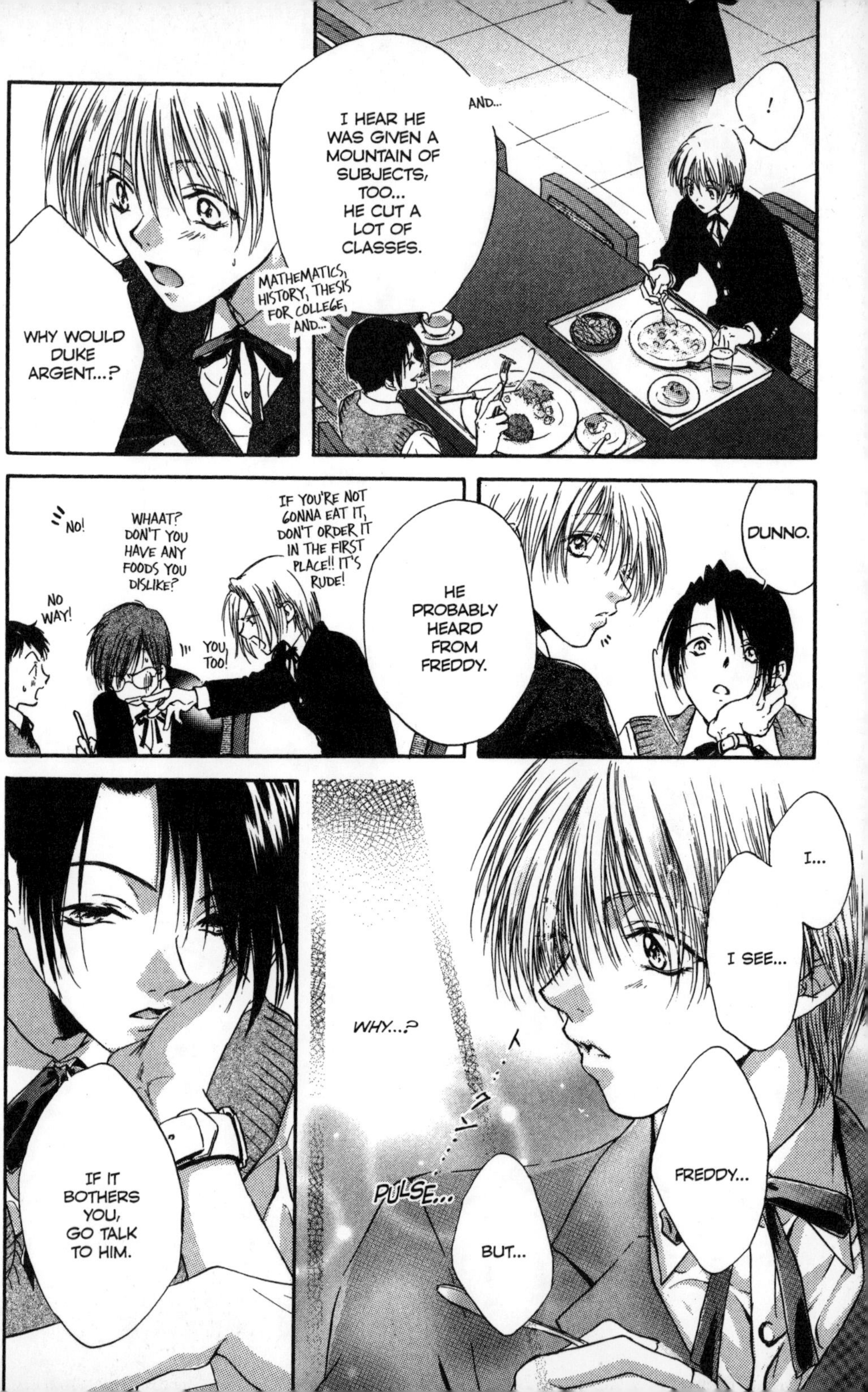
AND...
!
I HEAR HE WAS GIVEN A MOUNTAIN OF SUBJECTS, TOO... HE CUT A LOT OF CLASSES.
MATHEMATICS, HISTORY, THESIS FOR COLLEGE, AND...
WHY WOULD DUKE ARGENT...?
DUNNO.
HE PROBABLY HEARD FROM FREDDY.
IF YOU'RE NOT GONNA EAT IT, DON'T ORDER IT IN THE FIRST PLACE!! IT'S RUDE!
WHAAT? DON'T YOU HAVE ANY FOODS YOU DISLIKE?
NO!
YOU, TOO!
NO WAY!
I...
I SEE...
FREDDY...
BUT...
PULSE...
WHY...?
IF IT BOTHERS YOU, GO TALK TO HIM.

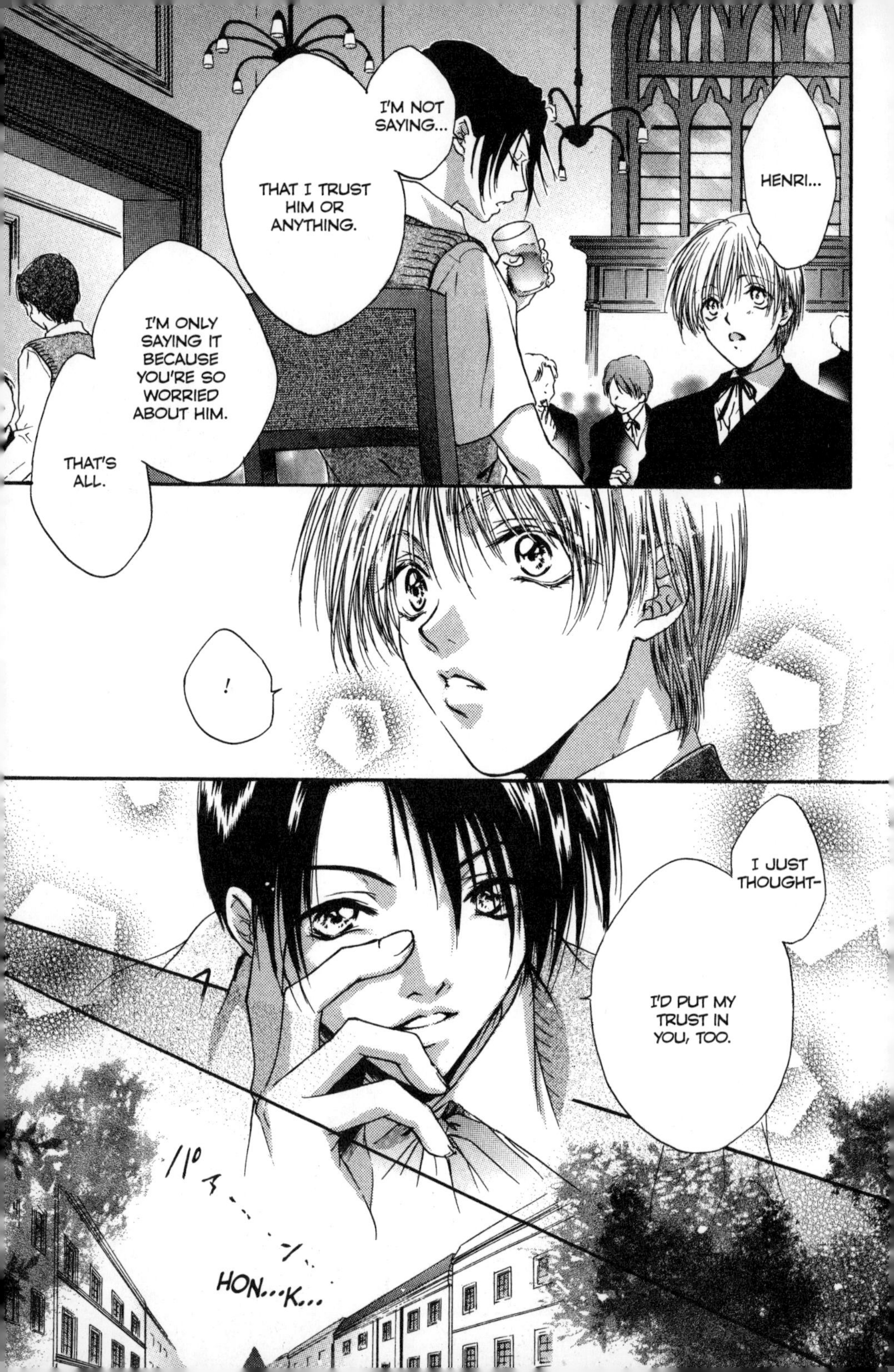
HENRI...
I'M NOT SAYING...
THAT I TRUST HIM OR ANYTHING.
I'M ONLY SAYING IT BECAUSE YOU'RE SO WORRIED ABOUT HIM.
THAT'S ALL.
!
I JUST THOUGHT-
I'D PUT MY TRUST IN YOU, TOO.
HON...K...

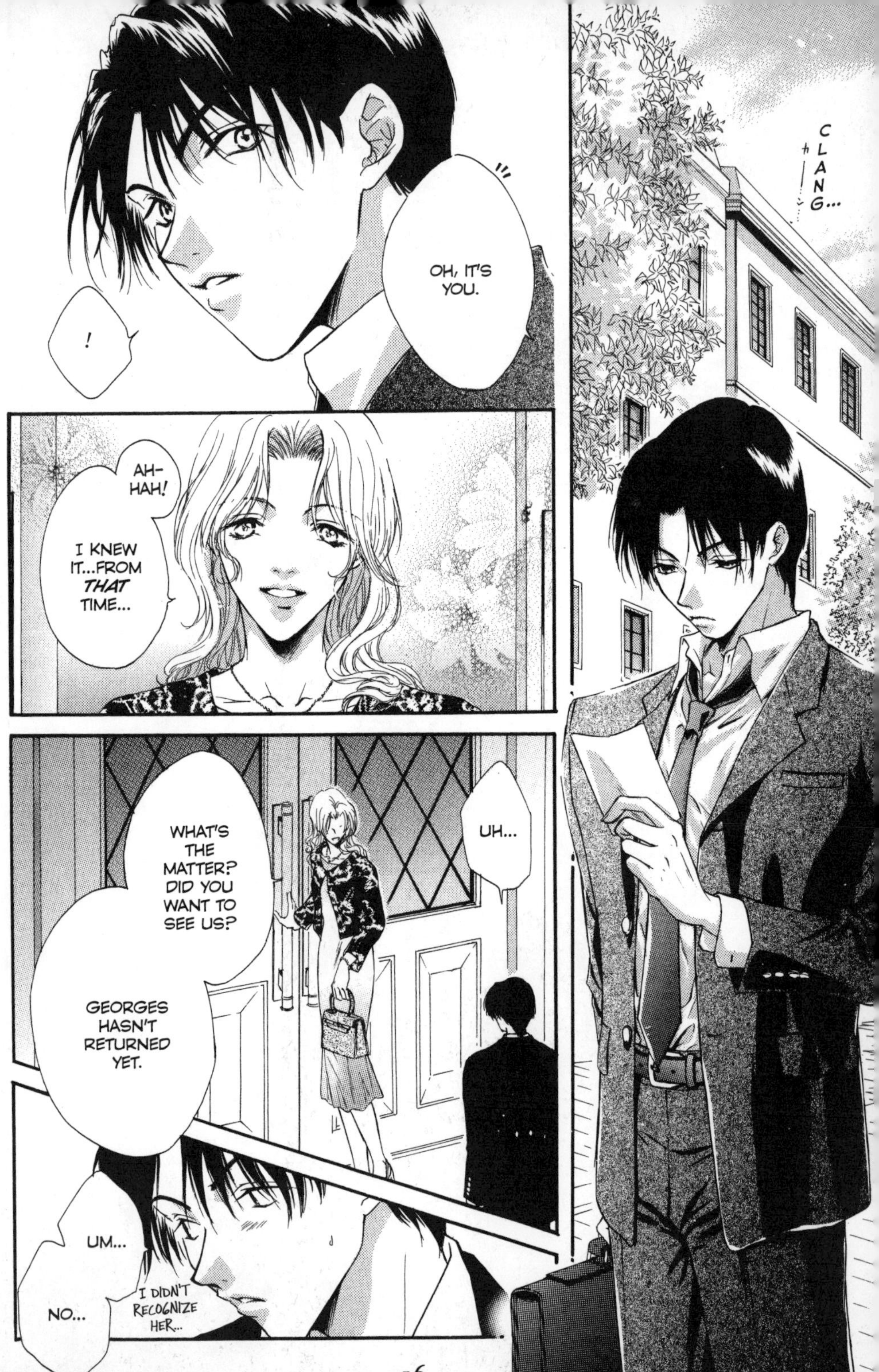
CLANG...
OH, IT'S YOU.
!
AH-HAH!
I KNEW IT...FROM *THAT* TIME...
UH...
WHAT'S THE MATTER? DID YOU WANT TO SEE US?
GEORGES HASN'T RETURNED YET.
UM...
NO...
I DIDN'T RECOGNIZE HER...

FOR THAT TIME...

WHAT?

IT'S MONEY FOR THE TAXI...AND THE CLEANING FEE FOR THE SHEETS.

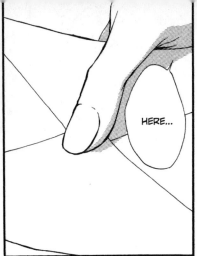

HERE...

OH.

YOU DIDN'T HAVE TO...

WORRY ABOUT ANY OF THAT...

THANK YOU...

...
...

YOU CAME ALL THE WAY DOWN HERE JUST FOR THIS?

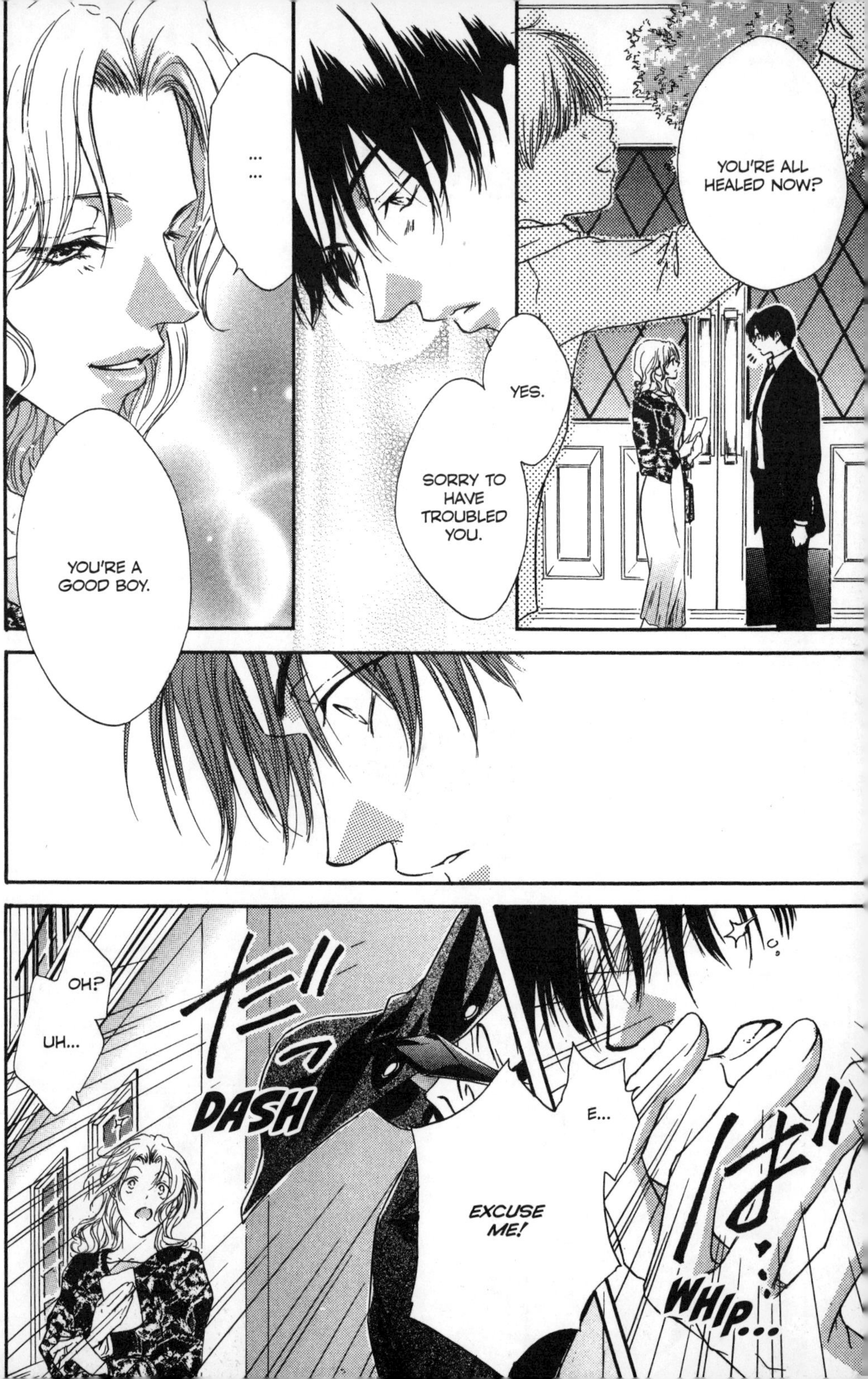
YOU'RE ALL HEALED NOW?
YES.
SORRY TO HAVE TROUBLED YOU.
...
...
YOU'RE A GOOD BOY.
ば
WHIP...
E...
EXCUSE ME!
だっ
DASH
OH?
UH...

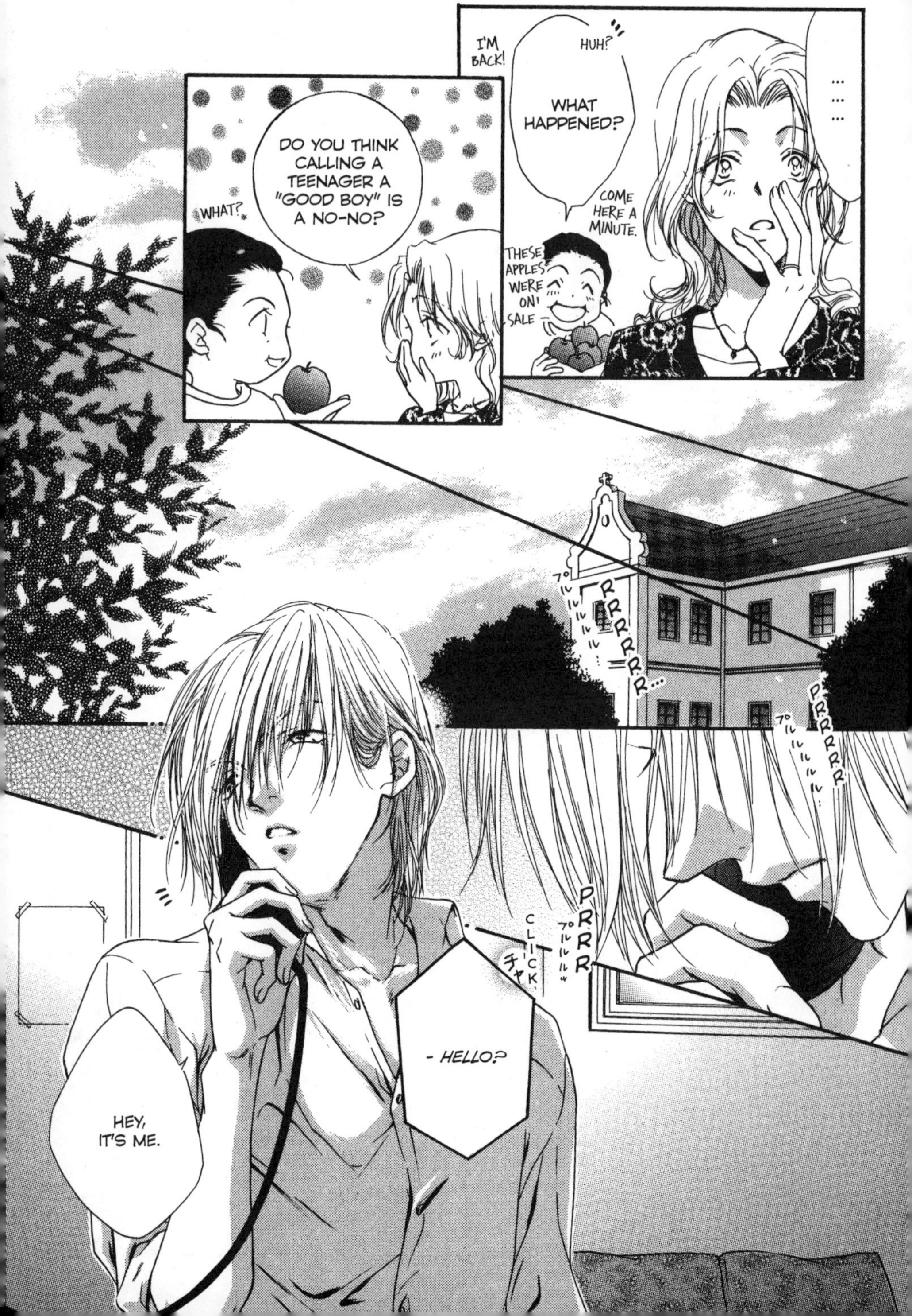
...
...
...
HUH?
WHAT HAPPENED?
I'M BACK!
COME HERE A MINUTE.
THESE APPLES WERE ON SALE
DO YOU THINK CALLING A TEENAGER A "GOOD BOY" IS A NO-NO?
WHAT?
PRRRRR
プルルル…
プルルル…
RRRRRRR...
PRRR
プルルル
CLICK
チャ
- HELLO?
HEY, IT'S ME.

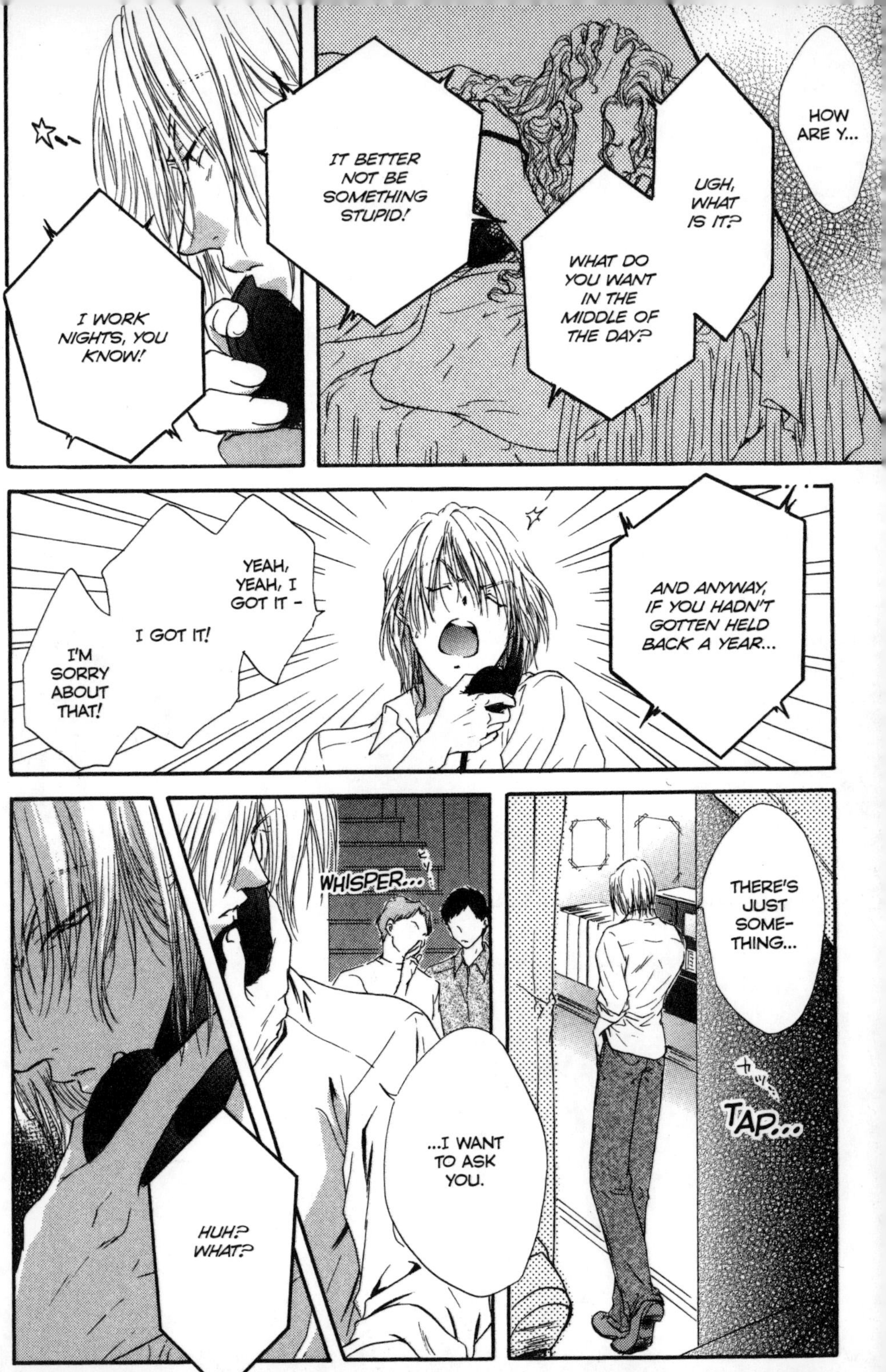

HOW ARE Y...
UGH, WHAT IS IT?
WHAT DO YOU WANT IN THE MIDDLE OF THE DAY?
IT BETTER NOT BE SOMETHING STUPID!
I WORK NIGHTS, YOU KNOW!
AND ANYWAY, IF YOU HADN'T GOTTEN HELD BACK A YEAR...
YEAH, YEAH, I GOT IT -
I GOT IT!
I'M SORRY ABOUT THAT!
THERE'S JUST SOME-THING...
TAP...
WHISPER...
...I WANT TO ASK YOU.
HUH? WHAT?

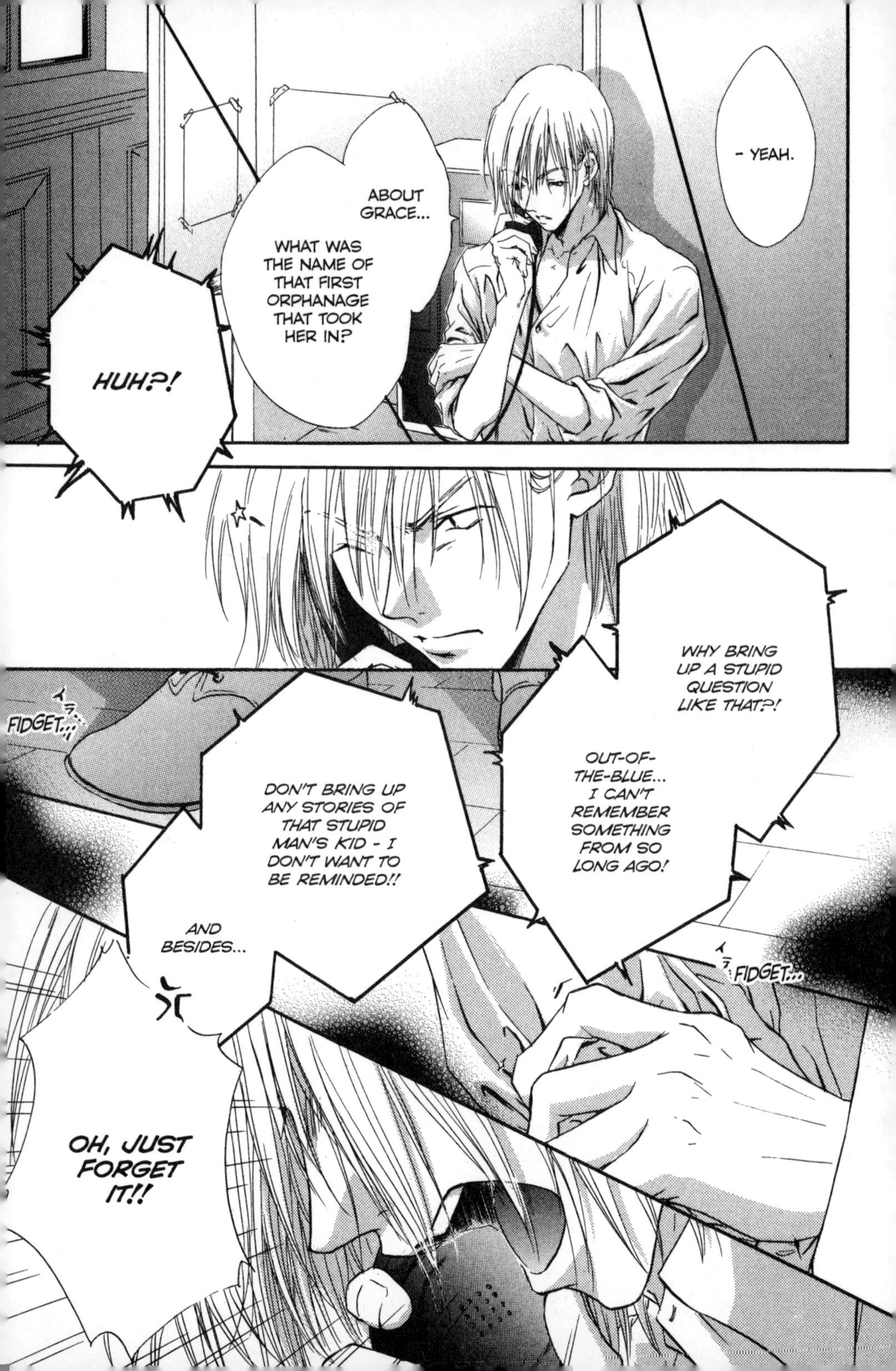
- YEAH.
ABOUT GRACE...
WHAT WAS THE NAME OF THAT FIRST ORPHANAGE THAT TOOK HER IN?
HUH?!
WHY BRING UP A STUPID QUESTION LIKE THAT?!
OUT-OF-THE-BLUE... I CAN'T REMEMBER SOMETHING FROM SO LONG AGO!
FIDGET...
DON'T BRING UP ANY STORIES OF THAT STUPID MAN'S KID - I DON'T WANT TO BE REMINDED!!
AND BESIDES...
FIDGET...
OH, JUST FORGET IT!!

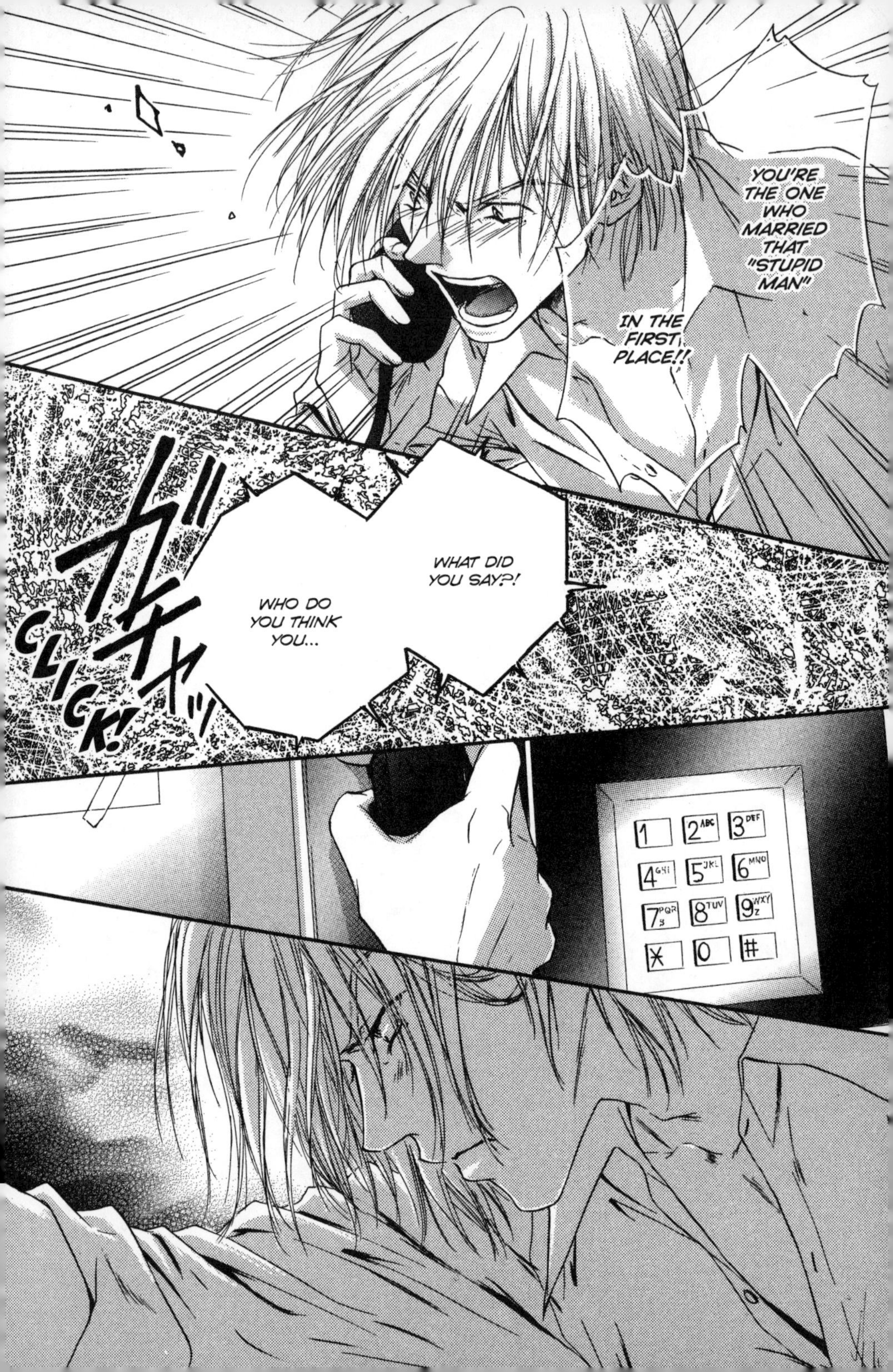
YOU'RE THE ONE WHO MARRIED THAT "STUPID MAN"
IN THE FIRST PLACE!!
WHAT DID YOU SAY?!
WHO DO YOU THINK YOU...
ガチャッ
CLICK!

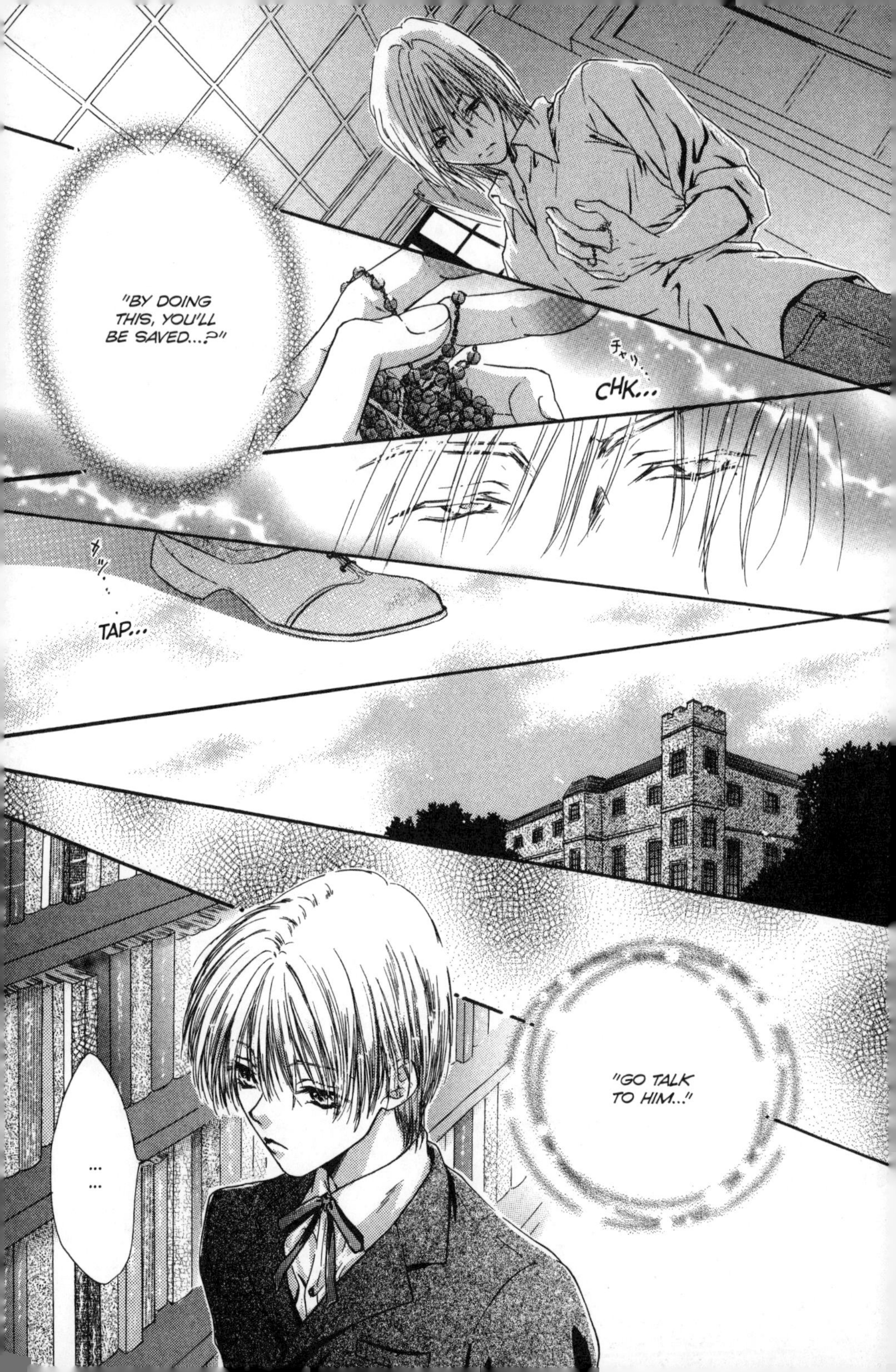
"BY DOING THIS, YOU'LL BE SAVED...?"
チャリ…
CHK...
タッ…
TAP...
"GO TALK TO HIM..."
... ...

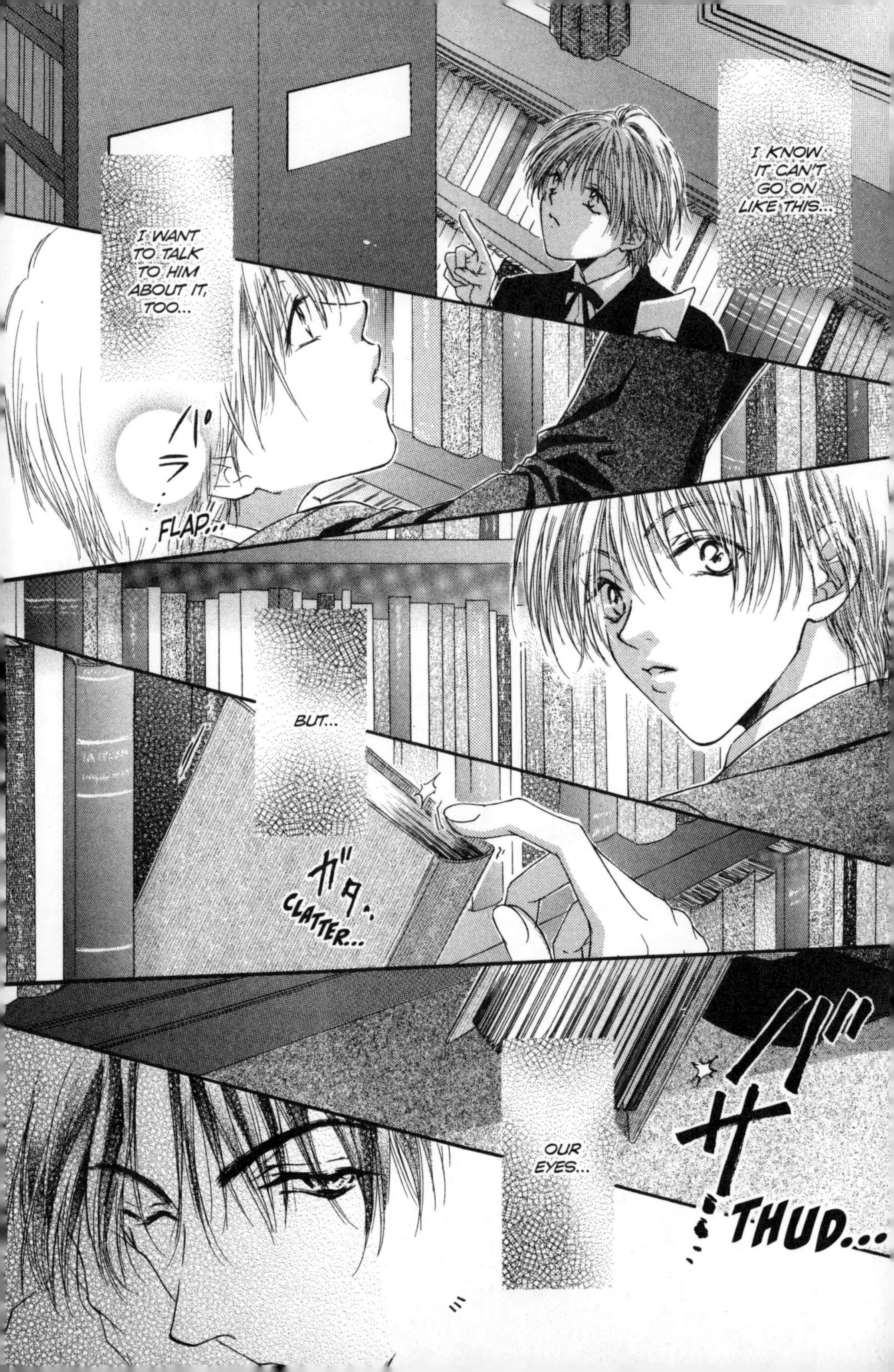
I KNOW IT CAN'T GO ON LIKE THIS...
I WANT TO TALK TO HIM ABOUT IT, TOO...
パラ
FLAP...
BUT...
ガタ..
CLATTER...
バサ
THUD...
OUR EYES...

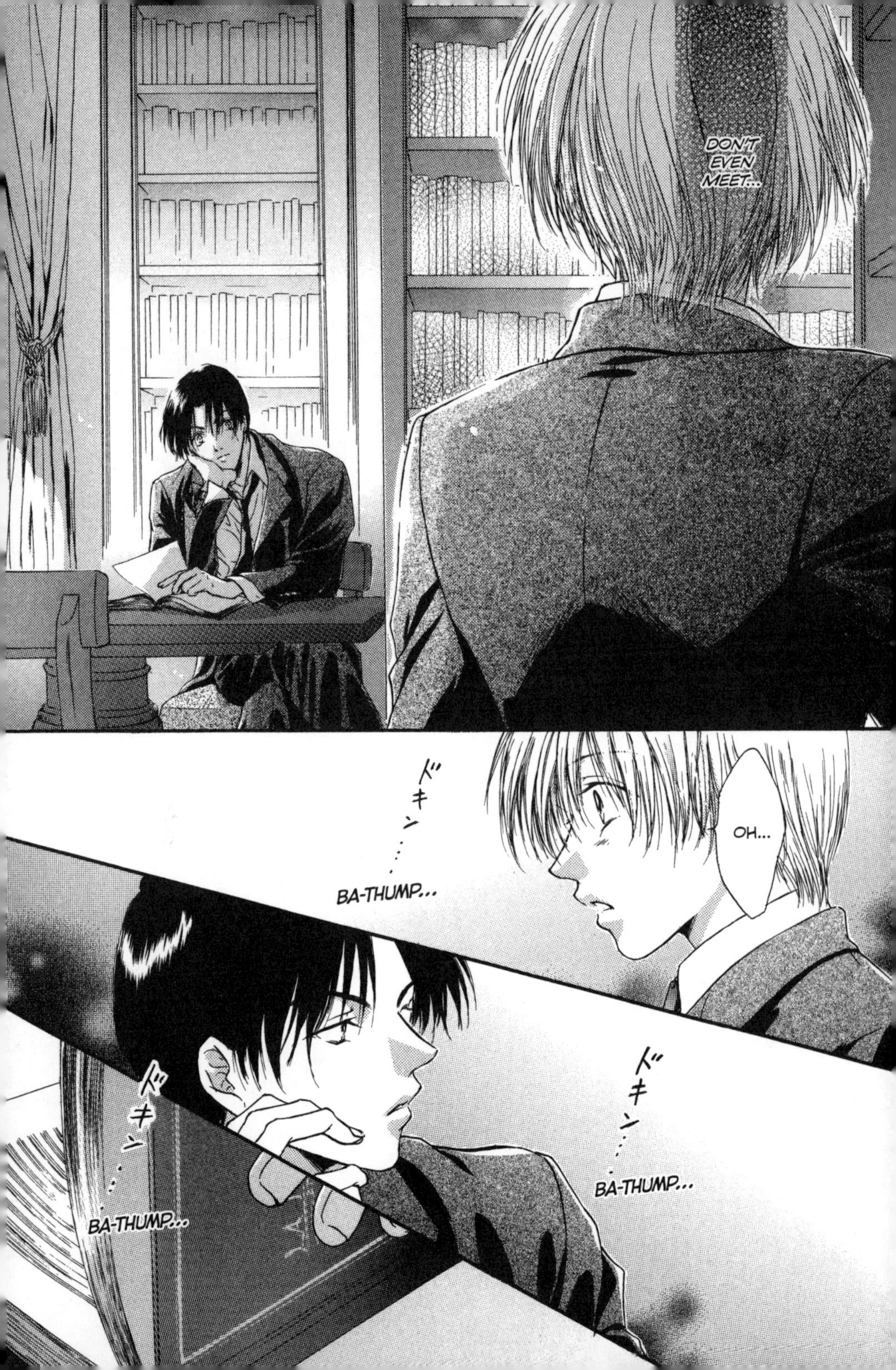
DON'T EVEN MEET...
OH...
ドキン…
BA-THUMP...
ドキン…
BA-THUMP...
ドキン…
BA-THUMP...

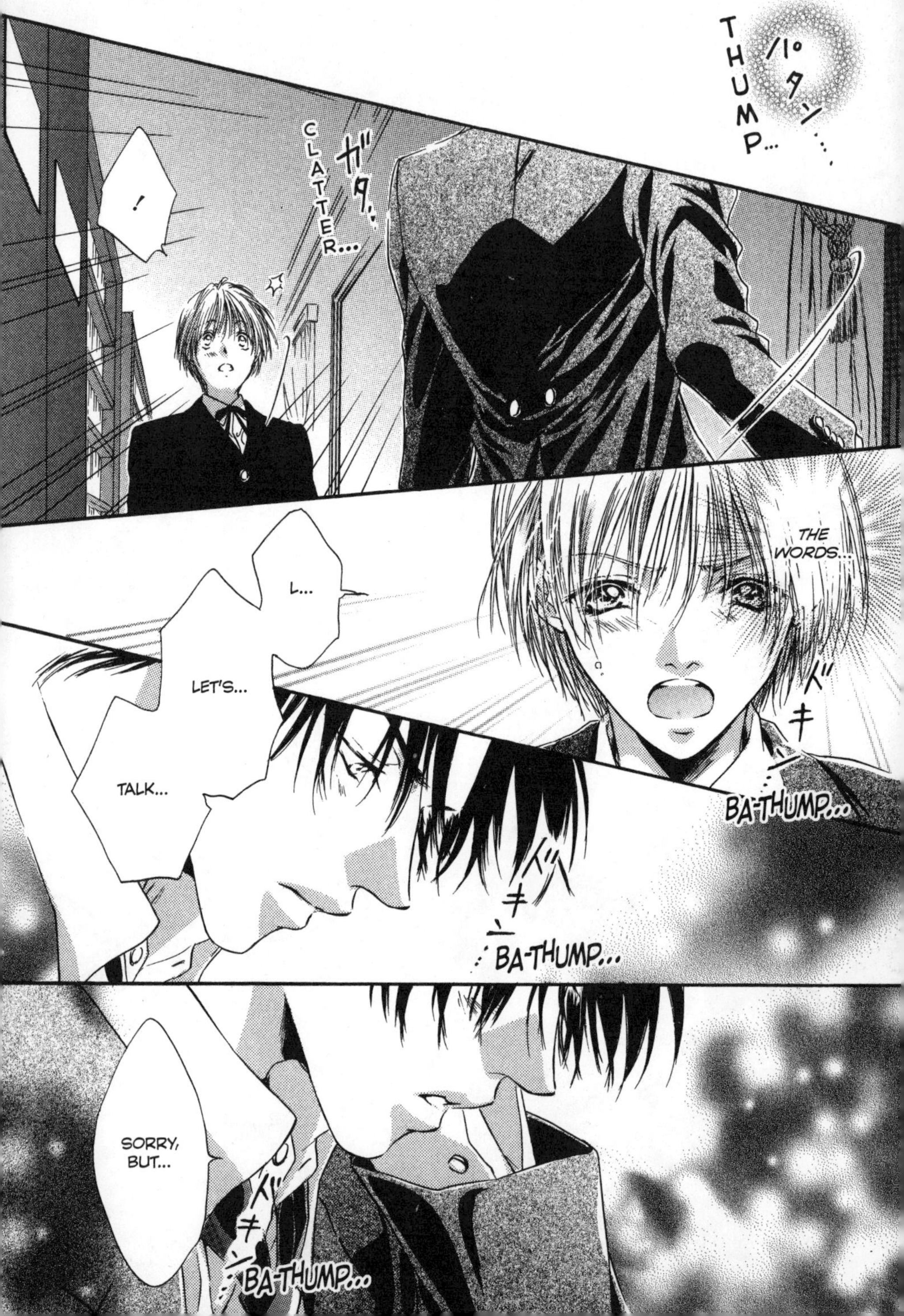
パタン…
THUMP...
ガタ…
CLATTER...
!
THE WORDS...
ドキン
BA-THUMP...
L...
LET'S...
TALK...
ドキン
BA-THUMP...
SORRY, BUT...
ドキン
BA-THUMP...

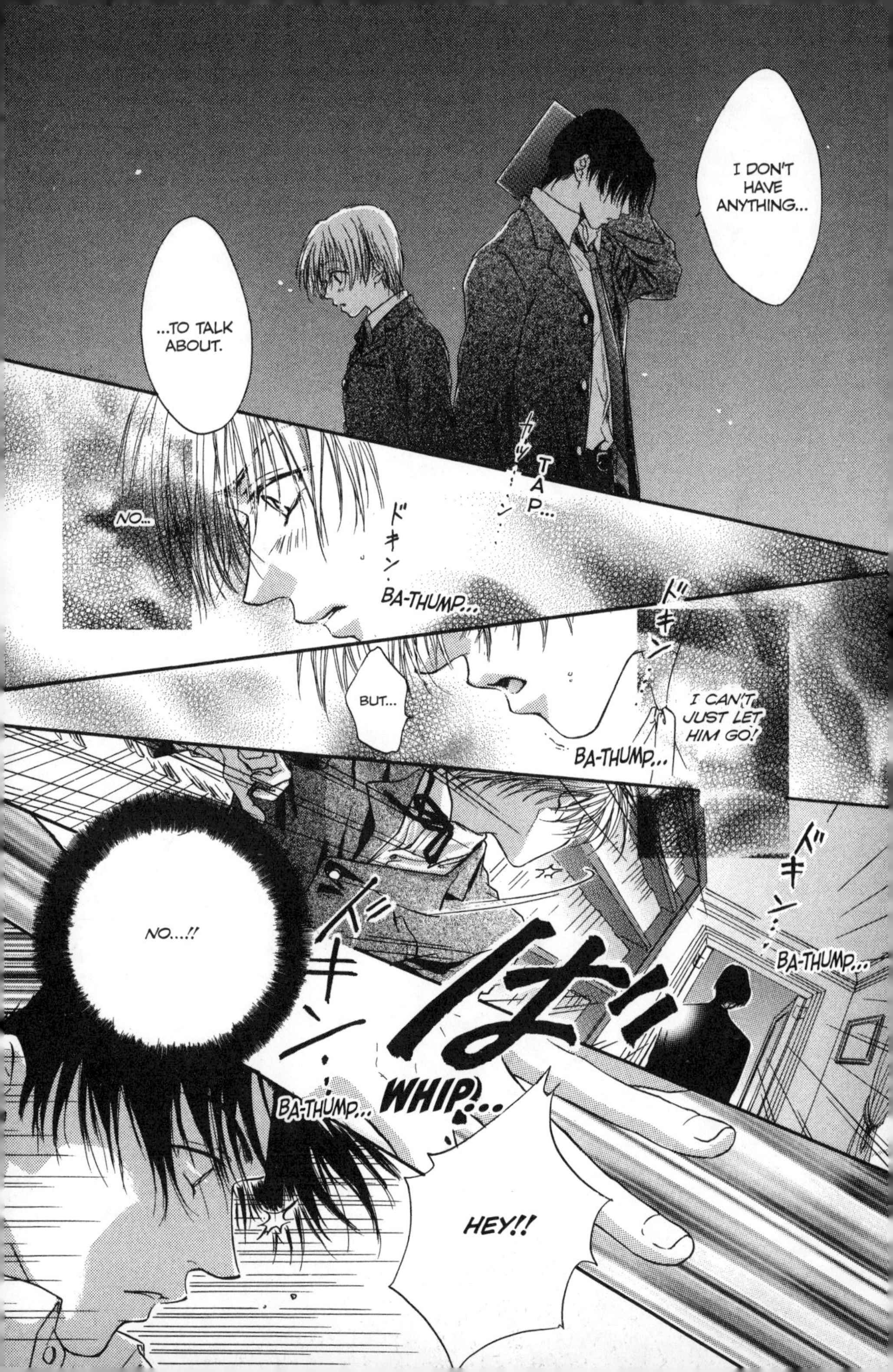

I DON'T HAVE ANYTHING...
...TO TALK ABOUT.
TAP...
NO...
BA-THUMP...
BUT...
I CAN'T JUST LET HIM GO!
BA-THUMP...
BA-THUMP...
NO...!!
BA-THUMP...
WHIP...
HEY!!

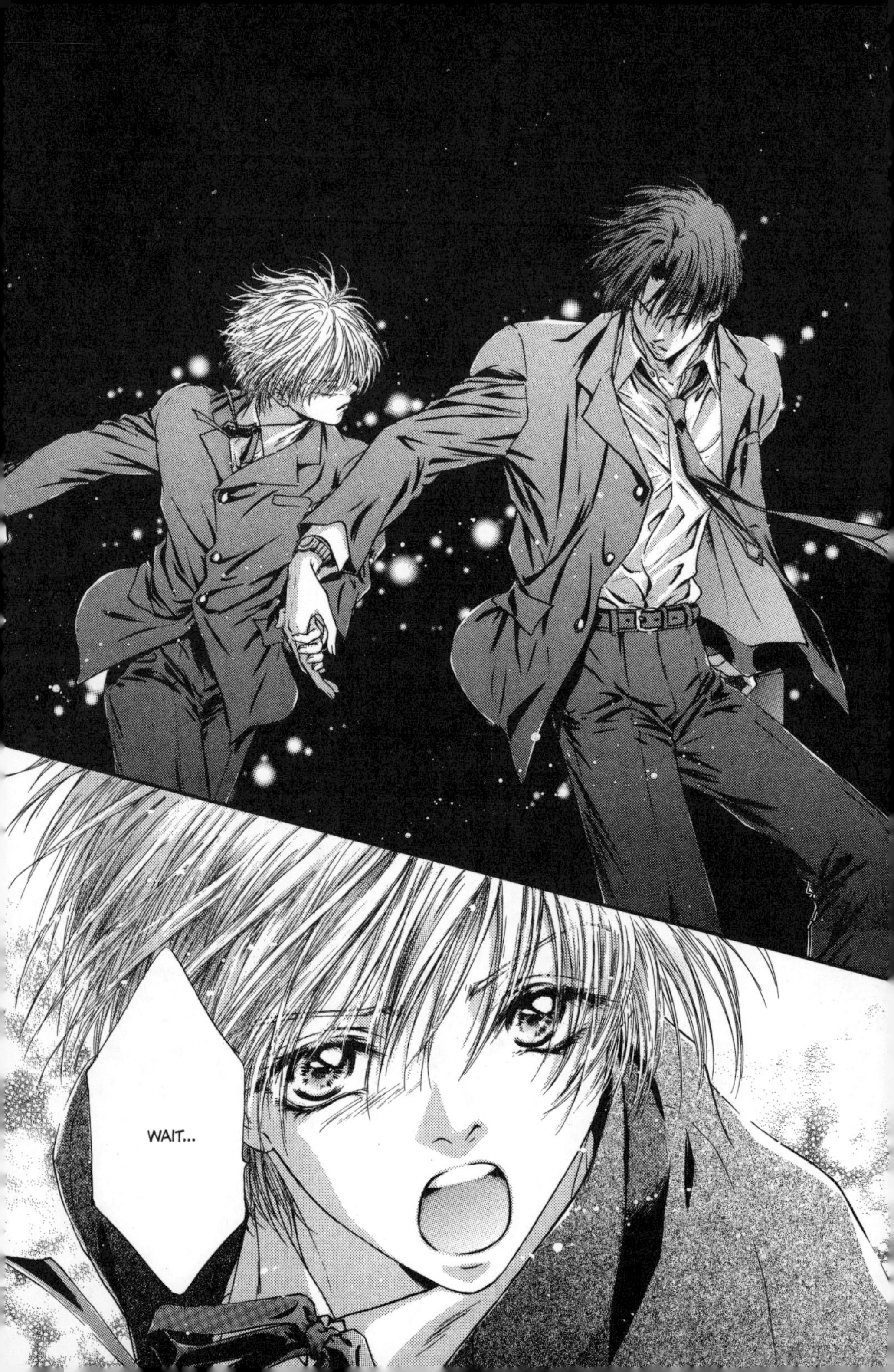
WAIT...

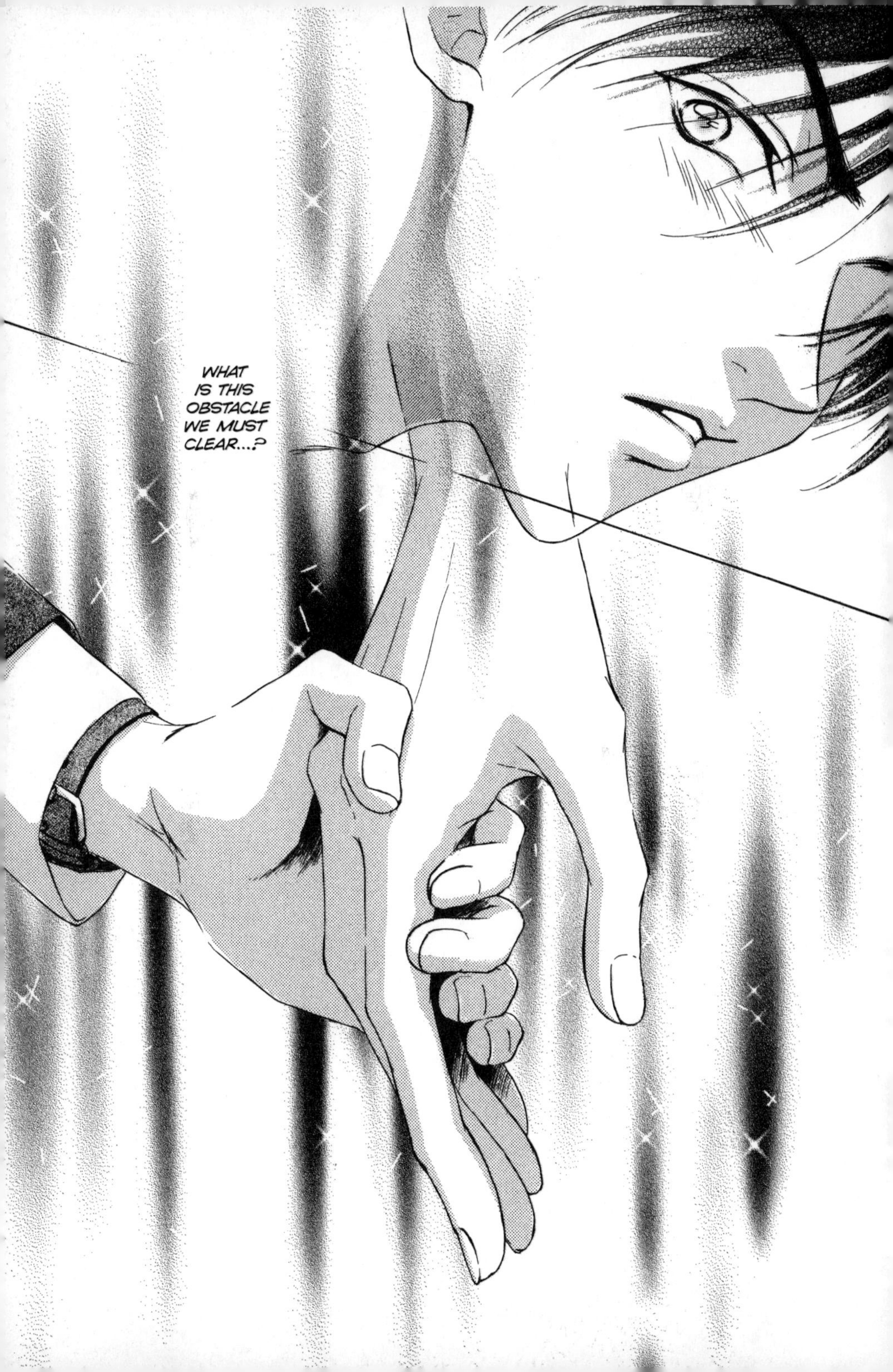
WHAT IS THIS OBSTACLE WE MUST CLEAR...?

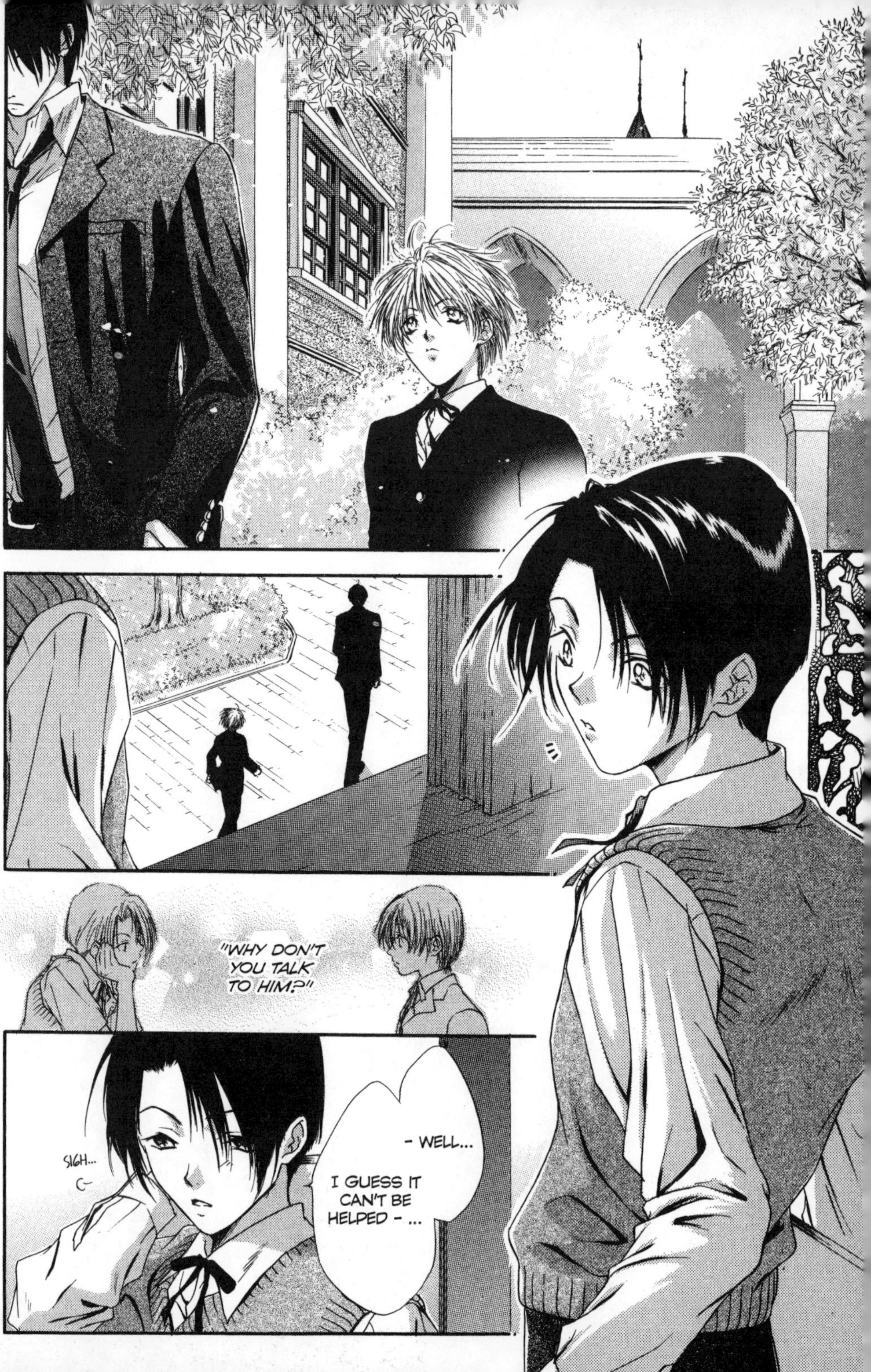
"WHY DON'T YOU TALK TO HIM?"
- WELL...
I GUESS IT CAN'T BE HELPED - ...
SIGH...

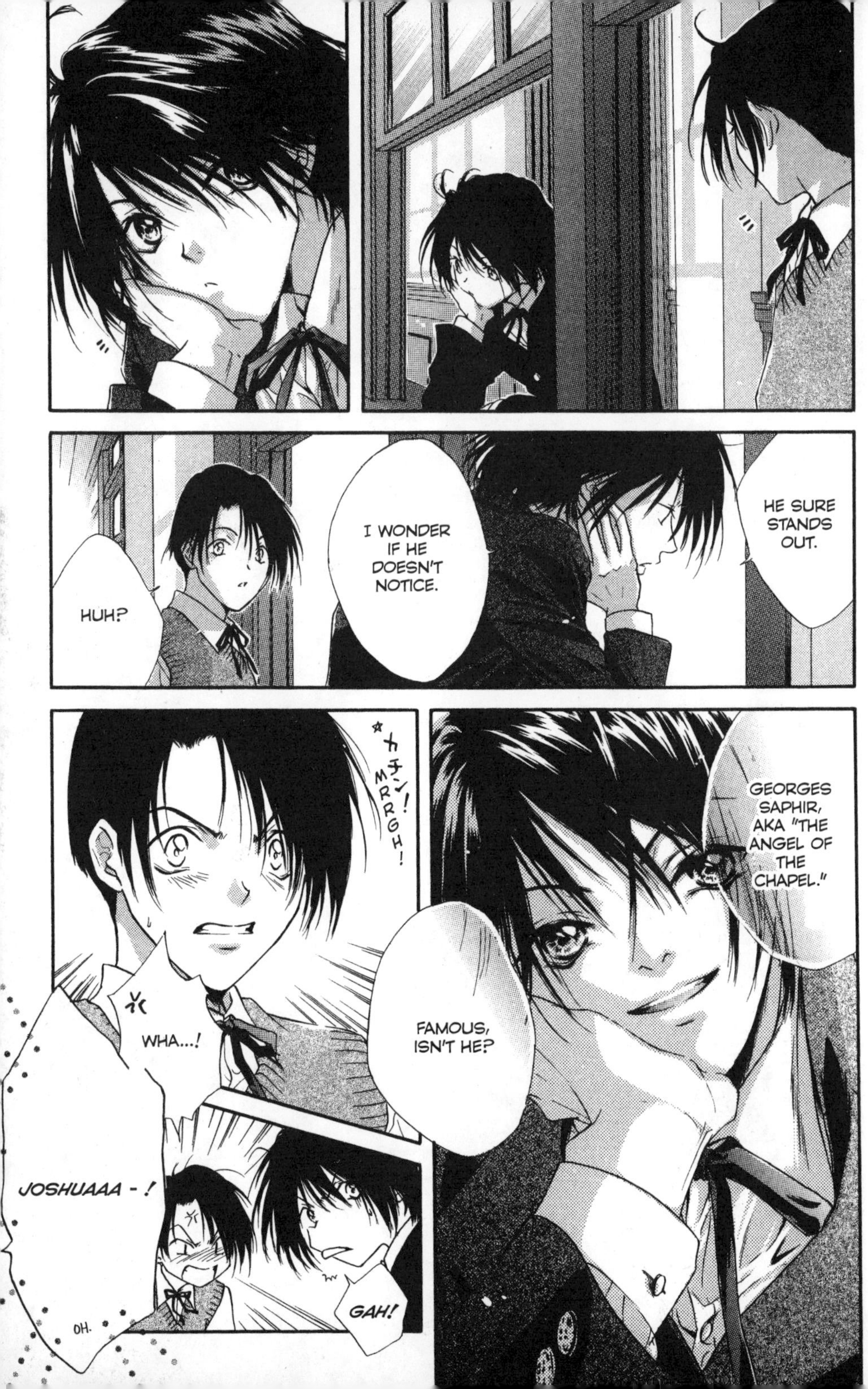
HE SURE STANDS OUT.
I WONDER IF HE DOESN'T NOTICE.
HUH?
GEORGES SAPHIR, AKA "THE ANGEL OF THE CHAPEL."
FAMOUS, ISN'T HE?
カチン!
MRRGH!
WHA...!
GAH!
JOSHUAAA - !
OH.

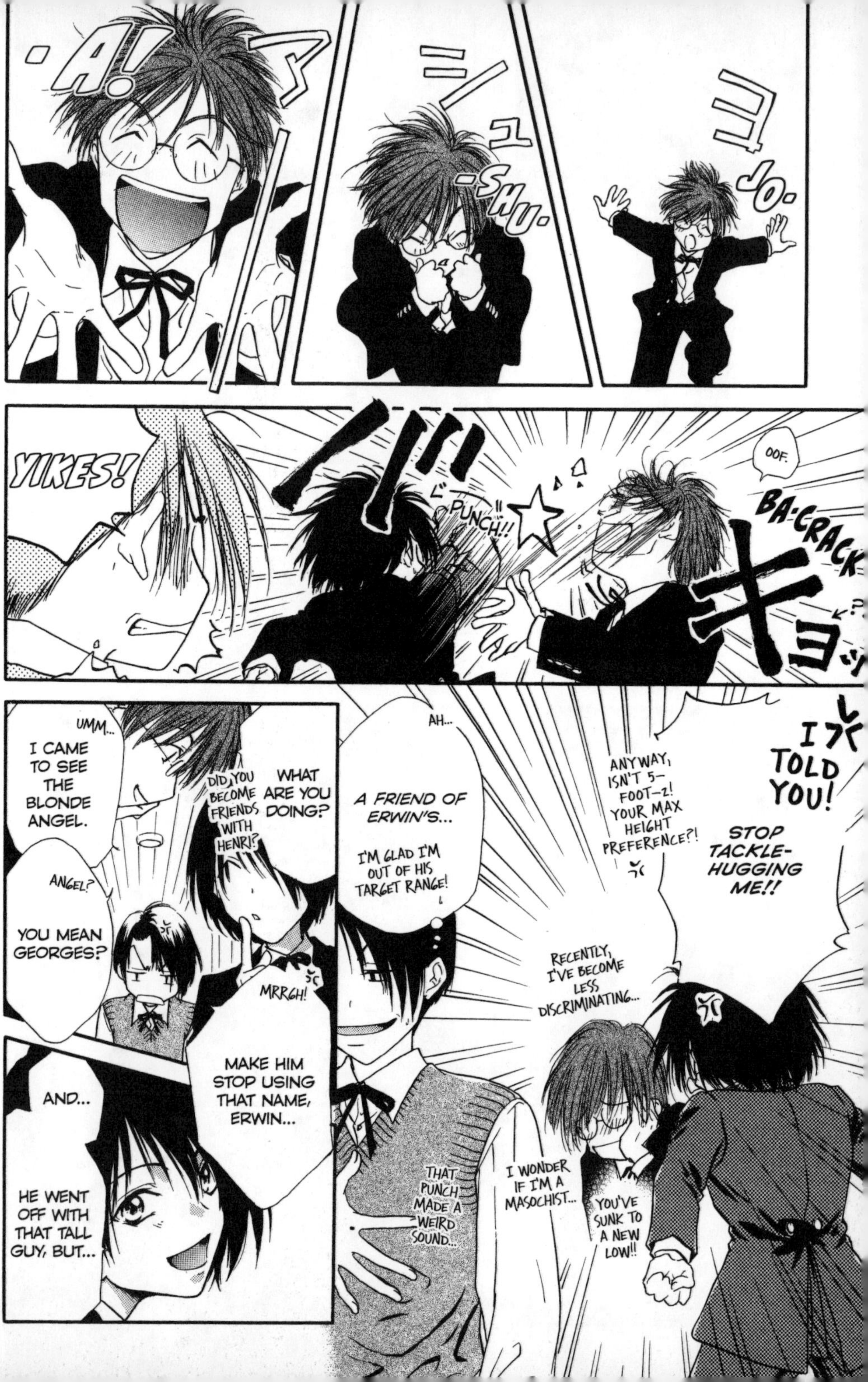
ヨ
JO-
ニシュ
-SHU-
-A!
ア
OOF.
BA-CRACK
キョッ
?
バ
PUNCH!!
YIKES!
I TOLD YOU!
STOP TACKLE-HUGGING ME!!
ANYWAY, ISN'T 5-FOOT-2! YOUR MAX HEIGHT PREFERENCE?!
RECENTLY, I'VE BECOME LESS DISCRIMINATING...
YOU'VE SUNK TO A NEW LOW!!
I WONDER IF I'M A MASOCHIST...
THAT PUNCH MADE A WEIRD SOUND...
AH...
A FRIEND OF ERWIN'S...
I'M GLAD I'M OUT OF HIS TARGET RANGE!
WHAT ARE YOU DOING?
DID YOU BECOME FRIENDS WITH HENRI?
UMM... I CAME TO SEE THE BLONDE ANGEL.
ANGEL?
YOU MEAN GEORGES?
MRRGH!
MAKE HIM STOP USING THAT NAME, ERWIN...
AND...
HE WENT OFF WITH THAT TALL GUY, BUT...

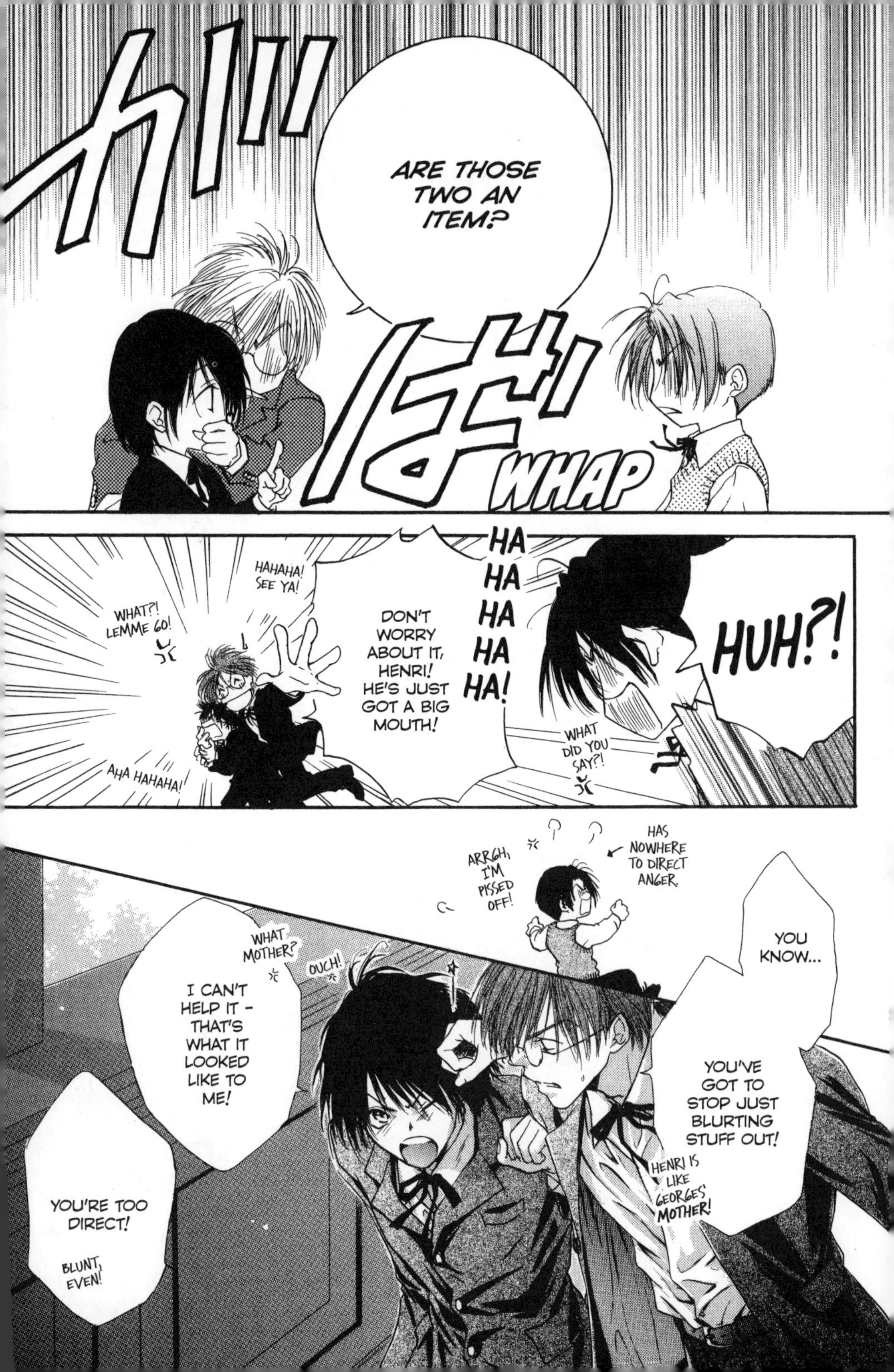
ARE THOSE TWO AN ITEM?
WHAP
HUH?!
HA HA HA HA HA!
WHAT DID YOU SAY?!
DON'T WORRY ABOUT IT, HENRI! HE'S JUST GOT A BIG MOUTH!
HAHAHA! SEE YA!
WHAT?! LEMME GO!
AHA HAHAHA!
HAS NOWHERE TO DIRECT ANGER.
ARRGH, I'M PISSED OFF!
YOU KNOW...
YOU'VE GOT TO STOP JUST BLURTING STUFF OUT!
HENRI IS LIKE GEORGES' MOTHER!
OUCH!
WHAT MOTHER?
I CAN'T HELP IT - THAT'S WHAT IT LOOKED LIKE TO ME!
YOU'RE TOO DIRECT!
BLUNT, EVEN!

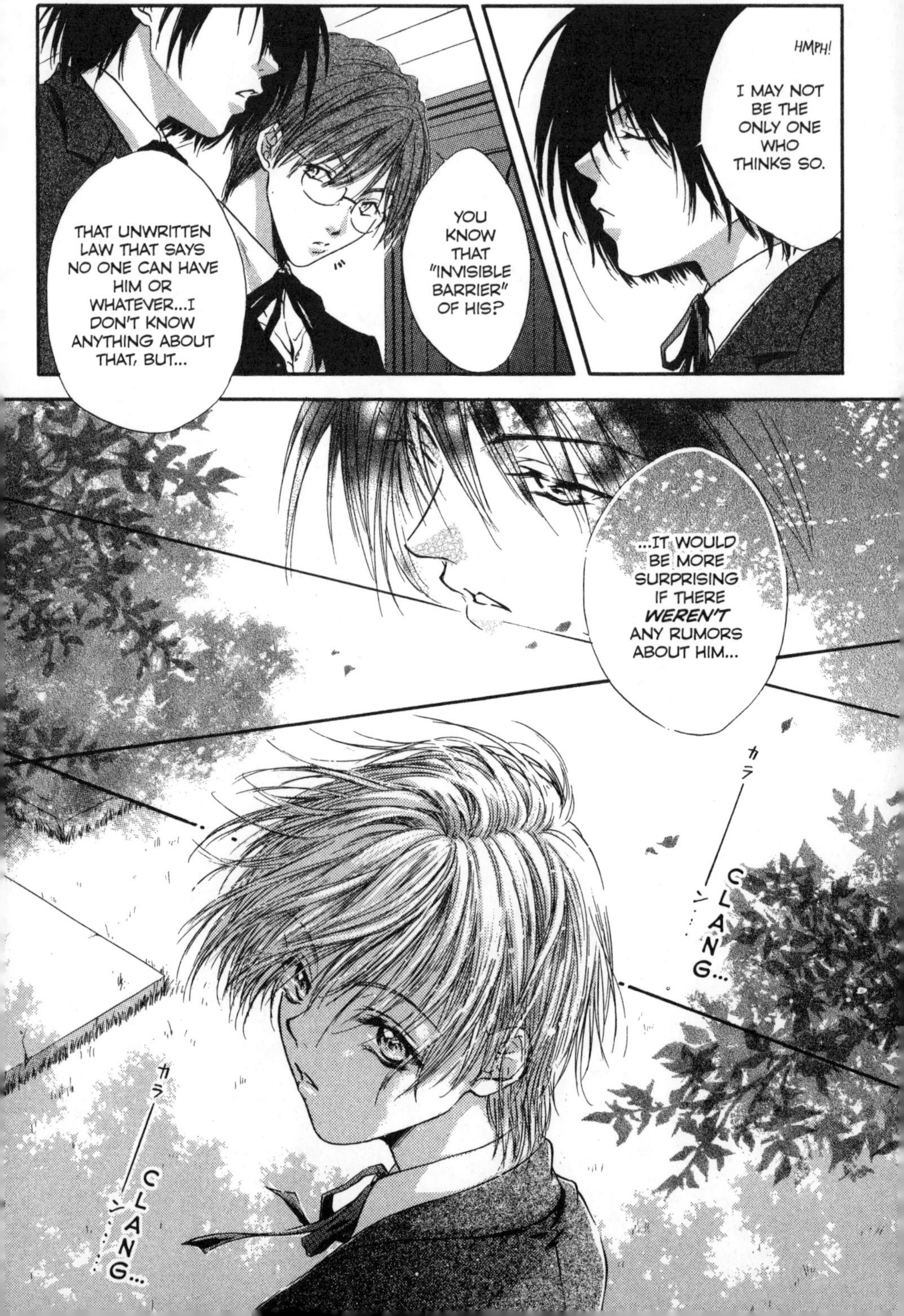
HMPH!
I MAY NOT BE THE ONLY ONE WHO THINKS SO.
YOU KNOW THAT "INVISIBLE BARRIER" OF HIS?
THAT UNWRITTEN LAW THAT SAYS NO ONE CAN HAVE HIM OR WHATEVER...I DON'T KNOW ANYTHING ABOUT THAT, BUT...
...IT WOULD BE MORE SURPRISING IF THERE ***WEREN'T*** ANY RUMORS ABOUT HIM...
カラ—ン...
CLANG...
カラ—ン...
CLANG...

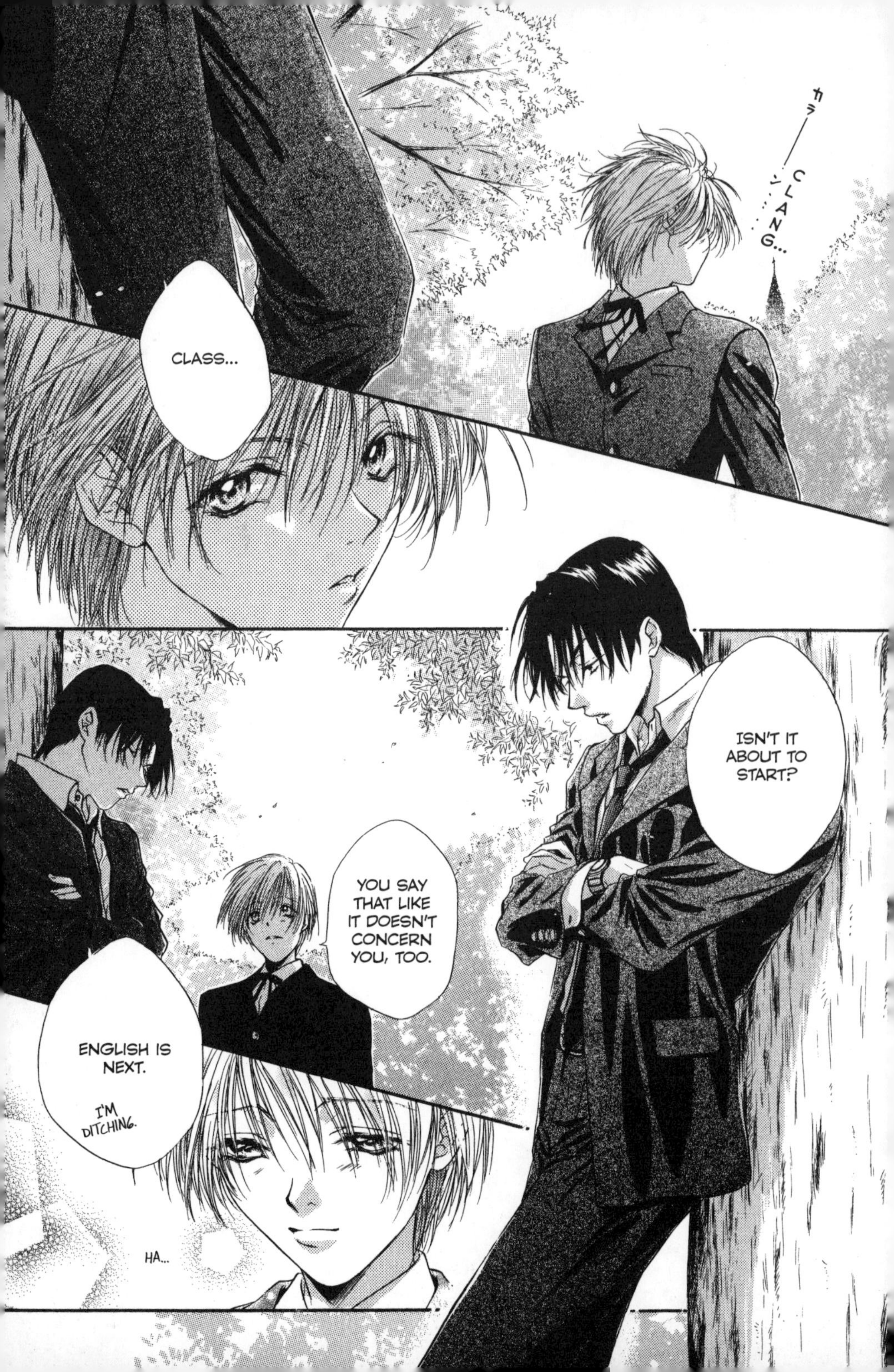
カラーン…
CLANG...
CLASS...
ISN'T IT ABOUT TO START?
YOU SAY THAT LIKE IT DOESN'T CONCERN YOU, TOO.
ENGLISH IS NEXT.
I'M DITCHING.
HA...

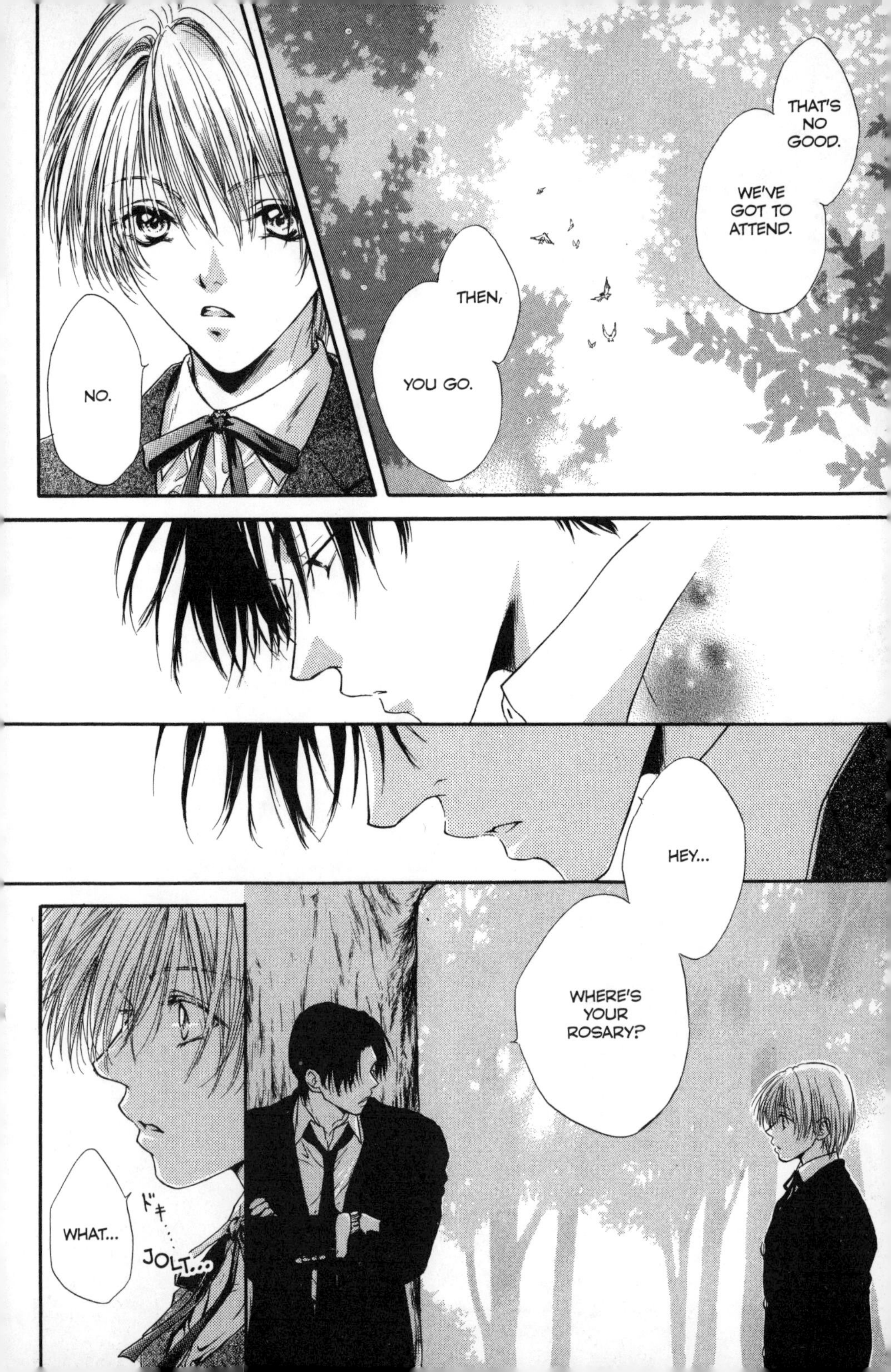
THAT'S NO GOOD.
WE'VE GOT TO ATTEND.
THEN,
YOU GO.
NO.
HEY...
WHERE'S YOUR ROSARY?
WHAT...
ドキ...
JOLT...

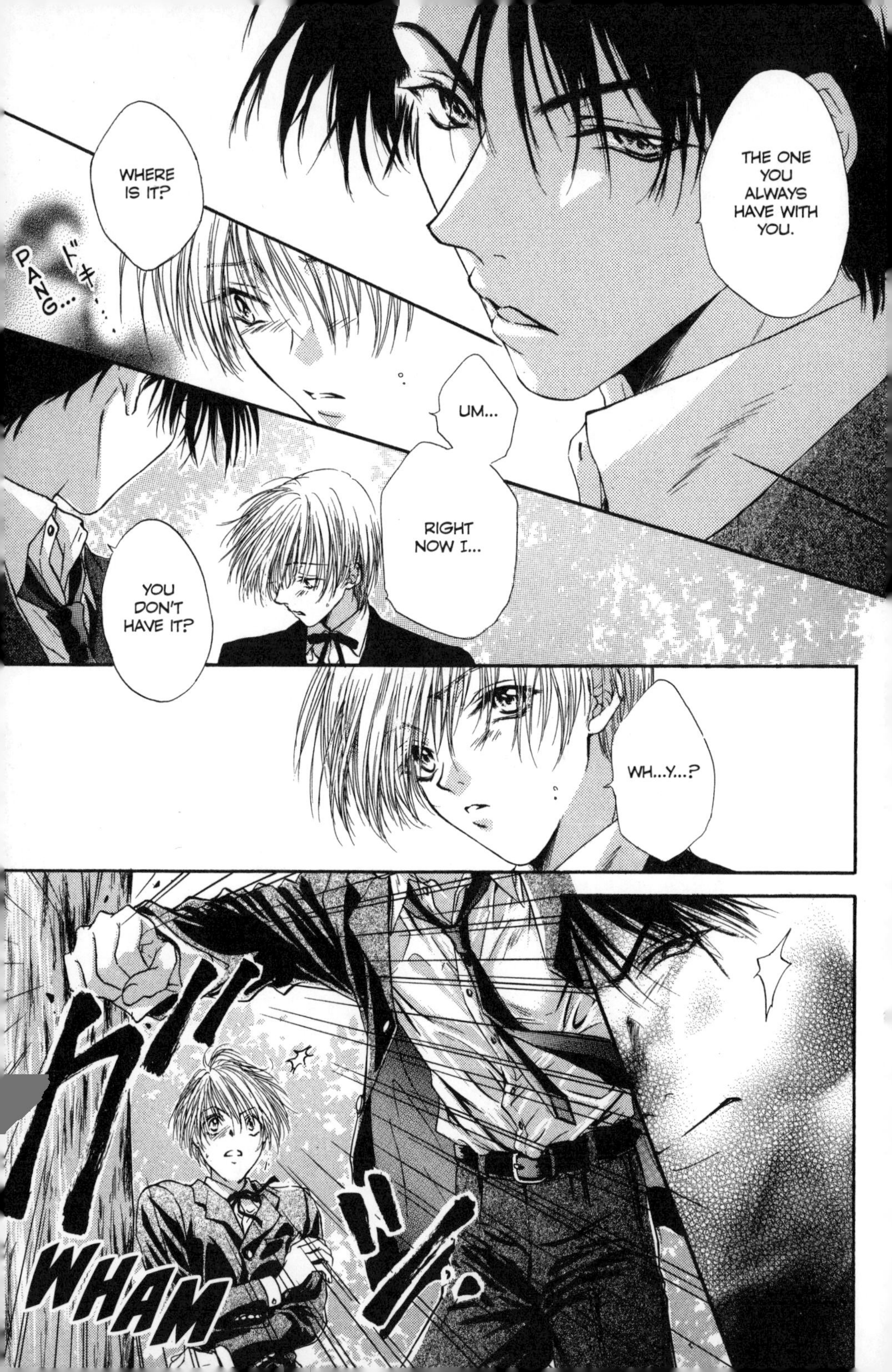
THE ONE YOU ALWAYS HAVE WITH YOU.
WHERE IS IT?
ドキ…
PANG…
UM...
RIGHT NOW I...
YOU DON'T HAVE IT?
WH...Y...?
WHAM

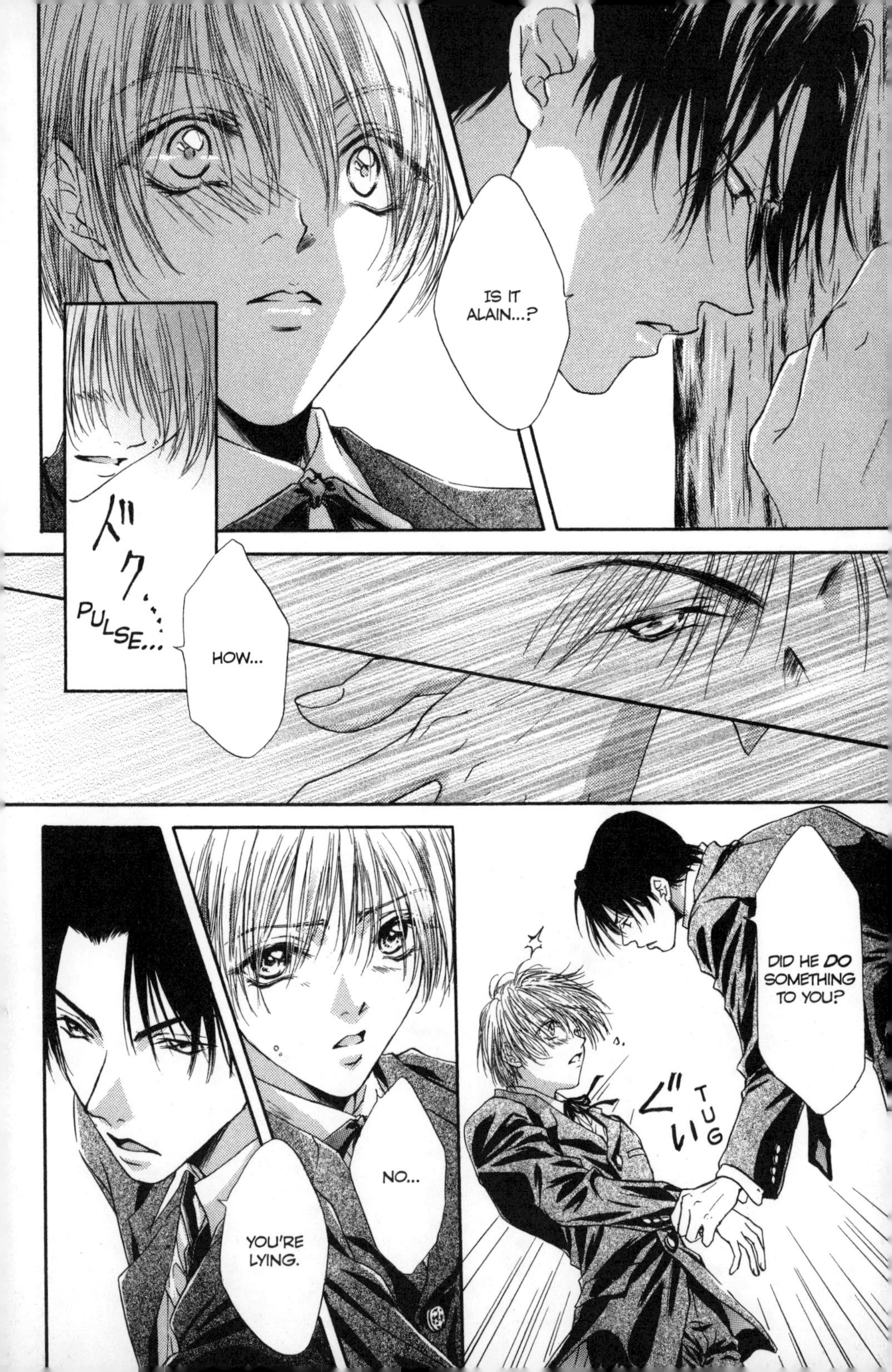

IS IT ALAIN...?
ドク…
PULSE...
HOW...
DID HE *DO* SOMETHING TO YOU?
ぐい
TUG
NO...
YOU'RE LYING.

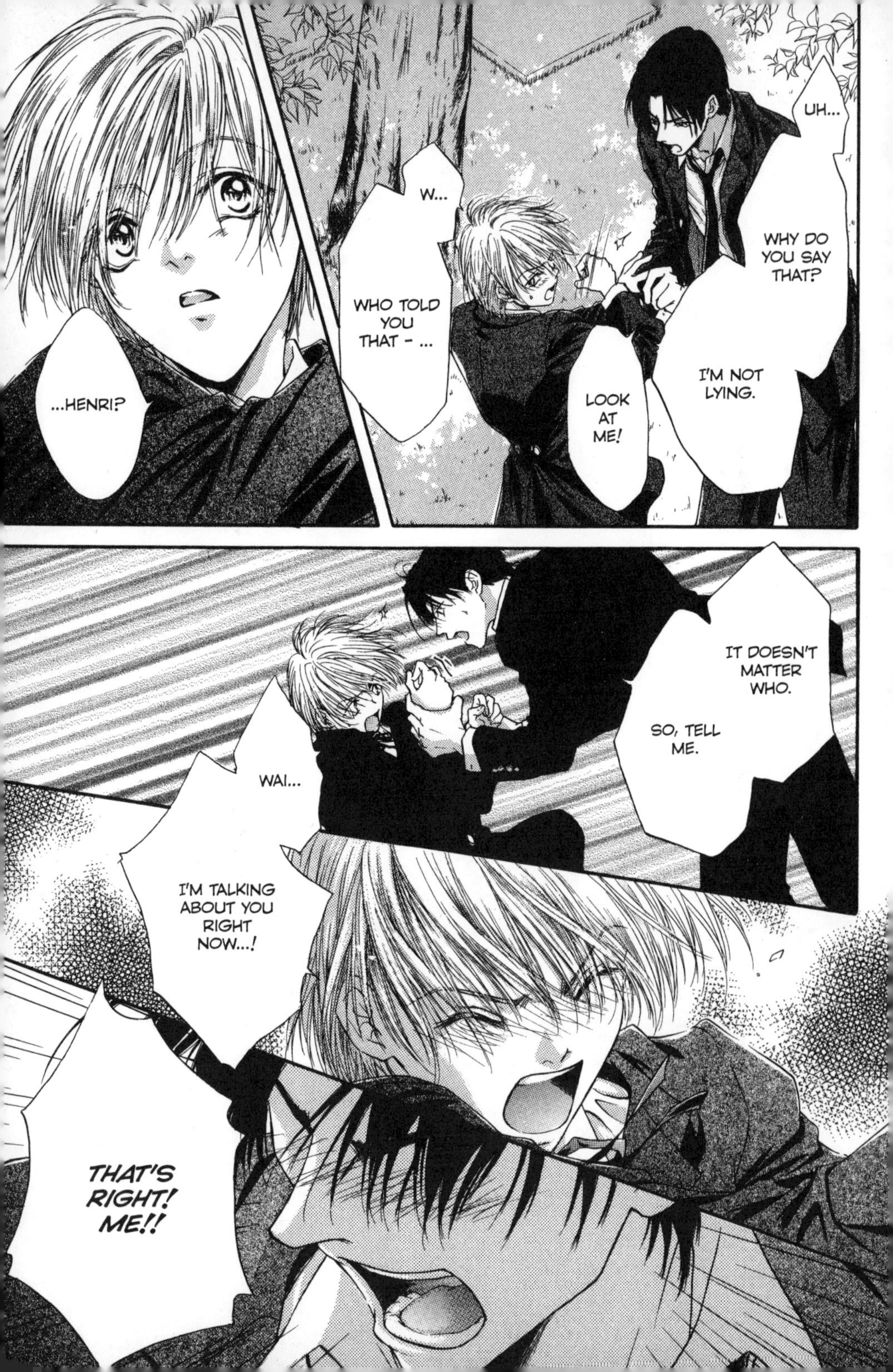
UH...
WHY DO YOU SAY THAT?
I'M NOT LYING.
LOOK AT ME!
W...
WHO TOLD YOU THAT - ...
...HENRI?
IT DOESN'T MATTER WHO.
SO, TELL ME.
WAI...
I'M TALKING ABOUT YOU RIGHT NOW...!
THAT'S RIGHT! ME!!

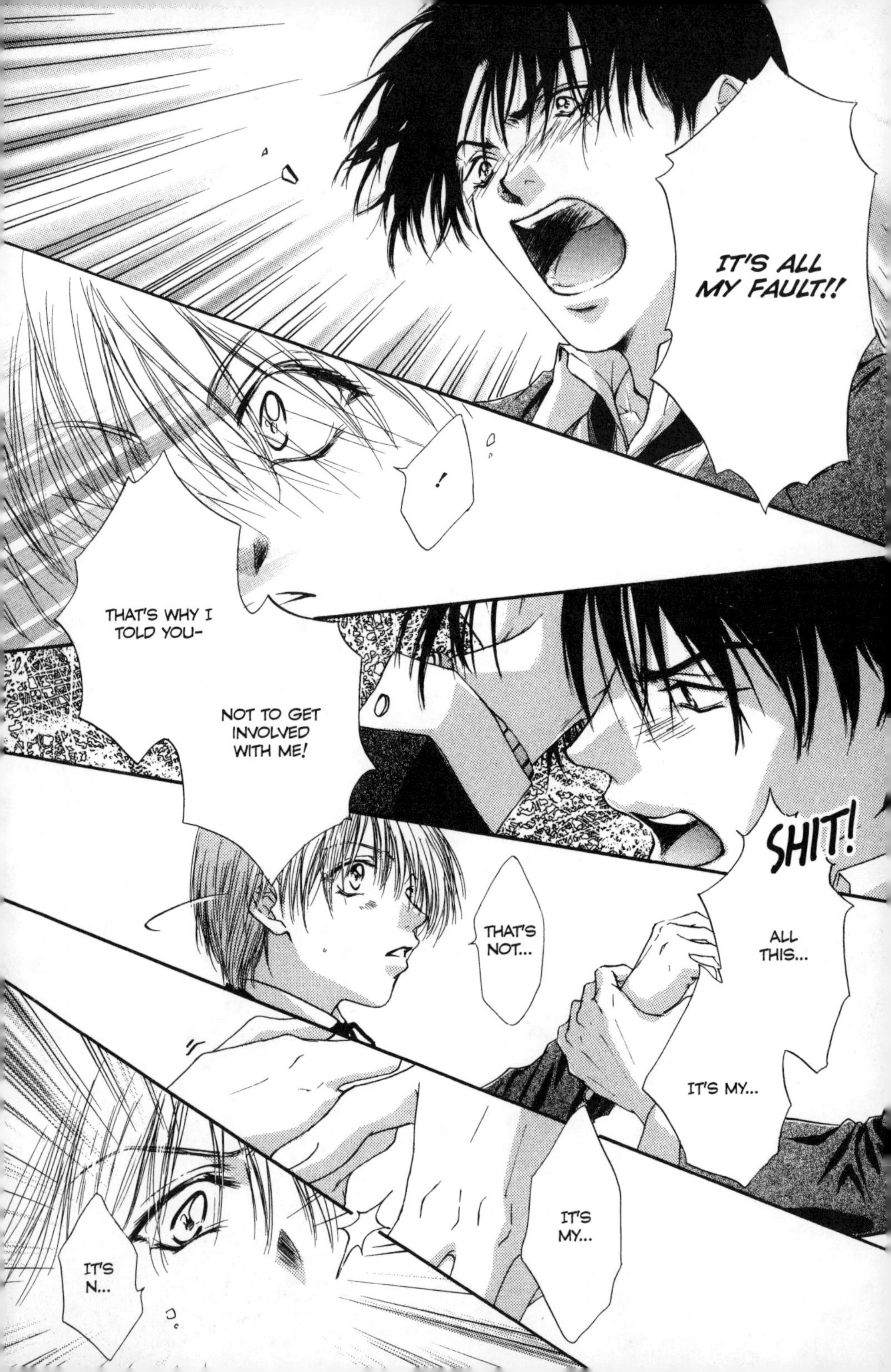
IT'S ALL MY FAULT!!
!
THAT'S WHY I TOLD YOU-
NOT TO GET INVOLVED WITH ME!
SHIT!
ALL THIS...
IT'S MY...
THAT'S NOT...
IT'S MY...
IT'S N...

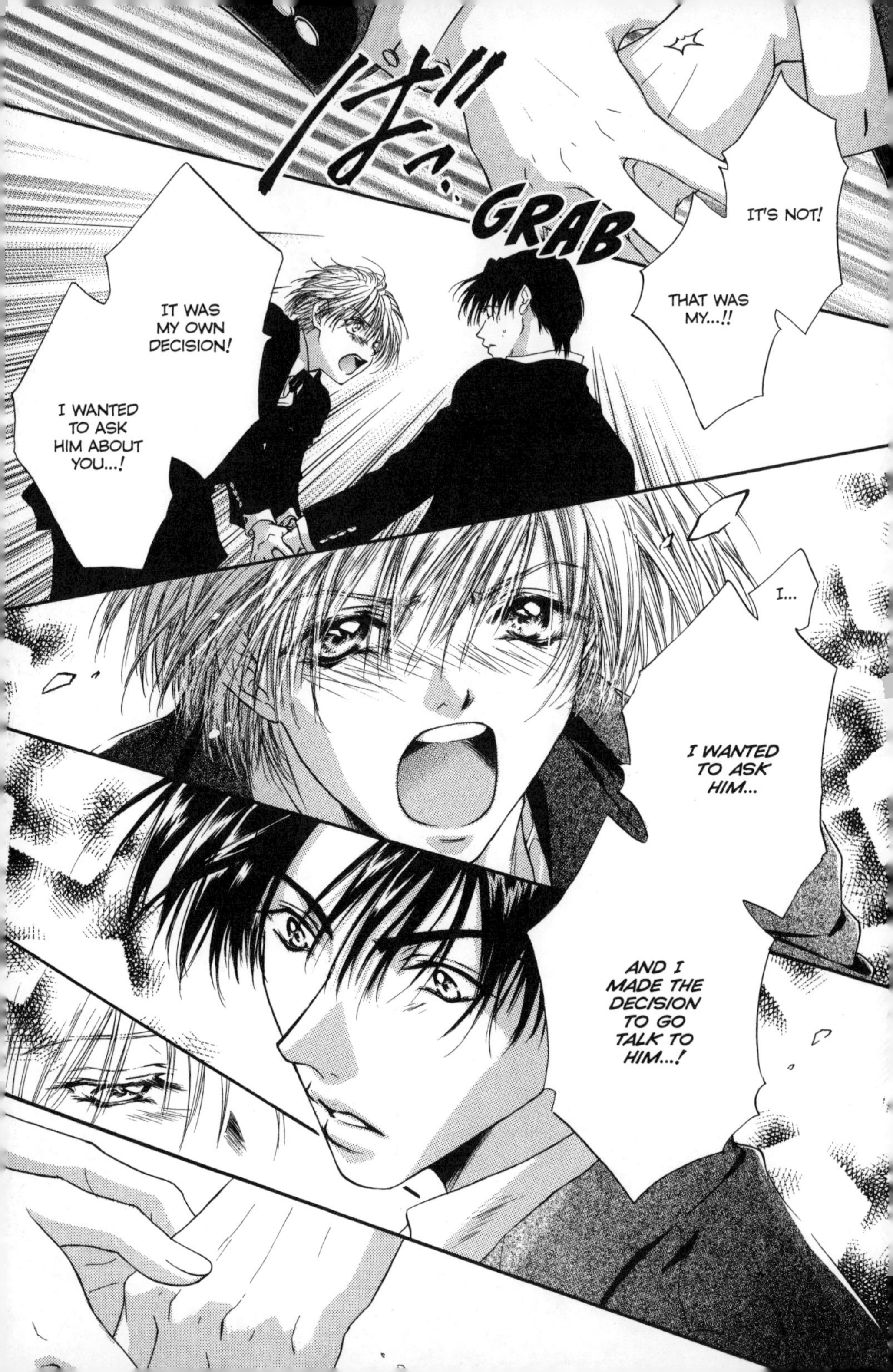
GRAB
IT'S NOT!
THAT WAS MY...!!
IT WAS MY OWN DECISION!
I WANTED TO ASK HIM ABOUT YOU...!
I...
I WANTED TO ASK HIM...
AND I MADE THE DECISION TO GO TALK TO HIM...!

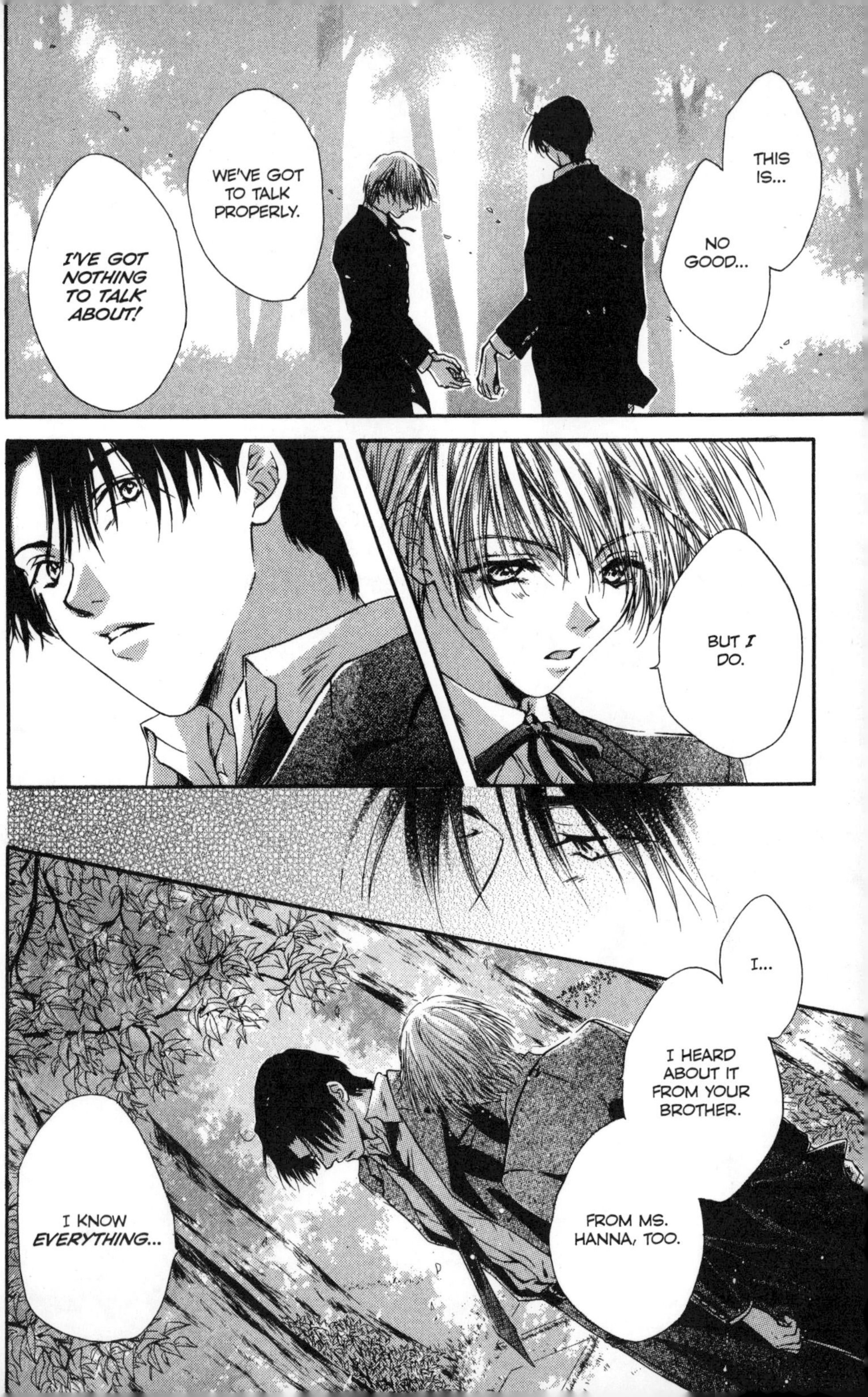
THIS IS... NO GOOD...
WE'VE GOT TO TALK PROPERLY.
I'VE GOT NOTHING TO TALK ABOUT!
BUT *I* DO.
I...
I HEARD ABOUT IT FROM YOUR BROTHER.
FROM MS. HANNA, TOO.
I KNOW *EVERYTHING*...

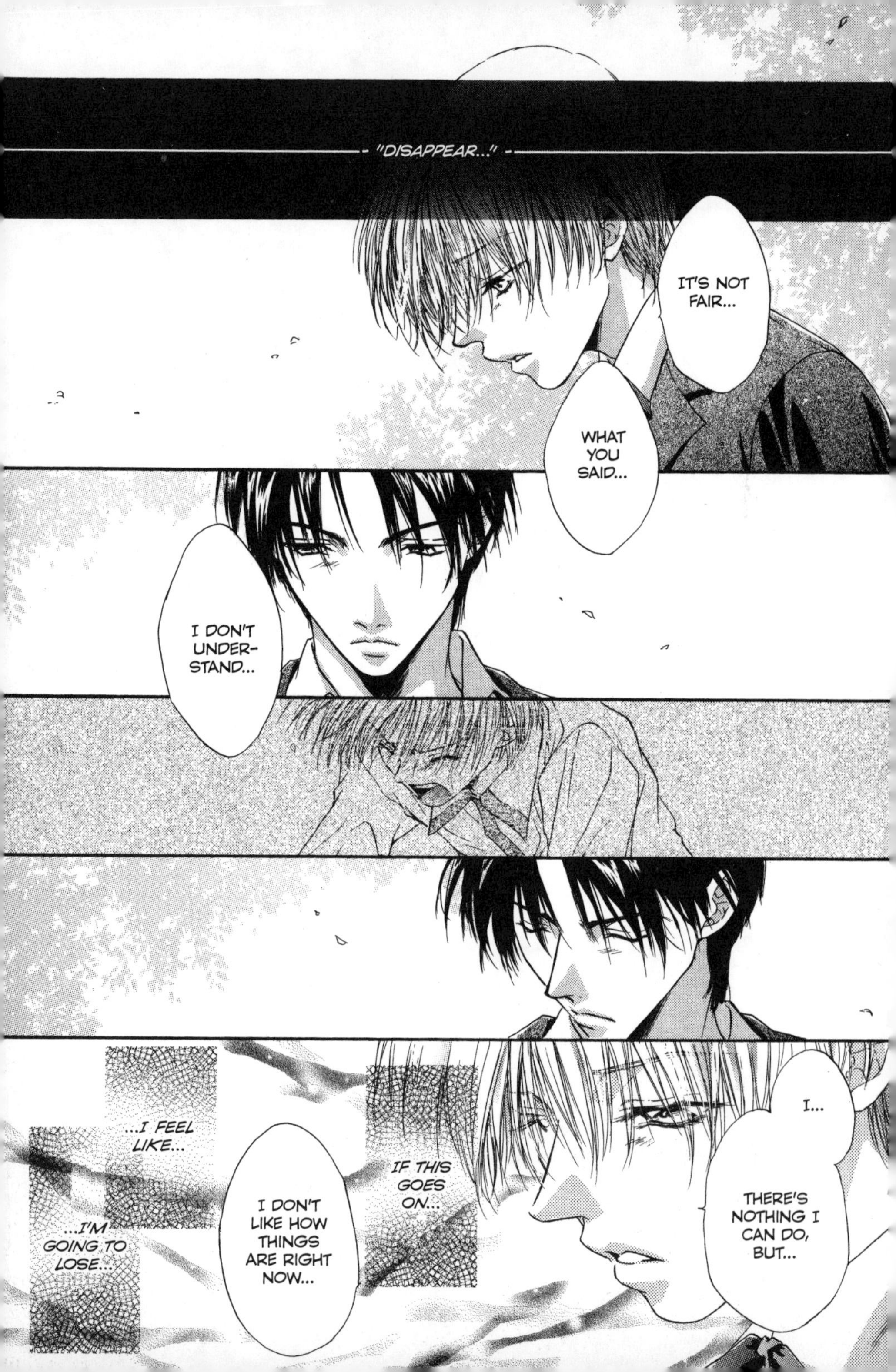
"DISAPPEAR..."
IT'S NOT FAIR...
WHAT YOU SAID...
I DON'T UNDER-STAND...
I...
THERE'S NOTHING I CAN DO, BUT...
IF THIS GOES ON...
I DON'T LIKE HOW THINGS ARE RIGHT NOW...
...I FEEL LIKE...
...I'M GOING TO LOSE...

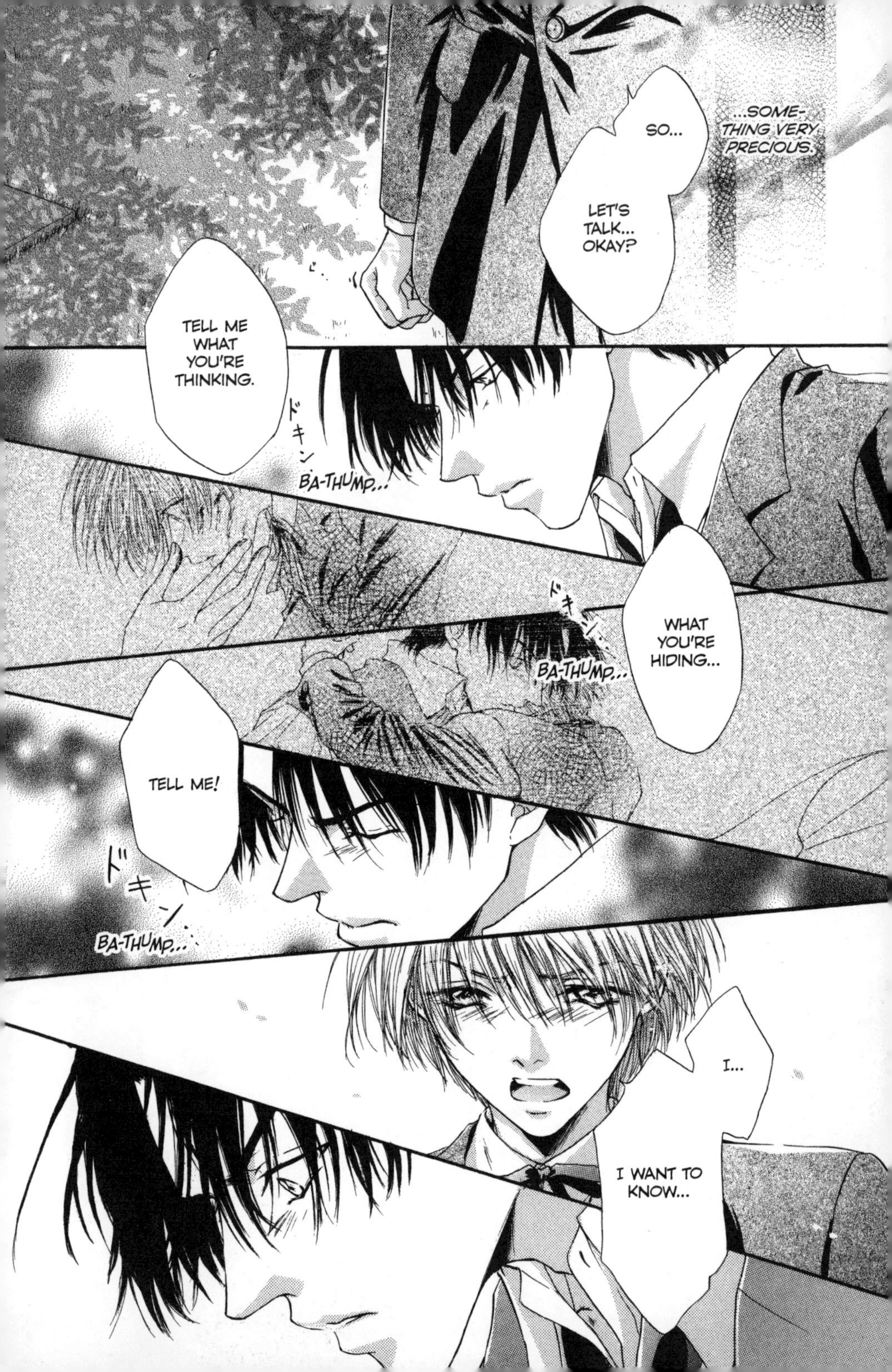

...SOME-THING VERY PRECIOUS.
SO...
LET'S TALK... OKAY?
TELL ME WHAT YOU'RE THINKING.
ドキン
BA-THUMP...
WHAT YOU'RE HIDING...
ドキン
BA-THUMP...
TELL ME!
ドキン
BA-THUMP...
I...
I WANT TO KNOW...

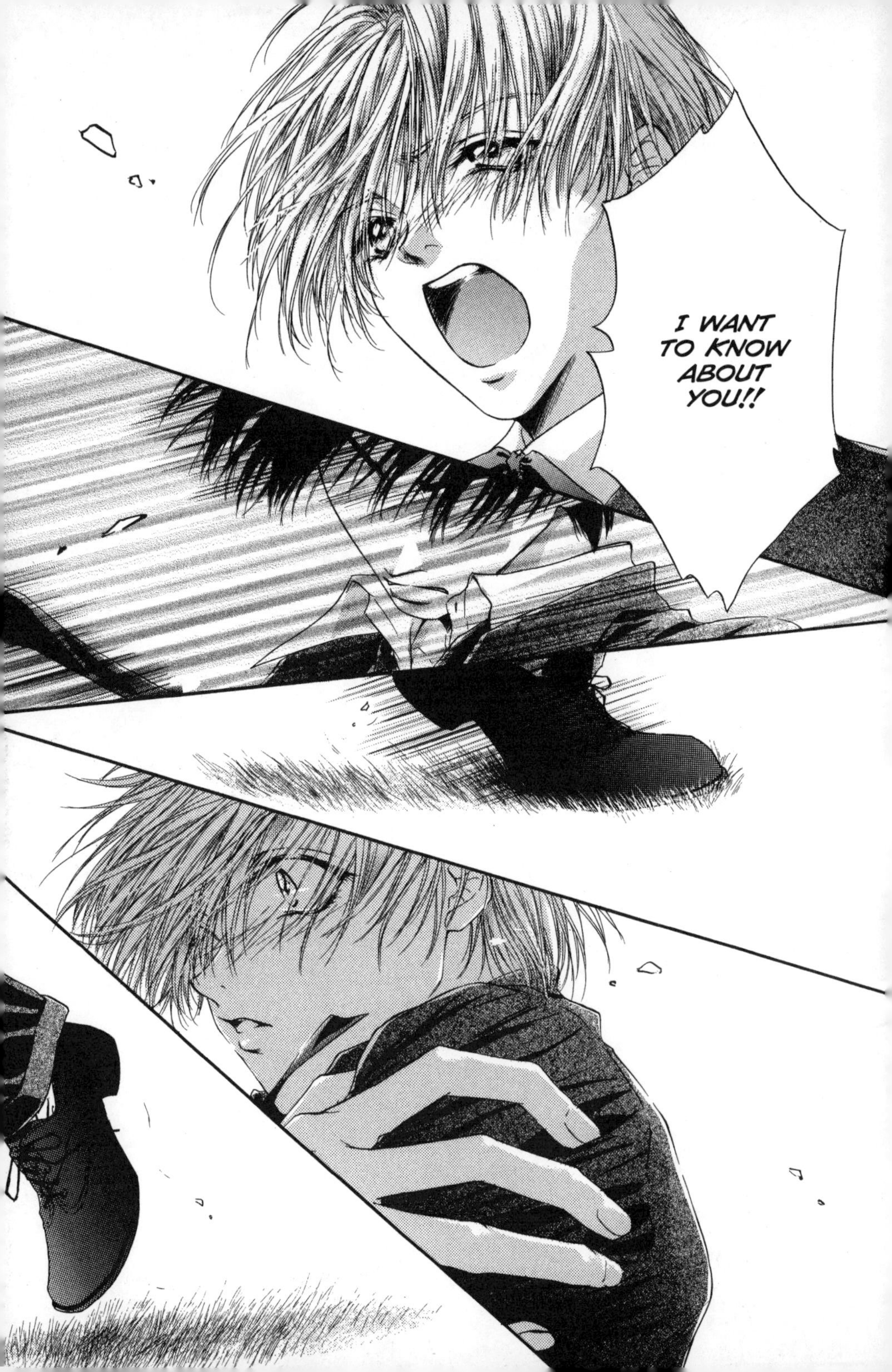
I WANT TO KNOW ABOUT YOU!!

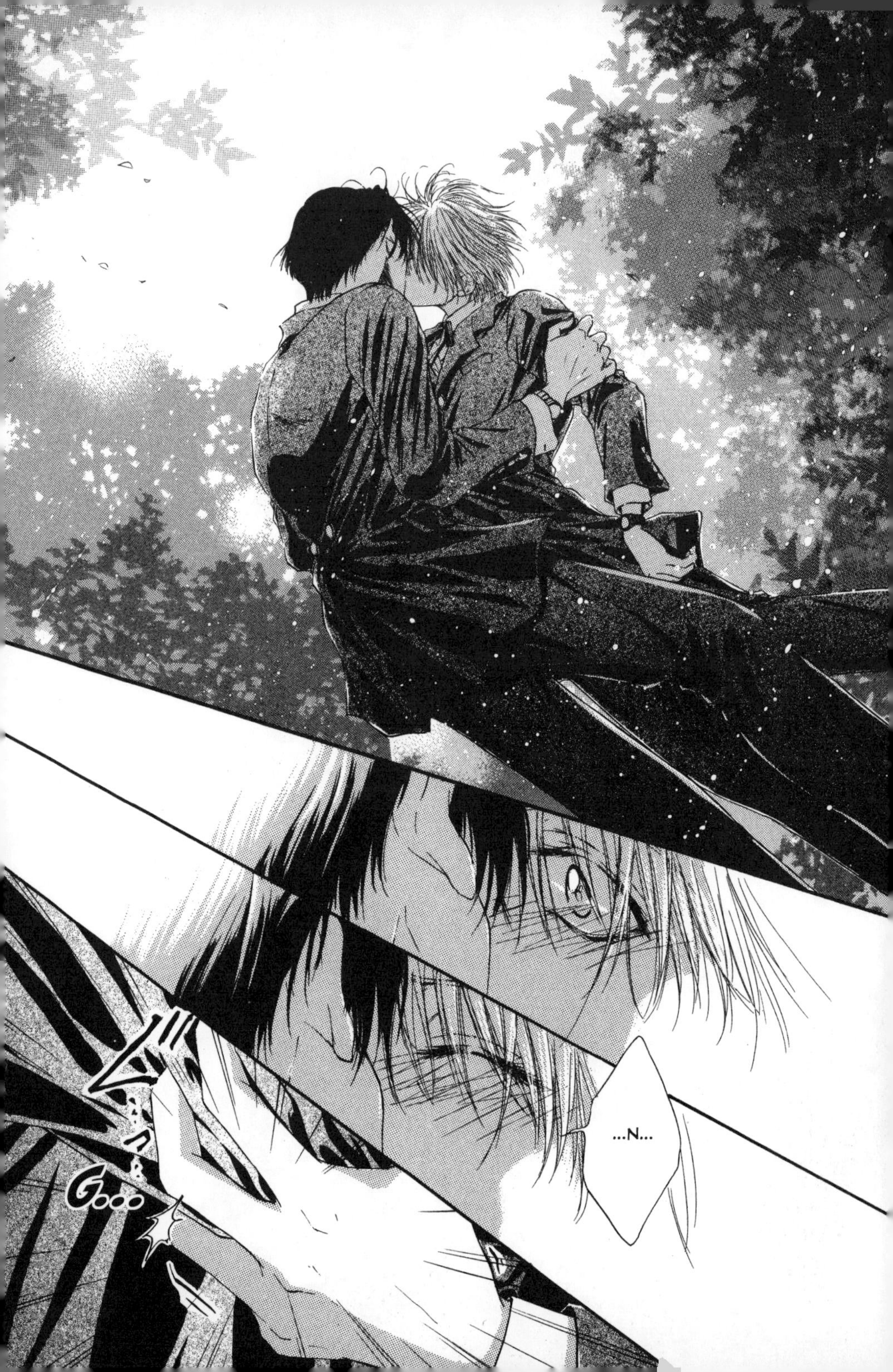
...N...
Goo

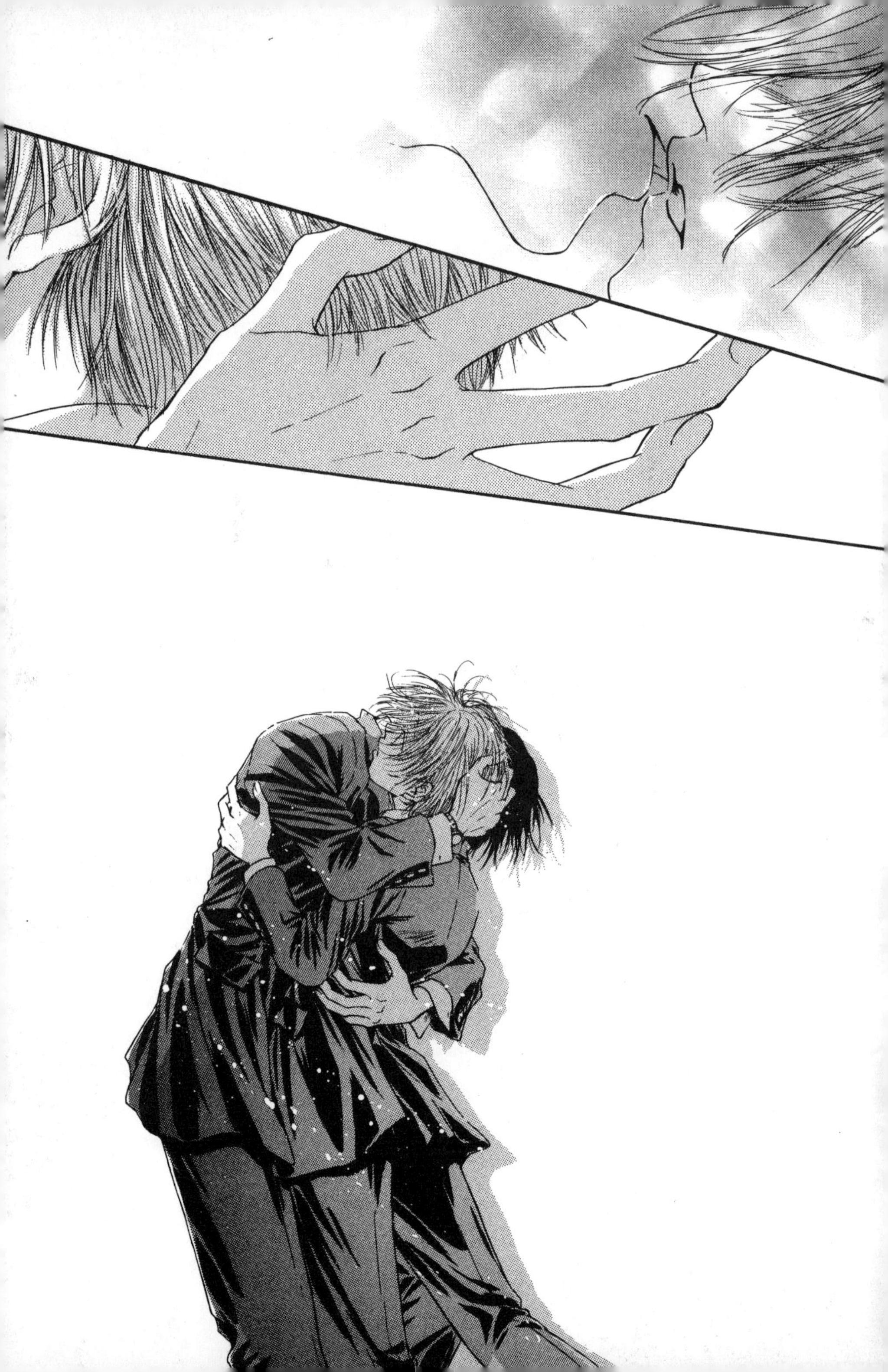

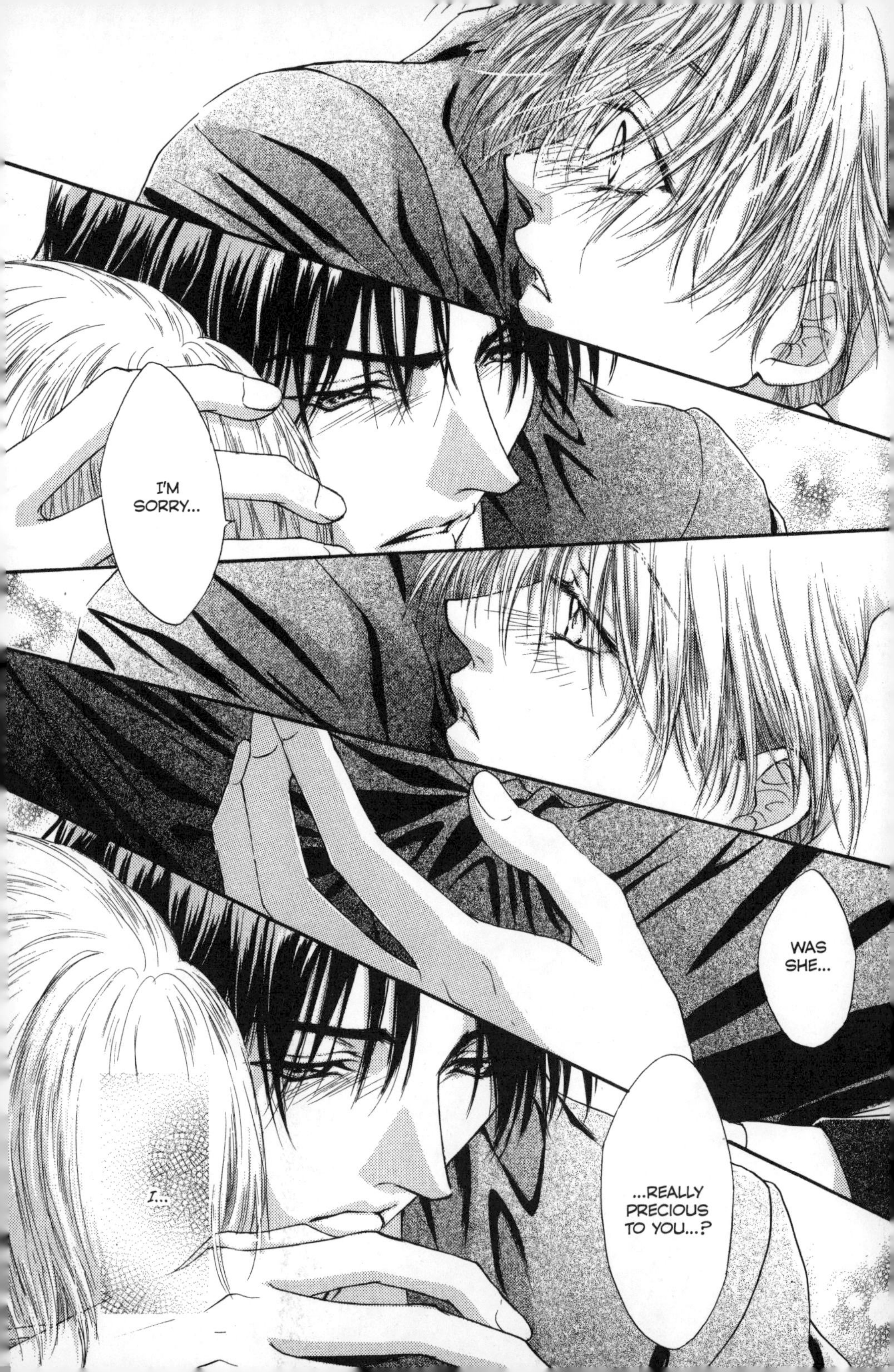
I'M SORRY...
WAS SHE...
...REALLY PRECIOUS TO YOU...?
I...

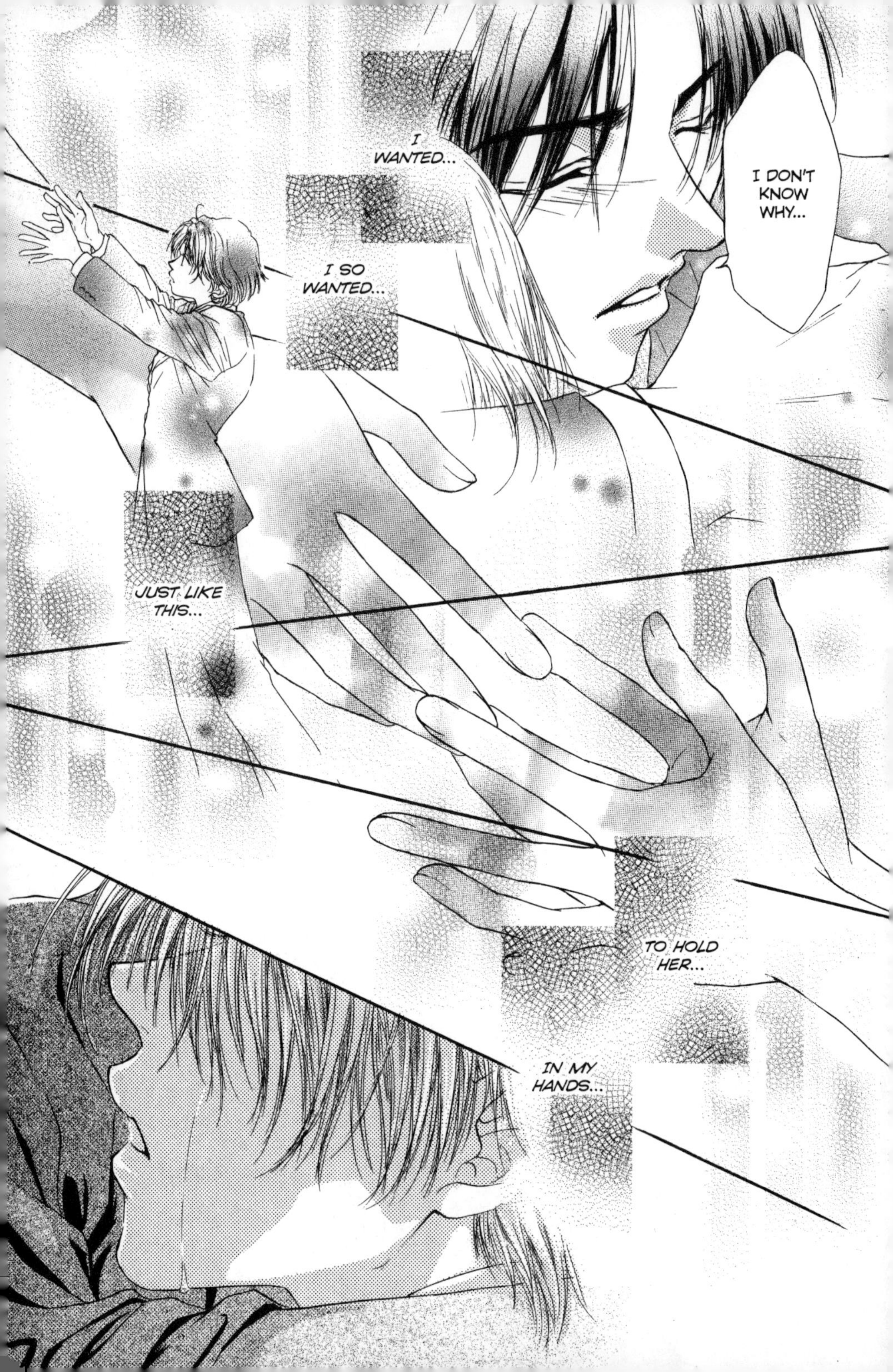
I DON'T KNOW WHY...
I WANTED...
I SO WANTED...
JUST LIKE THIS...
TO HOLD HER...
IN MY HANDS...

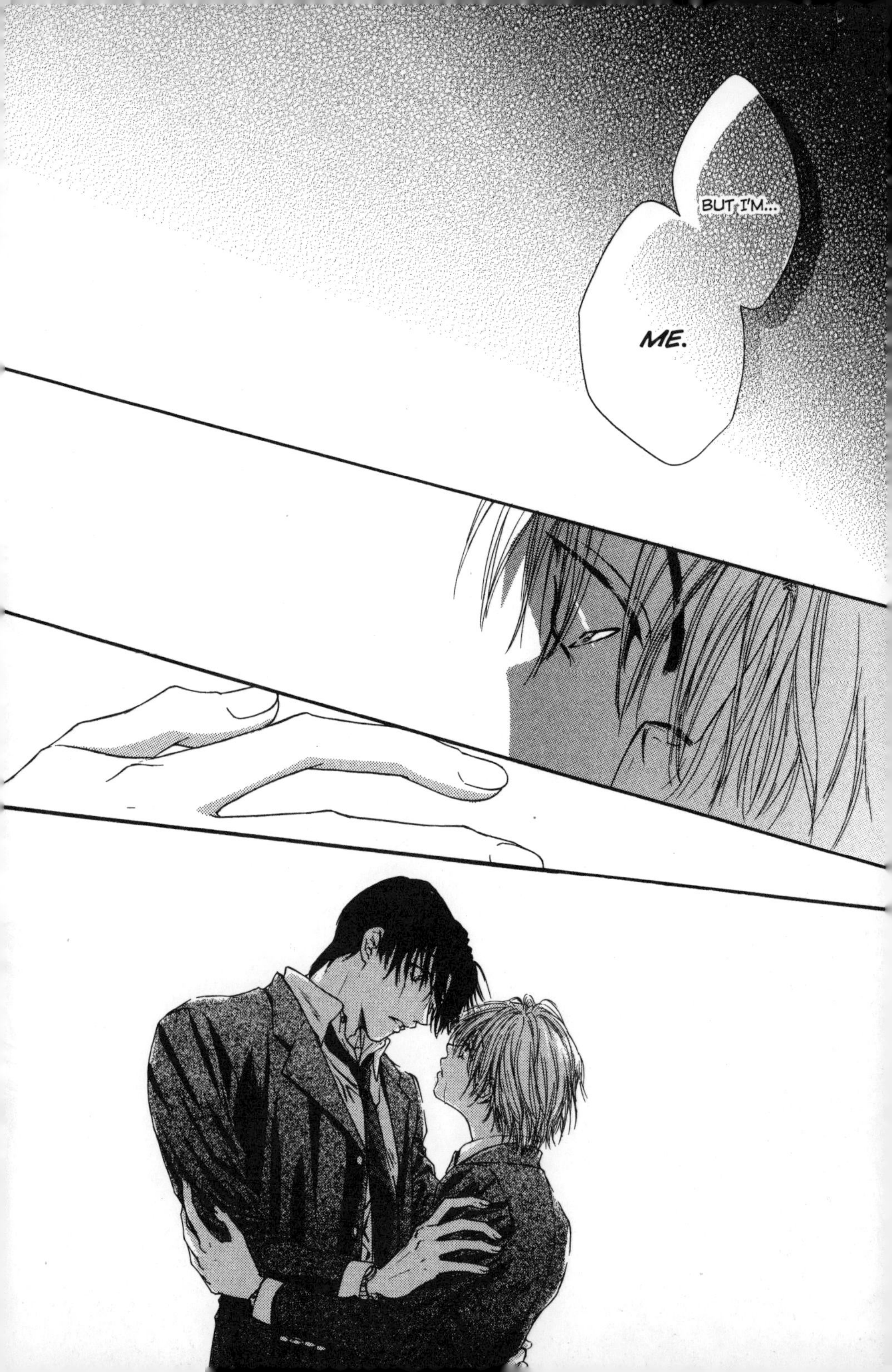
BUT I'M...
ME.

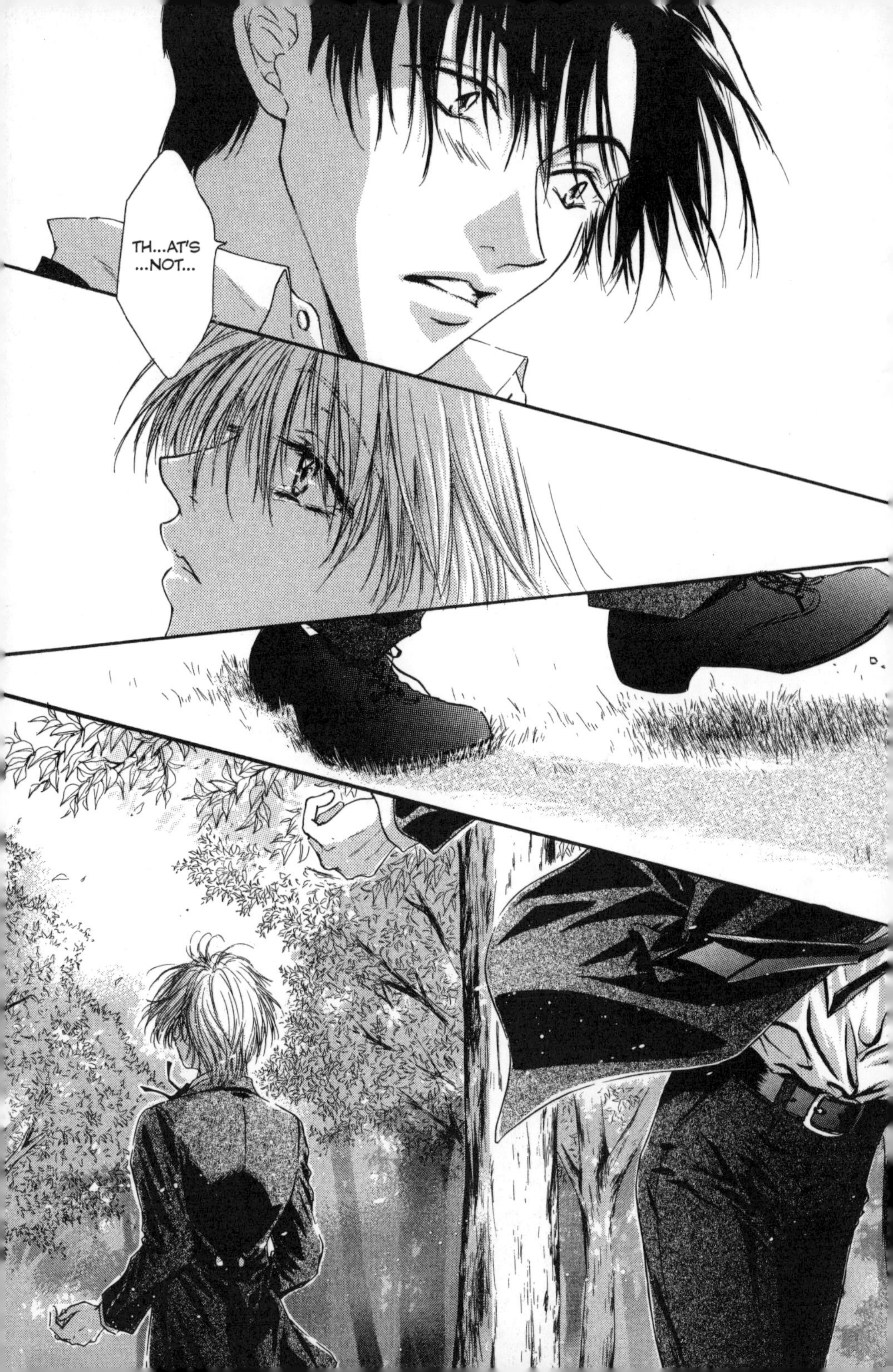
TH...AT'S ...NOT...

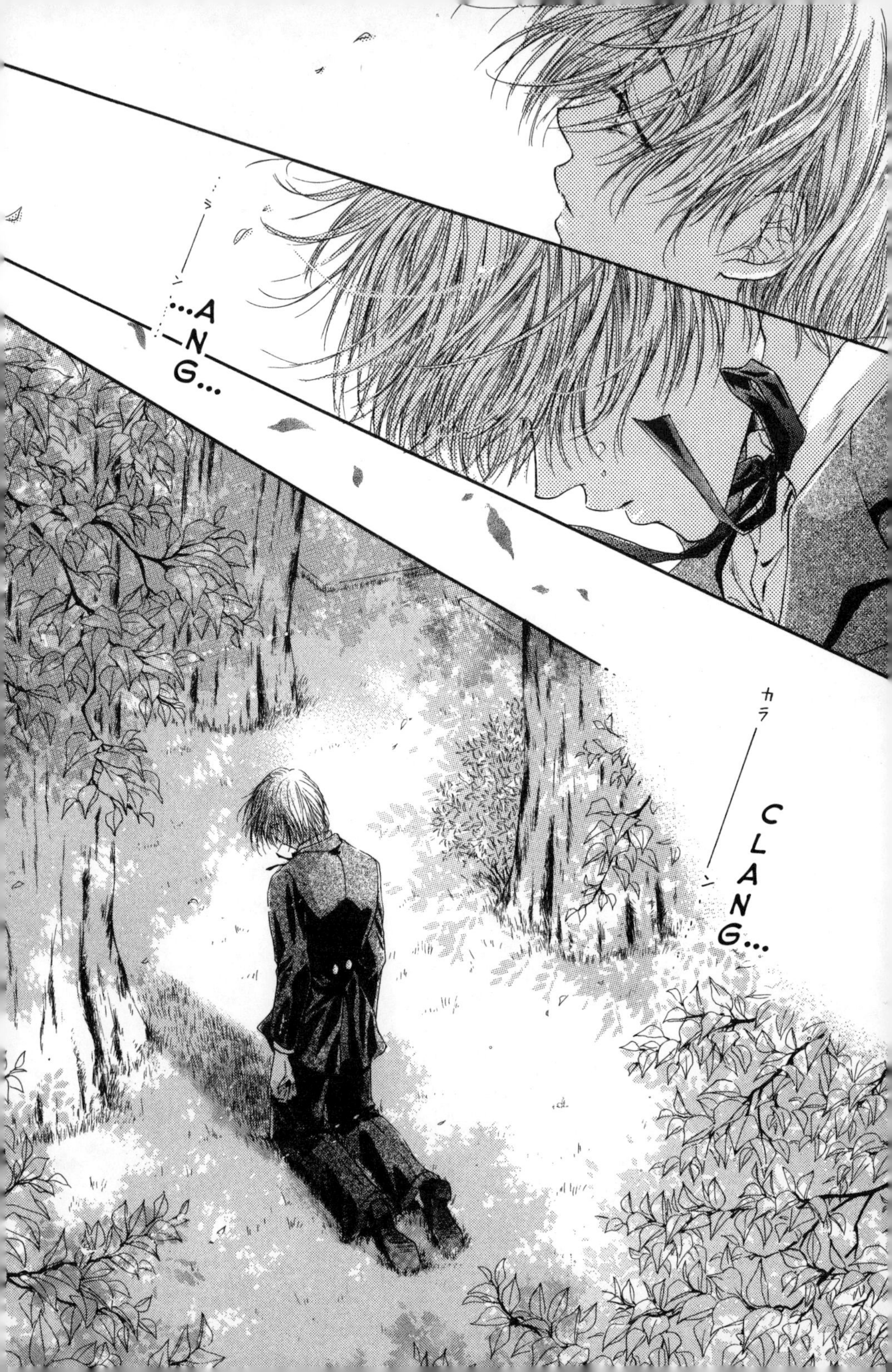

カラーン
...ANG...
カラーン
CLANG...

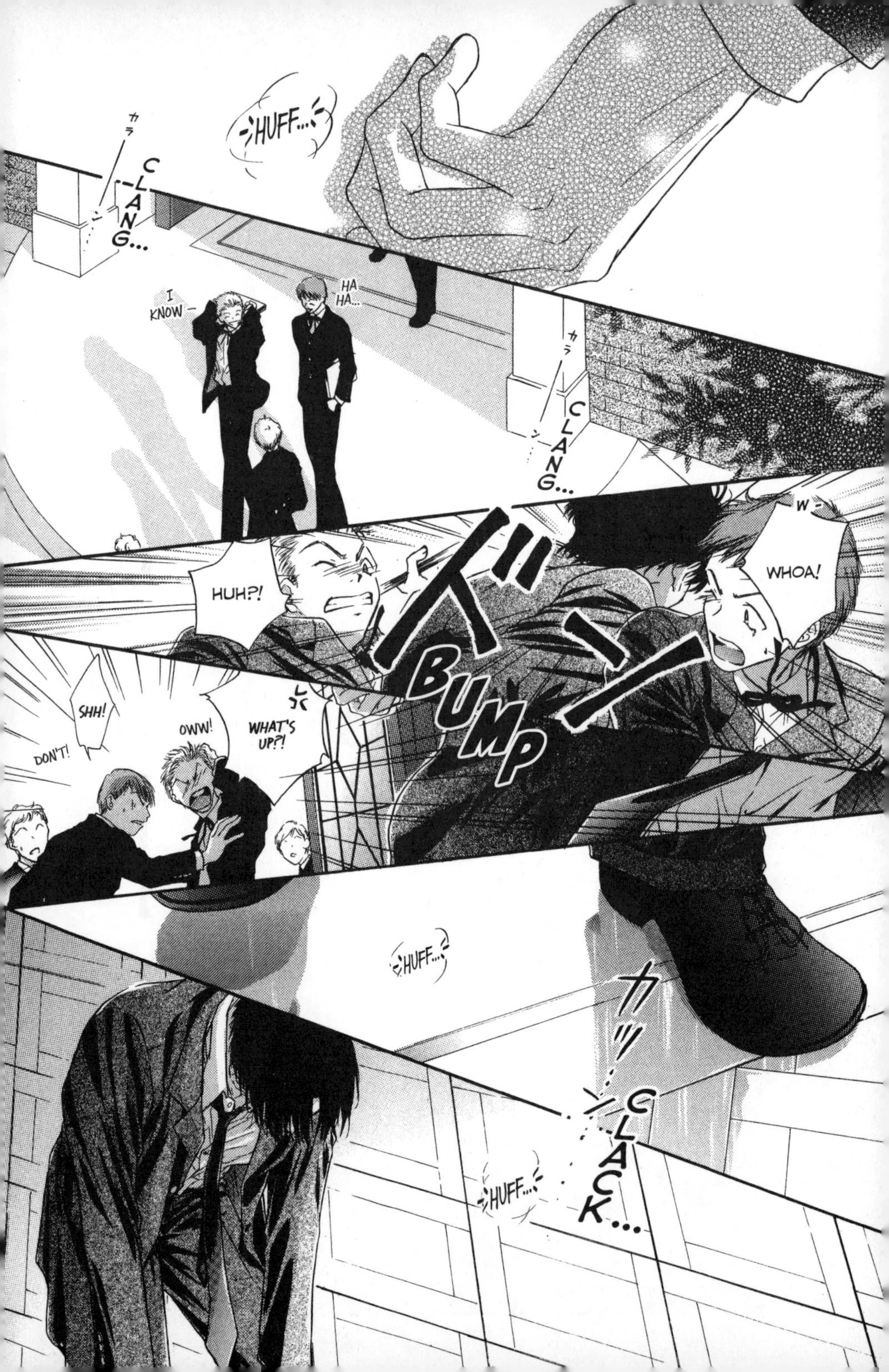

HUFF...
CLANG...
CLANG...
HA HA...
I KNOW
W-
WHOA!
BUMP
HUH?!
WHAT'S UP?!
OWW!
SHH!
DON'T!
CLACK...
HUFF...
HUFF...

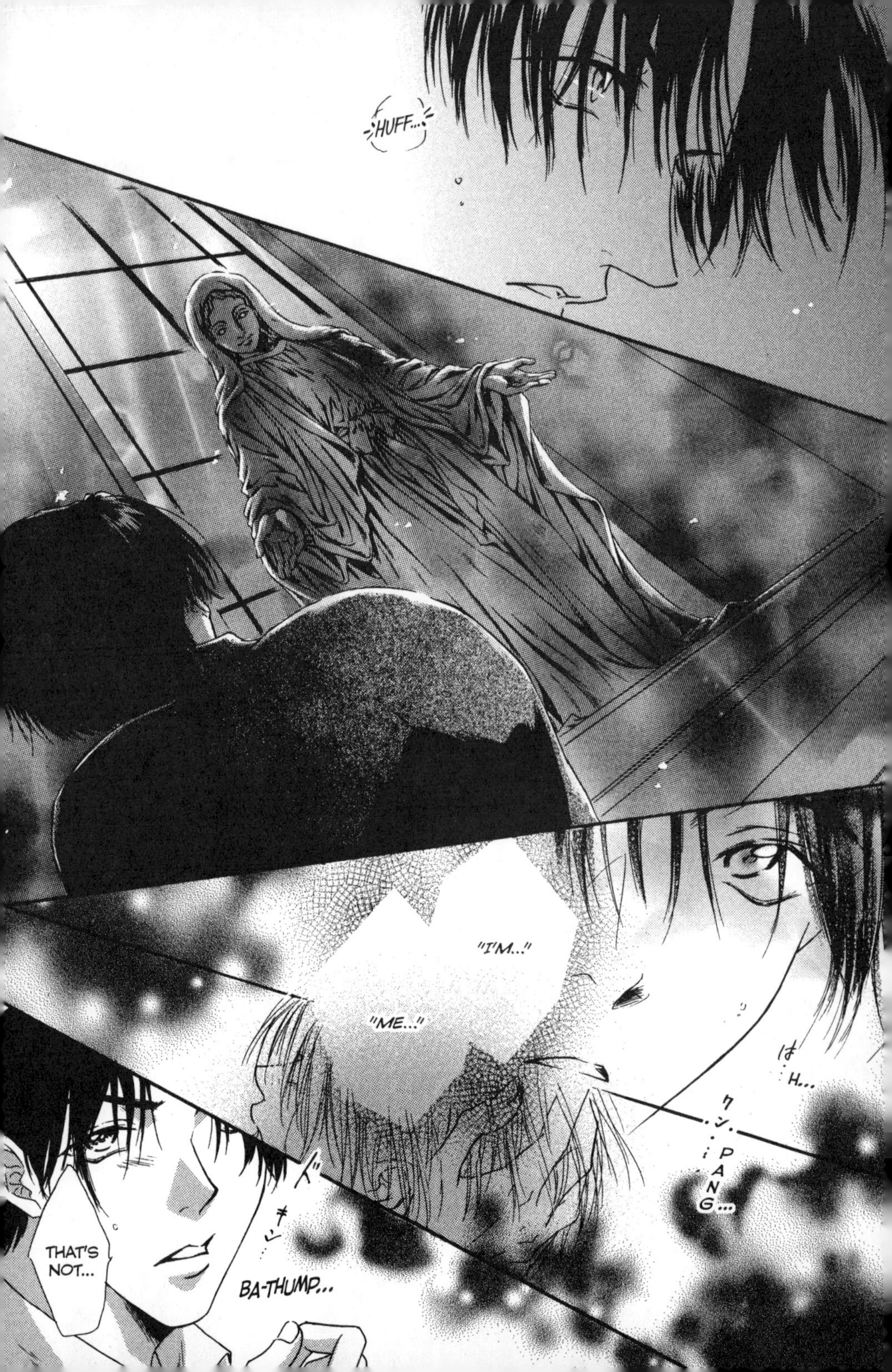
HUFF...
"I'M..."
"ME..."
は H...
クン PANG...
ドキン BA-THUMP...
THAT'S NOT...

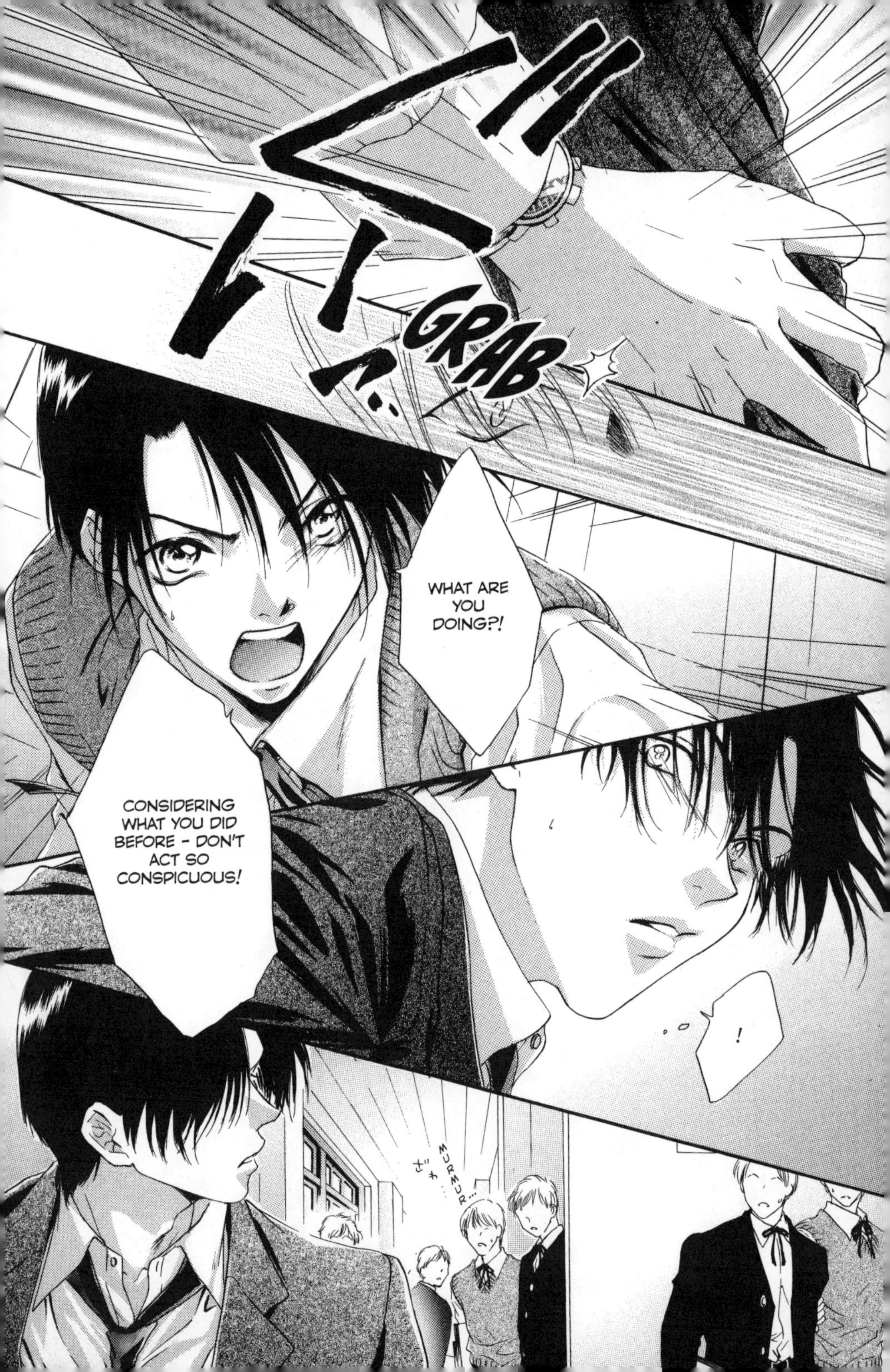
GRAB
WHAT ARE YOU DOING?!
CONSIDERING WHAT YOU DID BEFORE - DON'T ACT SO CONSPICUOUS!
!
MURMUR...

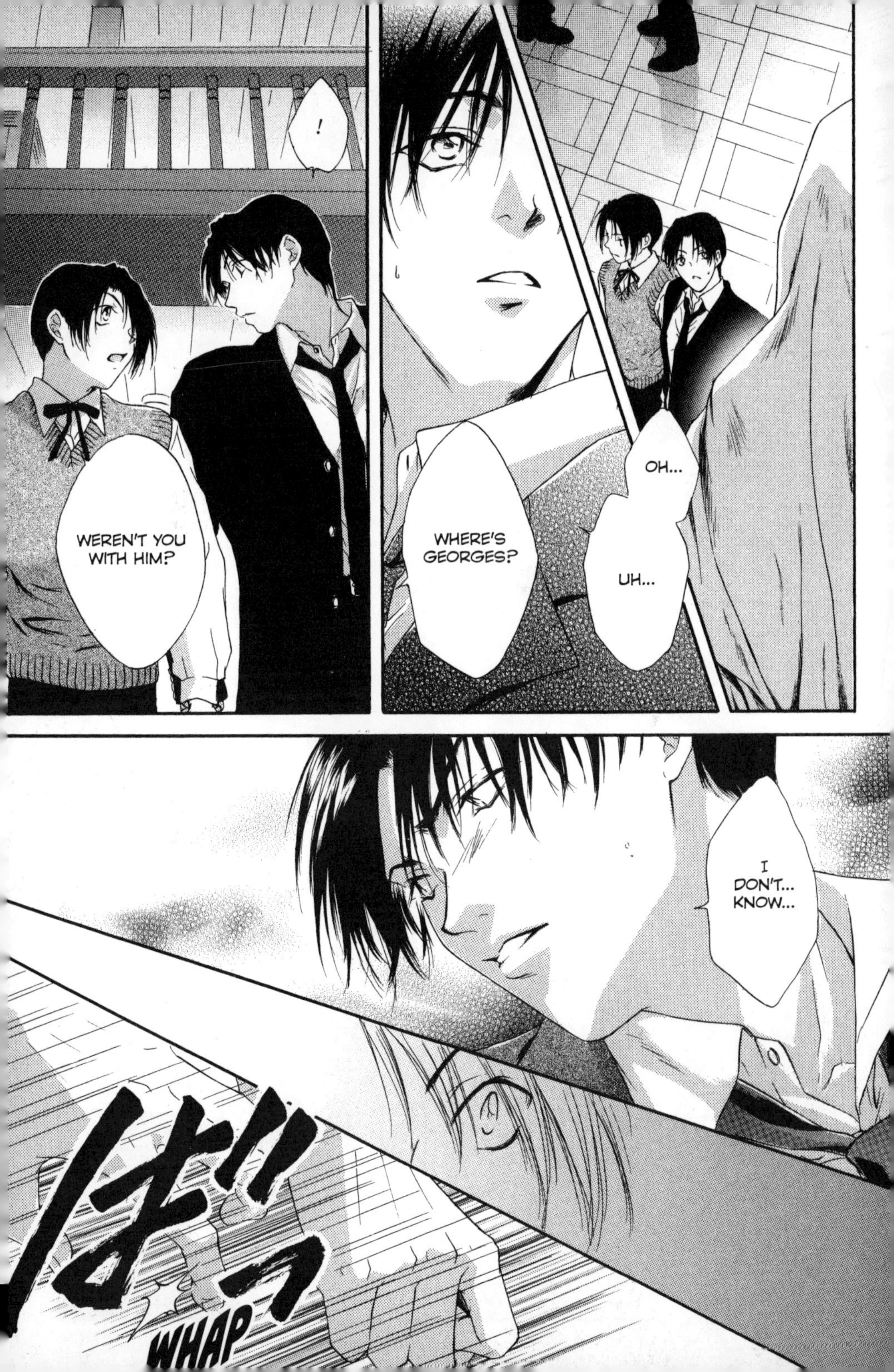
!
WEREN'T YOU WITH HIM?
WHERE'S GEORGES?
OH...
UH...
I DON'T... KNOW...
WHAP

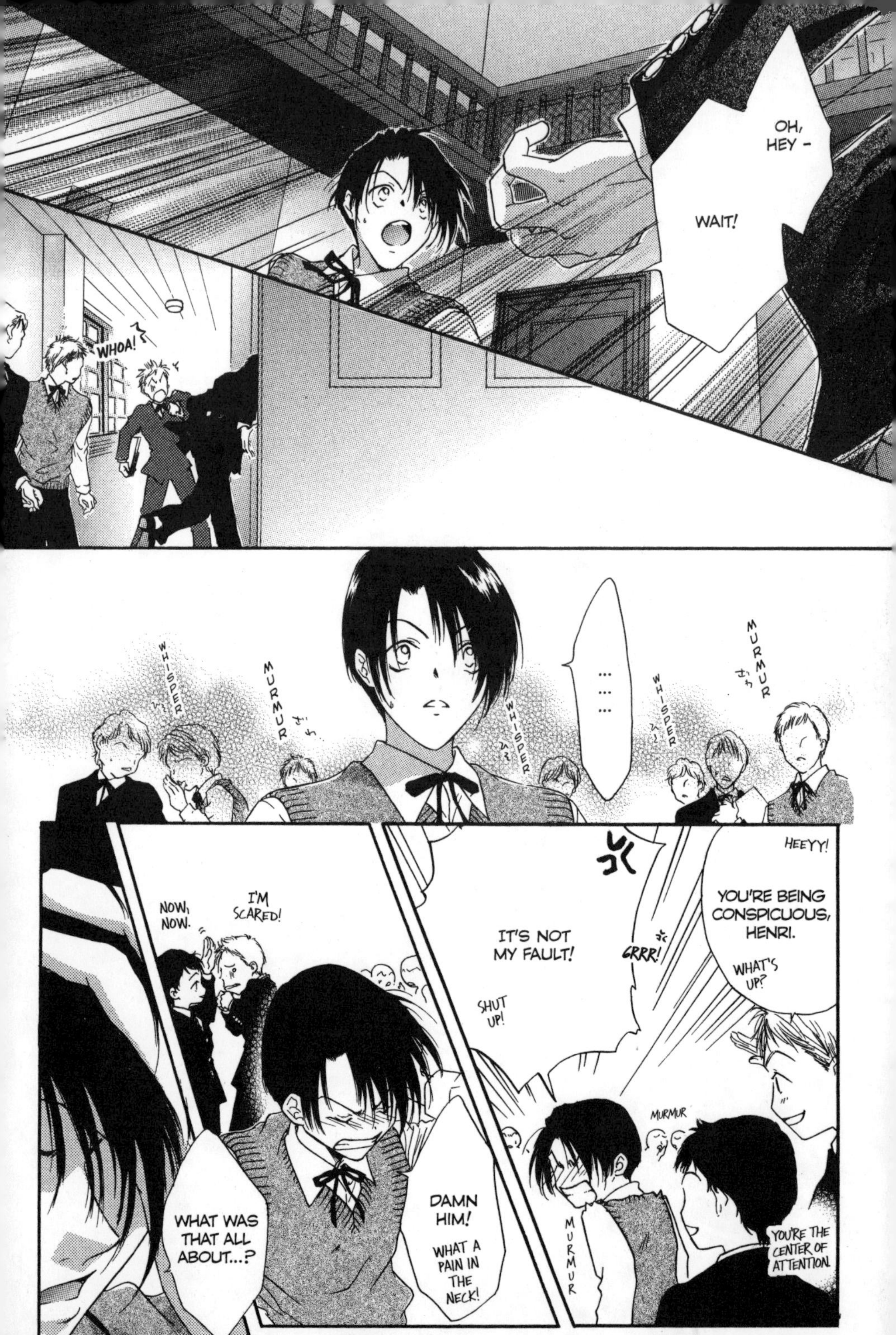
OH, HEY -
WAIT!
WHOA!
MURMUR
WHISPER
...
...
...
MURMUR
WHISPER
HEEYY!
YOU'RE BEING CONSPICUOUS, HENRI.
WHAT'S UP?
IT'S NOT MY FAULT!
GRRR!
SHUT UP!
MURMUR
MURMUR
YOU'RE THE CENTER OF ATTENTION.
I'M SCARED!
NOW, NOW.
DAMN HIM!
WHAT A PAIN IN THE NECK!
WHAT WAS THAT ALL ABOUT...?

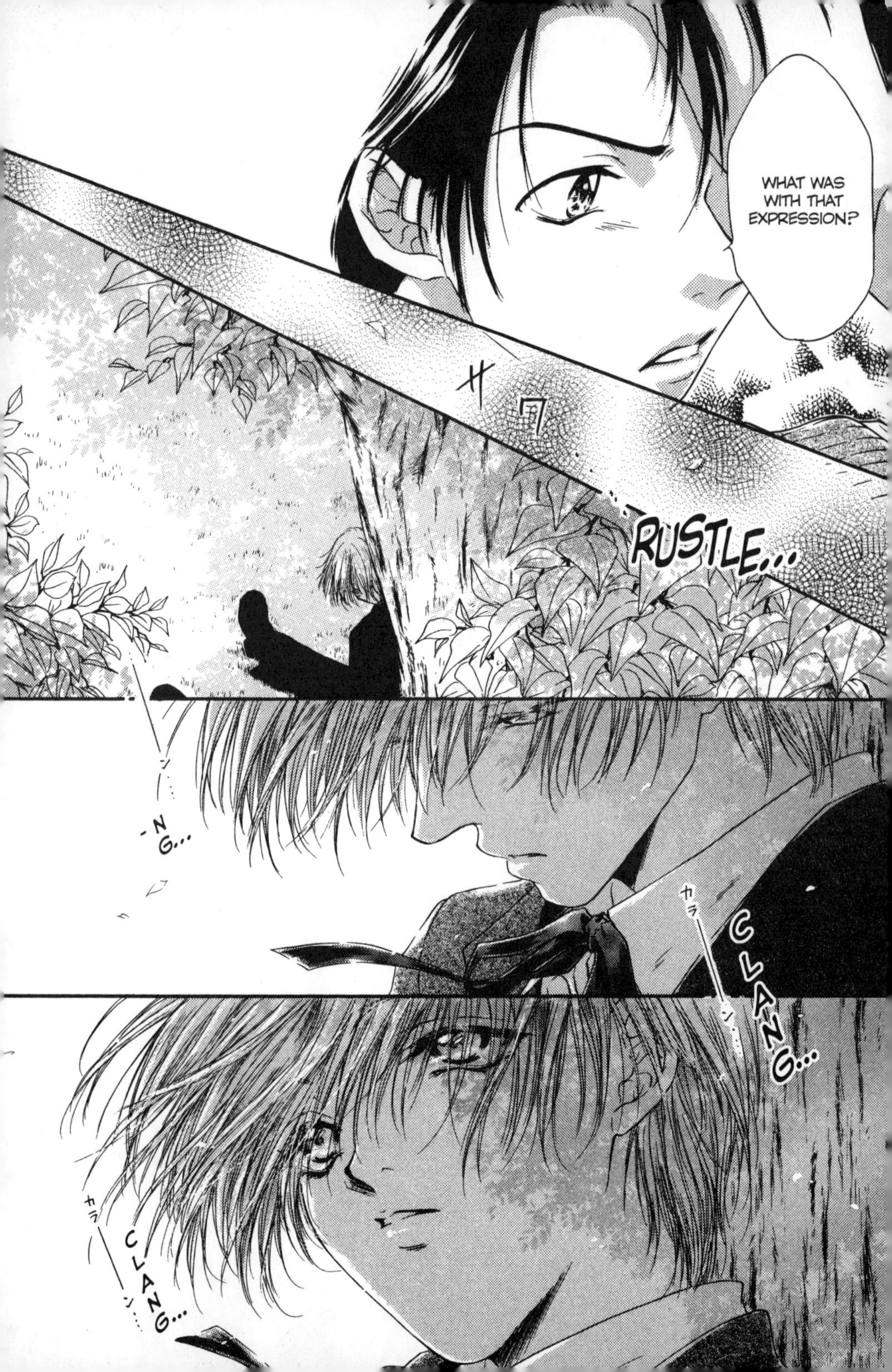

WHAT WAS WITH THAT EXPRESSION?
RUSTLE...
CLANG...
-NG...
CLANG...

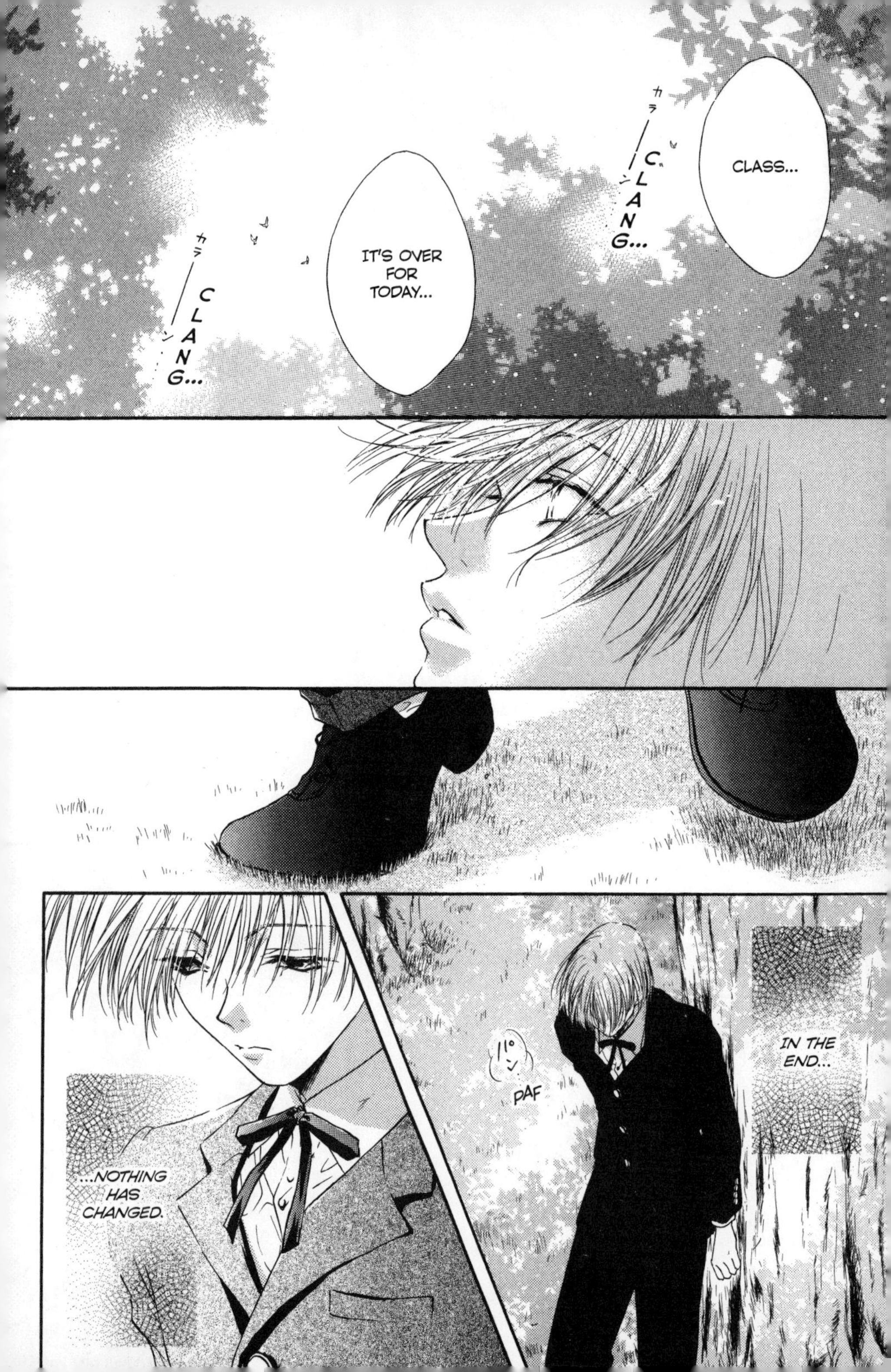
CLASS...
CLANG...
IT'S OVER FOR TODAY...
CLANG...
IN THE END...
PAF
...NOTHING HAS CHANGED.

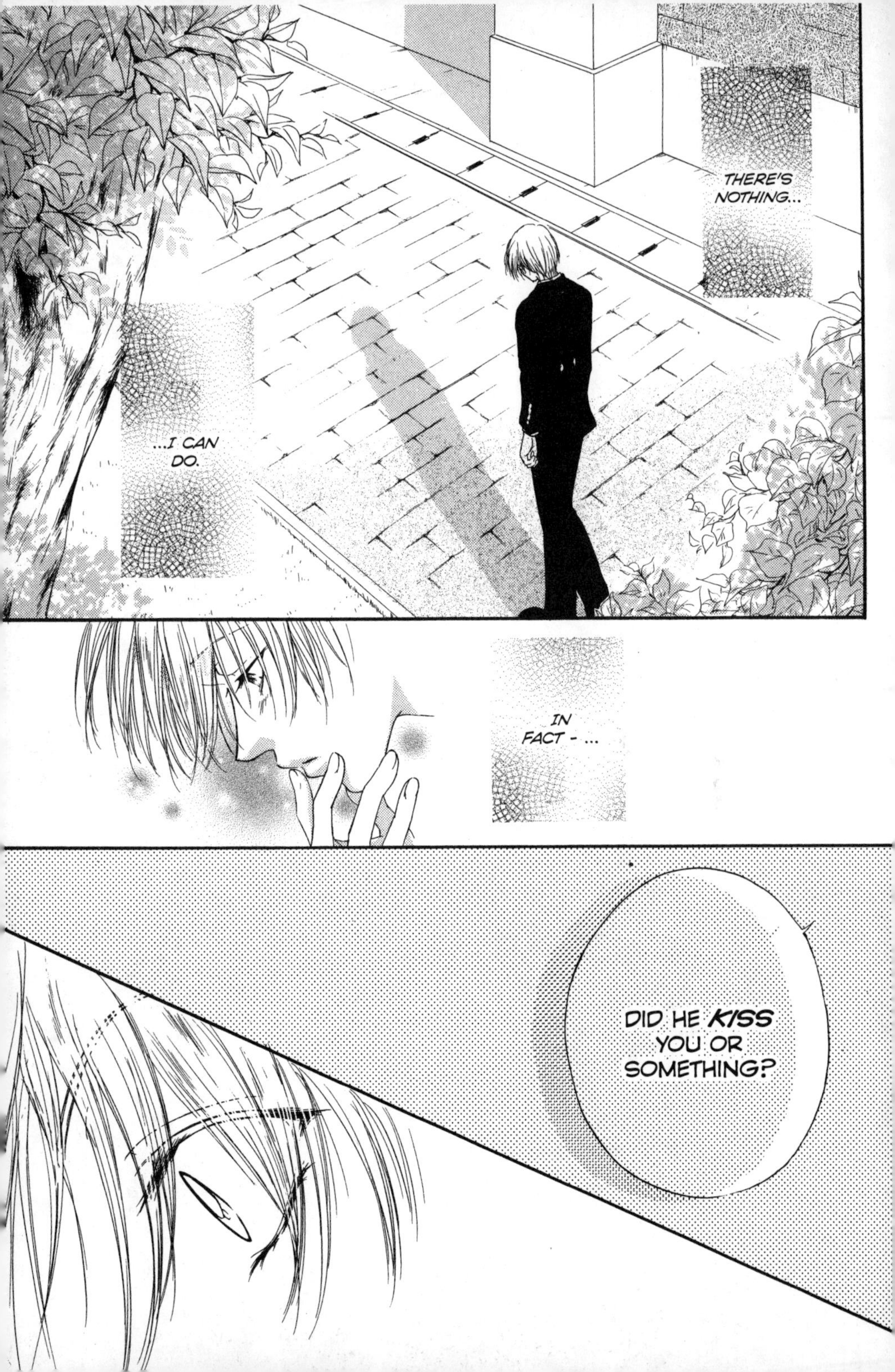
THERE'S NOTHING...
...I CAN DO.
IN FACT - ...
DID HE **KISS** YOU OR SOMETHING?

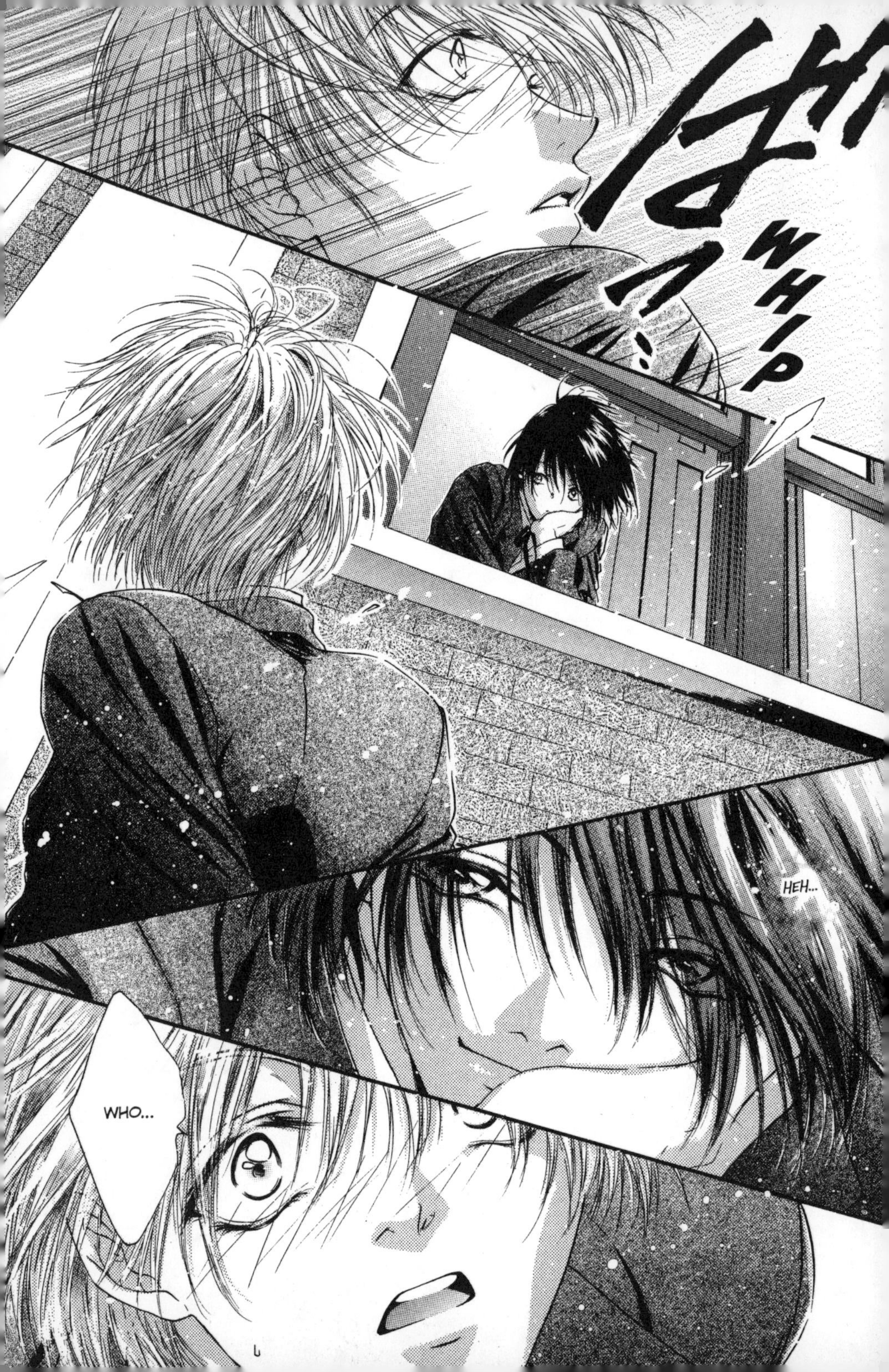
はっ
WHIP
HEH...
WHO...

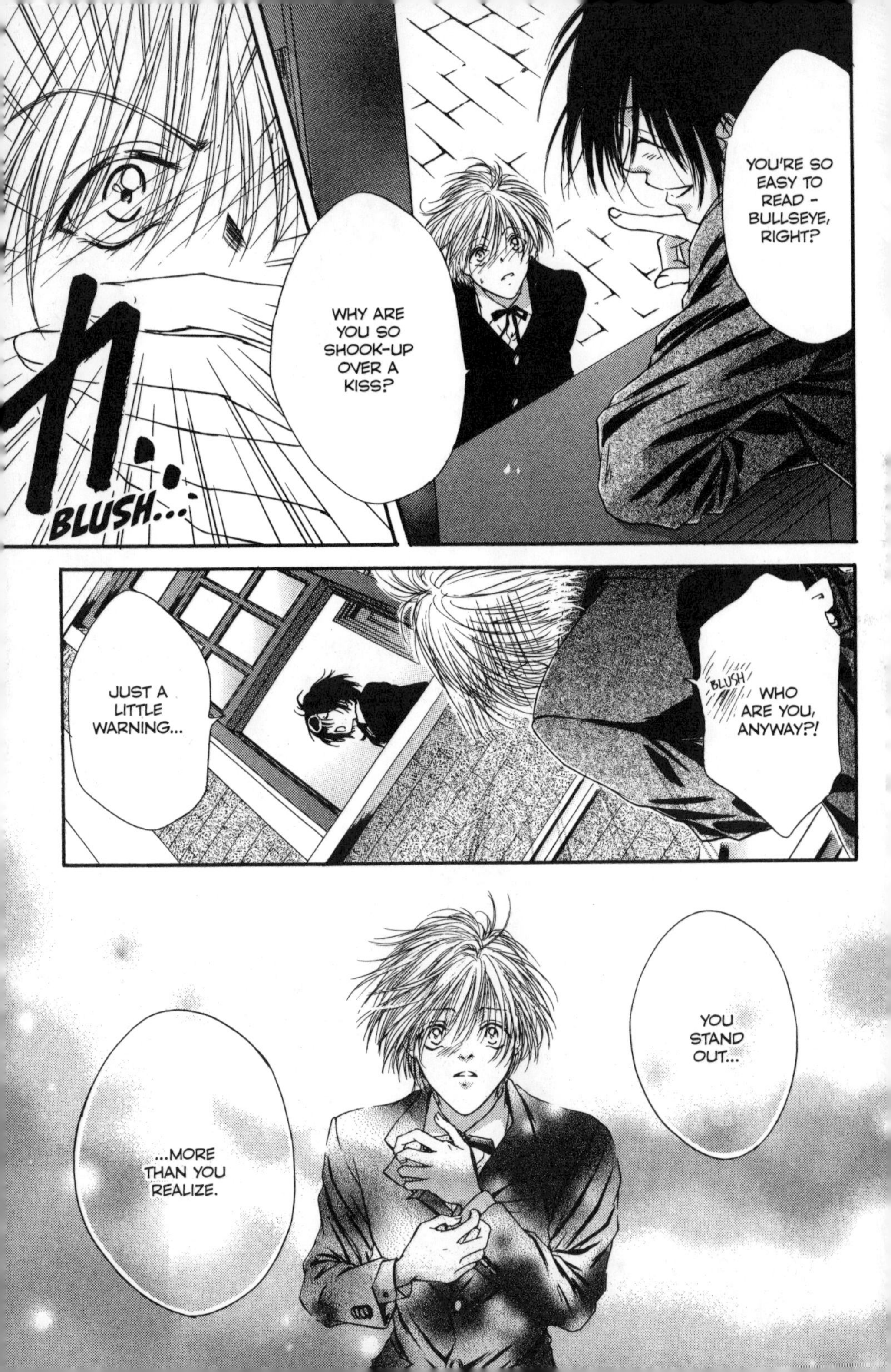
YOU'RE SO EASY TO READ - BULLSEYE, RIGHT?
WHY ARE YOU SO SHOOK-UP OVER A KISS?
BLUSH...
BLUSH
WHO ARE YOU, ANYWAY?!
JUST A LITTLE WARNING...
YOU STAND OUT...
...MORE THAN YOU REALIZE.

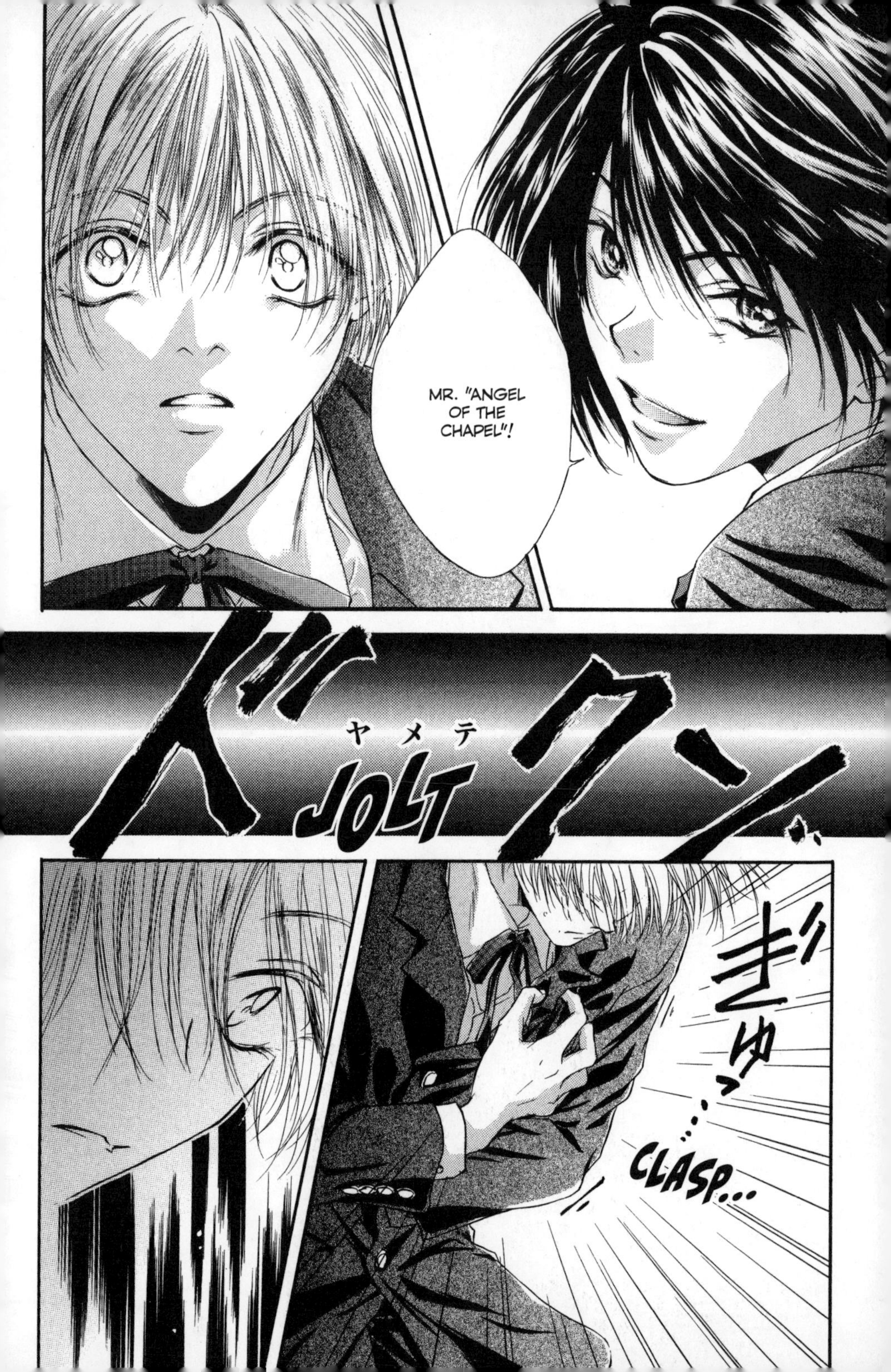
MR. "ANGEL OF THE CHAPEL"!
ドクン
ヤメテ
JOLT
きゅっ
CLASP...

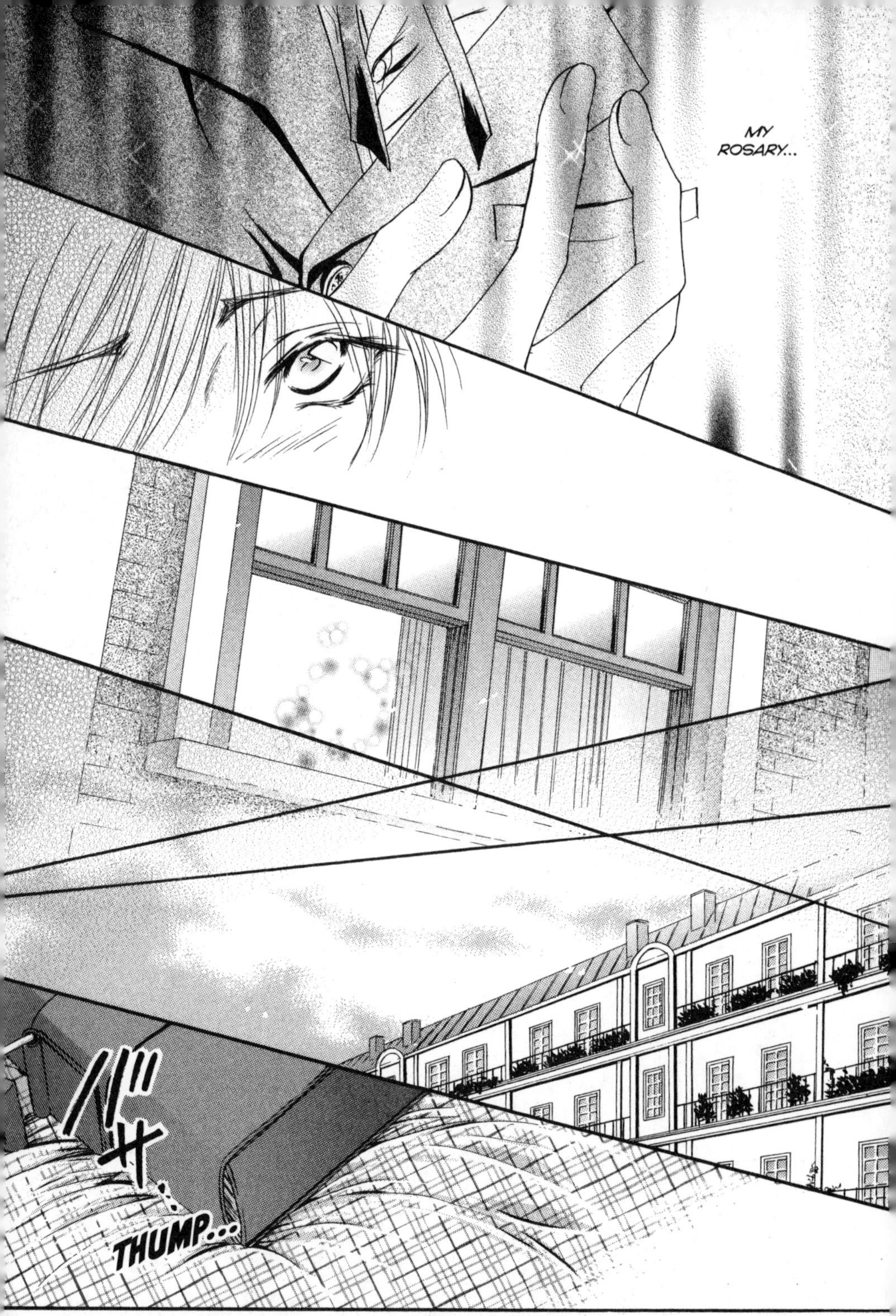
MY ROSARY...
バサ...
THUMP...

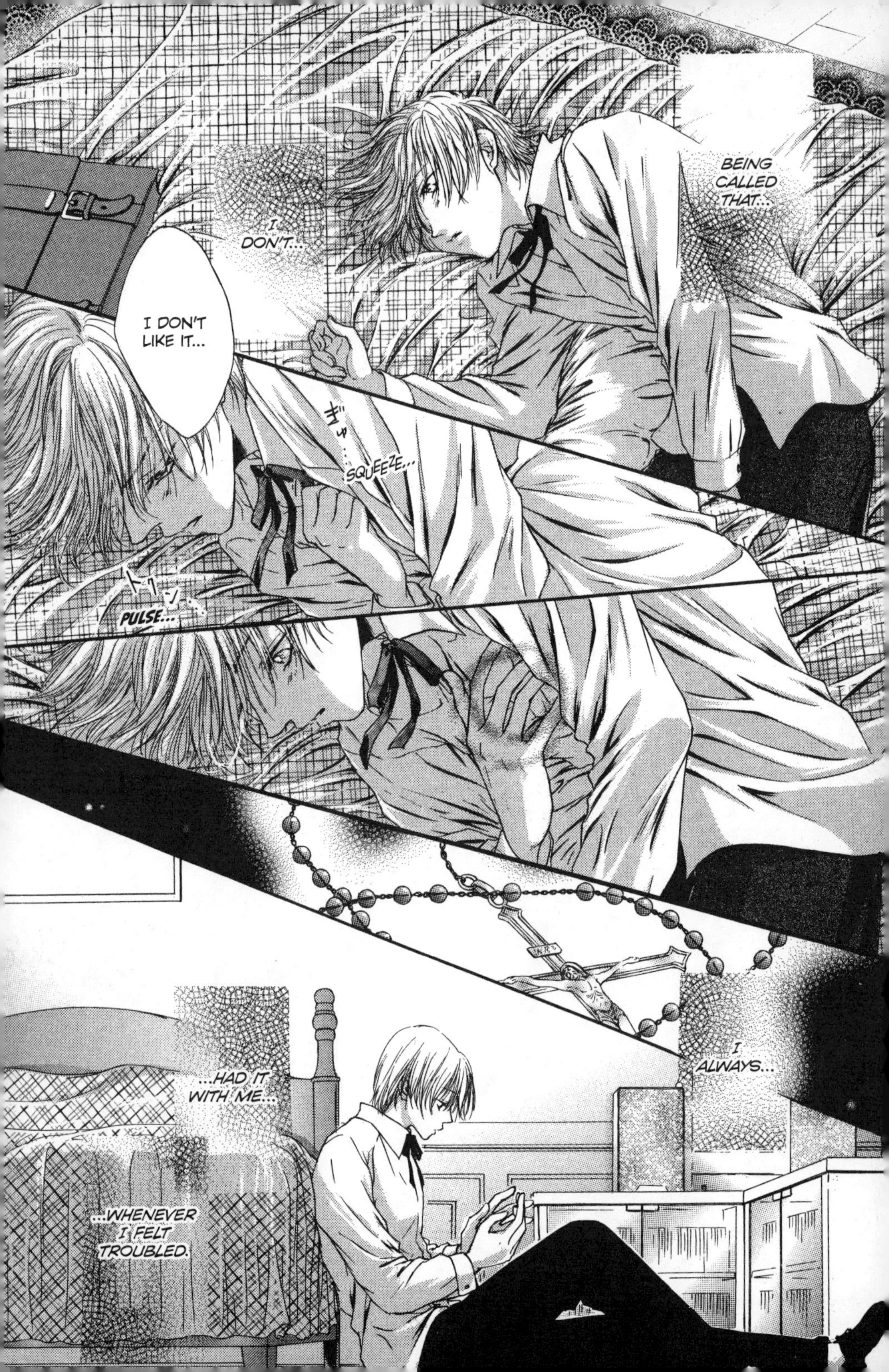

BEING CALLED THAT...
I DON'T...
I DON'T LIKE IT...
ぎゅ
SQUEEZE...
トクン
PULSE...
I ALWAYS...
...HAD IT WITH ME...
...WHENEVER I FELT TROUBLED.

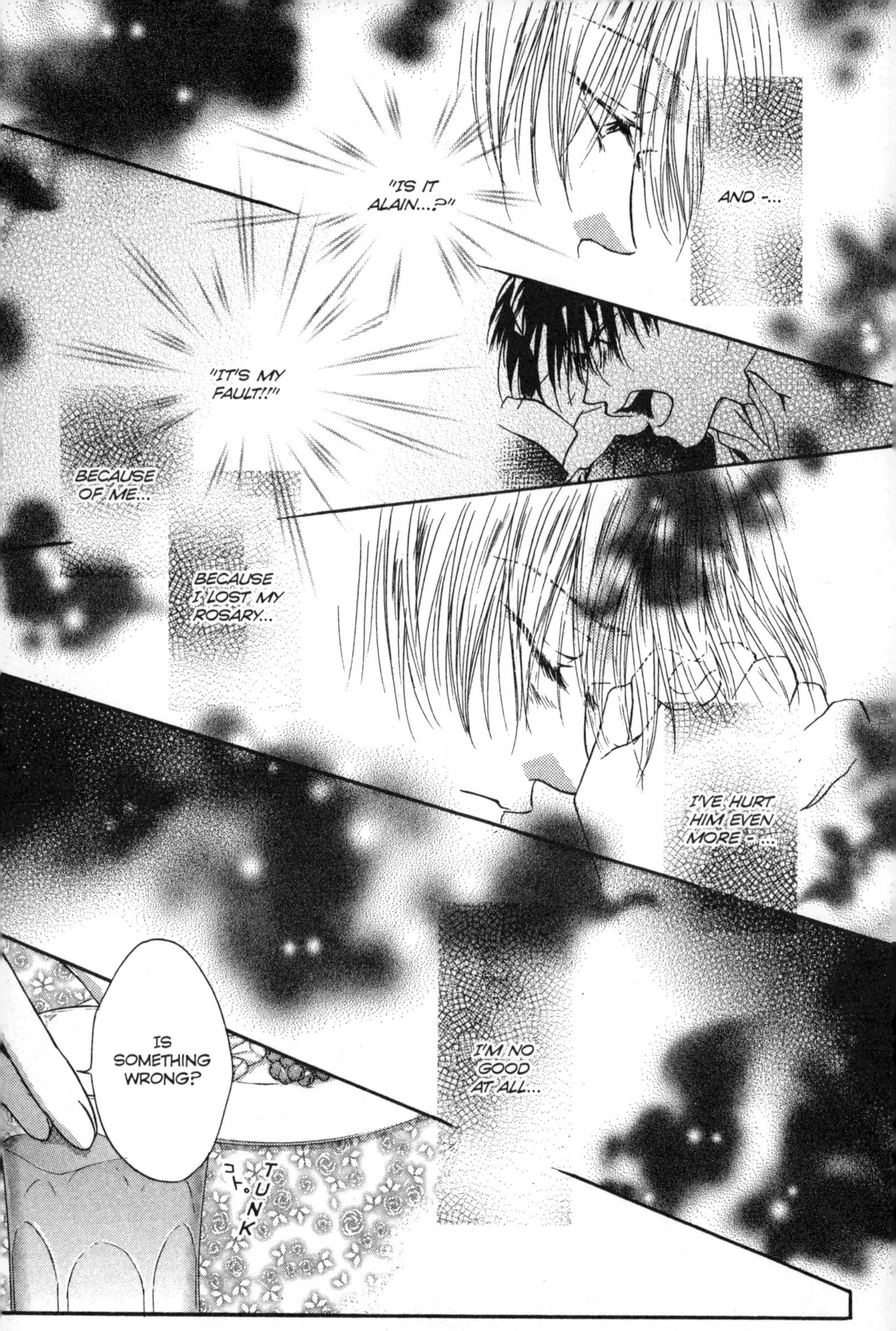
"IS IT ALAIN...?"
AND -...
"IT'S MY FAULT!!"
BECAUSE OF ME...
BECAUSE I LOST MY ROSARY...
I'VE HURT HIM EVEN MORE -...
I'M NO GOOD AT ALL...
IS SOMETHING WRONG?
TUNK

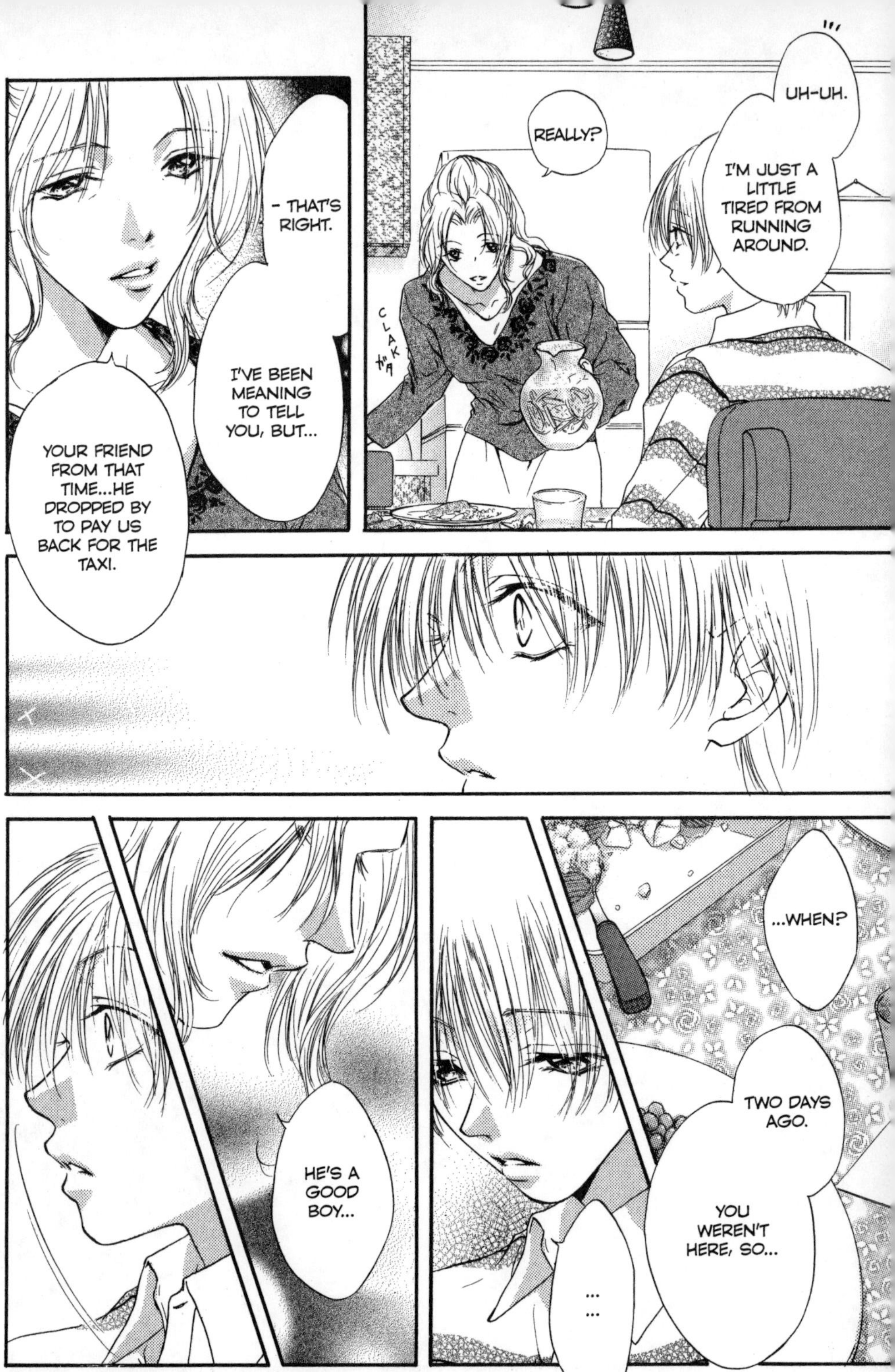
UH-UH.
I'M JUST A LITTLE TIRED FROM RUNNING AROUND.
REALLY?
CLAK
- THAT'S RIGHT.
I'VE BEEN MEANING TO TELL YOU, BUT...
YOUR FRIEND FROM THAT TIME...HE DROPPED BY TO PAY US BACK FOR THE TAXI.
...WHEN?
TWO DAYS AGO.
YOU WEREN'T HERE, SO...
... ...
HE'S A GOOD BOY...

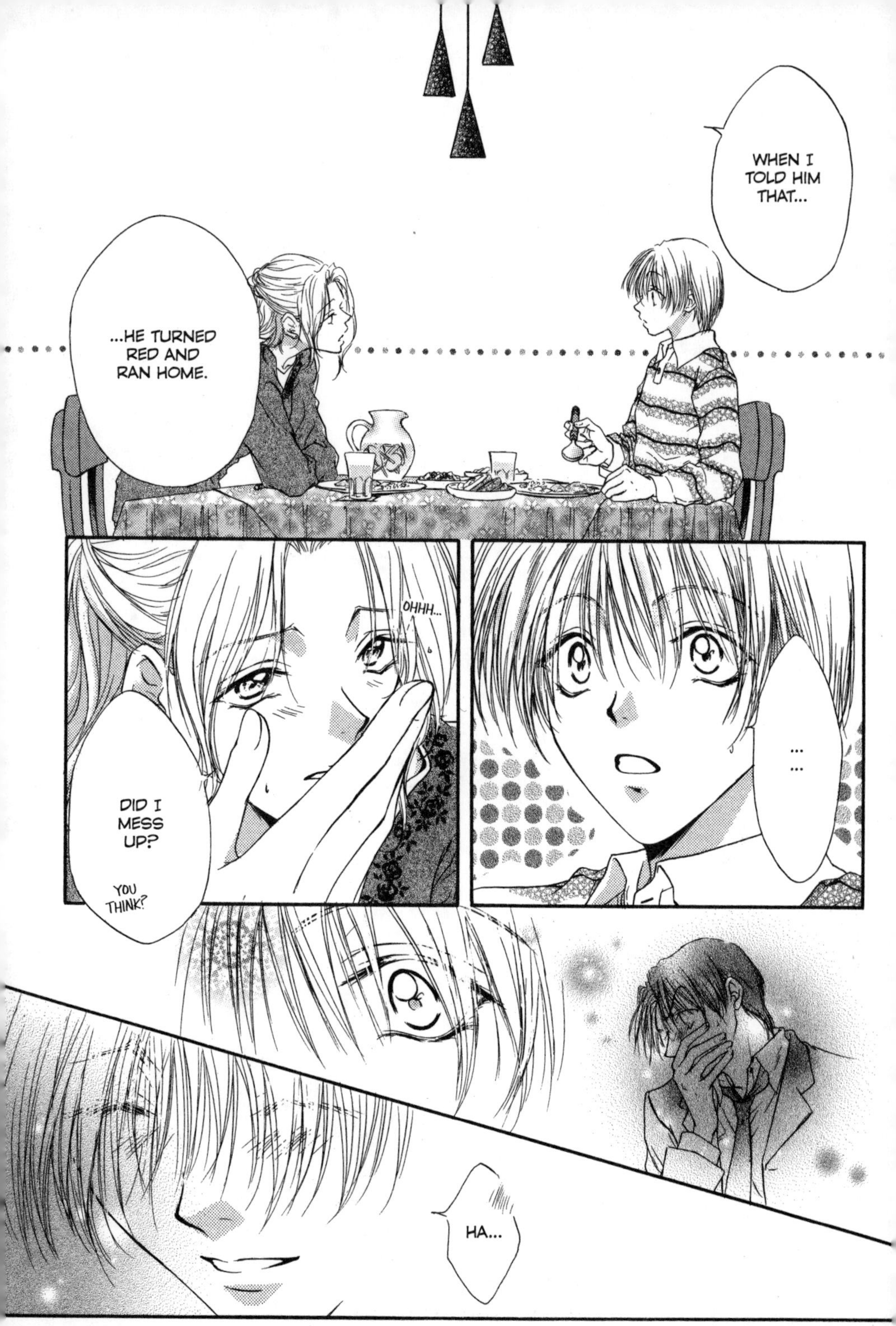
WHEN I TOLD HIM THAT...
...HE TURNED RED AND RAN HOME.
... ...
OHHH...
DID I MESS UP?
YOU THINK?
HA...

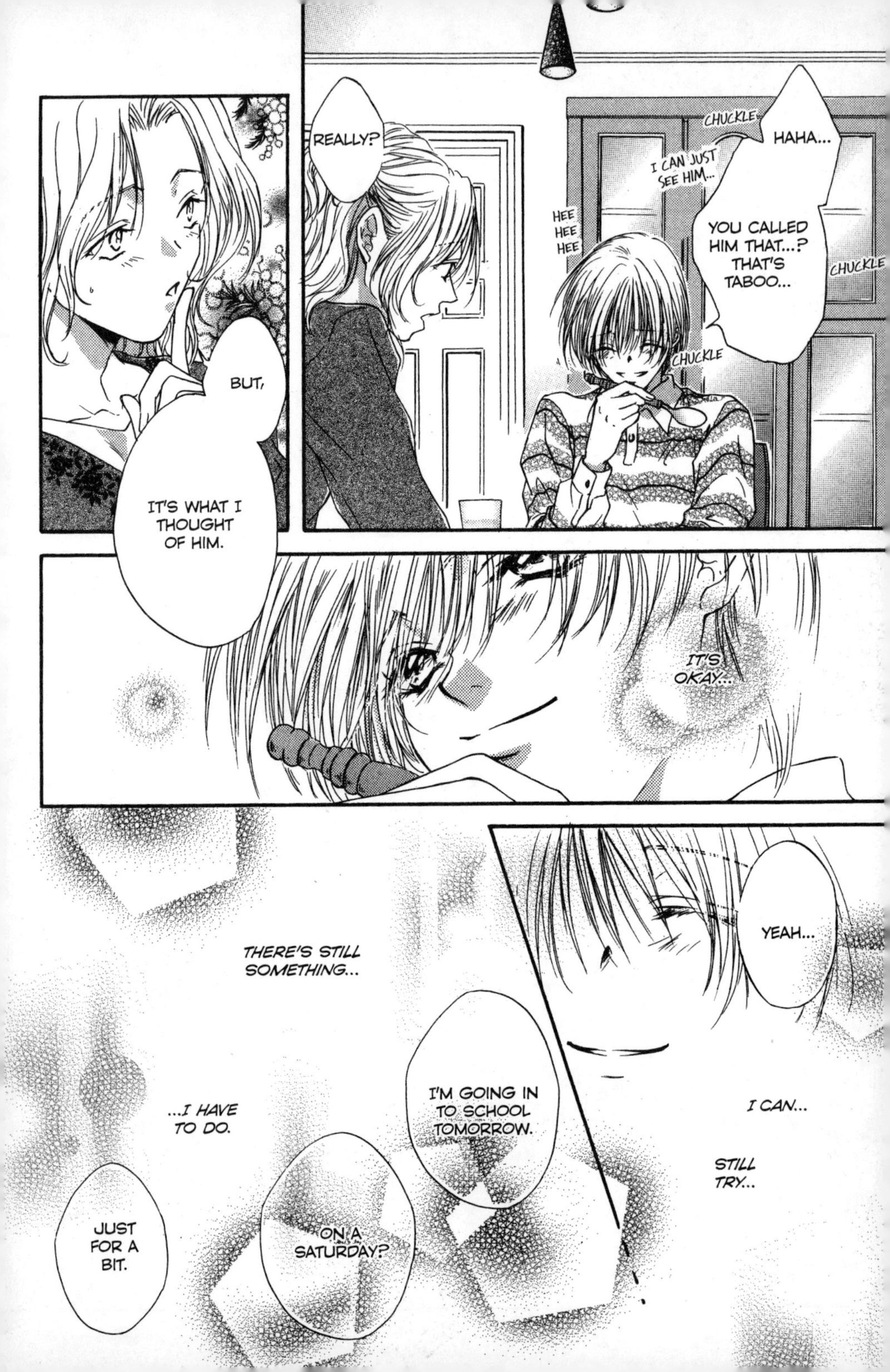
HAHA...
CHUCKLE
I CAN JUST SEE HIM...
YOU CALLED HIM THAT...? THAT'S TABOO...
CHUCKLE
HEE HEE HEE
CHUCKLE
REALLY?
BUT,
IT'S WHAT I THOUGHT OF HIM.
IT'S OKAY...
YEAH...
I CAN...
STILL TRY...
THERE'S STILL SOMETHING...
...I HAVE TO DO.
I'M GOING IN TO SCHOOL TOMORROW.
ON A SATURDAY?
JUST FOR A BIT.

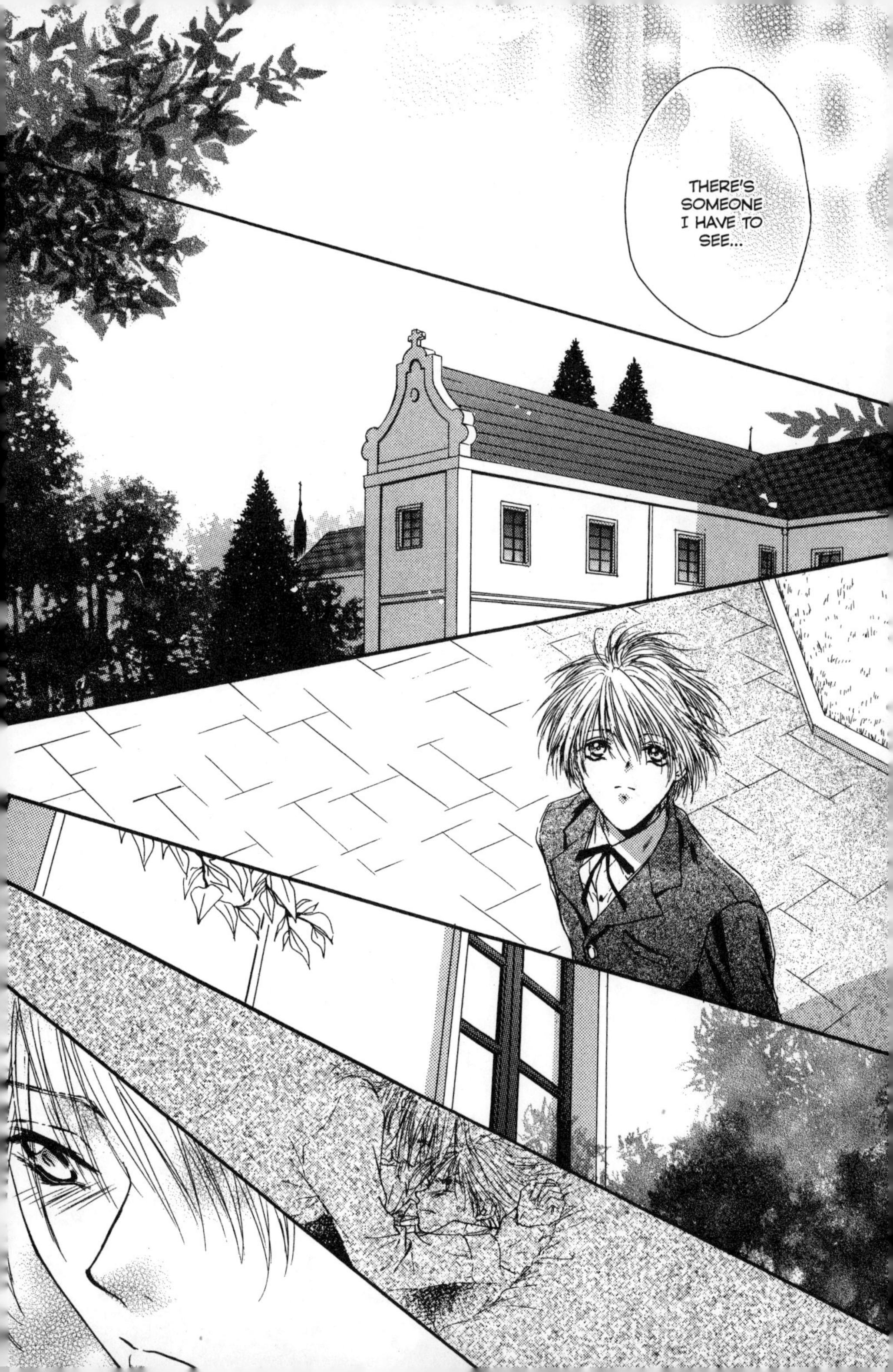
THERE'S SOMEONE I HAVE TO SEE...

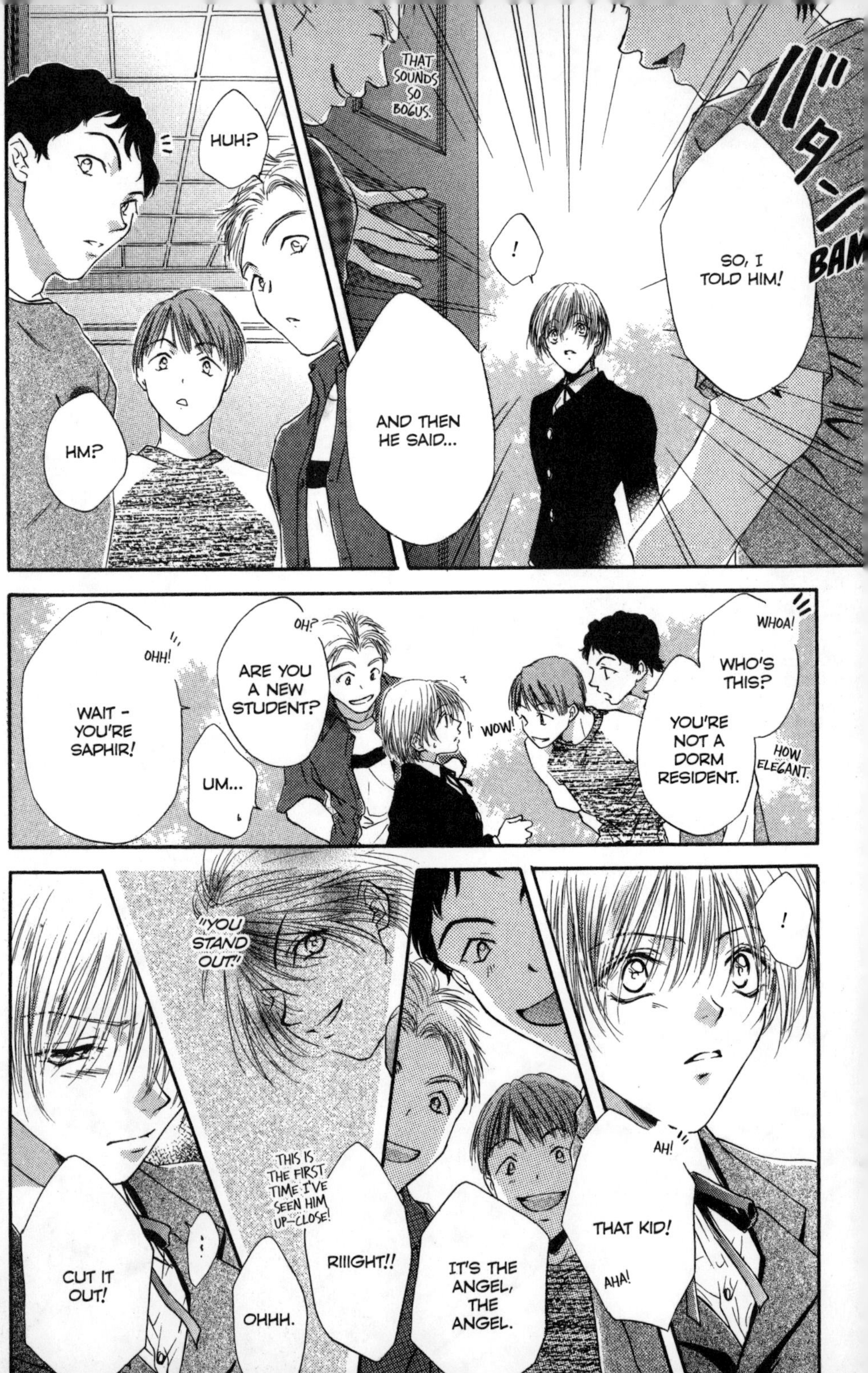
BAM
SO, I TOLD HIM!
!
THAT SOUNDS SO BOGUS.
AND THEN HE SAID...
HUH?
HM?
WHOA!
WHO'S THIS?
YOU'RE NOT A DORM RESIDENT.
HOW ELEGANT.
WOW!
OH?
ARE YOU A NEW STUDENT?
OHH!
WAIT - YOU'RE SAPHIR!
UM...
!
AH!
THAT KID!
AHA!
IT'S THE ANGEL, THE ANGEL.
RIIIGHT!!
THIS IS THE FIRST TIME I'VE SEEN HIM UP-CLOSE!
OHHH.
"YOU STAND OUT!"
...
CUT IT OUT!

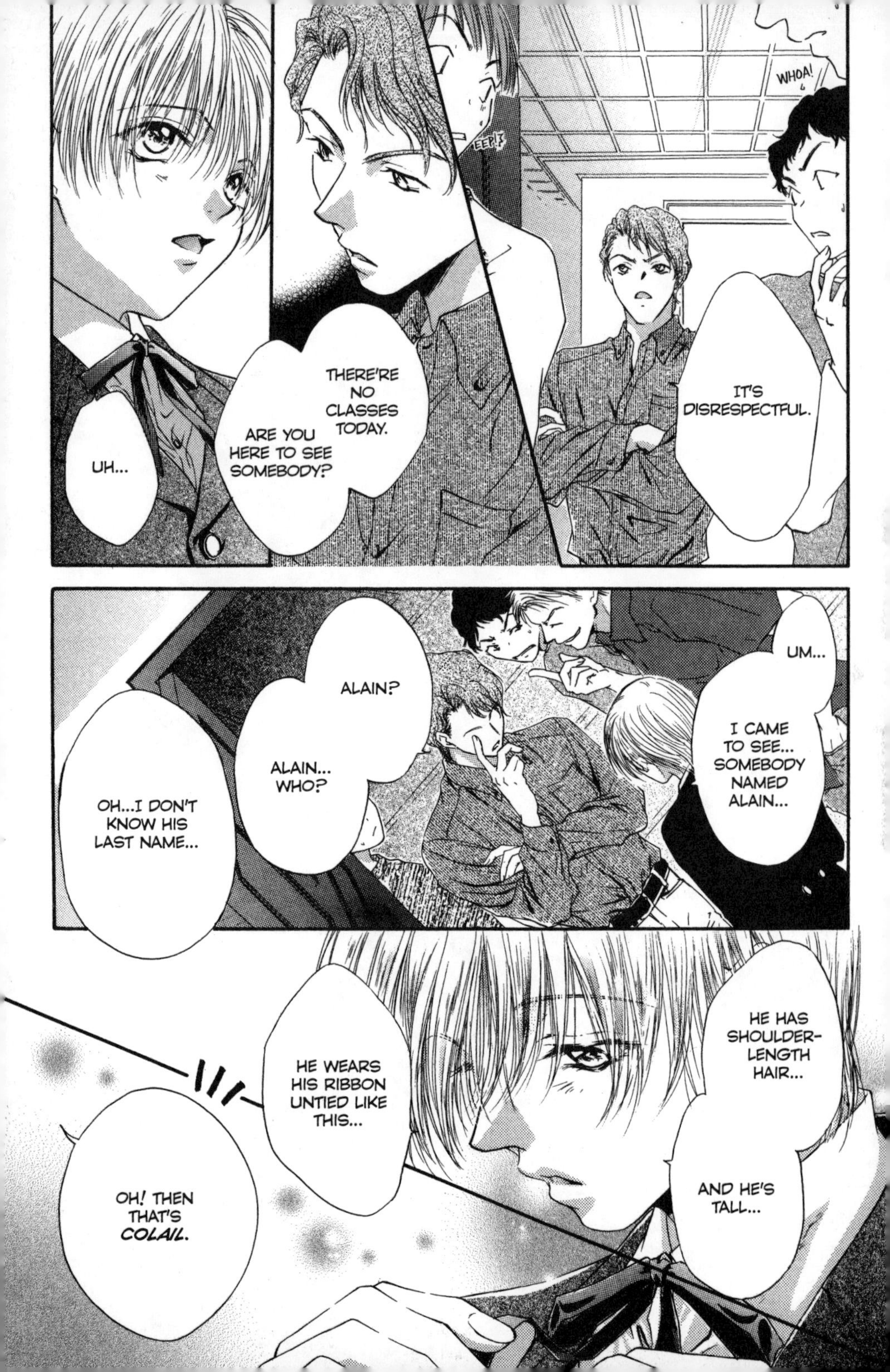
WHOA!
IT'S DISRESPECTFUL.
EEP!
THERE'RE NO CLASSES TODAY.
ARE YOU HERE TO SEE SOMEBODY?
UH...
UM...
I CAME TO SEE... SOMEBODY NAMED ALAIN...
ALAIN?
ALAIN... WHO?
OH...I DON'T KNOW HIS LAST NAME...
HE HAS SHOULDER-LENGTH HAIR...
AND HE'S TALL...
HE WEARS HIS RIBBON UNTIED LIKE THIS...
OH! THEN THAT'S *COLAIL*.

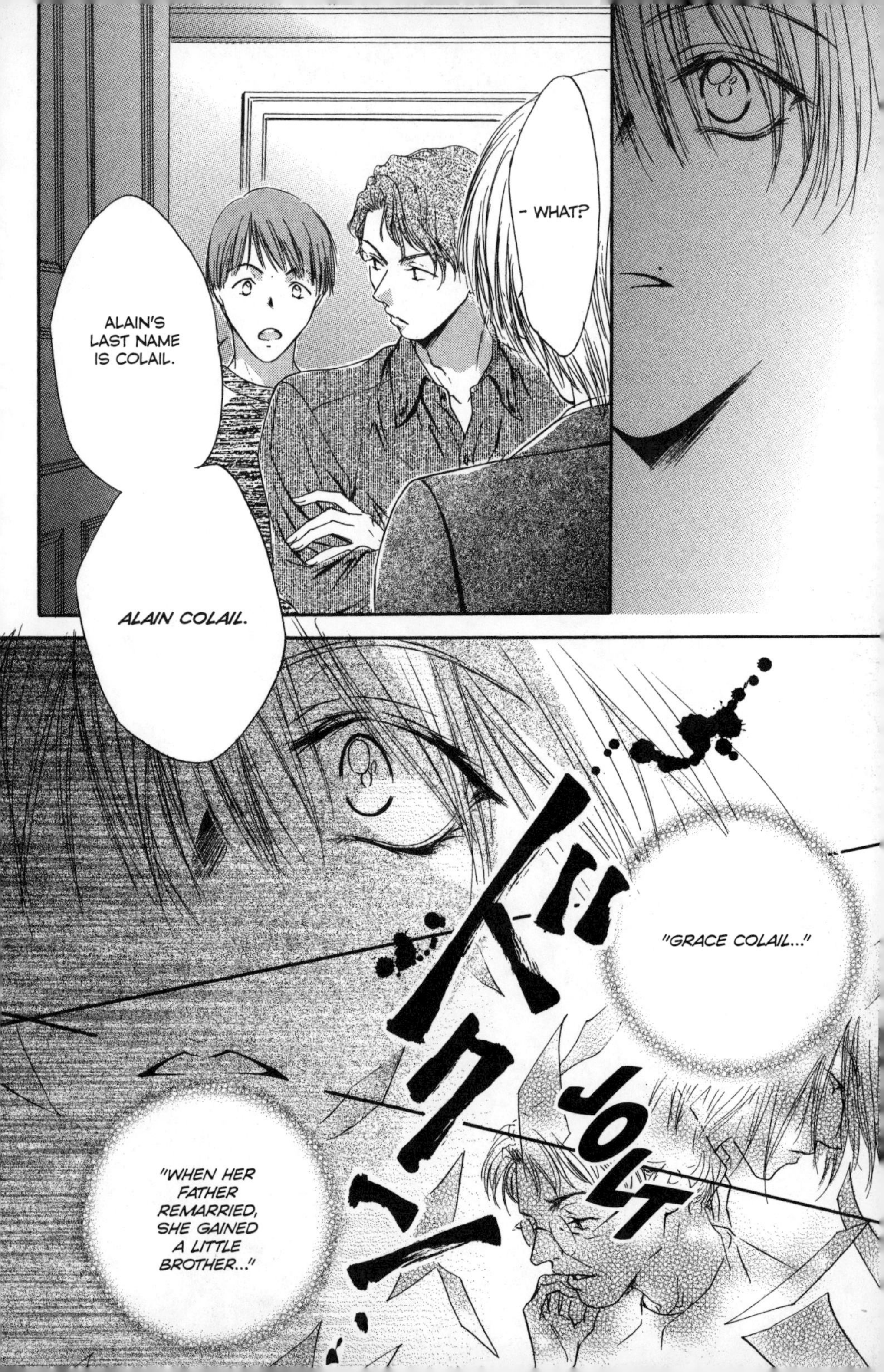
- WHAT?
ALAIN'S LAST NAME IS COLAIL.
ALAIN COLAIL.
"GRACE COLAIL..."
JOLT
"WHEN HER FATHER REMARRIED, SHE GAINED A LITTLE BROTHER..."

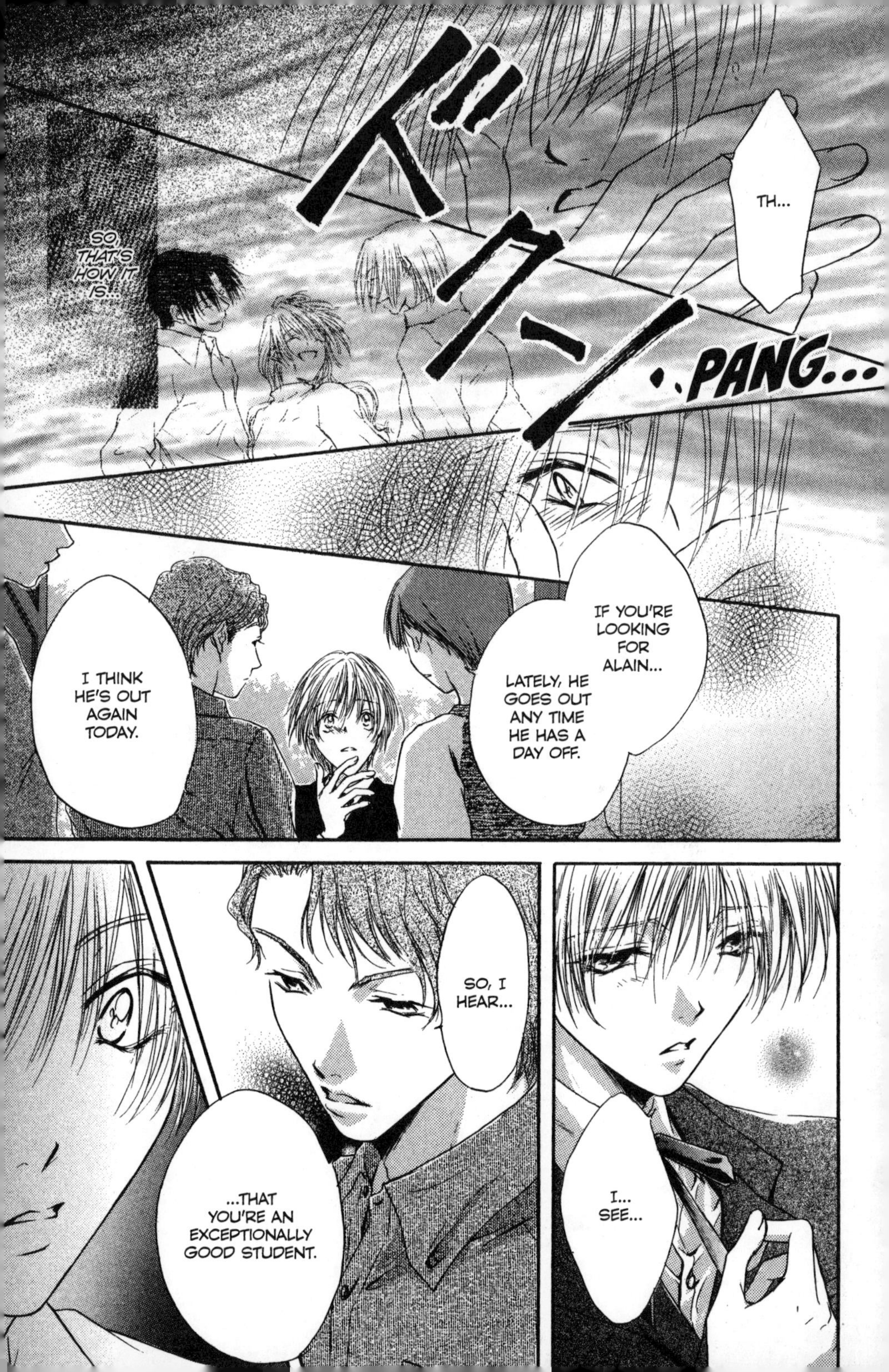
TH...
PANG...
SO, THAT'S HOW IT IS...
IF YOU'RE LOOKING FOR ALAIN...
LATELY, HE GOES OUT ANY TIME HE HAS A DAY OFF.
I THINK HE'S OUT AGAIN TODAY.
I... SEE...
SO, I HEAR...
...THAT YOU'RE AN EXCEPTIONALLY GOOD STUDENT.

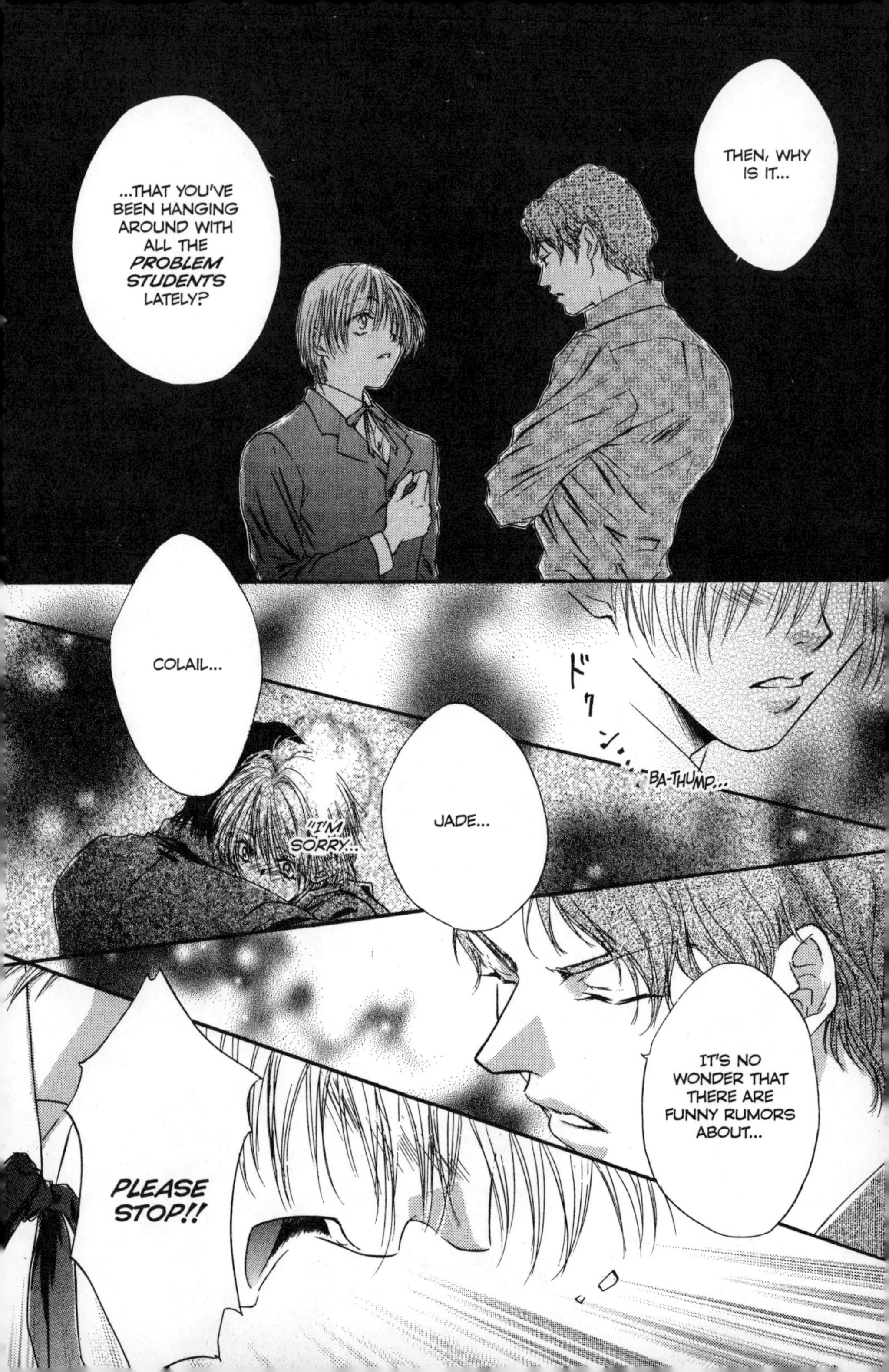
THEN, WHY IS IT...
...THAT YOU'VE BEEN HANGING AROUND WITH ALL THE *PROBLEM STUDENTS* LATELY?
COLAIL...
ドクン
BA-THUMP...
JADE...
"I'M SORRY..."
IT'S NO WONDER THAT THERE ARE FUNNY RUMORS ABOUT...
PLEASE STOP!!

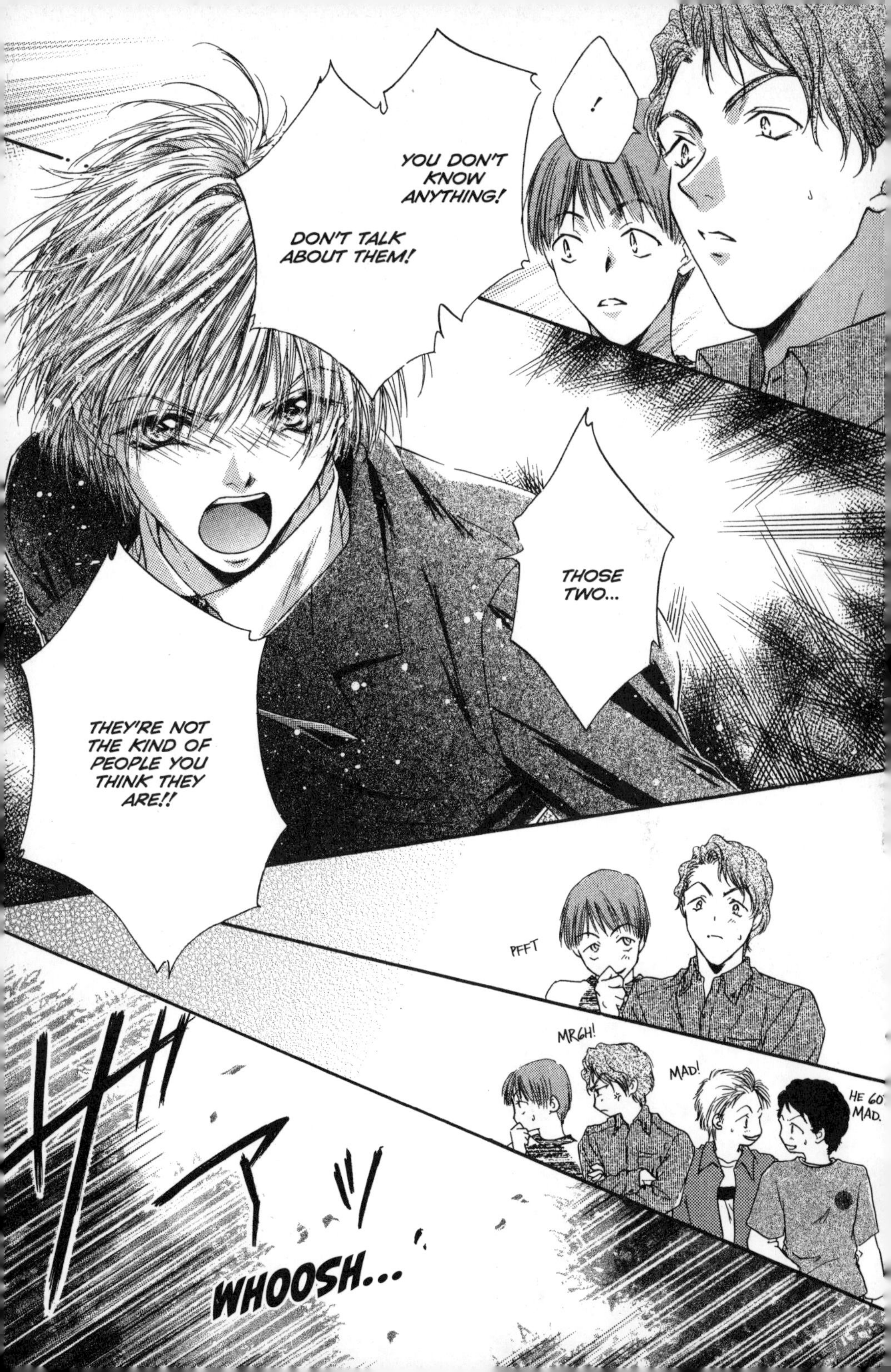
!
YOU DON'T KNOW ANYTHING!
DON'T TALK ABOUT THEM!
THOSE TWO...
THEY'RE NOT THE KIND OF PEOPLE YOU THINK THEY ARE!!
PFFT
HE GO MAD.
MAD!
MRGH!
WHOOSH...

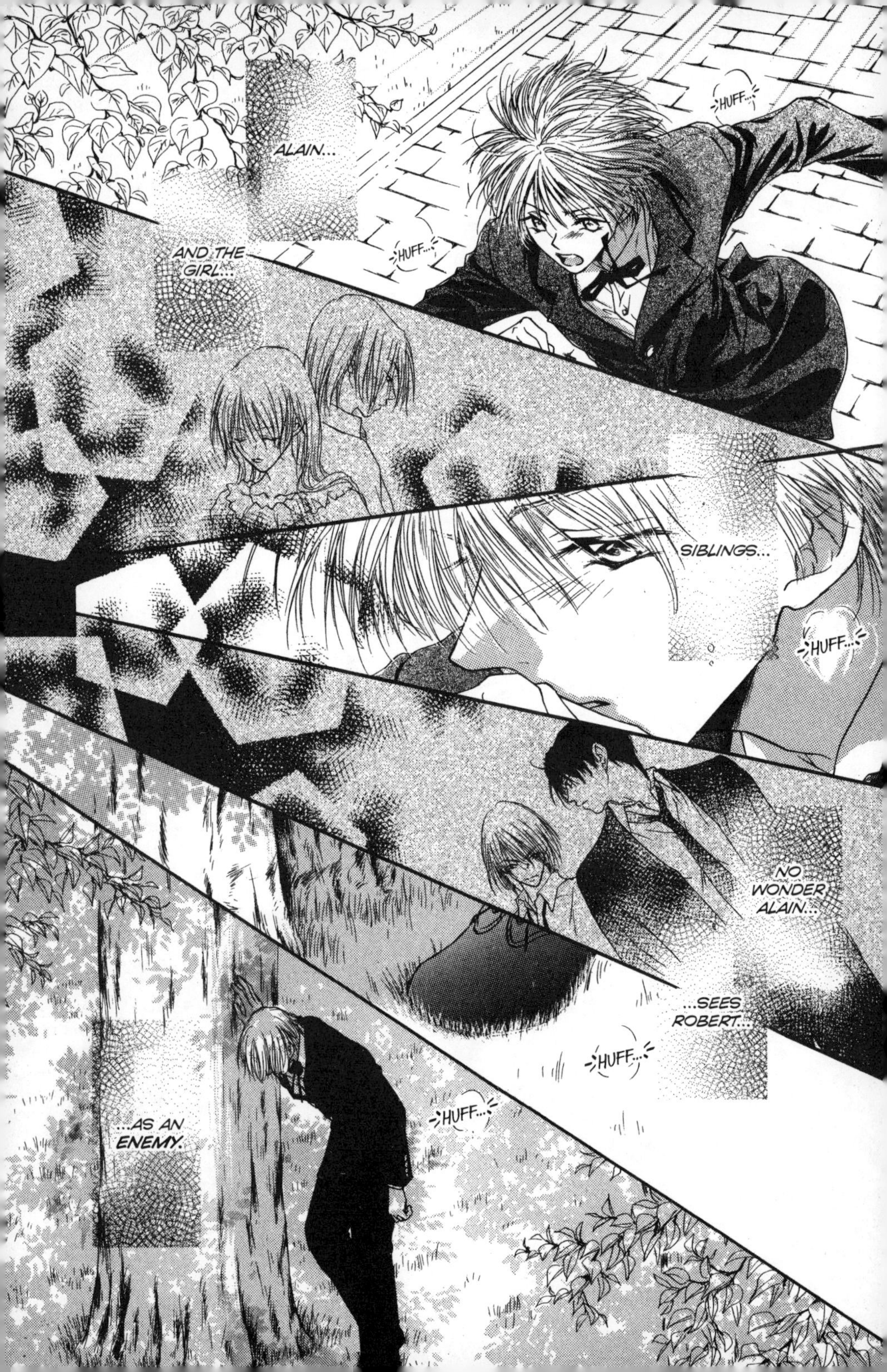
HUFF...
ALAIN...
HUFF...
AND THE GIRL...
SIBLINGS...
HUFF...
NO WONDER ALAIN...
...SEES ROBERT...
HUFF...
HUFF...
...AS AN ENEMY.

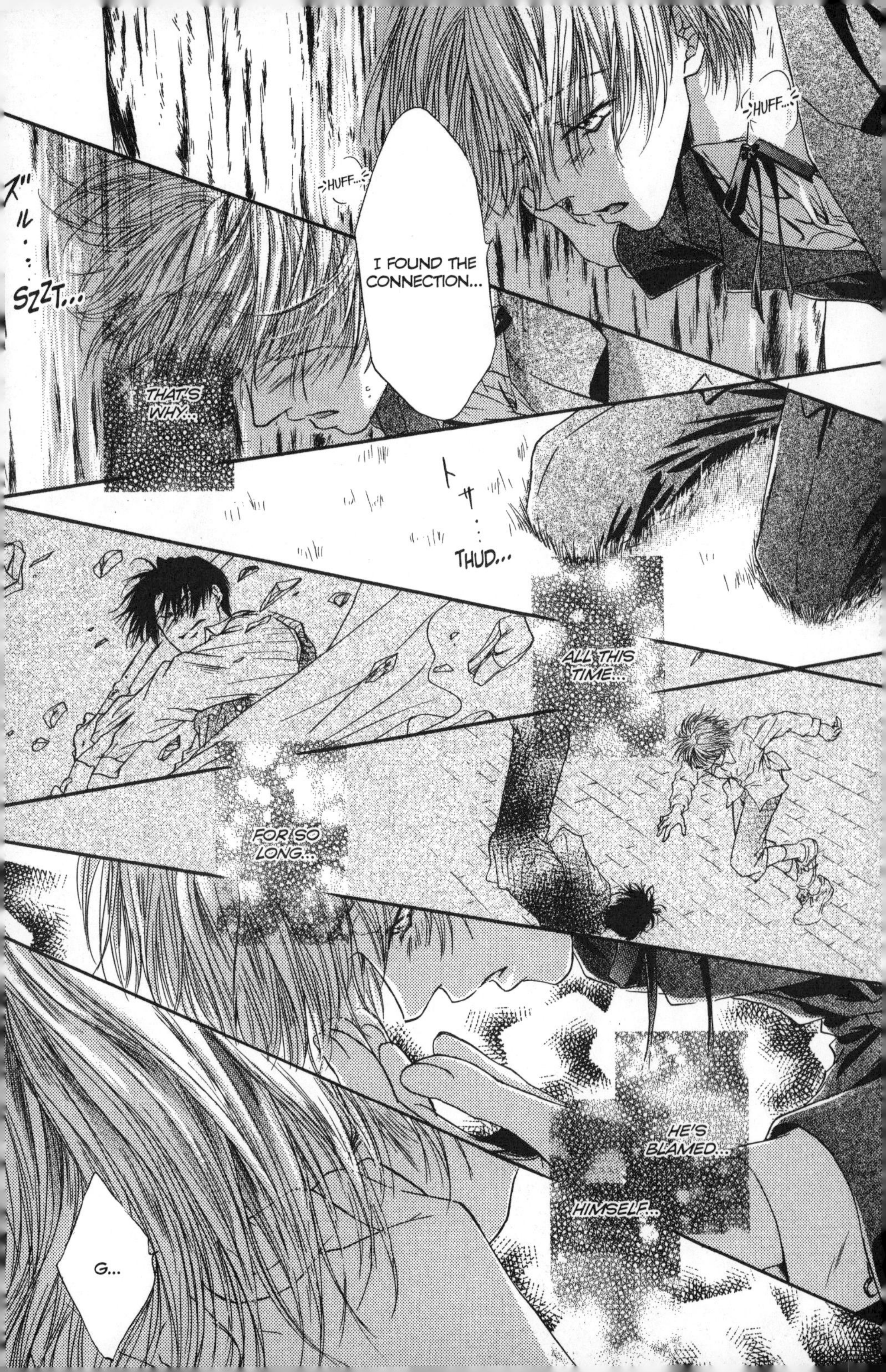
HUFF...
HUFF...
I FOUND THE CONNECTION...
ズル・・・
SZZT...
THAT'S WHY...
トサ・・・
THUD...
ALL THIS TIME...
FOR SO LONG...
HE'S BLAMED...
HIMSELF...
G...

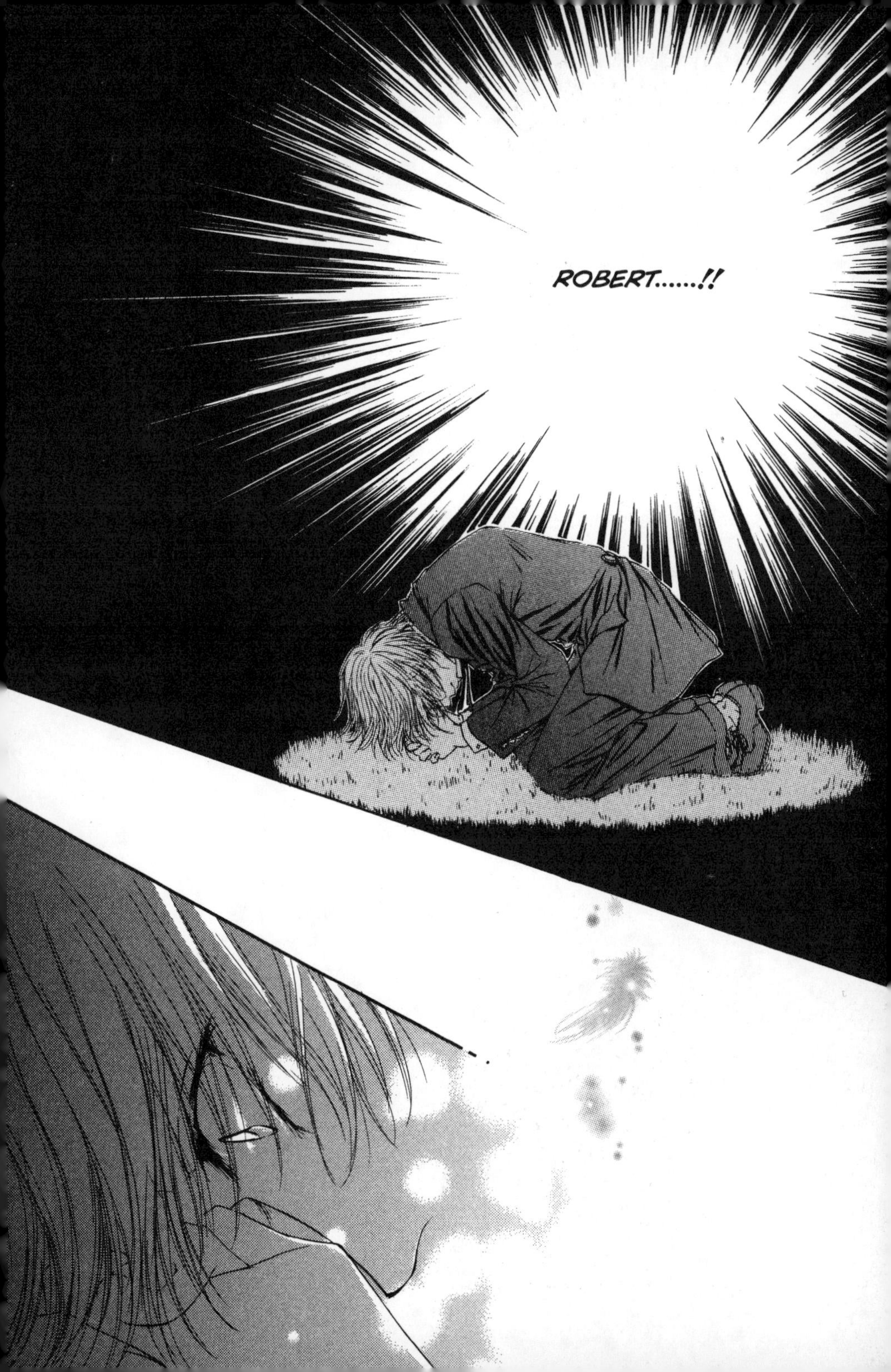
ROBERT......!!

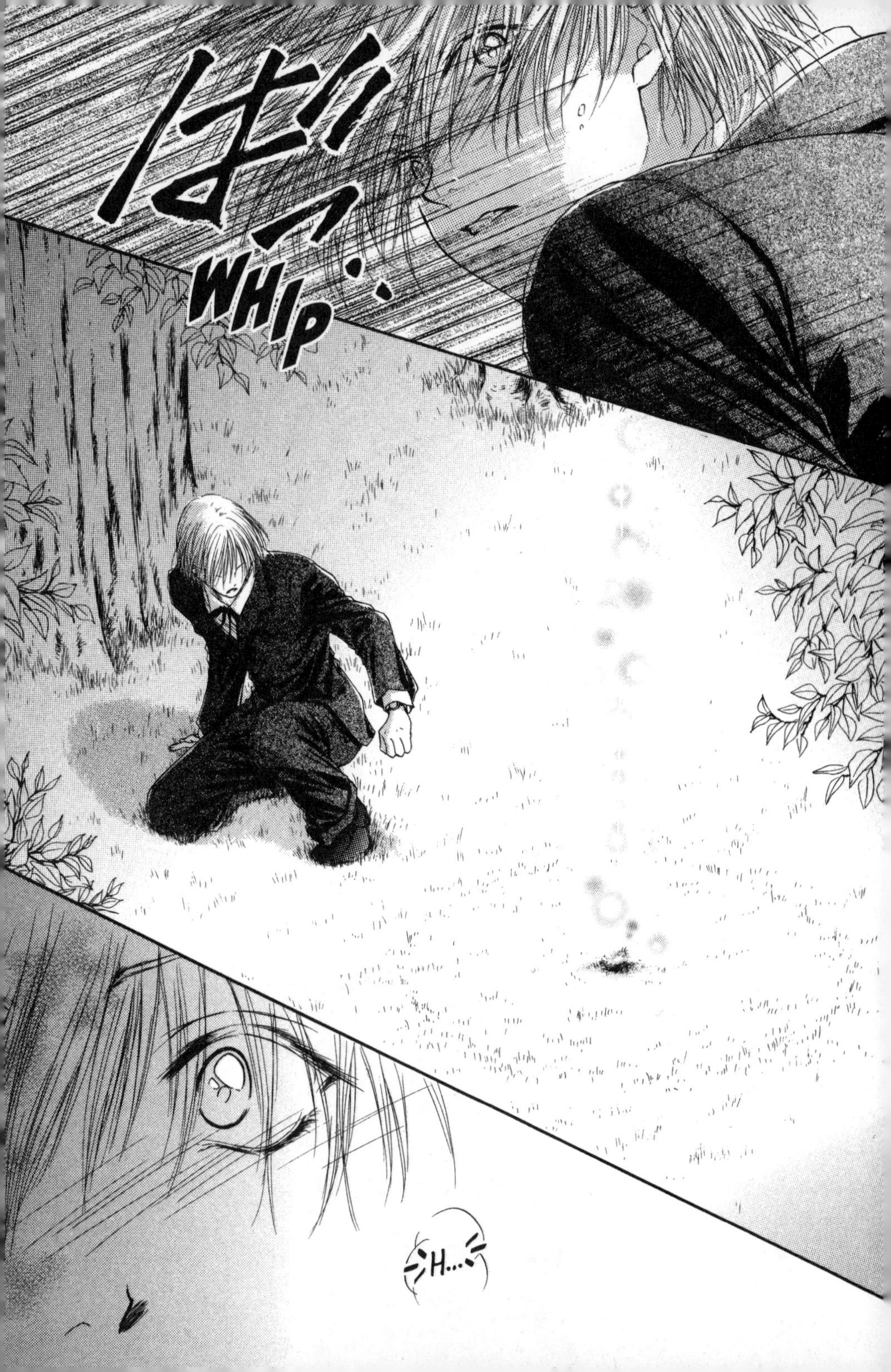
はっ
WHIP
H...

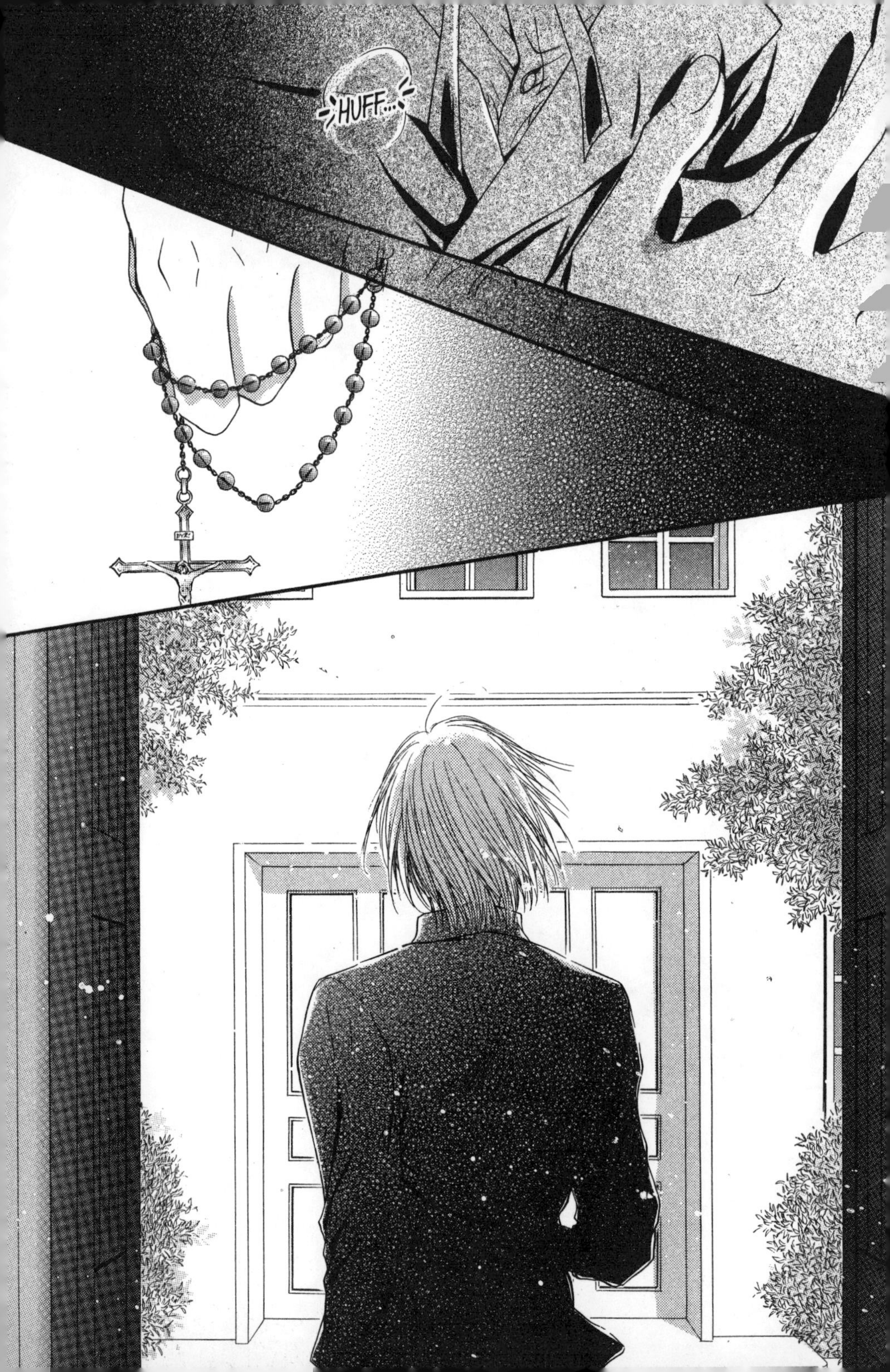
HUFF...

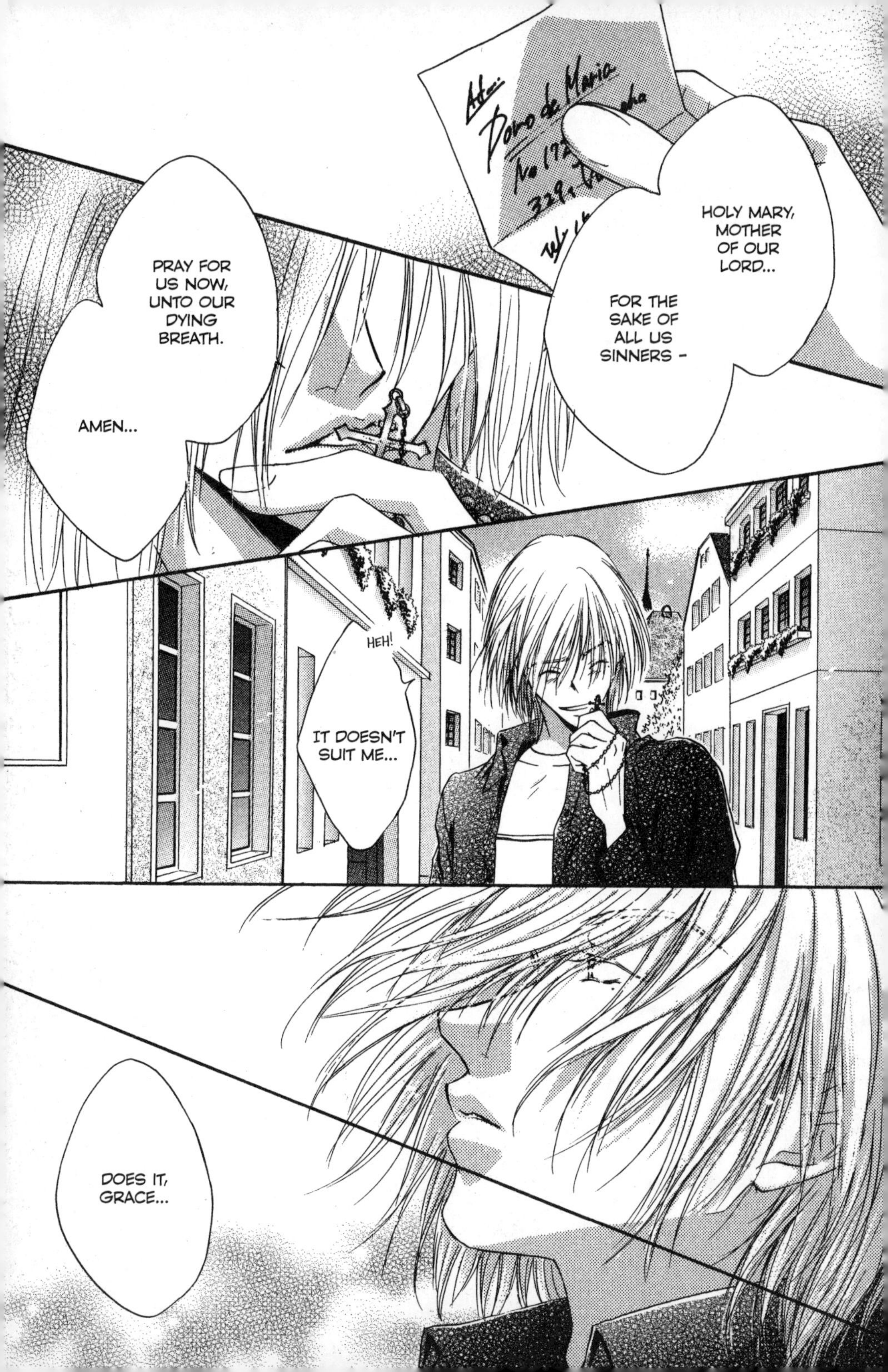
HOLY MARY, MOTHER OF OUR LORD...
FOR THE SAKE OF ALL US SINNERS -
PRAY FOR US NOW, UNTO OUR DYING BREATH.
AMEN...
HEH!
IT DOESN'T SUIT ME...
DOES IT, GRACE...

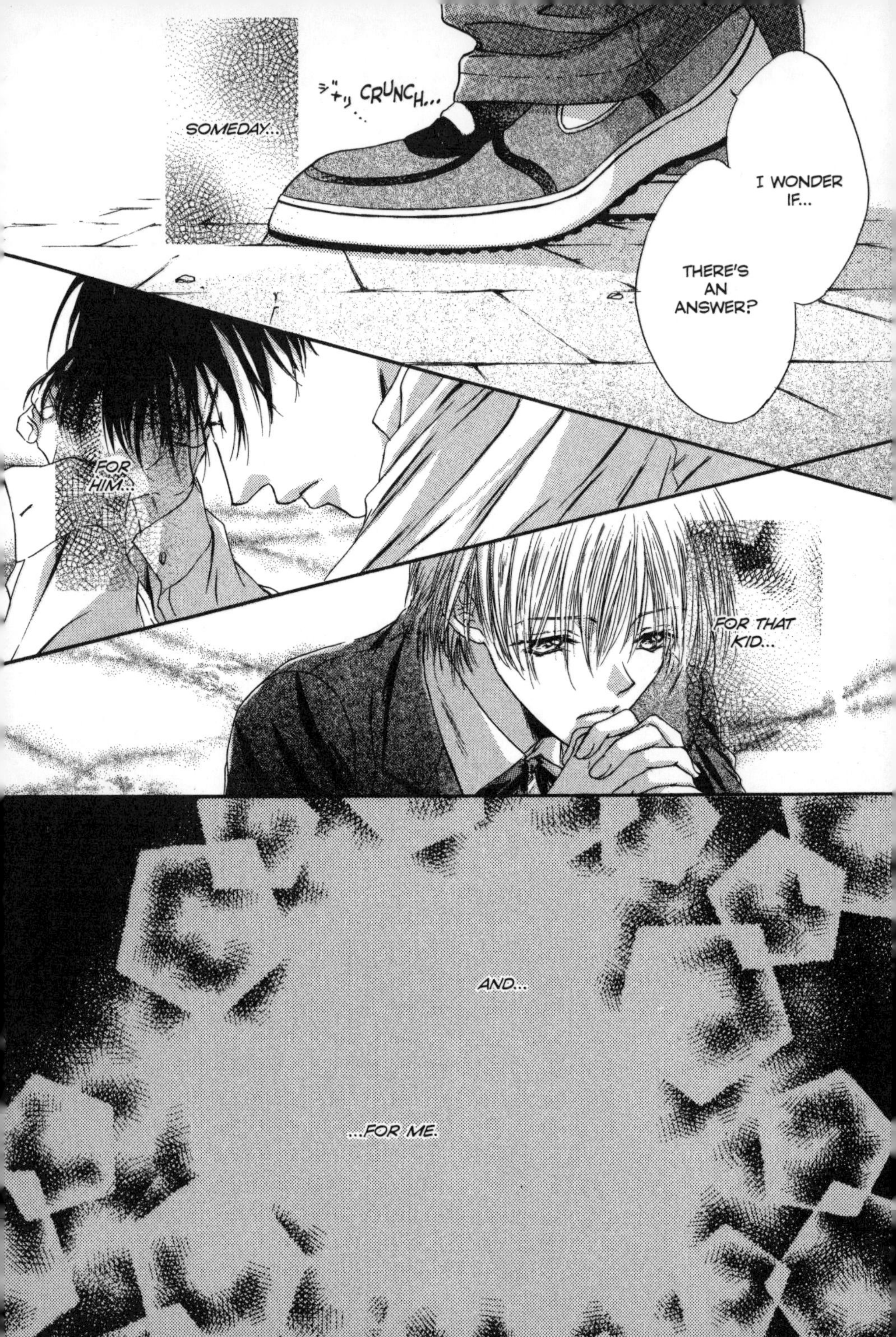
CRUNCH...
SOMEDAY...
I WONDER IF...
THERE'S AN ANSWER?
FOR HIM...
FOR THAT KID...
AND...
...FOR ME.

AVE MARIA◆END

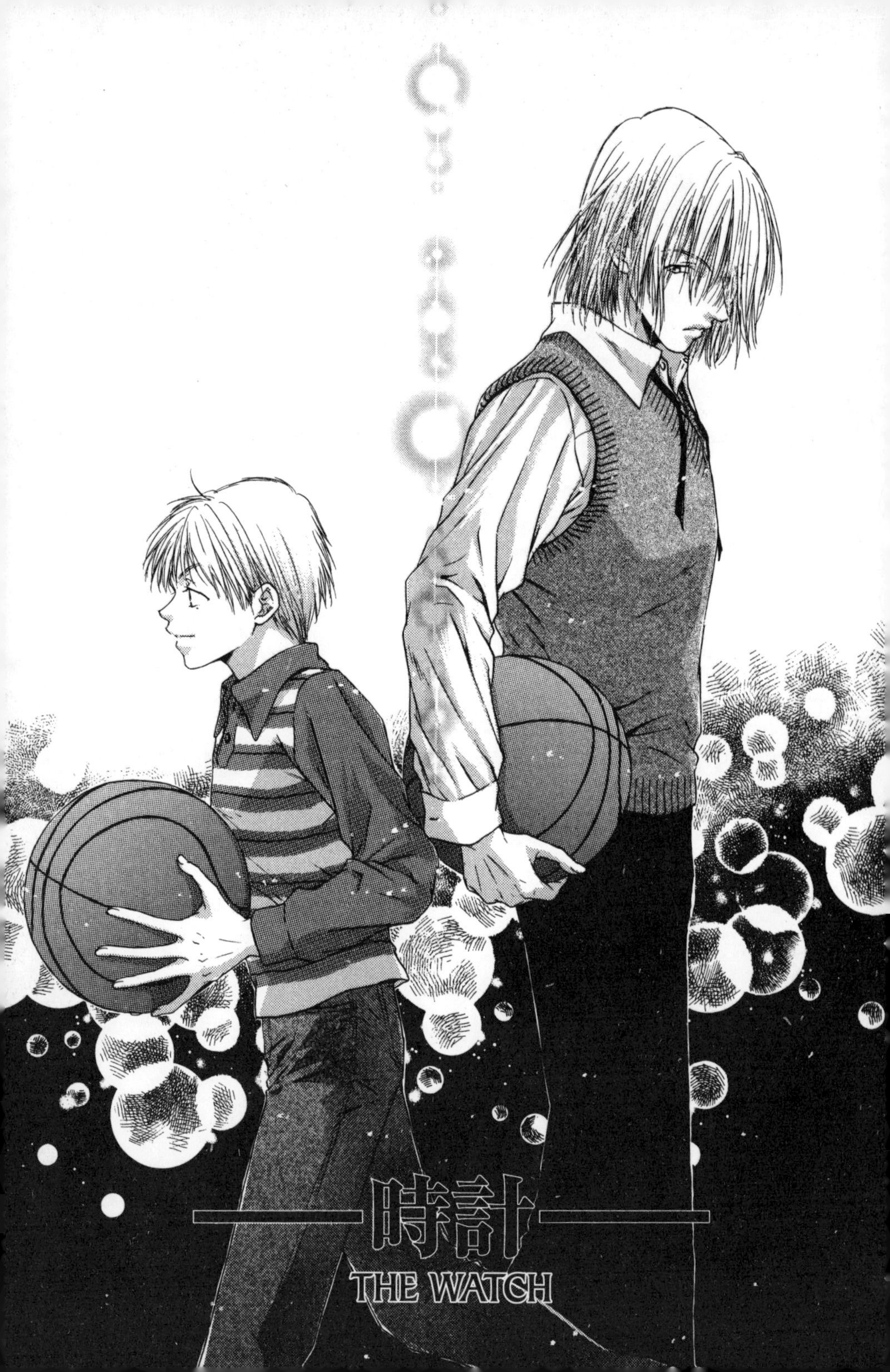
時計
THE WATCH

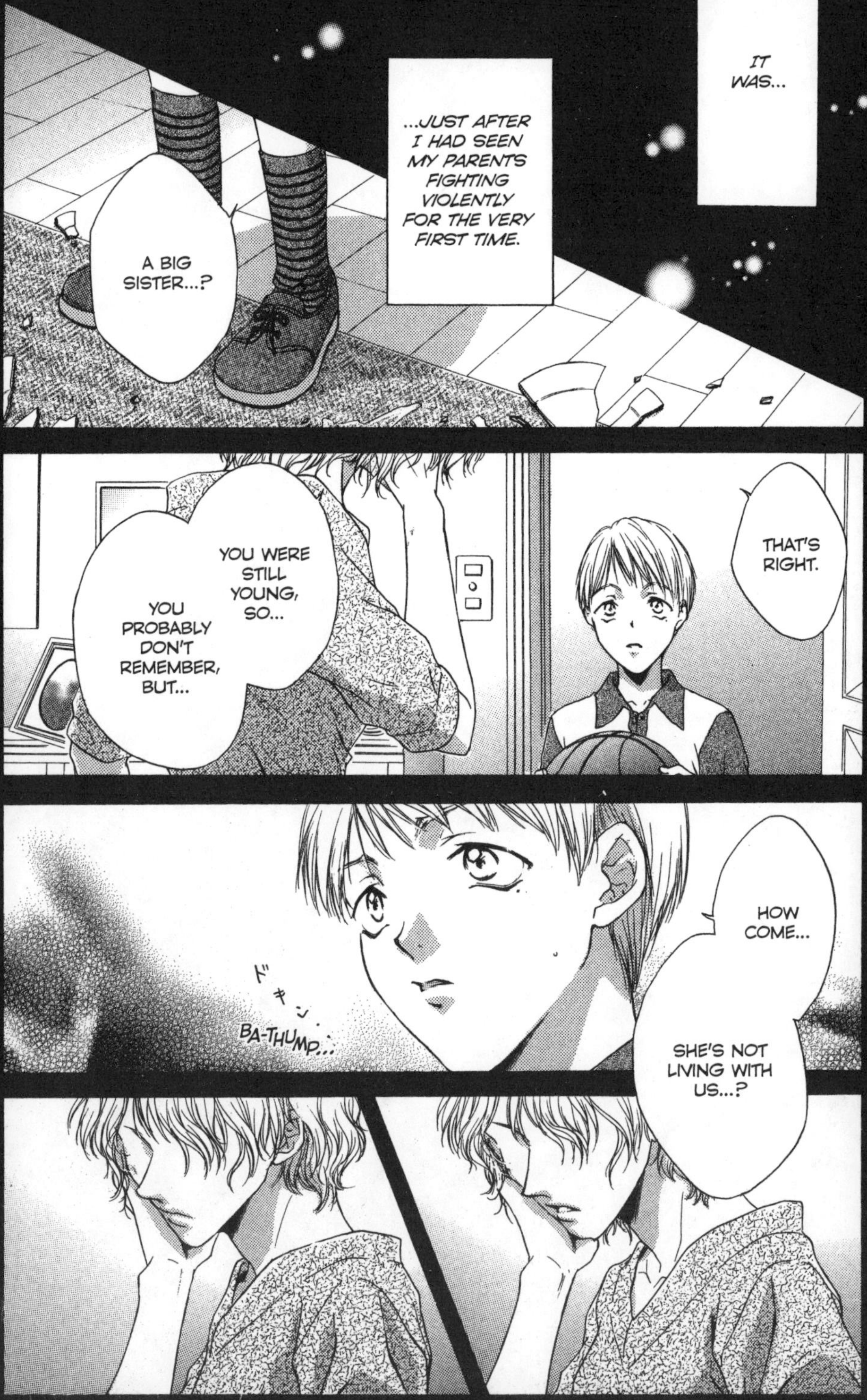
IT WAS...
...JUST AFTER I HAD SEEN MY PARENTS FIGHTING VIOLENTLY FOR THE VERY FIRST TIME.
A BIG SISTER...?
THAT'S RIGHT.
YOU WERE STILL YOUNG, SO...
YOU PROBABLY DON'T REMEMBER, BUT...
HOW COME...
SHE'S NOT LIVING WITH US...?
ドキン。
BA-THUMP...

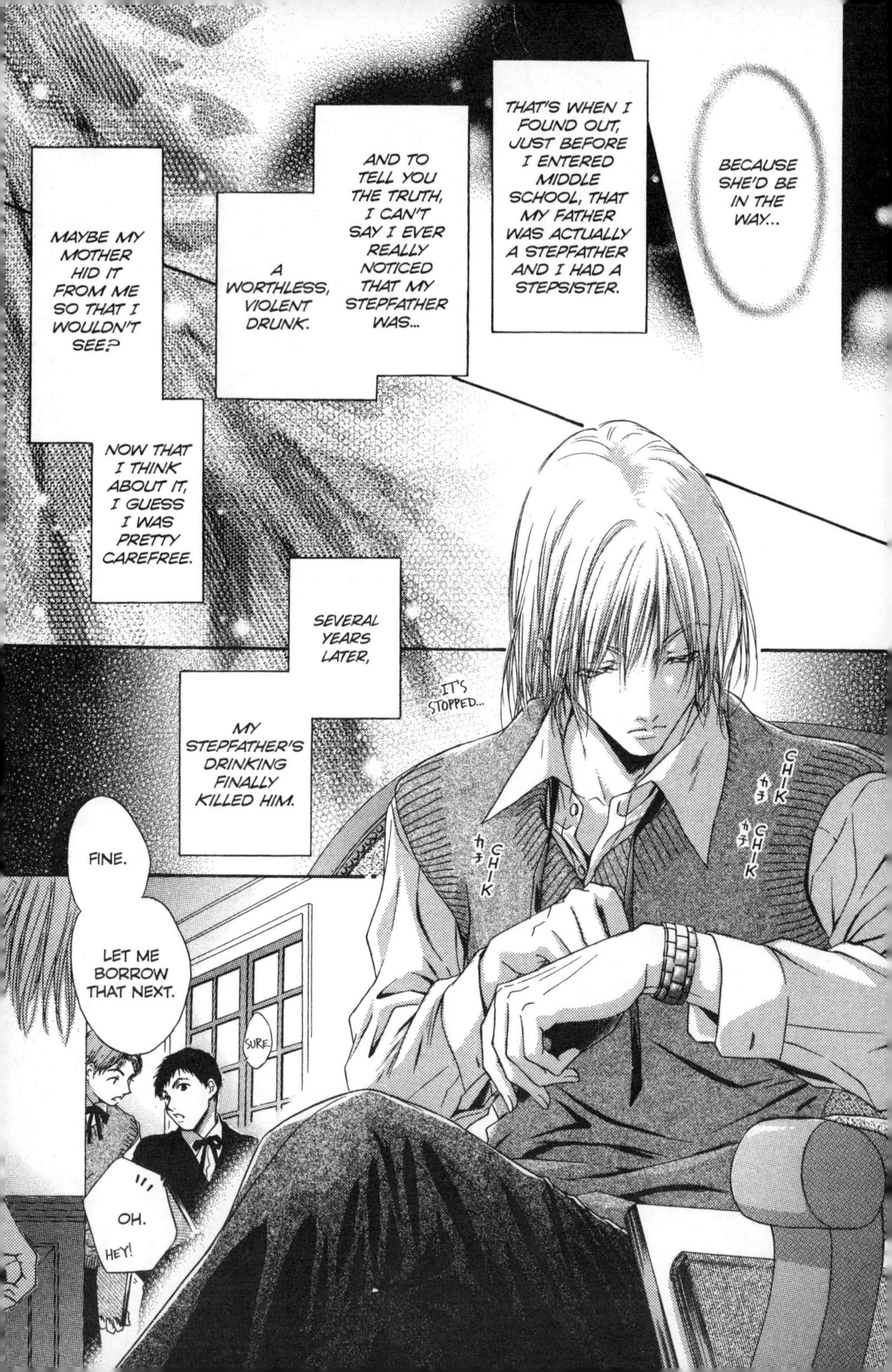
BECAUSE SHE'D BE IN THE WAY...
THAT'S WHEN I FOUND OUT, JUST BEFORE I ENTERED MIDDLE SCHOOL, THAT MY FATHER WAS ACTUALLY A STEPFATHER AND I HAD A STEPSISTER.
AND TO TELL YOU THE TRUTH, I CAN'T SAY I EVER REALLY NOTICED THAT MY STEPFATHER WAS...
A WORTHLESS, VIOLENT DRUNK.
MAYBE MY MOTHER HID IT FROM ME SO THAT I WOULDN'T SEE?
NOW THAT I THINK ABOUT IT, I GUESS I WAS PRETTY CAREFREE.
SEVERAL YEARS LATER,
MY STEPFATHER'S DRINKING FINALLY KILLED HIM.
IT'S STOPPED...
CHIK カチ
CHIK カチ
CHIK カチ
FINE.
LET ME BORROW THAT NEXT.
SURE.
OH.
HEY!

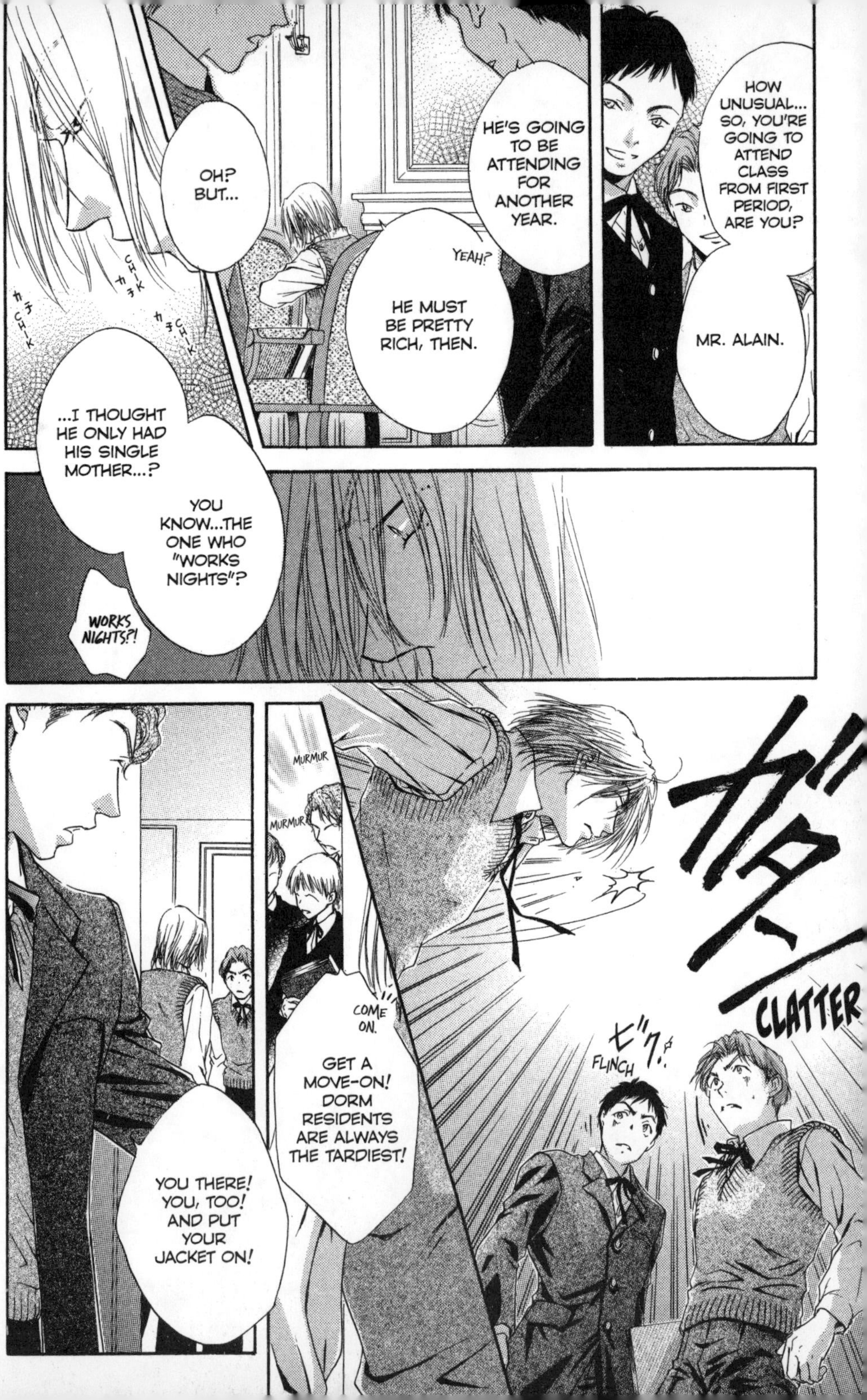
HOW UNUSUAL... SO, YOU'RE GOING TO ATTEND CLASS FROM FIRST PERIOD, ARE YOU?
MR. ALAIN.
HE'S GOING TO BE ATTENDING FOR ANOTHER YEAR.
YEAH?
HE MUST BE PRETTY RICH, THEN.
OH? BUT...
CHIK
CHIK
CHIK
...I THOUGHT HE ONLY HAD HIS SINGLE MOTHER...?
YOU KNOW...THE ONE WHO "WORKS NIGHTS"?
WORKS NIGHTS?!
CLATTER
FLINCH
MURMUR
MURMUR
COME ON.
GET A MOVE-ON! DORM RESIDENTS ARE ALWAYS THE TARDIEST!
YOU THERE! YOU, TOO! AND PUT YOUR JACKET ON!

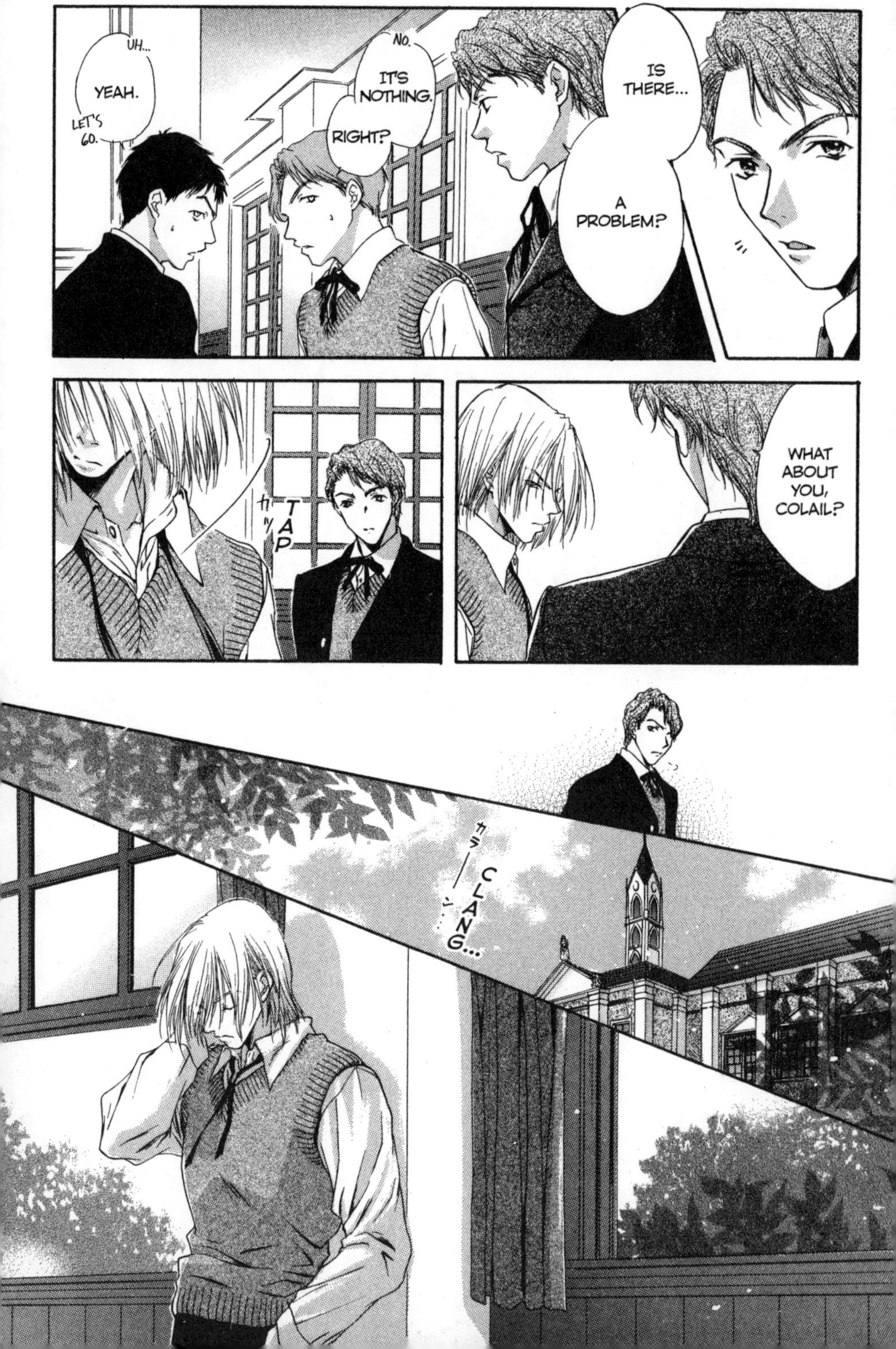
IS THERE...
A PROBLEM?
NO.
IT'S NOTHING.
RIGHT?
UH...
YEAH.
LET'S GO.
WHAT ABOUT YOU, COLAIL?
カッ
TAP
カラーン...
CLANG...

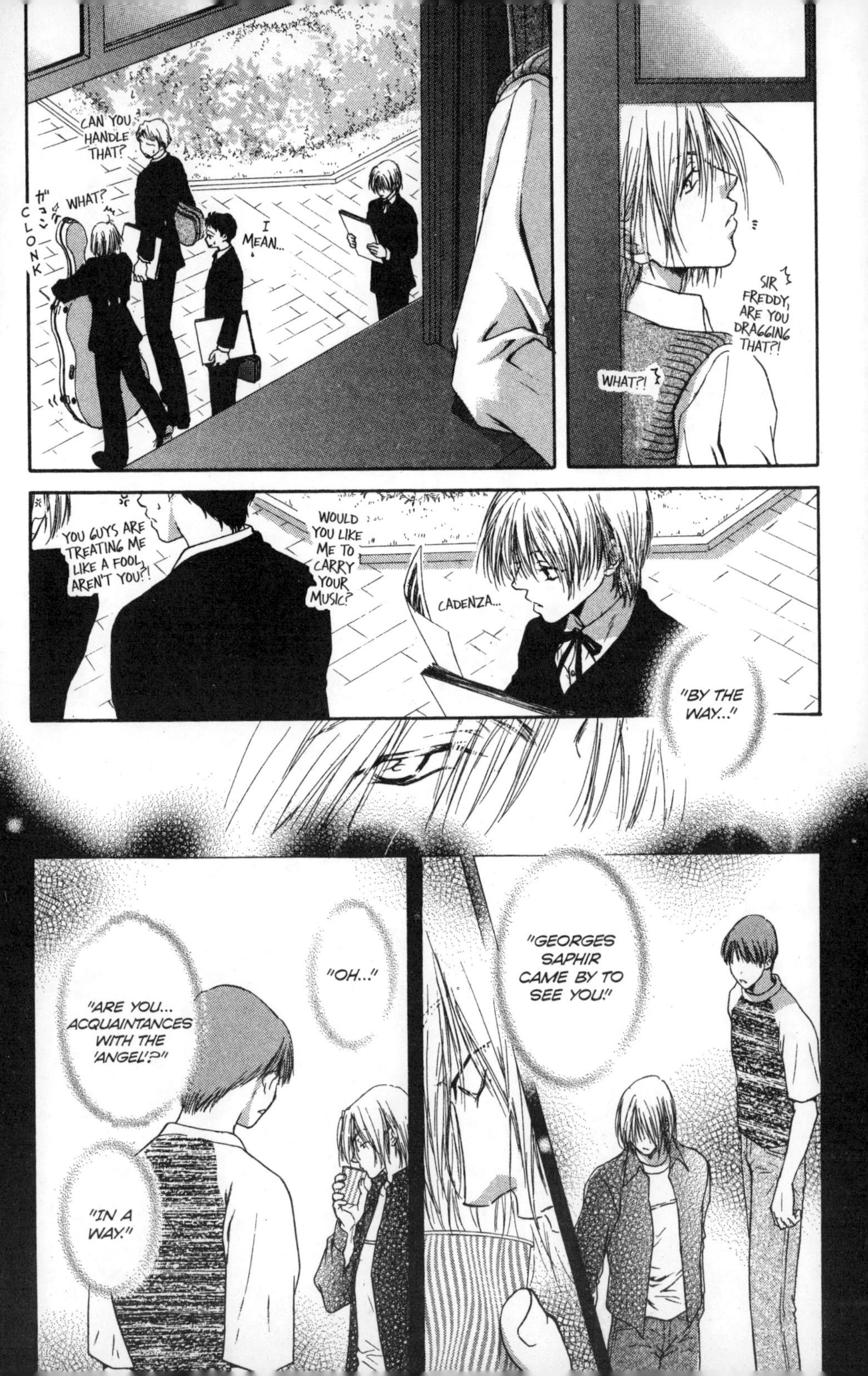
SIR FREDDY, ARE YOU DRAGGING THAT?!
WHAT?!
CAN YOU HANDLE THAT?
CLONK
WHAT?
I MEAN...
CADENZA...
WOULD YOU LIKE ME TO CARRY YOUR MUSIC?
YOU GUYS ARE TREATING ME LIKE A FOOL, AREN'T YOU?!
"BY THE WAY..."
"GEORGES SAPHIR CAME BY TO SEE YOU."
"OH..."
"ARE YOU... ACQUAINTANCES WITH THE 'ANGEL'?"
"IN A WAY."

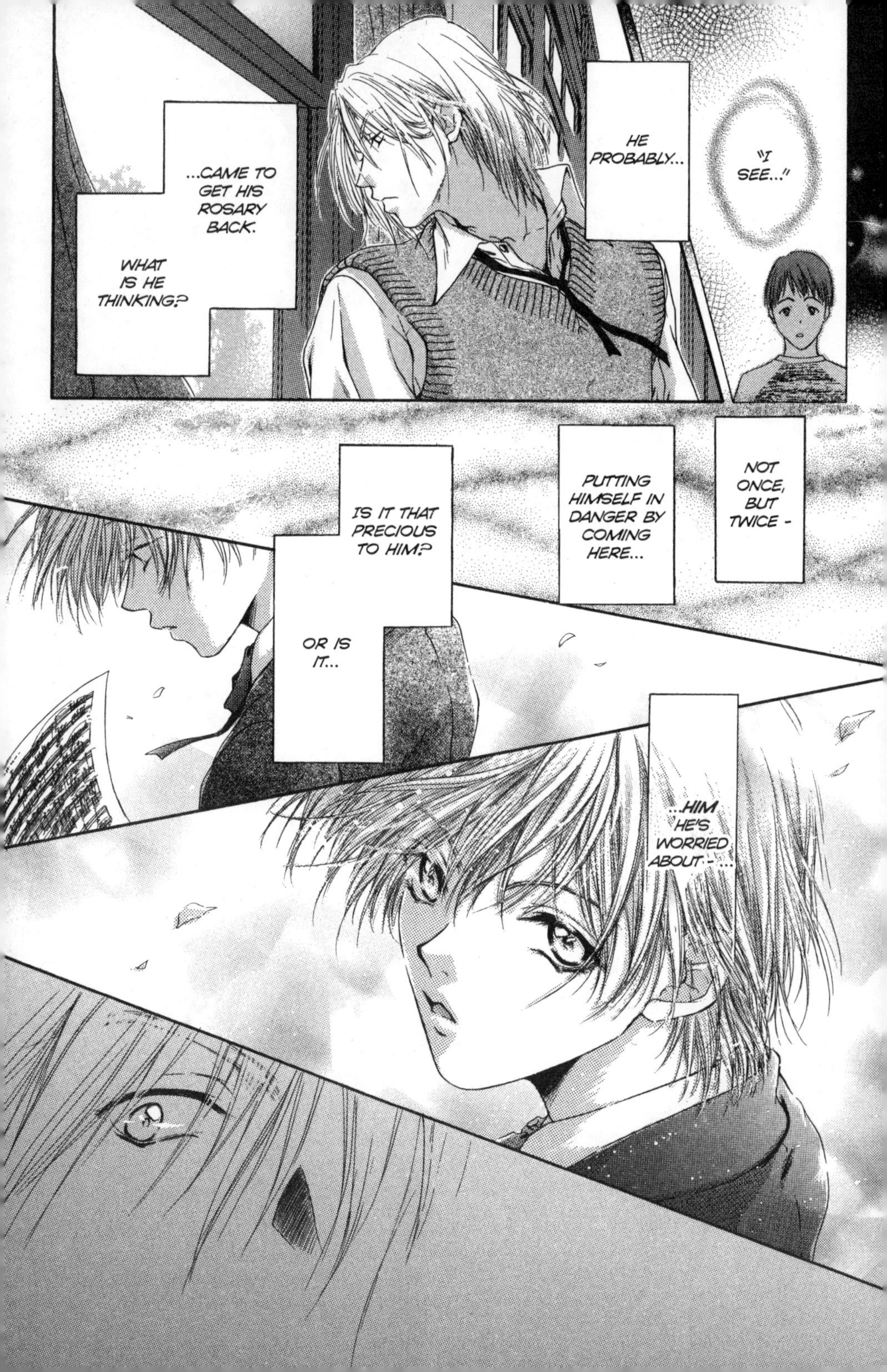
"I SEE..."
HE PROBABLY...
...CAME TO GET HIS ROSARY BACK.
WHAT IS HE THINKING?
NOT ONCE, BUT TWICE -
PUTTING HIMSELF IN DANGER BY COMING HERE...
IS IT THAT PRECIOUS TO HIM?
OR IS IT...
...HIM HE'S WORRIED ABOUT -...

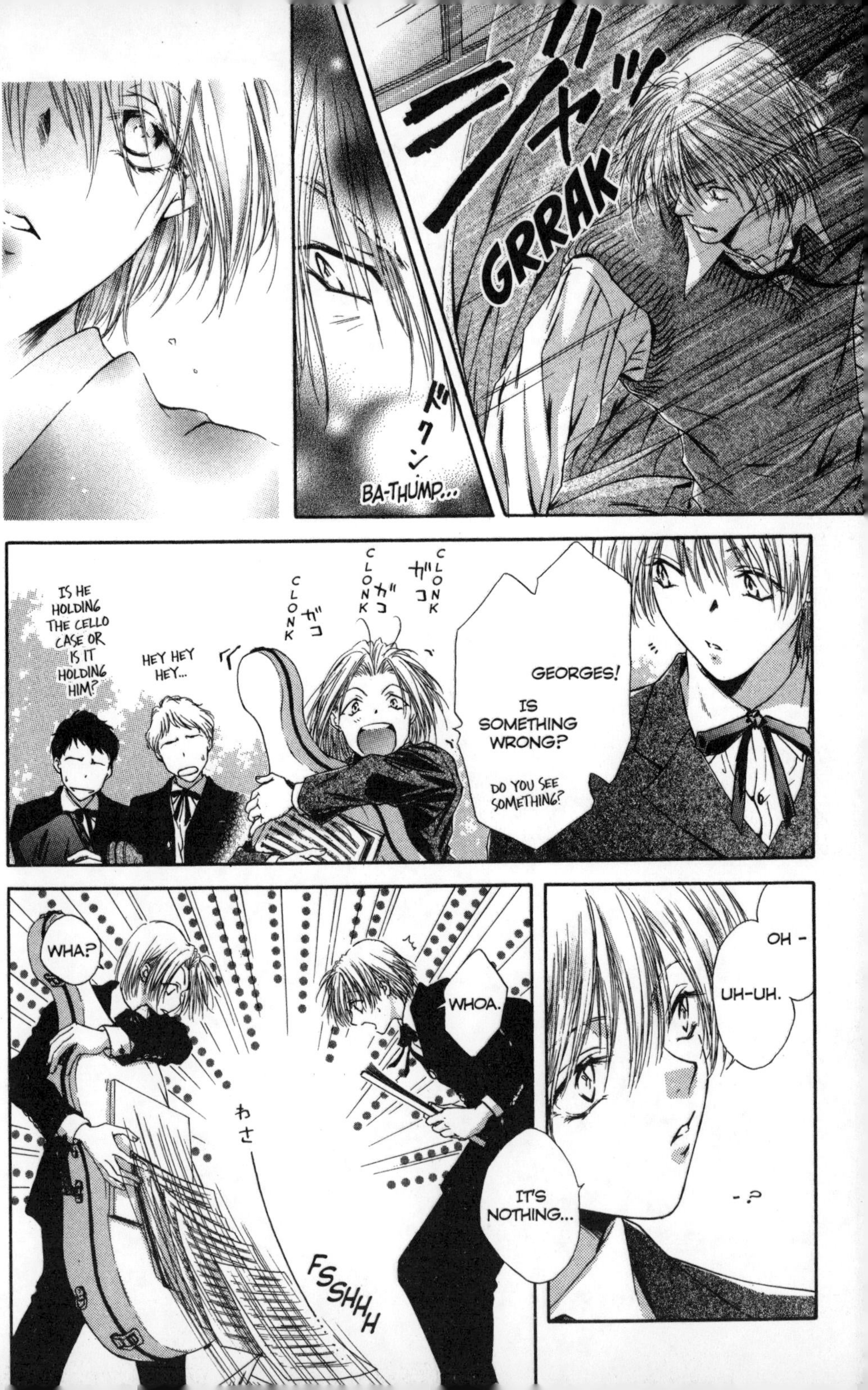

ジャッ
GRRAK
ドクン
BA-THUMP...
GEORGES!
IS SOMETHING WRONG?
DO YOU SEE SOMETHING?
CLONK ガコ
CLONK ガコ
CLONK ガコ
HEY HEY HEY...
IS HE HOLDING THE CELLO CASE OR IS IT HOLDING HIM?
OH -
UH-UH.
IT'S NOTHING...
-?
WHOA.
WHA?
わさ
FSSHHH

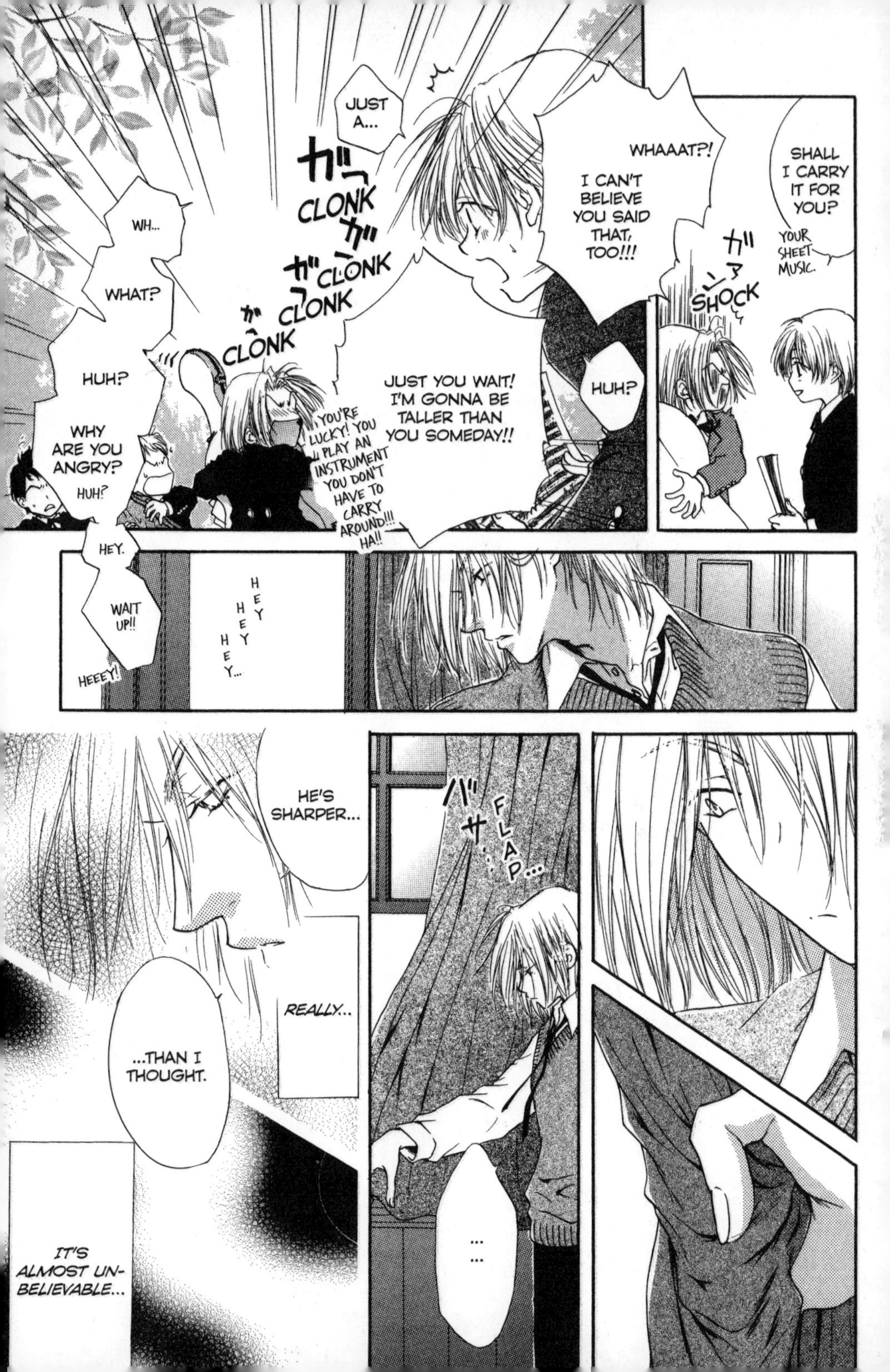

SHALL I CARRY IT FOR YOU?
YOUR SHEET MUSIC.
ガァン SHOCK
WHAAAT?!
I CAN'T BELIEVE YOU SAID THAT, TOO!!!
HUH?
JUST A...
JUST YOU WAIT! I'M GONNA BE TALLER THAN YOU SOMEDAY!!
YOU'RE LUCKY! YOU PLAY AN INSTRUMENT YOU DON'T HAVE TO CARRY AROUND!!! HA!!
ガッ CLONK
ガッ CLONK
ガッ CLONK
ガッ CLONK
WH...
WHAT?
HUH?
WHY ARE YOU ANGRY?
HUH?
HEY.
WAIT UP!!
HEEEY!
HEY HEY HEY HEY...
バサ FLAP...
...
...
HE'S SHARPER...
...THAN I THOUGHT.
REALLY...
IT'S ALMOST UN-BELIEVABLE...

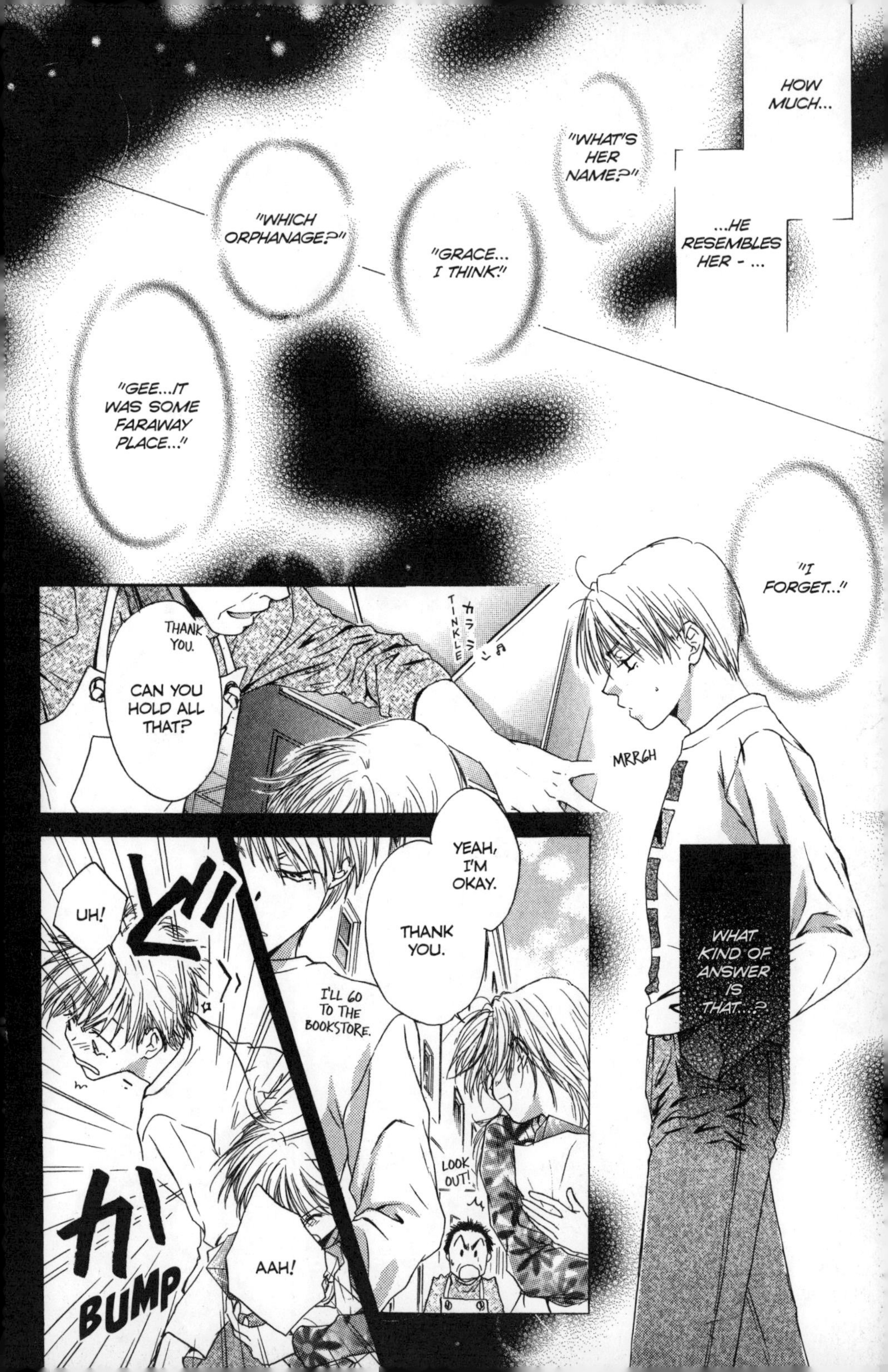
HOW MUCH...
...HE RESEMBLES HER - ...
"WHAT'S HER NAME?"
"GRACE... I THINK."
"WHICH ORPHANAGE?"
"GEE...IT WAS SOME FARAWAY PLACE..."
"I FORGET..."
MRRGH
WHAT KIND OF ANSWER IS THAT...?
TINKLE
THANK YOU.
CAN YOU HOLD ALL THAT?
YEAH, I'M OKAY.
THANK YOU.
I'LL GO TO THE BOOKSTORE.
LOOK OUT!
UH!
AAH!
BUMP

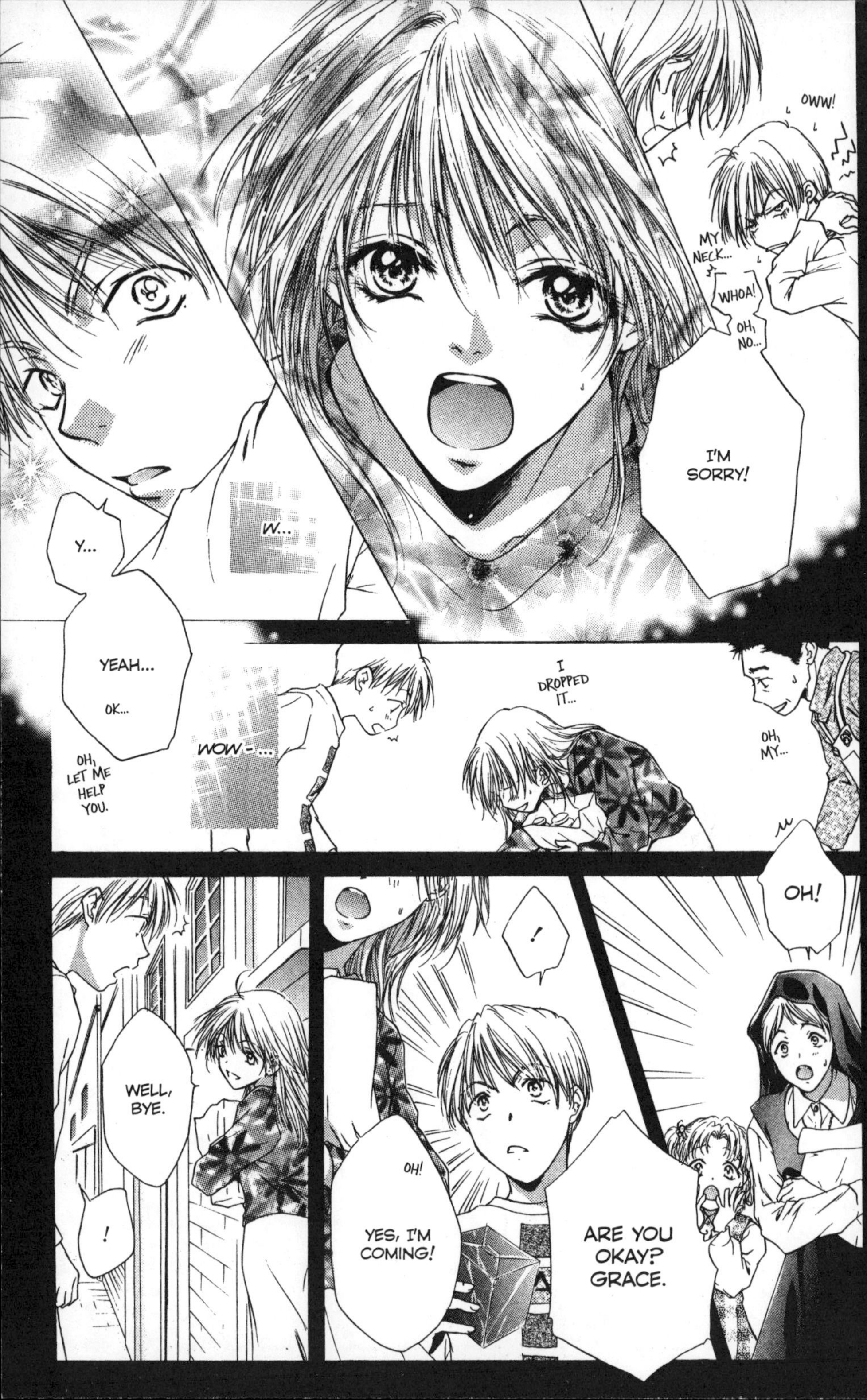
OWW!
MY NECK...
WHOA!
OH, NO...
I'M SORRY!
W...
Y...
YEAH... OK...
OH, MY...
I DROPPED IT...
WOW-...
OH, LET ME HELP YOU.
OH!
!
ARE YOU OKAY? GRACE.
OH!
YES, I'M COMING!
WELL, BYE.
!

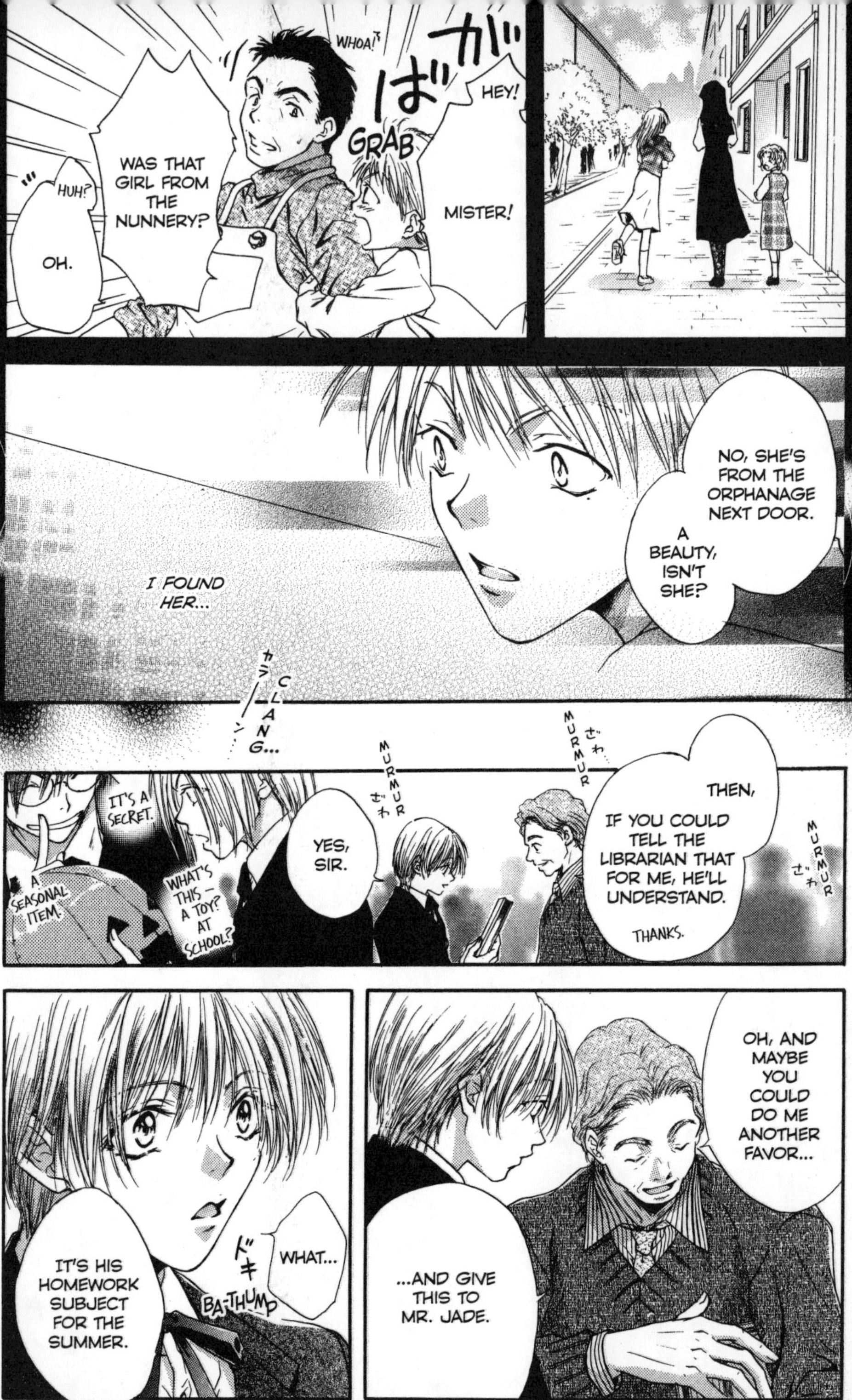
HEY!
MISTER!
GRAB
WHOA!
WAS THAT GIRL FROM THE NUNNERY?
HUH?
OH.
NO, SHE'S FROM THE ORPHANAGE NEXT DOOR.
A BEAUTY, ISN'T SHE?
I FOUND HER...
CLANG...
MURMUR
THEN, IF YOU COULD TELL THE LIBRARIAN THAT FOR ME, HE'LL UNDERSTAND.
THANKS.
MURMUR
MURMUR
YES, SIR.
WHAT'S THIS— A TOY? AT SCHOOL?
IT'S A SECRET.
A SEASONAL ITEM.
OH, AND MAYBE YOU COULD DO ME ANOTHER FAVOR...
...AND GIVE THIS TO MR. JADE.
WHAT...
BA-THUMP
IT'S HIS HOMEWORK SUBJECT FOR THE SUMMER.

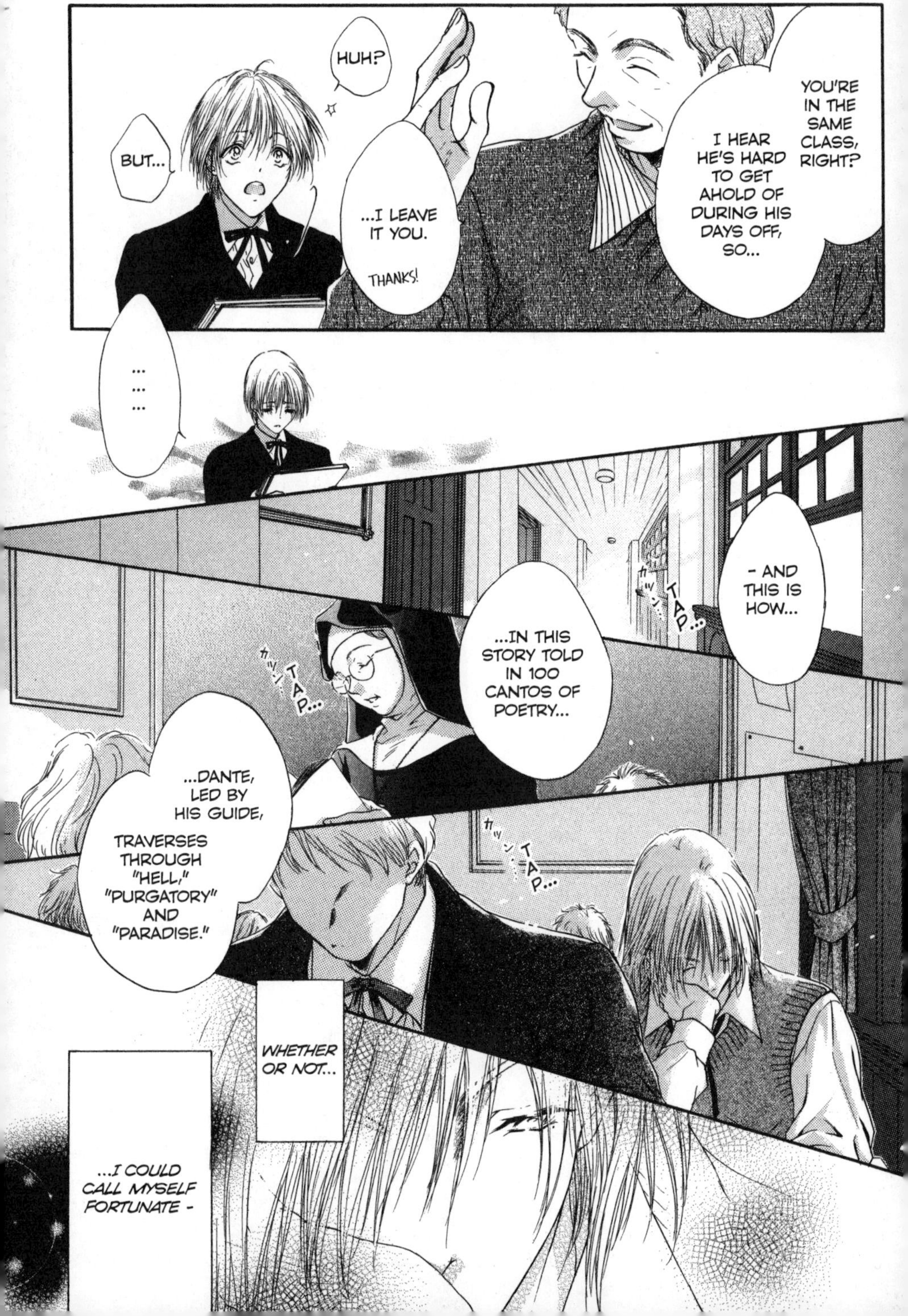
YOU'RE IN THE SAME CLASS, RIGHT?
I HEAR HE'S HARD TO GET AHOLD OF DURING HIS DAYS OFF, SO...
...I LEAVE IT YOU.
THANKS!
HUH?
BUT...
...
...
...
- AND THIS IS HOW...
TAP...
...IN THIS STORY TOLD IN 100 CANTOS OF POETRY...
TAP...
...DANTE, LED BY HIS GUIDE,
TRAVERSES THROUGH "HELL," "PURGATORY" AND "PARADISE."
TAP...
WHETHER OR NOT...
...I COULD CALL MYSELF FORTUNATE -

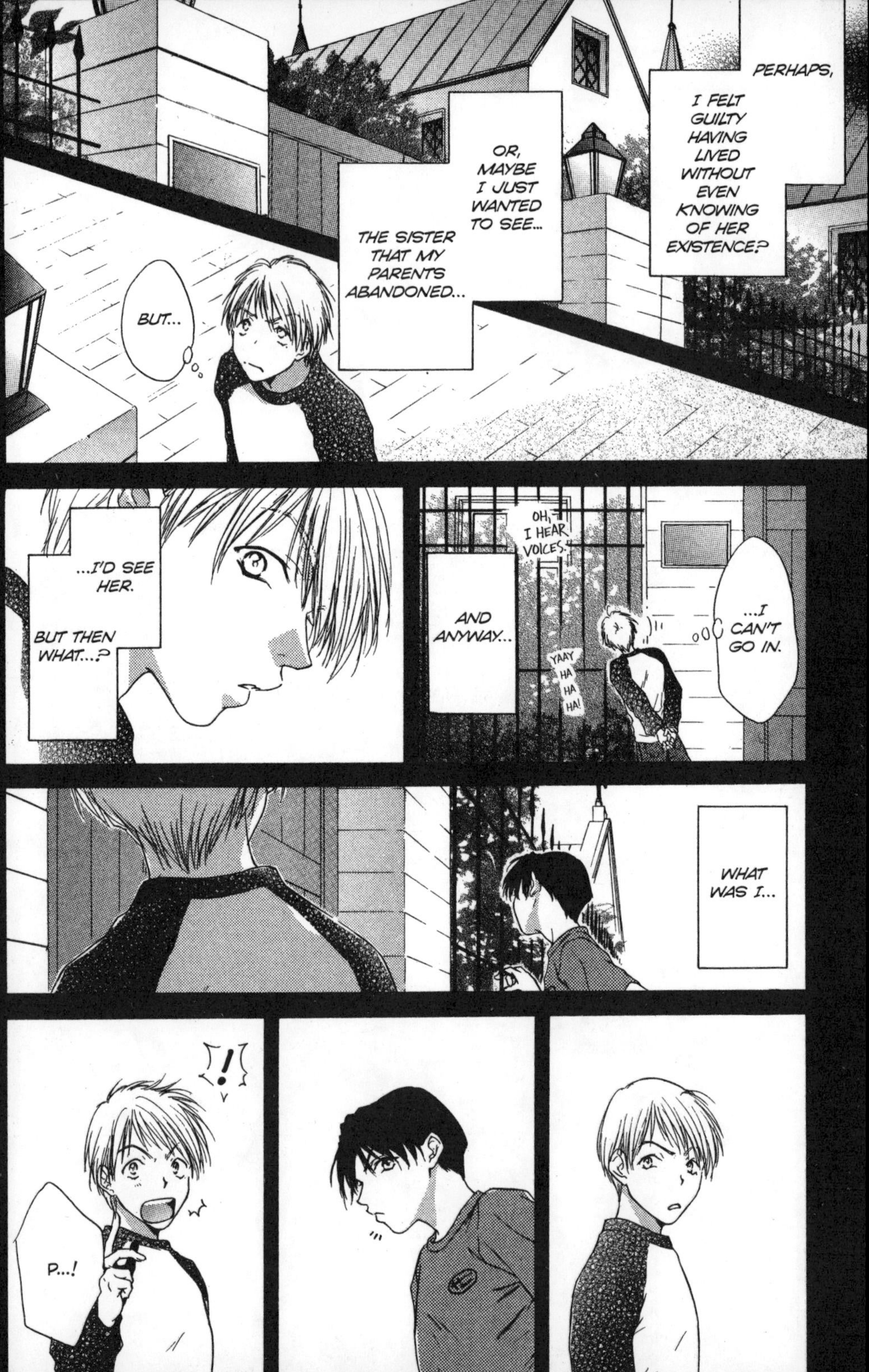
PERHAPS, I FELT GUILTY HAVING LIVED WITHOUT EVEN KNOWING OF HER EXISTENCE?
OR, MAYBE I JUST WANTED TO SEE...
THE SISTER THAT MY PARENTS ABANDONED...
BUT...
...I CAN'T GO IN.
OH, I HEAR VOICES.
AND ANYWAY...
YAAY HA HA HA!
...I'D SEE HER.
BUT THEN WHAT...?
WHAT WAS I...
!
P...!

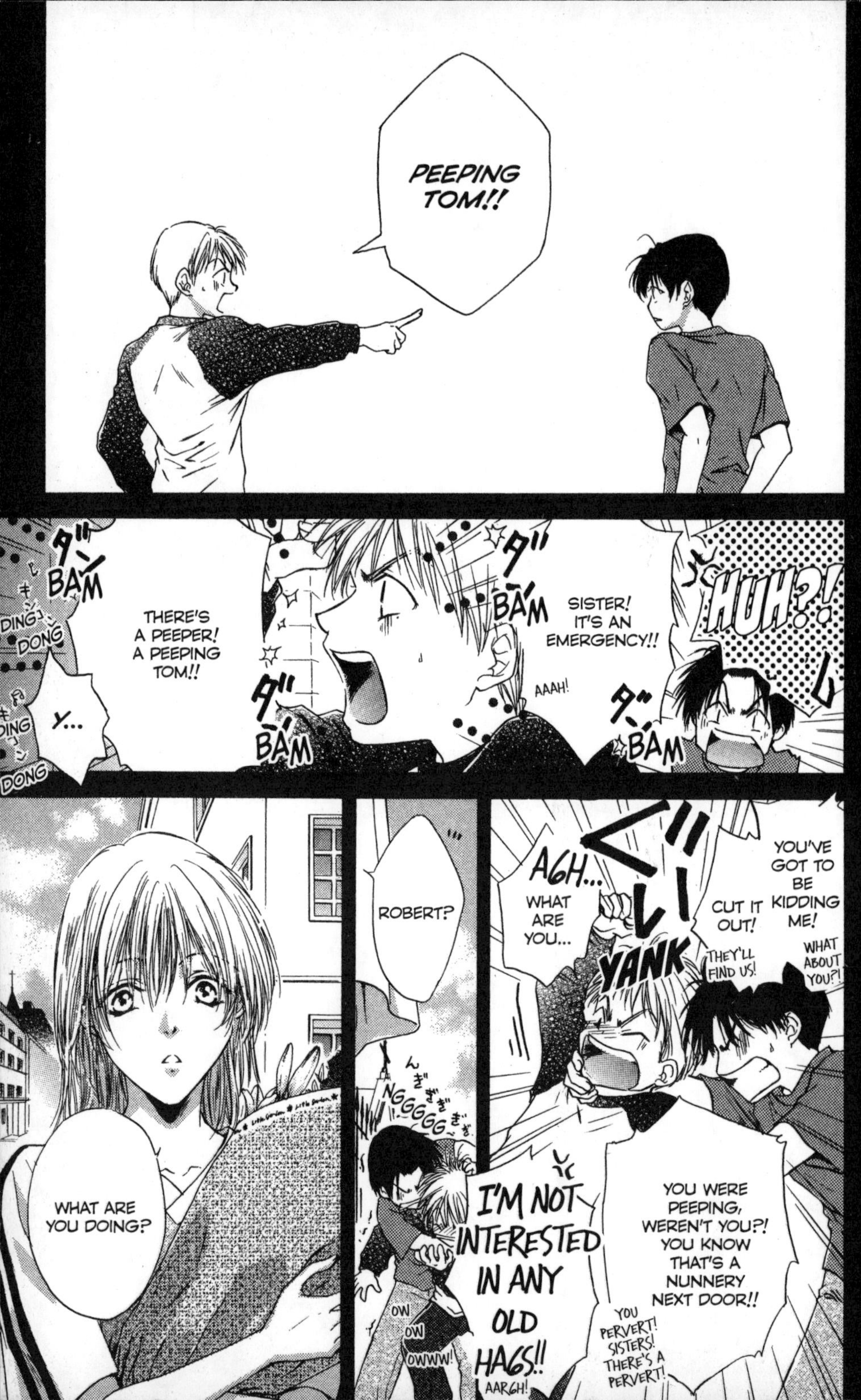
PEEPING TOM!!
HUH?!
SISTER! IT'S AN EMERGENCY!!
AAAH!
ダ BAM
ダ BAM
ダ BAM
ダン BAM
THERE'S A PEEPER! A PEEPING TOM!!
DING DONG
DING DONG
Y...
YOU'VE GOT TO BE KIDDING ME!
CUT IT OUT!
AGH... WHAT ARE YOU...
YANK
THEY'LL FIND US!
WHAT ABOUT YOU?!
YOU WERE PEEPING, WEREN'T YOU?! YOU KNOW THAT'S A NUNNERY NEXT DOOR!!
YOU PERVERT! SISTERS! THERE'S A PERVERT!
I'M NOT INTERESTED IN ANY OLD HAGS!!
AARGH!
OW OW OWWW!
NGGGGG
ROBERT?
WHAT ARE YOU DOING?

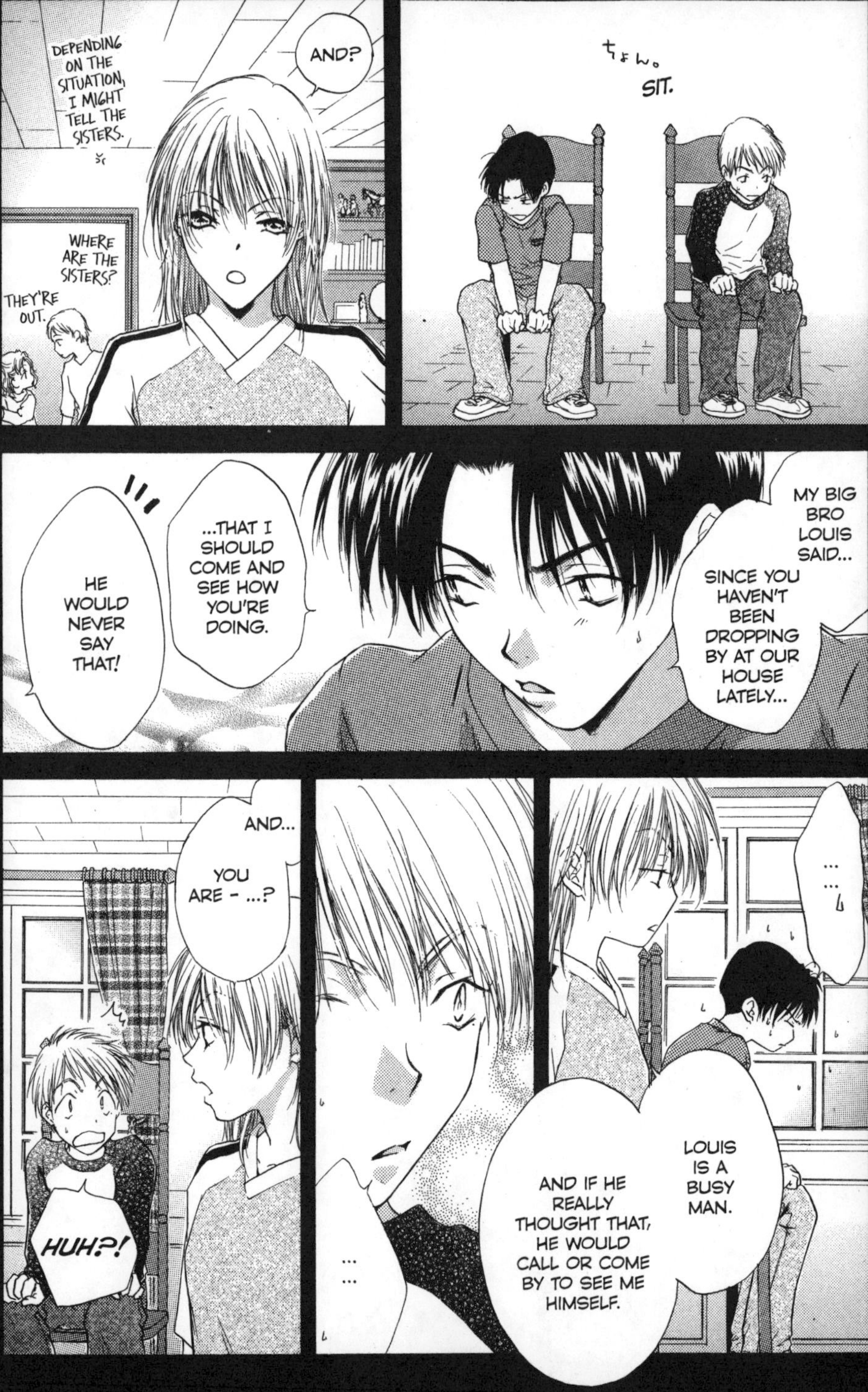
ちょん。
SIT.
AND?
DEPENDING ON THE SITUATION, I MIGHT TELL THE SISTERS.
WHERE ARE THE SISTERS?
THEY'RE OUT.
MY BIG BRO LOUIS SAID...
SINCE YOU HAVEN'T BEEN DROPPING BY AT OUR HOUSE LATELY...
...THAT I SHOULD COME AND SEE HOW YOU'RE DOING.
HE WOULD NEVER SAY THAT!
... ...
LOUIS IS A BUSY MAN.
AND IF HE REALLY THOUGHT THAT, HE WOULD CALL OR COME BY TO SEE ME HIMSELF.
... ...
AND...
YOU ARE - ...?
HUH?!

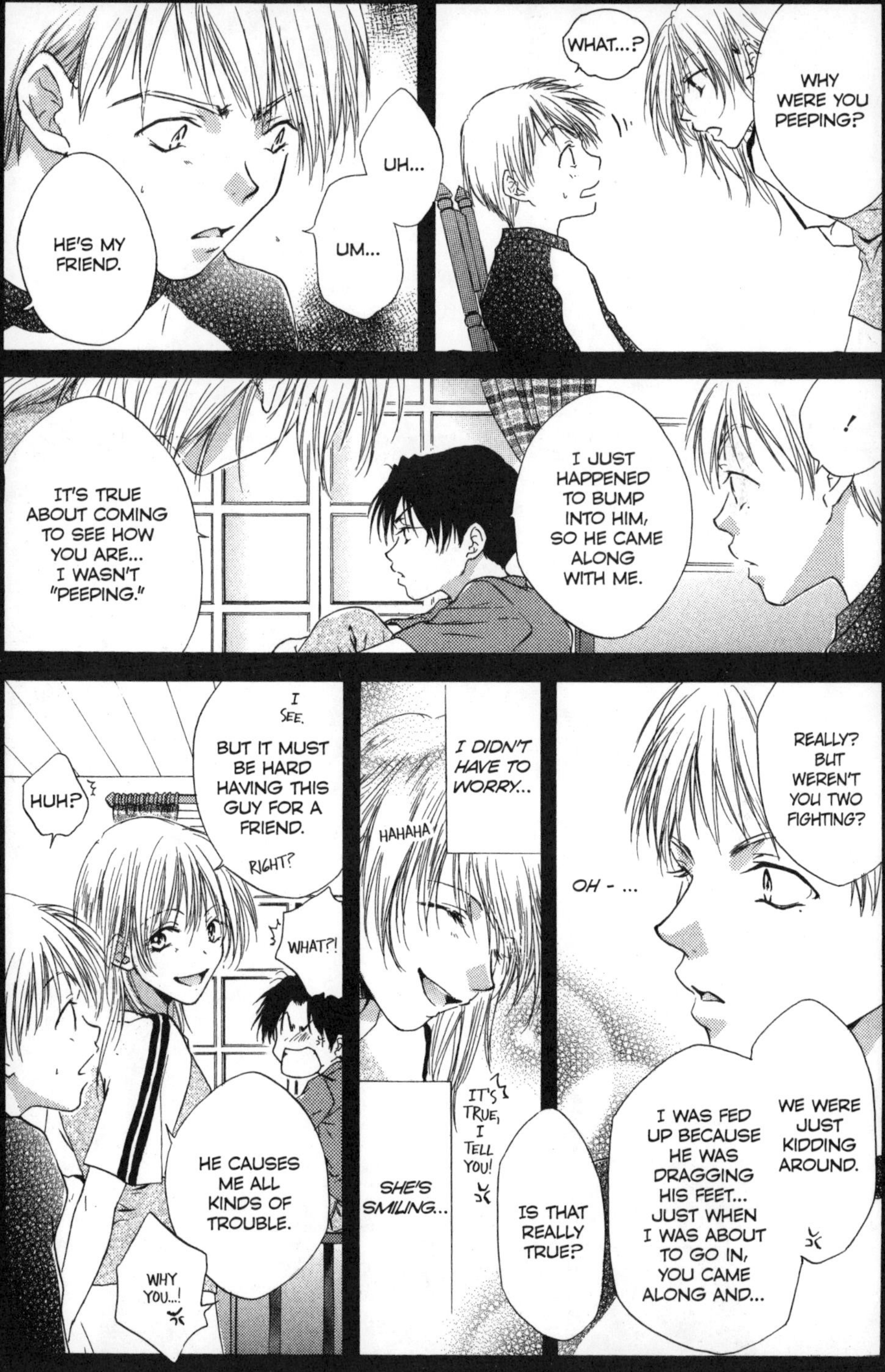
WHY WERE YOU PEEPING?
WHAT...?
UH...
UM...
HE'S MY FRIEND.
!
I JUST HAPPENED TO BUMP INTO HIM, SO HE CAME ALONG WITH ME.
IT'S TRUE ABOUT COMING TO SEE HOW YOU ARE... I WASN'T "PEEPING."
REALLY? BUT WEREN'T YOU TWO FIGHTING?
OH - ...
WE WERE JUST KIDDING AROUND.
I WAS FED UP BECAUSE HE WAS DRAGGING HIS FEET... JUST WHEN I WAS ABOUT TO GO IN, YOU CAME ALONG AND...
IT'S TRUE, I TELL YOU!
IS THAT REALLY TRUE?
I DIDN'T HAVE TO WORRY...
HAHAHA
SHE'S SMILING...
I SEE.
BUT IT MUST BE HARD HAVING THIS GUY FOR A FRIEND.
RIGHT?
HUH?
WHAT?!
HE CAUSES ME ALL KINDS OF TROUBLE.
WHY YOU...!

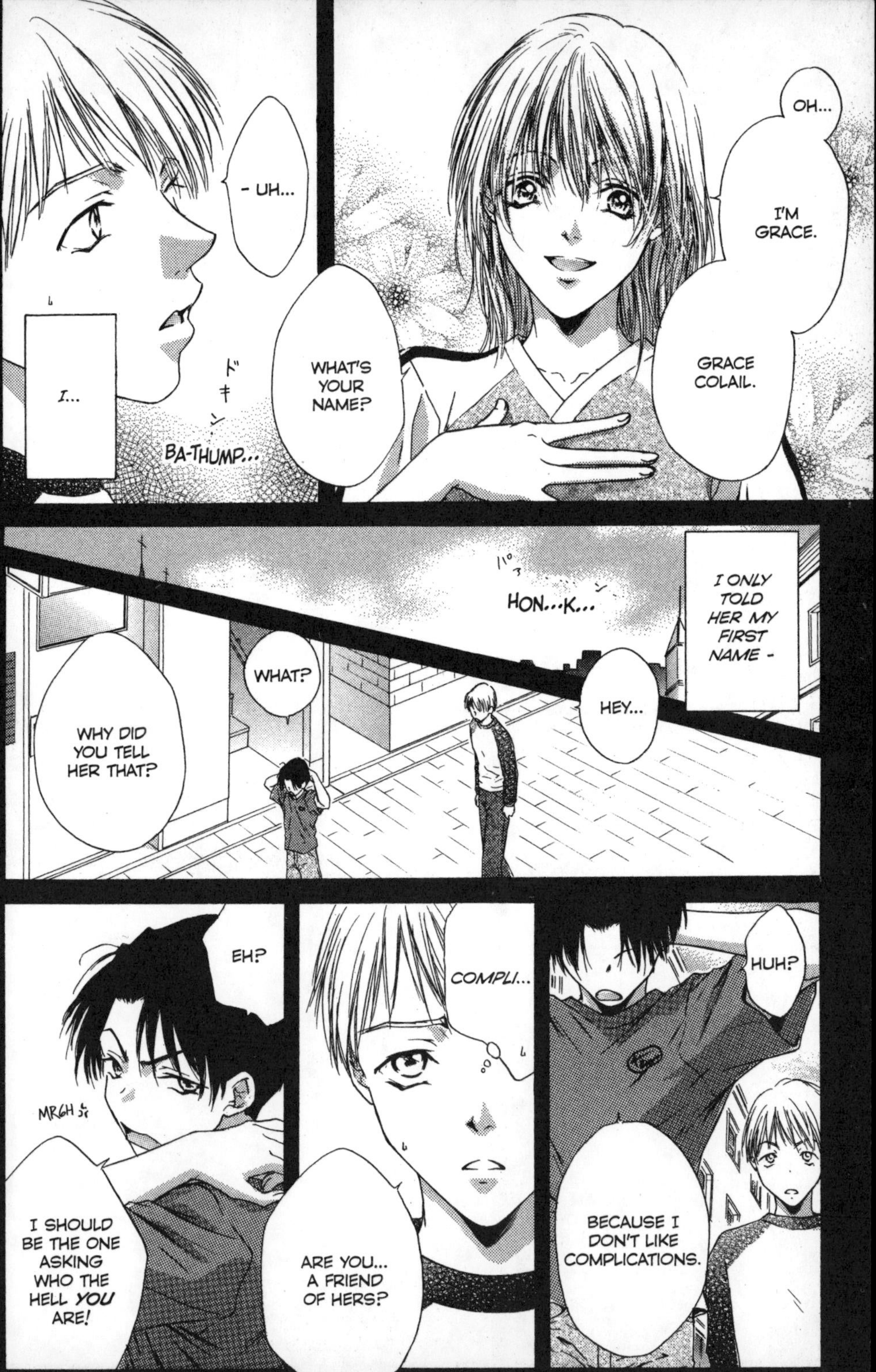
OH...
I'M GRACE.
GRACE COLAIL.
WHAT'S YOUR NAME?
- UH...
I...
ドキン
BA-THUMP...
I ONLY TOLD HER MY FIRST NAME -
HON...K...
HEY...
WHAT?
WHY DID YOU TELL HER THAT?
HUH?
BECAUSE I DON'T LIKE COMPLICATIONS.
COMPLI...
ARE YOU... A FRIEND OF HERS?
EH?
MRGH
I SHOULD BE THE ONE ASKING WHO THE HELL *YOU* ARE!

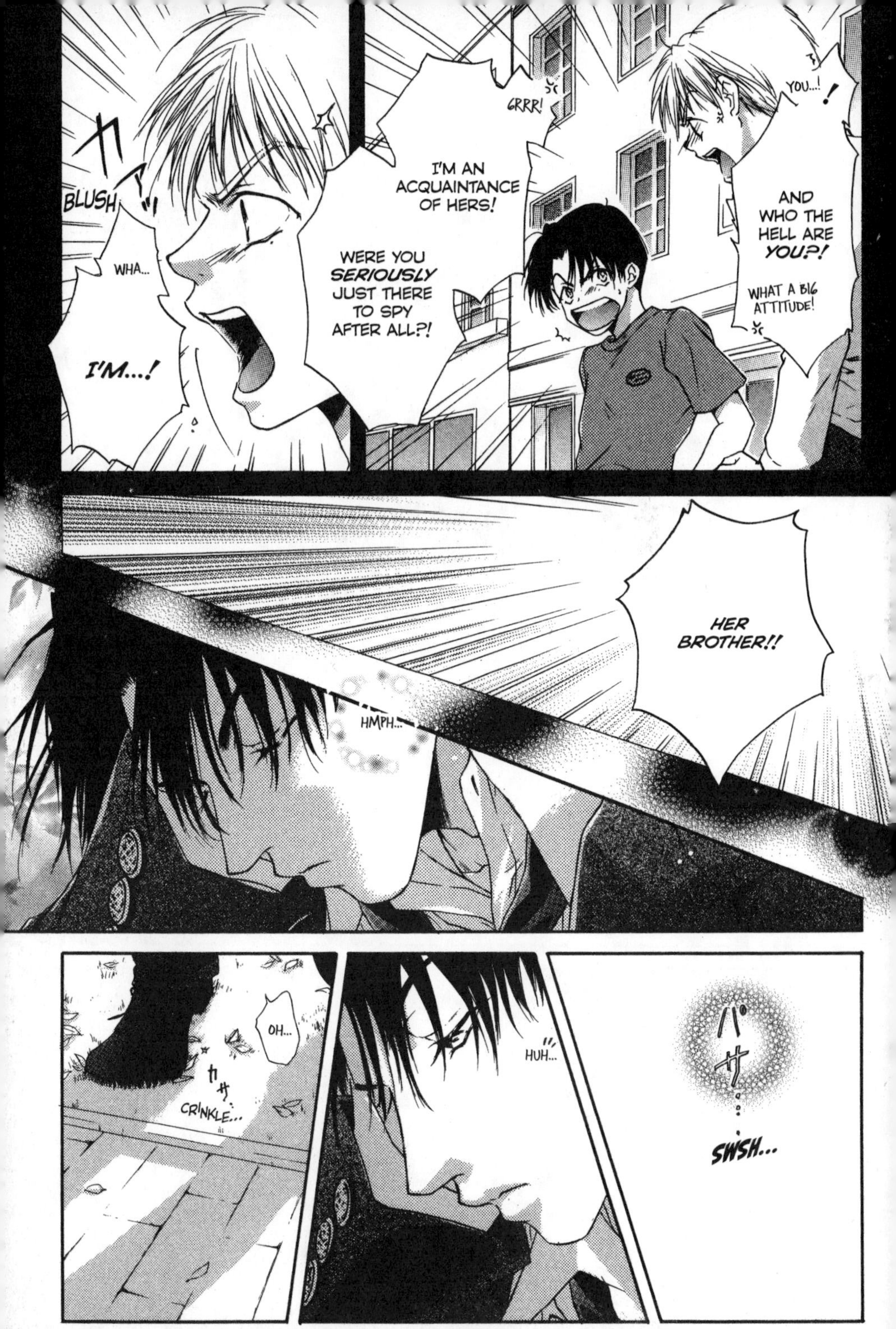
YOU...!
GRRR!
AND WHO THE HELL ARE YOU?!
I'M AN ACQUAINTANCE OF HERS!
WHAT A BIG ATTITUDE!
WERE YOU SERIOUSLY JUST THERE TO SPY AFTER ALL?!
BLUSH
WHA...
I'M...!
HER BROTHER!!
HMPH...
SWSH...
HUH...
OH...
CRINKLE...

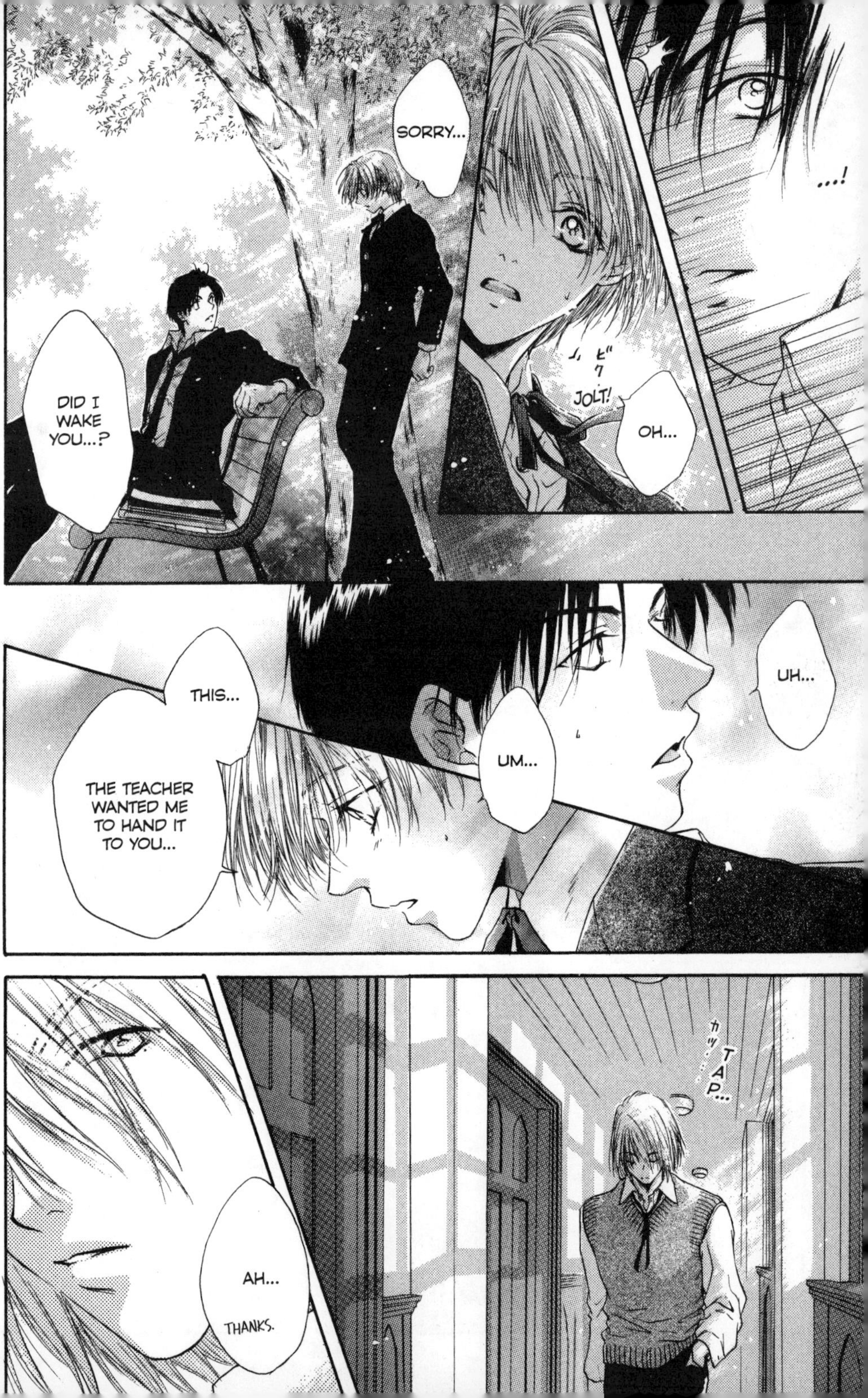
...!
ビク
JOLT!
OH...
SORRY...
DID I WAKE YOU...?
UH...
UM...
THIS...
THE TEACHER WANTED ME TO HAND IT TO YOU...
カツ…
TAP...
AH...
THANKS.

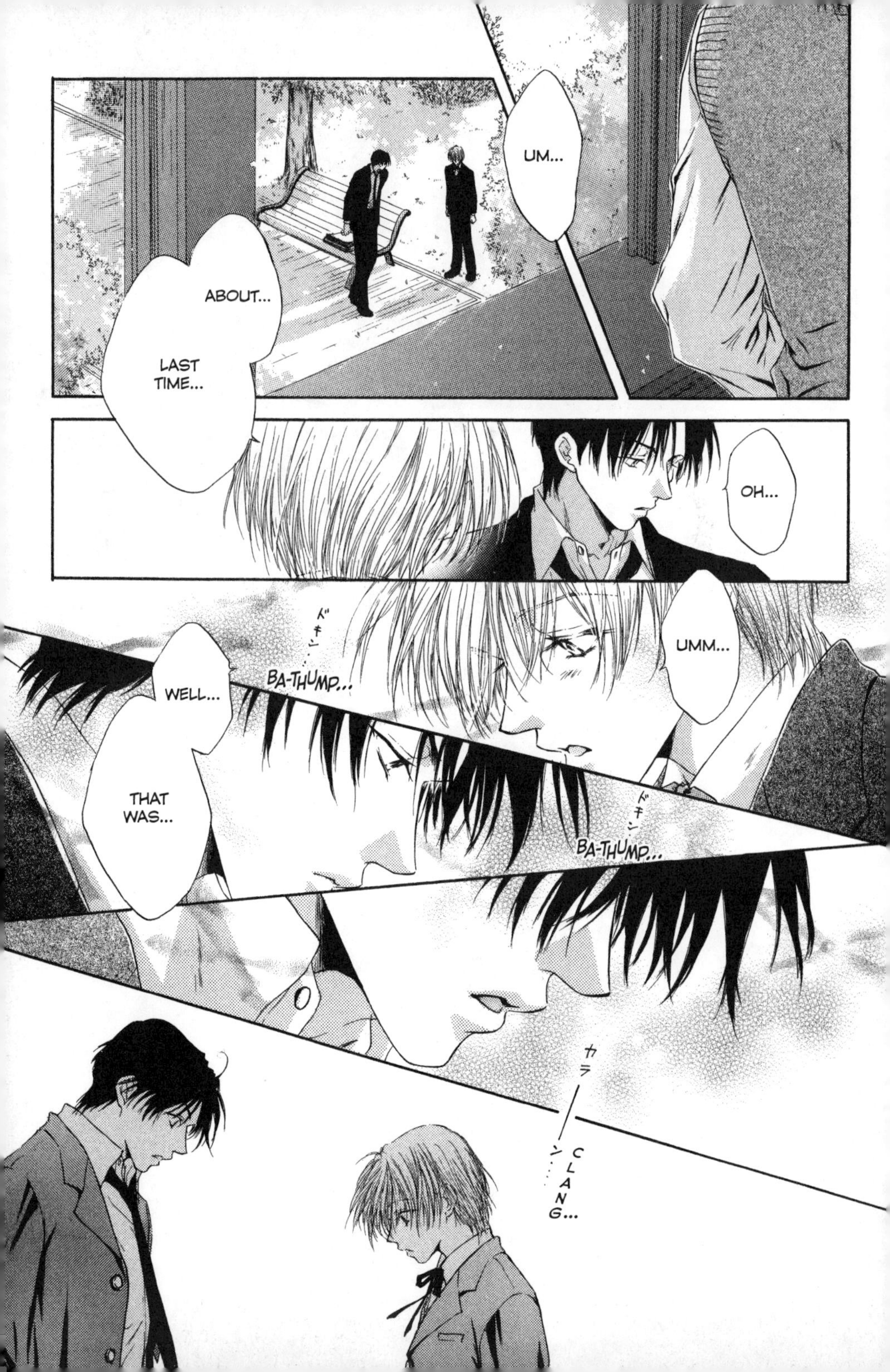
UM...
ABOUT...
LAST TIME...
OH...
UMM...
ドキン
BA-THUMP...
WELL...
THAT WAS...
ドキン
BA-THUMP...
カラーン...
CLANG...

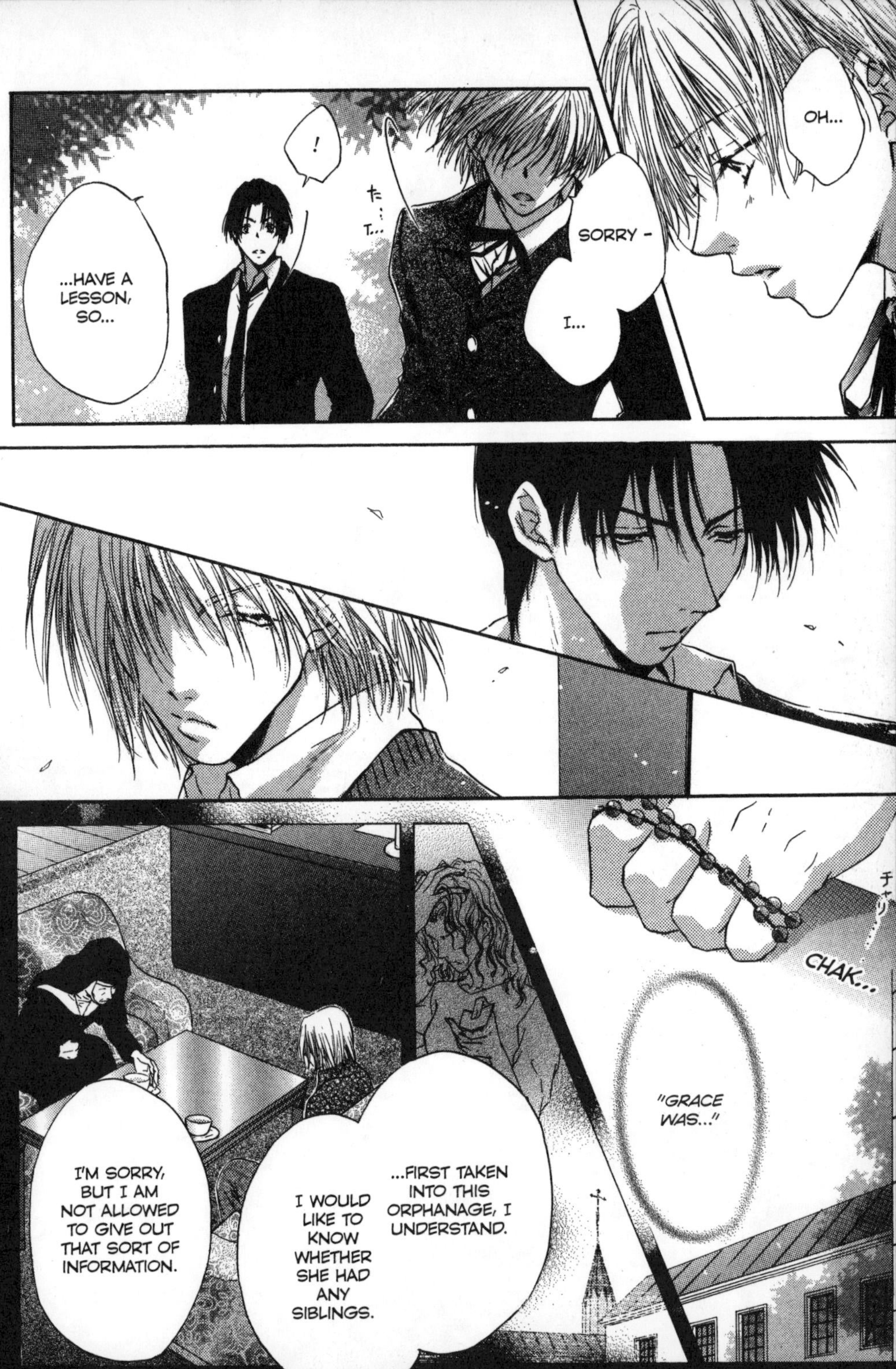
OH...
SORRY -
I...
T...
!
...HAVE A LESSON, SO...
CHAK...
"GRACE WAS..."
...FIRST TAKEN INTO THIS ORPHANAGE, I UNDERSTAND.
I WOULD LIKE TO KNOW WHETHER SHE HAD ANY SIBLINGS.
I'M SORRY, BUT I AM NOT ALLOWED TO GIVE OUT THAT SORT OF INFORMATION.

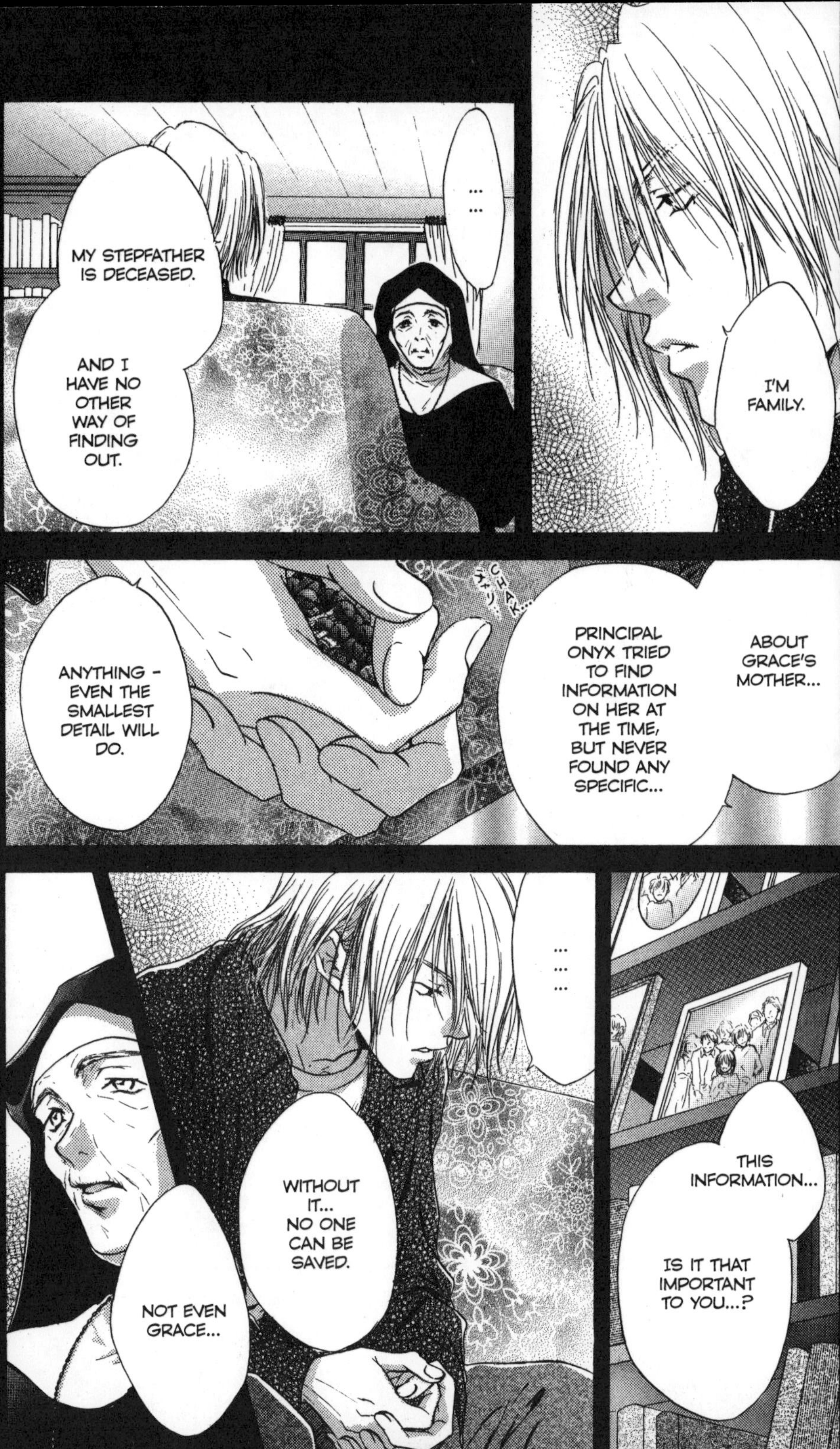
I'M FAMILY.
... ...
MY STEPFATHER IS DECEASED.
AND I HAVE NO OTHER WAY OF FINDING OUT.
ABOUT GRACE'S MOTHER...
PRINCIPAL ONYX TRIED TO FIND INFORMATION ON HER AT THE TIME, BUT NEVER FOUND ANY SPECIFIC...
CHAK...
ANYTHING - EVEN THE SMALLEST DETAIL WILL DO.
THIS INFORMATION...
IS IT THAT IMPORTANT TO YOU...?
... ...
WITHOUT IT... NO ONE CAN BE SAVED.
NOT EVEN GRACE...

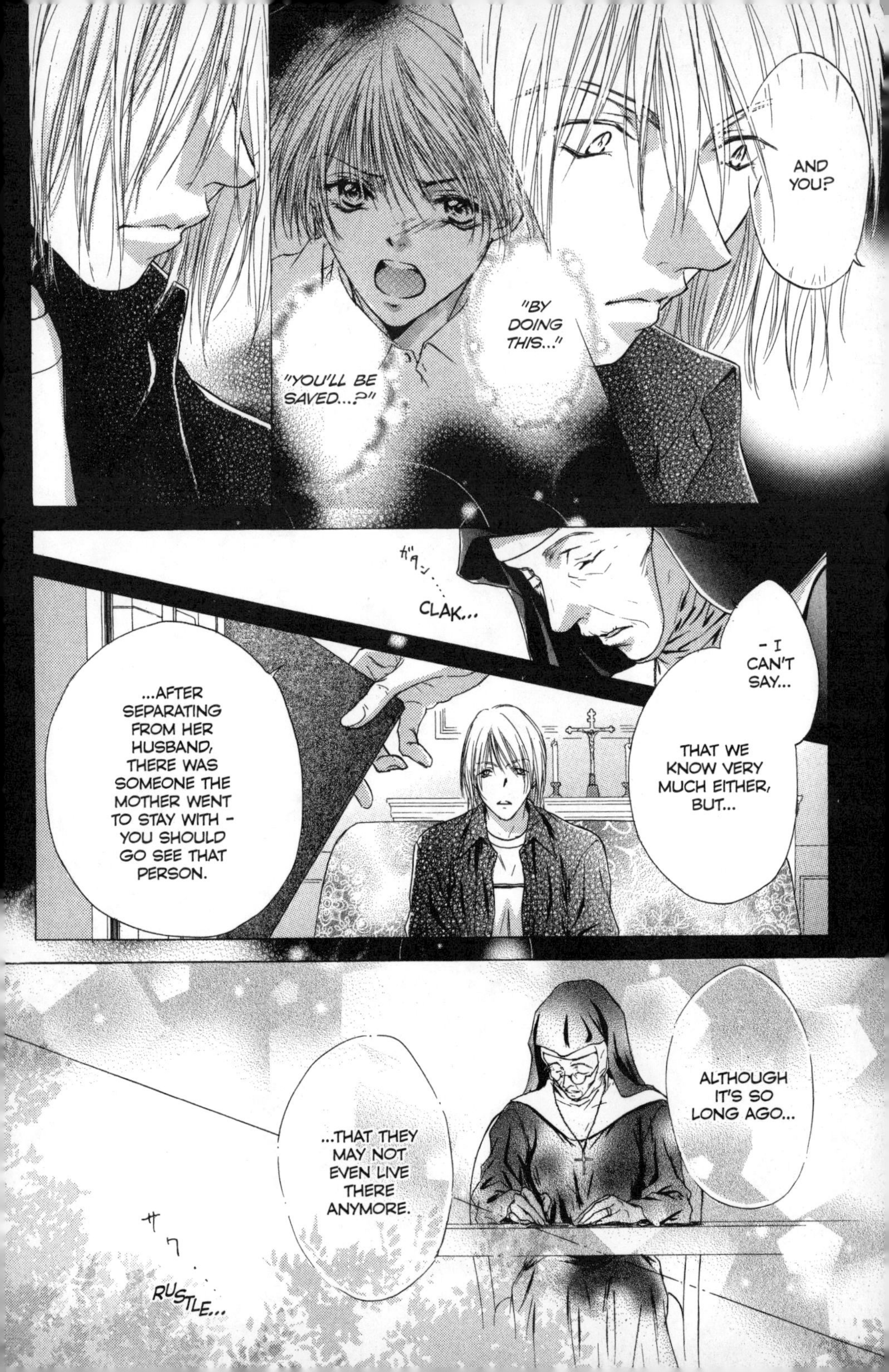
AND YOU?
"BY DOING THIS..."
"YOU'LL BE SAVED...?"
ガタン
CLAK...
- I CAN'T SAY...
THAT WE KNOW VERY MUCH EITHER, BUT...
...AFTER SEPARATING FROM HER HUSBAND, THERE WAS SOMEONE THE MOTHER WENT TO STAY WITH - YOU SHOULD GO SEE THAT PERSON.
ALTHOUGH IT'S SO LONG AGO...
...THAT THEY MAY NOT EVEN LIVE THERE ANYMORE.
サク
RUSTLE...

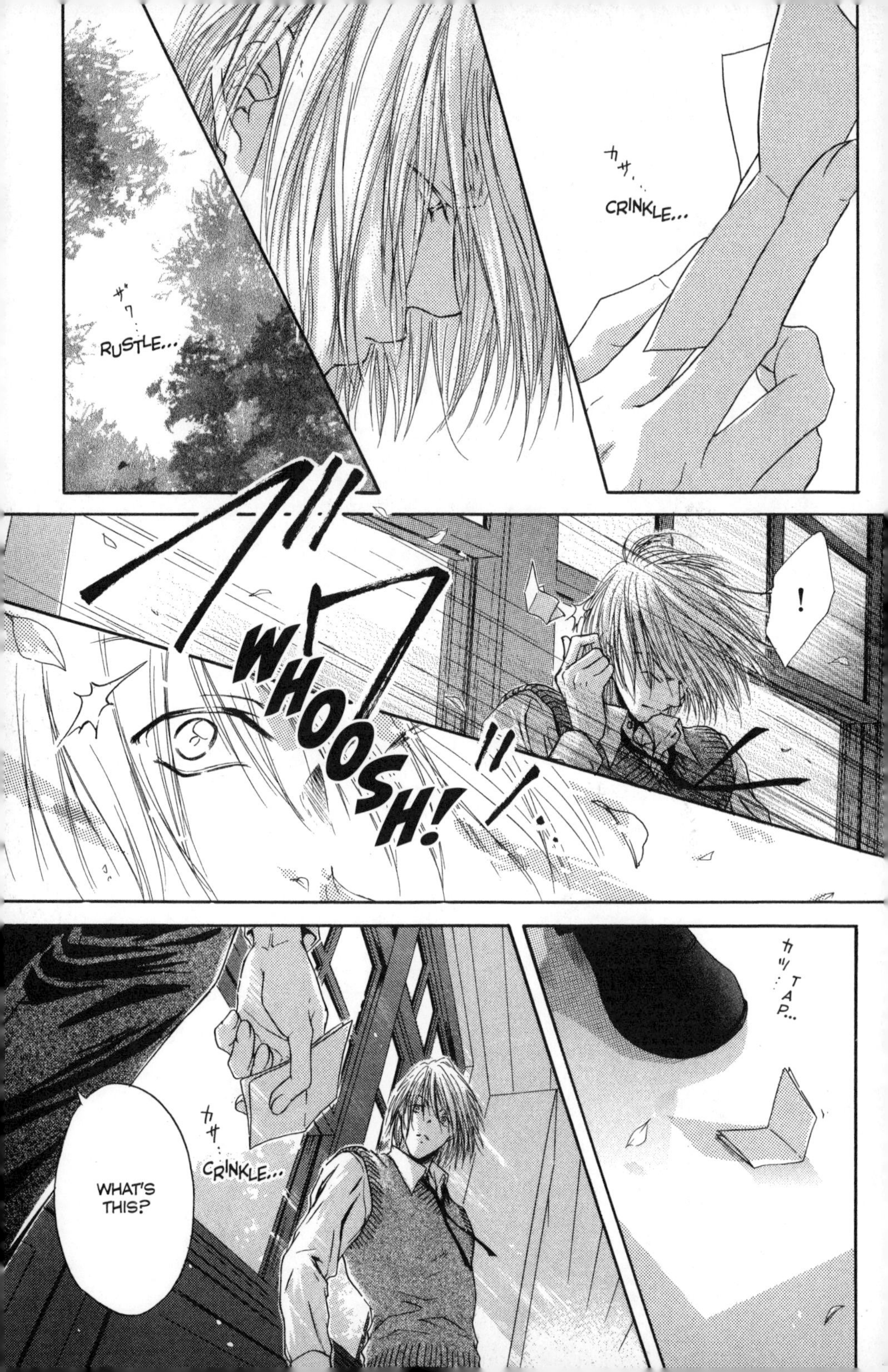
カサ…
CRINKLE...
ザワ…
RUSTLE...
!
WHOOSH!
カツ…
TAP...
カサ…
CRINKLE...
WHAT'S THIS?

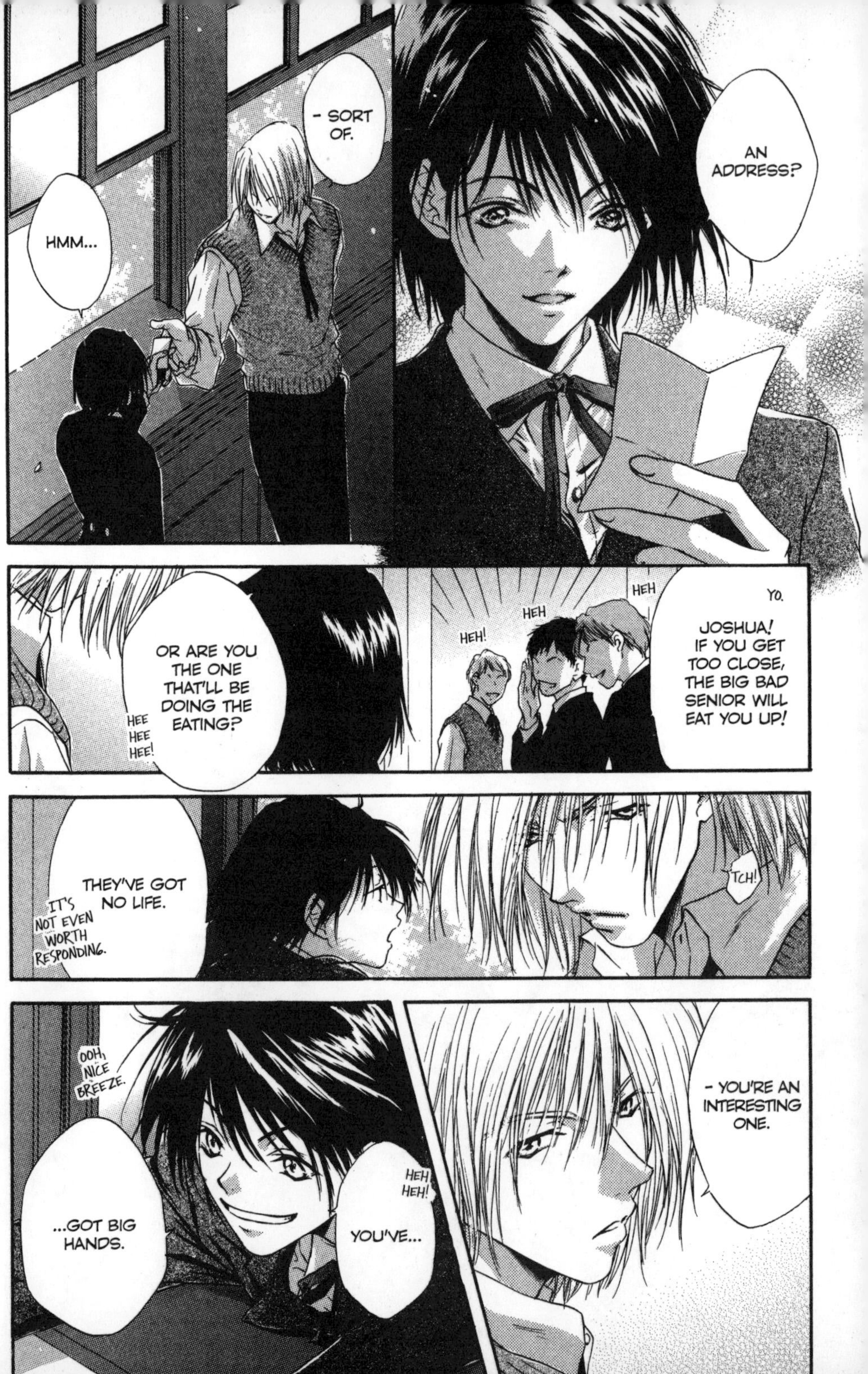
AN ADDRESS?
- SORT OF.
HMM...
YO.
JOSHUA! IF YOU GET TOO CLOSE, THE BIG BAD SENIOR WILL EAT YOU UP!
HEH
HEH
HEH!
OR ARE YOU THE ONE THAT'LL BE DOING THE EATING?
HEE HEE HEE!
TCH!
THEY'VE GOT NO LIFE.
IT'S NOT EVEN WORTH RESPONDING.
- YOU'RE AN INTERESTING ONE.
HEH HEH!
YOU'VE...
OOH, NICE BREEZE.
...GOT BIG HANDS.

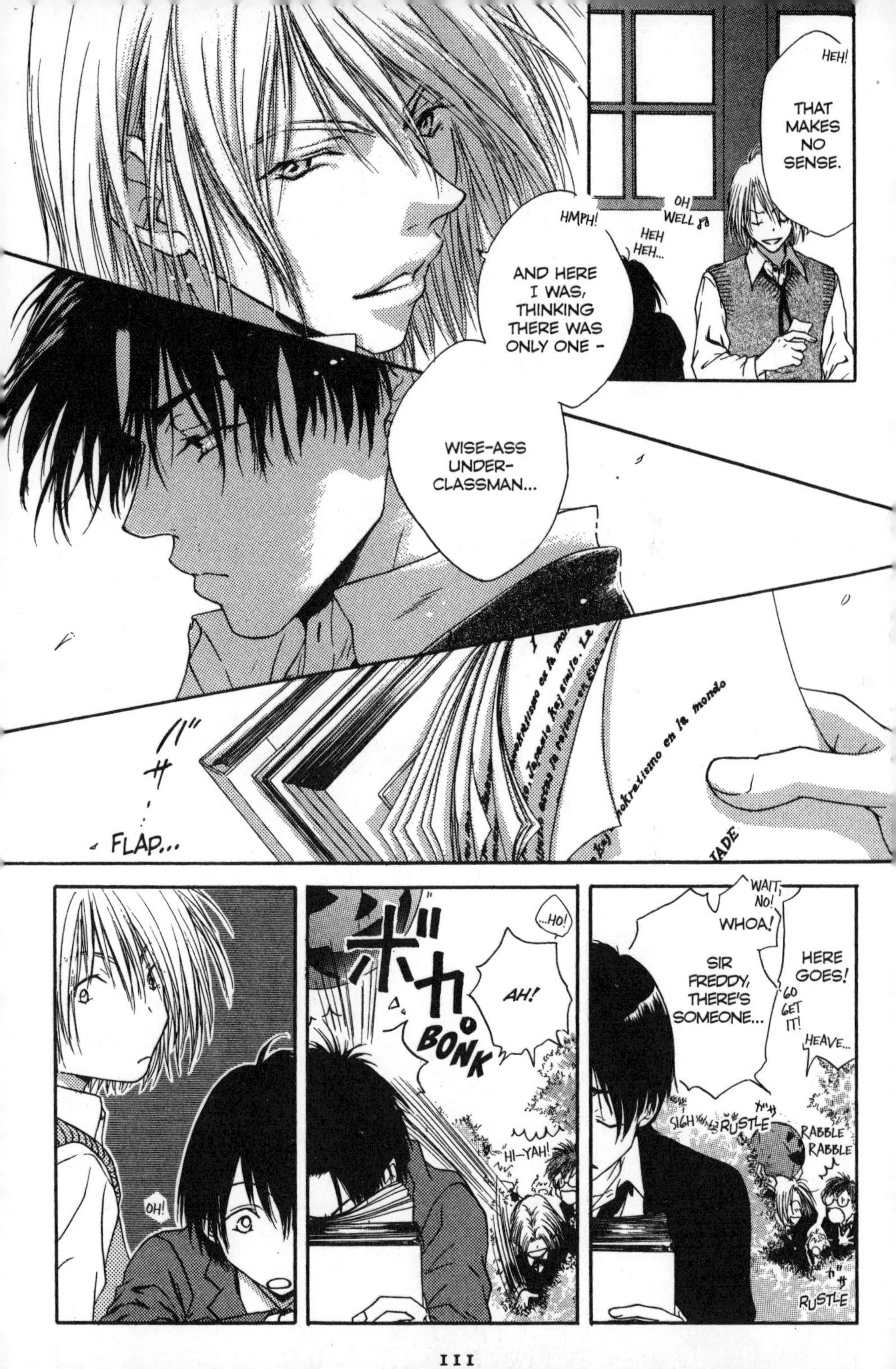
HEH!
THAT MAKES NO SENSE.
OH WELL
HEH HEH...
HMPH!
AND HERE I WAS, THINKING THERE WAS ONLY ONE -
WISE-ASS UNDER-CLASSMAN...
JADE
FLAP...
WAIT, NO!
HERE GOES!
GO GET IT!
WHOA!
SIR FREDDY, THERE'S SOMEONE...
HEAVE...
SIGH
RUSTLE
RABBLE RABBLE
RUSTLE
...HO!
AH!
BONK
HI-YAH!
OH!

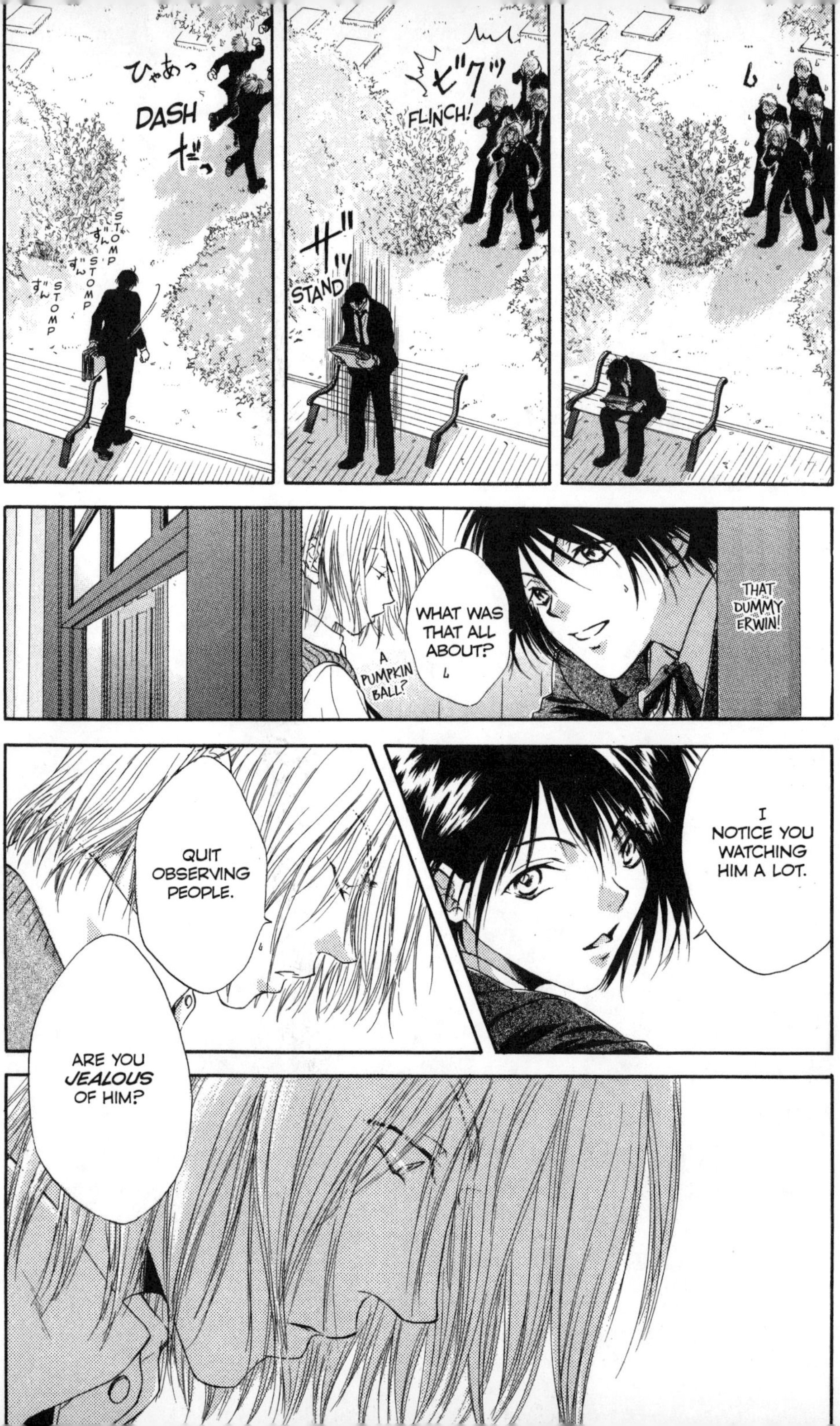

…
ム
ビクッ
FLINCH!
ザッ
STAND
ひゃあっ
DASH
だっ
ずん STOMP
ずん STOMP
ずん STOMP
THAT DUMMY ERWIN!
WHAT WAS THAT ALL ABOUT?
A PUMPKIN BALL?
I NOTICE YOU WATCHING HIM A LOT.
QUIT OBSERVING PEOPLE.
ARE YOU *JEALOUS* OF HIM?

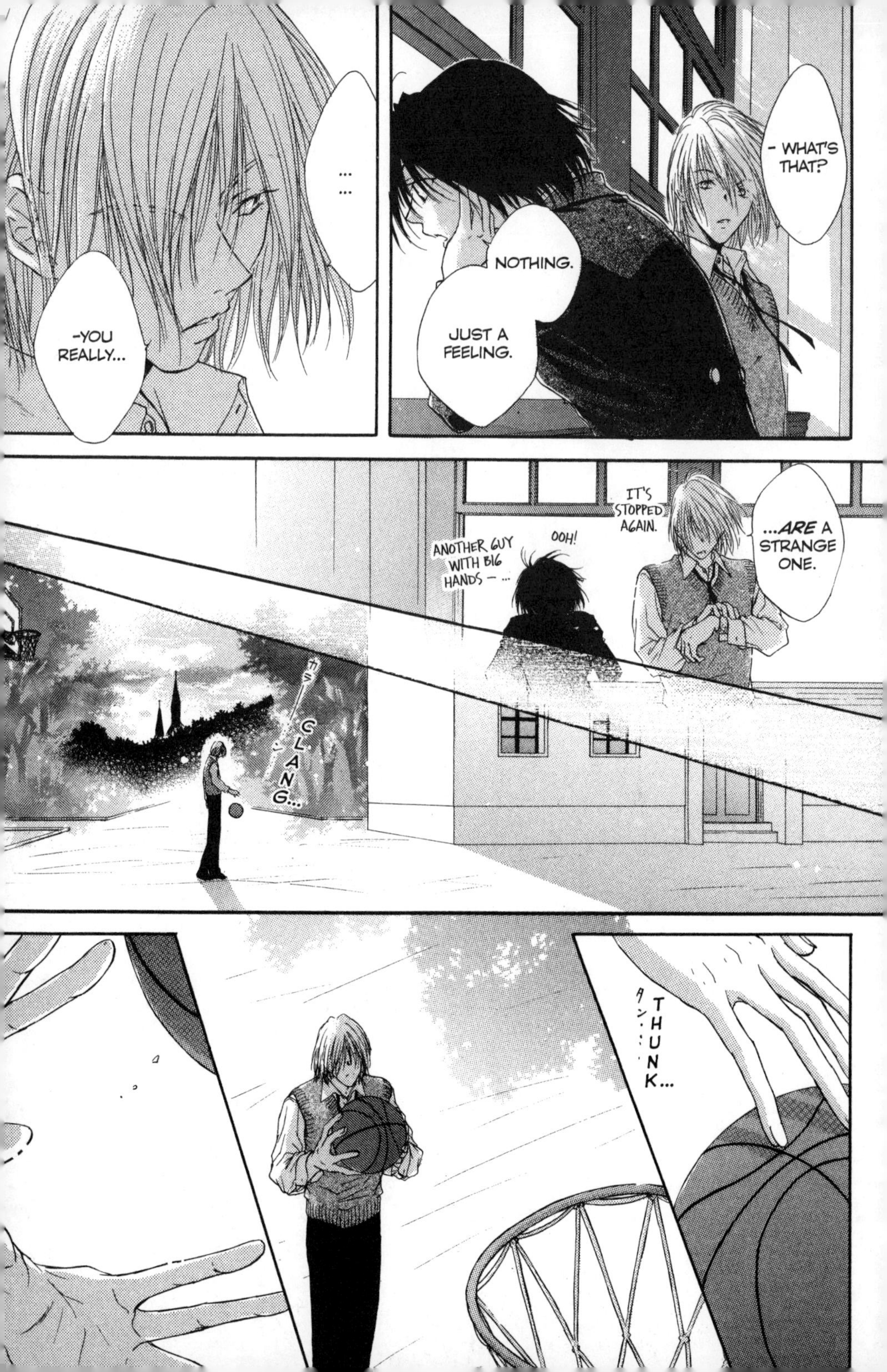
- WHAT'S THAT?
NOTHING.
JUST A FEELING.
...
...
-YOU REALLY...
...ARE A STRANGE ONE.
IT'S STOPPED AGAIN.
OOH!
ANOTHER GUY WITH BIG HANDS — ...
CLANG...
THUNK...

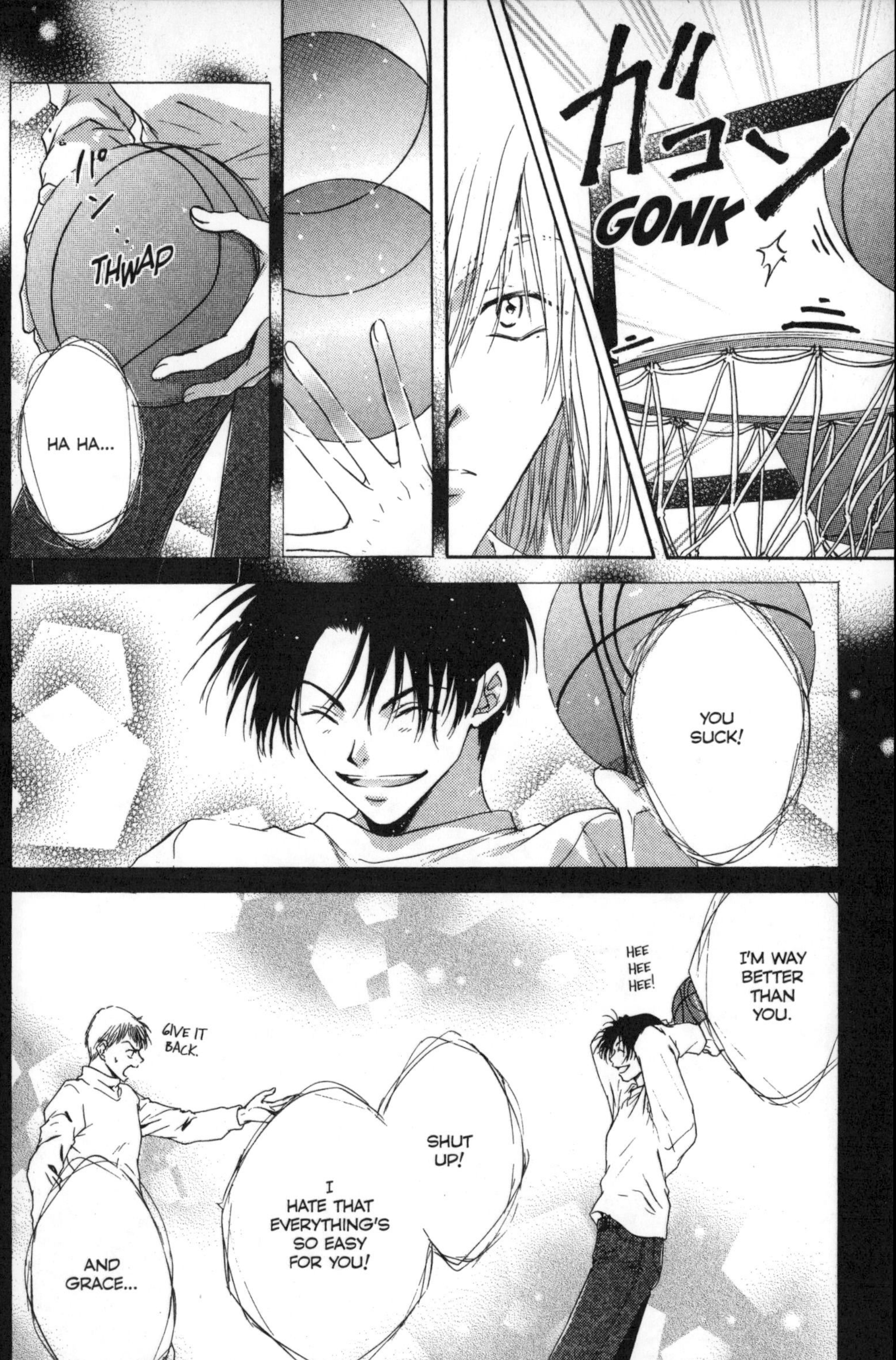

ガコン
GONK
パン
THWAP
HA HA...
YOU SUCK!
HEE HEE HEE!
I'M WAY BETTER THAN YOU.
GIVE IT BACK.
SHUT UP!
I HATE THAT EVERYTHING'S SO EASY FOR YOU!
AND GRACE...

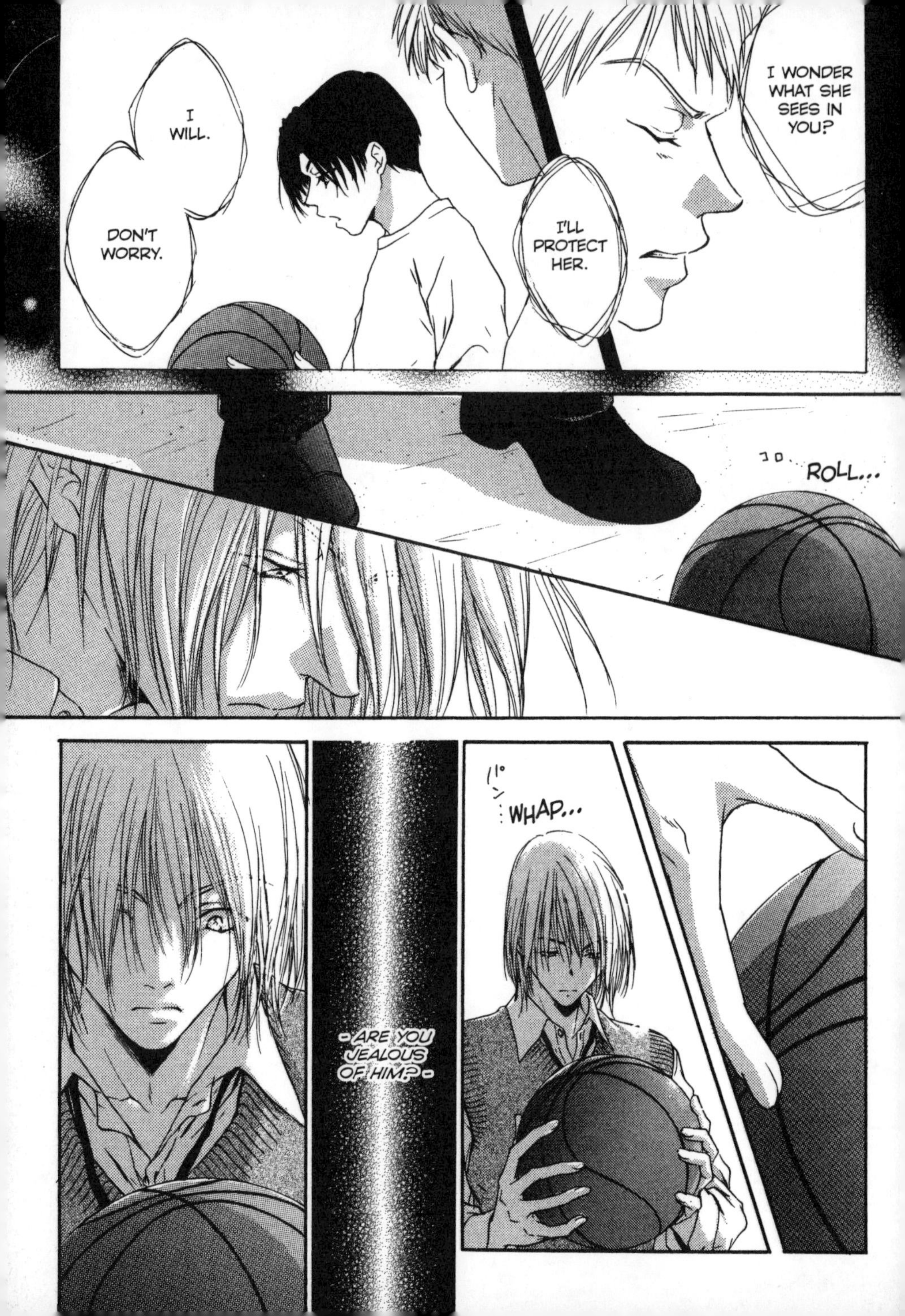
I WONDER WHAT SHE SEES IN YOU?
I'LL PROTECT HER.
I WILL.
DON'T WORRY.
コロ… ROLL…
パン WHAP…
-ARE YOU JEALOUS OF HIM?-

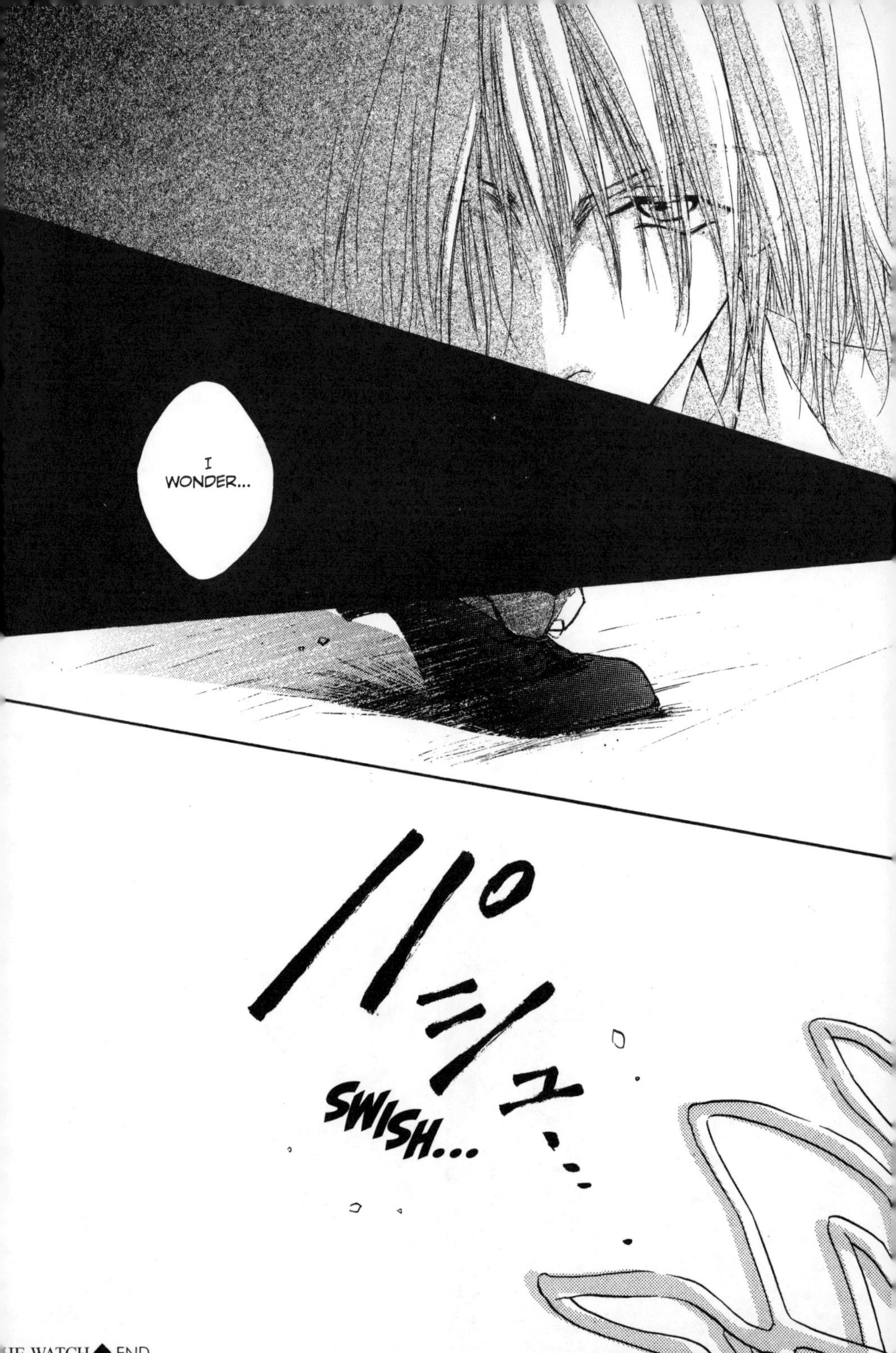
I WONDER...
パシュ…
SWISH...

HE WATCH ◆ END

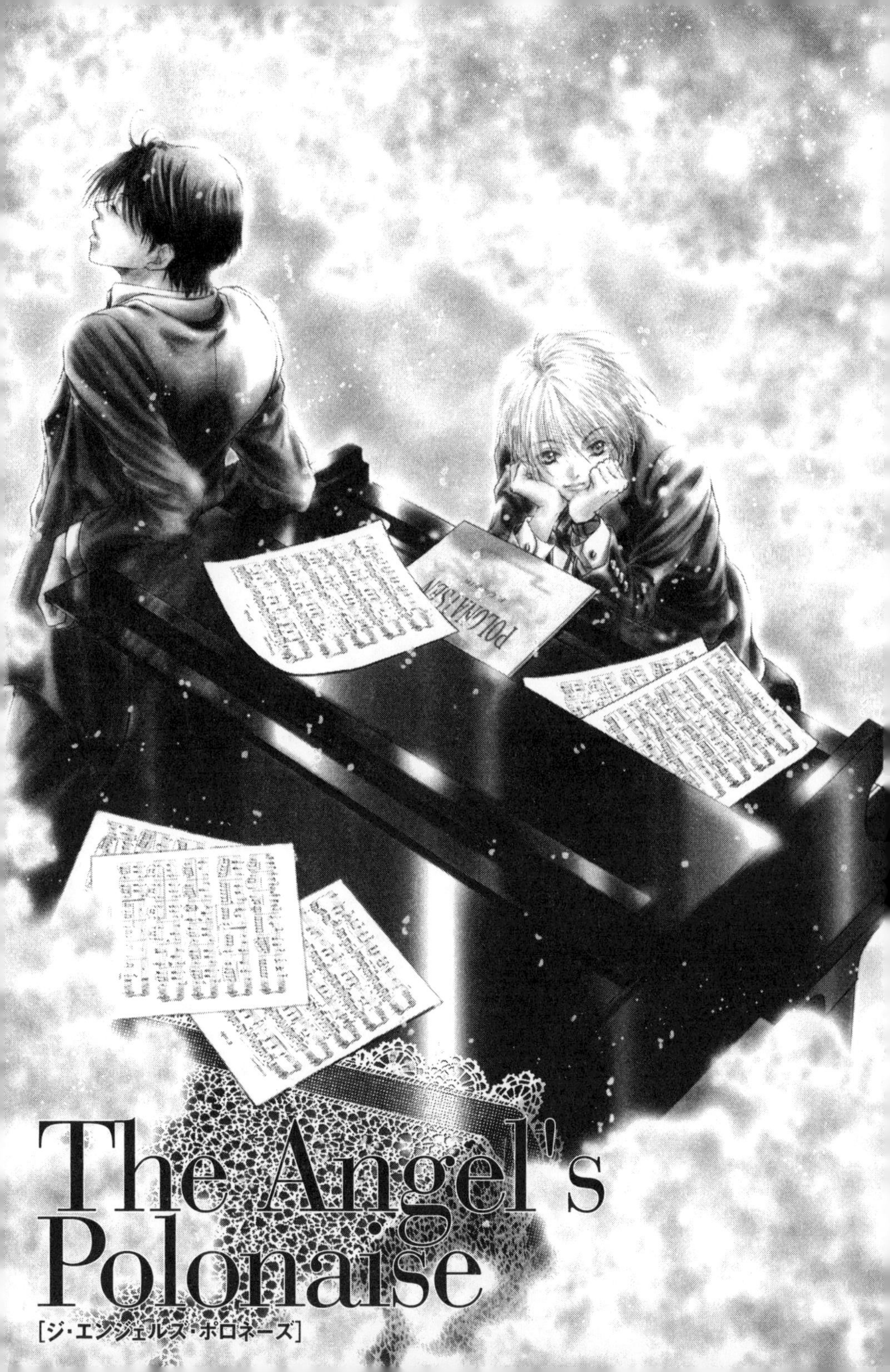

The Angel's Polonaise

[ジ・エンジェルズ・ポロネーズ]

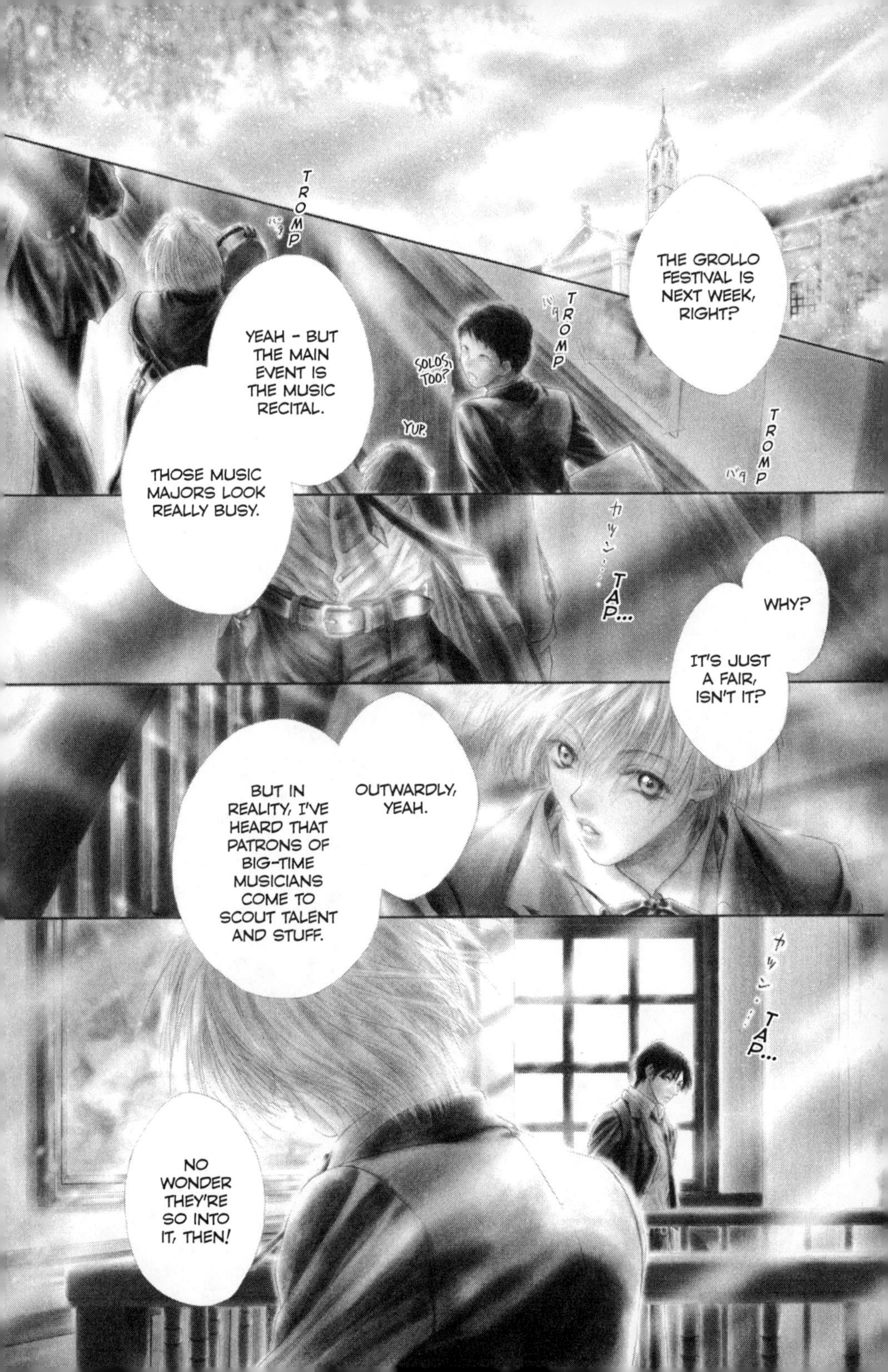
THE GROLLO FESTIVAL IS NEXT WEEK, RIGHT?
TROMP
TROMP
TROMP
YEAH - BUT THE MAIN EVENT IS THE MUSIC RECITAL.
SOLOS, TOO?
YUP.
THOSE MUSIC MAJORS LOOK REALLY BUSY.
TAP...
WHY?
IT'S JUST A FAIR, ISN'T IT?
OUTWARDLY, YEAH.
BUT IN REALITY, I'VE HEARD THAT PATRONS OF BIG-TIME MUSICIANS COME TO SCOUT TALENT AND STUFF.
TAP...
NO WONDER THEY'RE SO INTO IT, THEN!

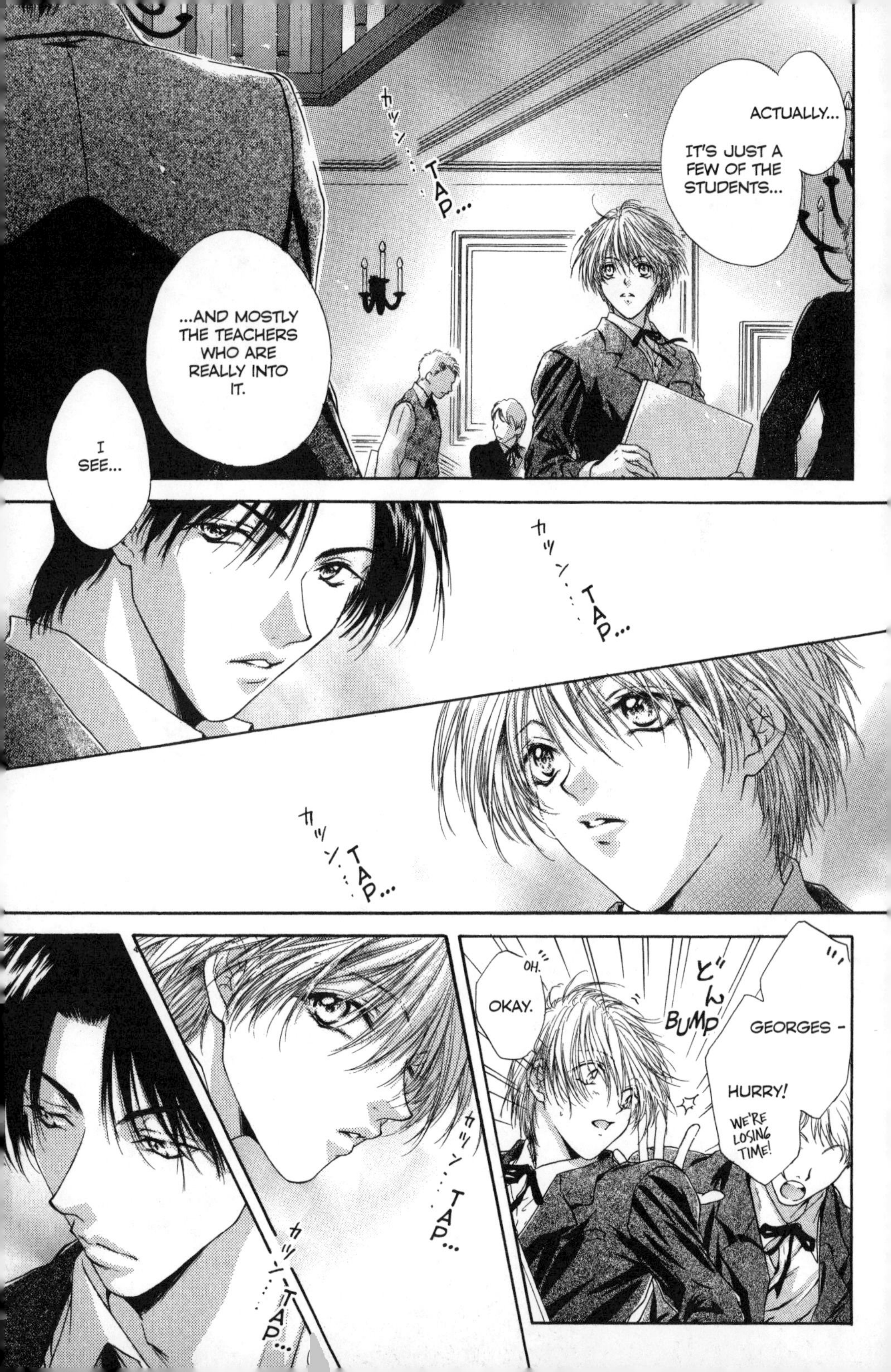
ACTUALLY...
IT'S JUST A FEW OF THE STUDENTS...
カツン... TAP...
...AND MOSTLY THE TEACHERS WHO ARE REALLY INTO IT.
I SEE...
カツン... TAP...
カツン... TAP...
GEORGES - HURRY! WE'RE LOSING TIME!
どん BUMP
OH. OKAY.
カツン... TAP...
カツン... TAP...

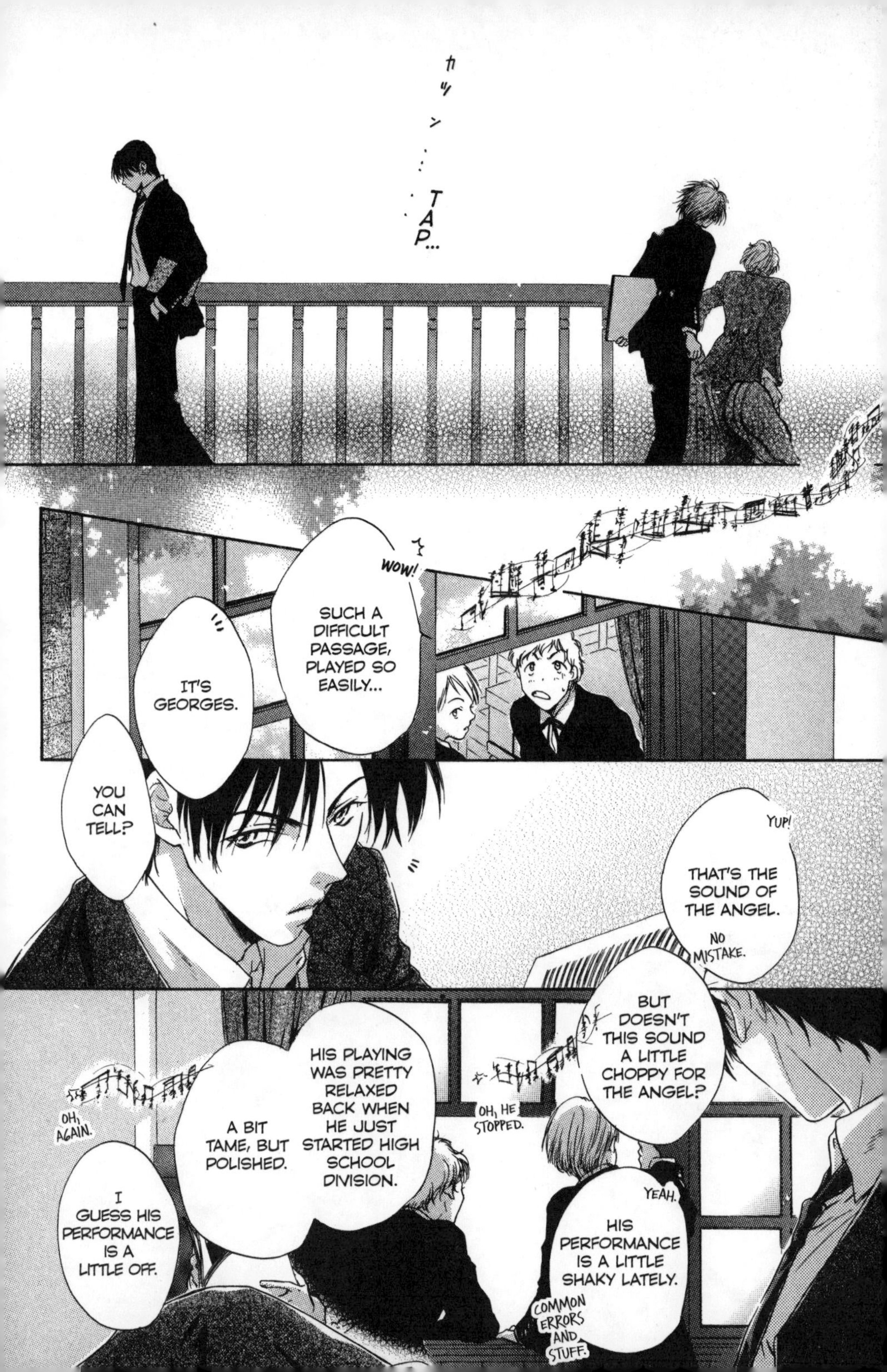
カッン・・・
TAP...
WOW!
SUCH A DIFFICULT PASSAGE, PLAYED SO EASILY...
IT'S GEORGES.
YOU CAN TELL?
YUP!
THAT'S THE SOUND OF THE ANGEL.
NO MISTAKE.
BUT DOESN'T THIS SOUND A LITTLE CHOPPY FOR THE ANGEL?
OH, HE STOPPED.
HIS PLAYING WAS PRETTY RELAXED BACK WHEN HE JUST STARTED HIGH SCHOOL DIVISION.
A BIT TAME, BUT POLISHED.
OH, AGAIN.
YEAH.
HIS PERFORMANCE IS A LITTLE SHAKY LATELY.
COMMON ERRORS AND STUFF.
I GUESS HIS PERFORMANCE IS A LITTLE OFF.

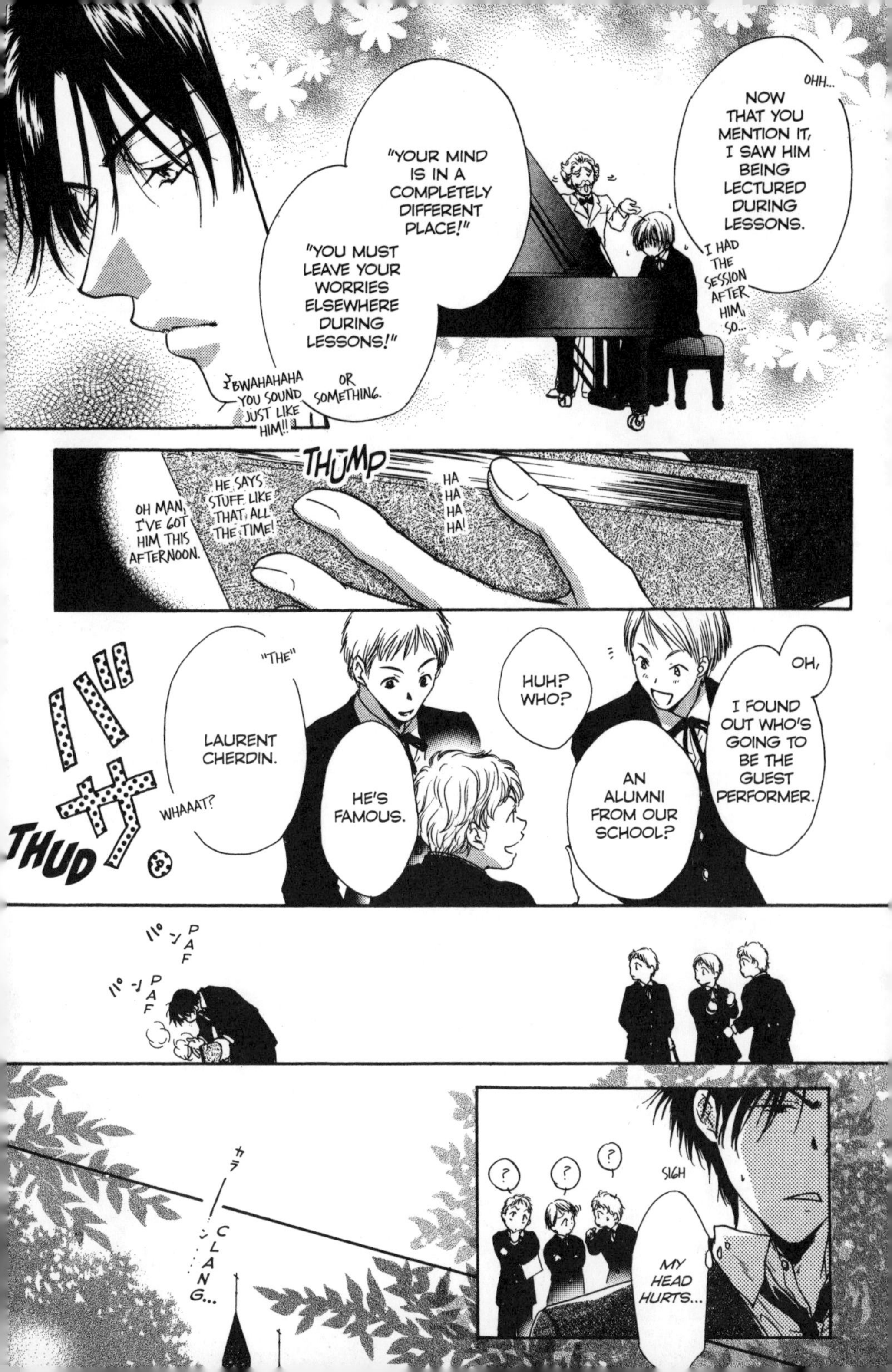
OHH... NOW THAT YOU MENTION IT, I SAW HIM BEING LECTURED DURING LESSONS.
I HAD THE SESSION AFTER HIM, SO...
"YOUR MIND IS IN A COMPLETELY DIFFERENT PLACE!" "YOU MUST LEAVE YOUR WORRIES ELSEWHERE DURING LESSONS!" OR SOMETHING.
BWAHAHAHA YOU SOUND JUST LIKE HIM!!
THUMP
HA HA HA HA!
HE SAYS STUFF LIKE THAT ALL THE TIME!
OH MAN, I'VE GOT HIM THIS AFTERNOON.
OH, I FOUND OUT WHO'S GOING TO BE THE GUEST PERFORMER.
HUH? WHO?
AN ALUMNI FROM OUR SCHOOL?
HE'S FAMOUS.
"THE" LAURENT CHERDIN.
WHAAAT?
THUD
PAF
PAF
SIGH
MY HEAD HURTS...
CLANG...

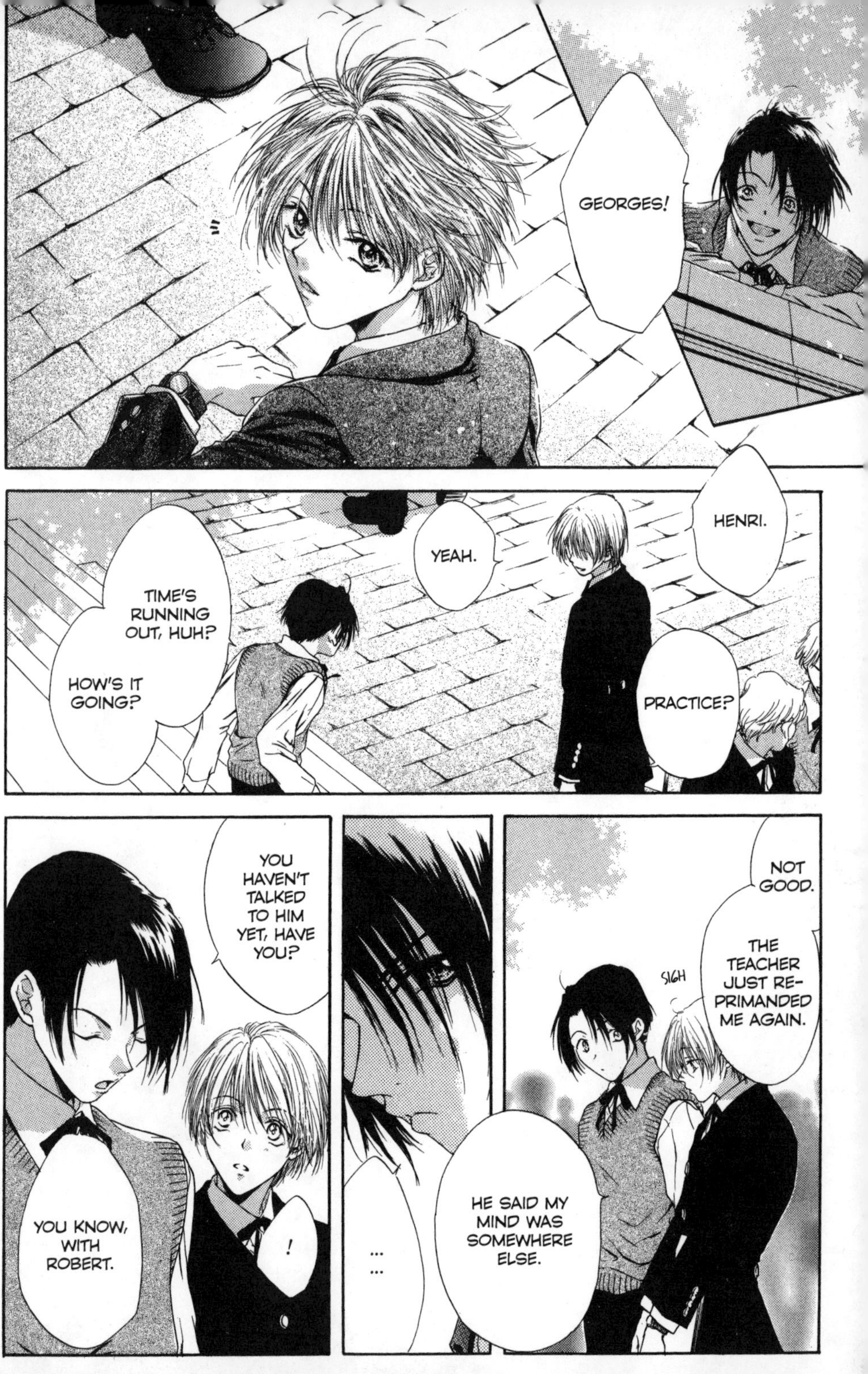
GEORGES!
HENRI.
PRACTICE?
YEAH.
TIME'S RUNNING OUT, HUH?
HOW'S IT GOING?
NOT GOOD.
SIGH
THE TEACHER JUST RE-PRIMANDED ME AGAIN.
HE SAID MY MIND WAS SOMEWHERE ELSE.
... ...
YOU HAVEN'T TALKED TO HIM YET, HAVE YOU?
YOU KNOW, WITH ROBERT.
!

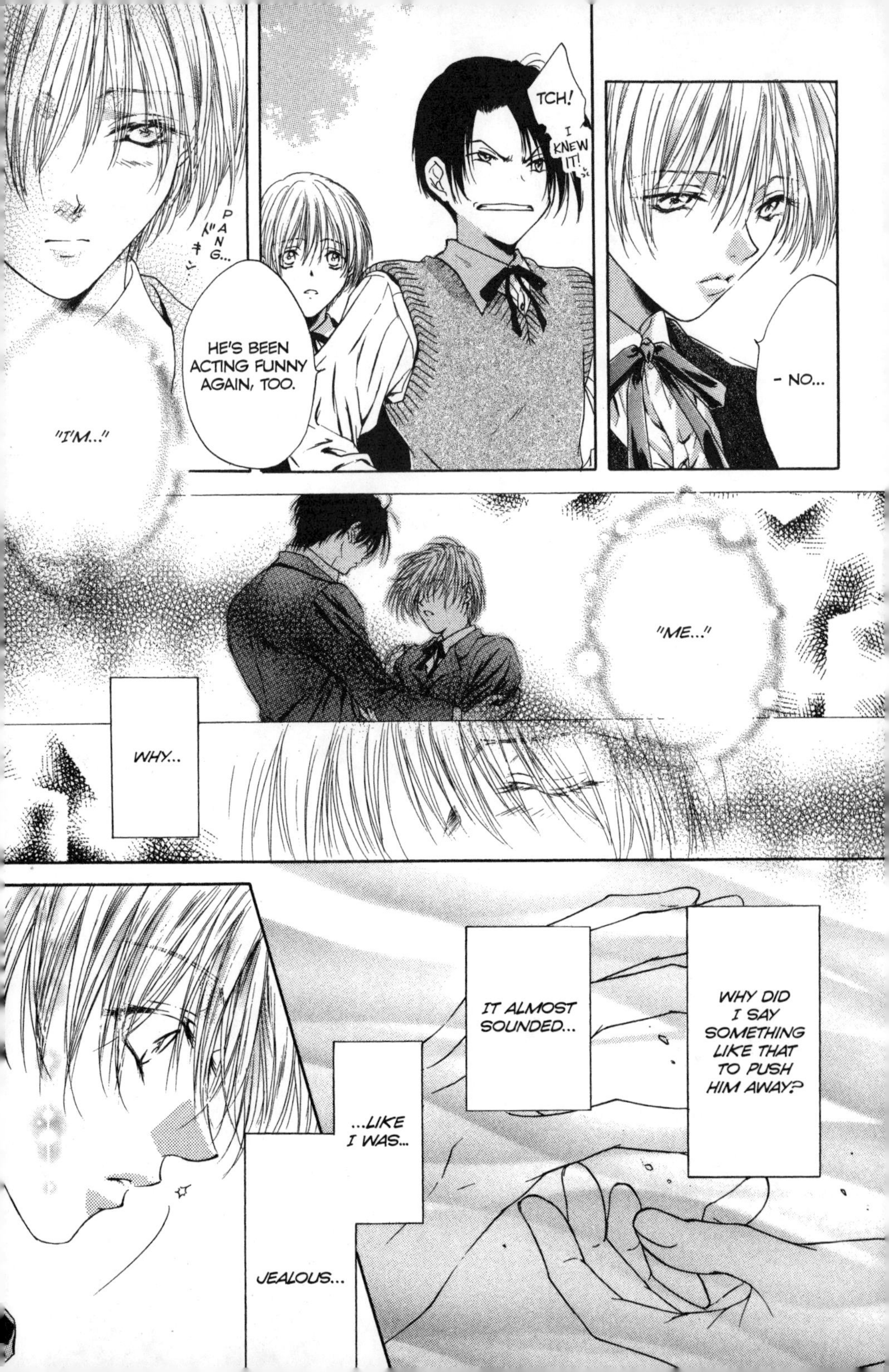

- NO...
TCH!
I KNEW IT!
HE'S BEEN ACTING FUNNY AGAIN, TOO.
PANG...
"I'M..."
"ME..."
WHY...
WHY DID I SAY SOMETHING LIKE THAT TO PUSH HIM AWAY?
IT ALMOST SOUNDED...
...LIKE I WAS...
JEALOUS...

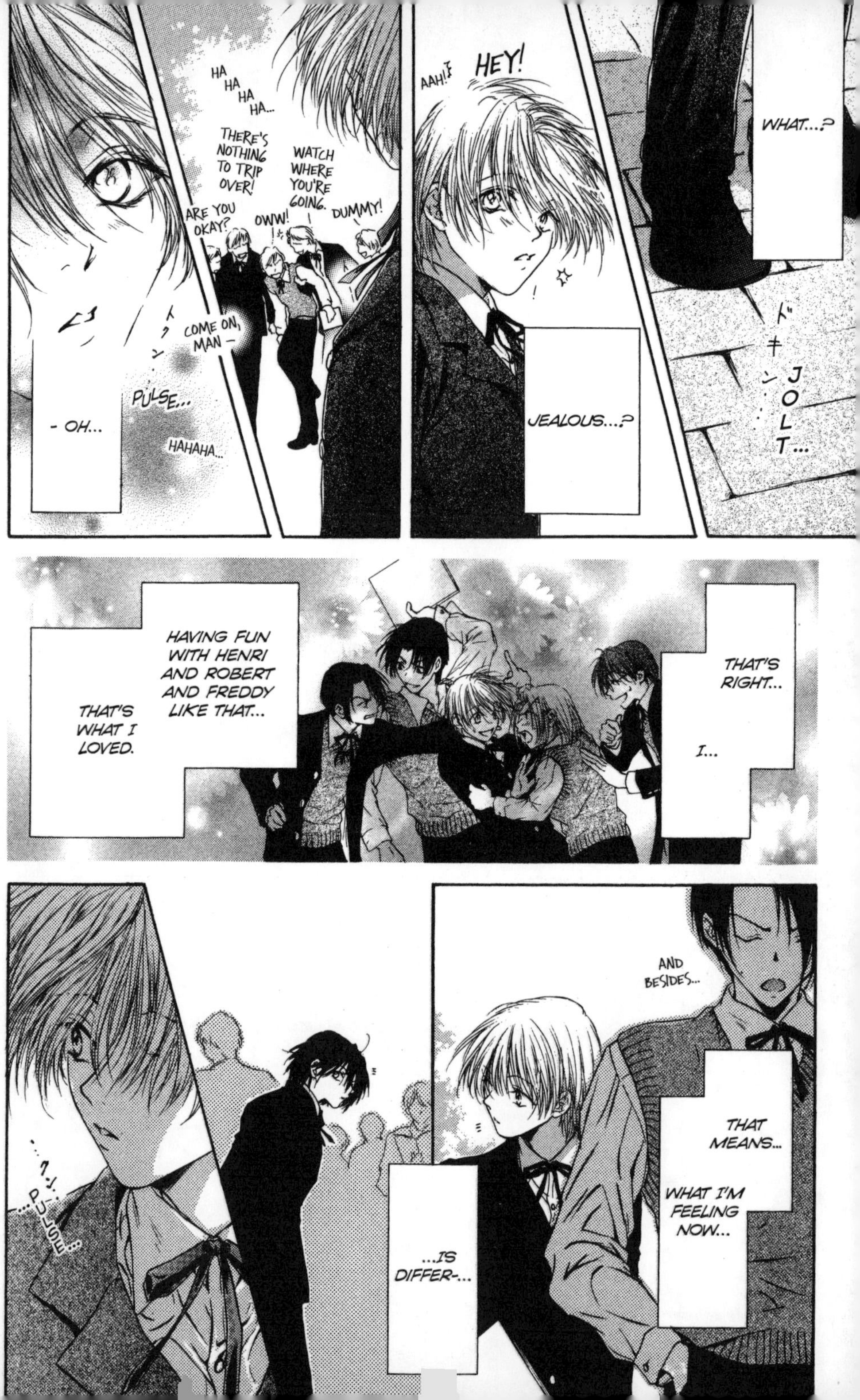
WHAT...?
ドキン
JOLT...
HEY!
AAH!
JEALOUS...?
HA HA HA HA...
WATCH WHERE YOU'RE GOING.
THERE'S NOTHING TO TRIP OVER!
DUMMY!
OWW!
ARE YOU OKAY?
COME ON, MAN—
トクン
PULSE...
HAHAHA...
- OH...
THAT'S RIGHT...
I...
HAVING FUN WITH HENRI AND ROBERT AND FREDDY LIKE THAT...
THAT'S WHAT I LOVED.
AND BESIDES...
THAT MEANS...
WHAT I'M FEELING NOW...
...IS DIFFER-...
トクン
...PULSE...

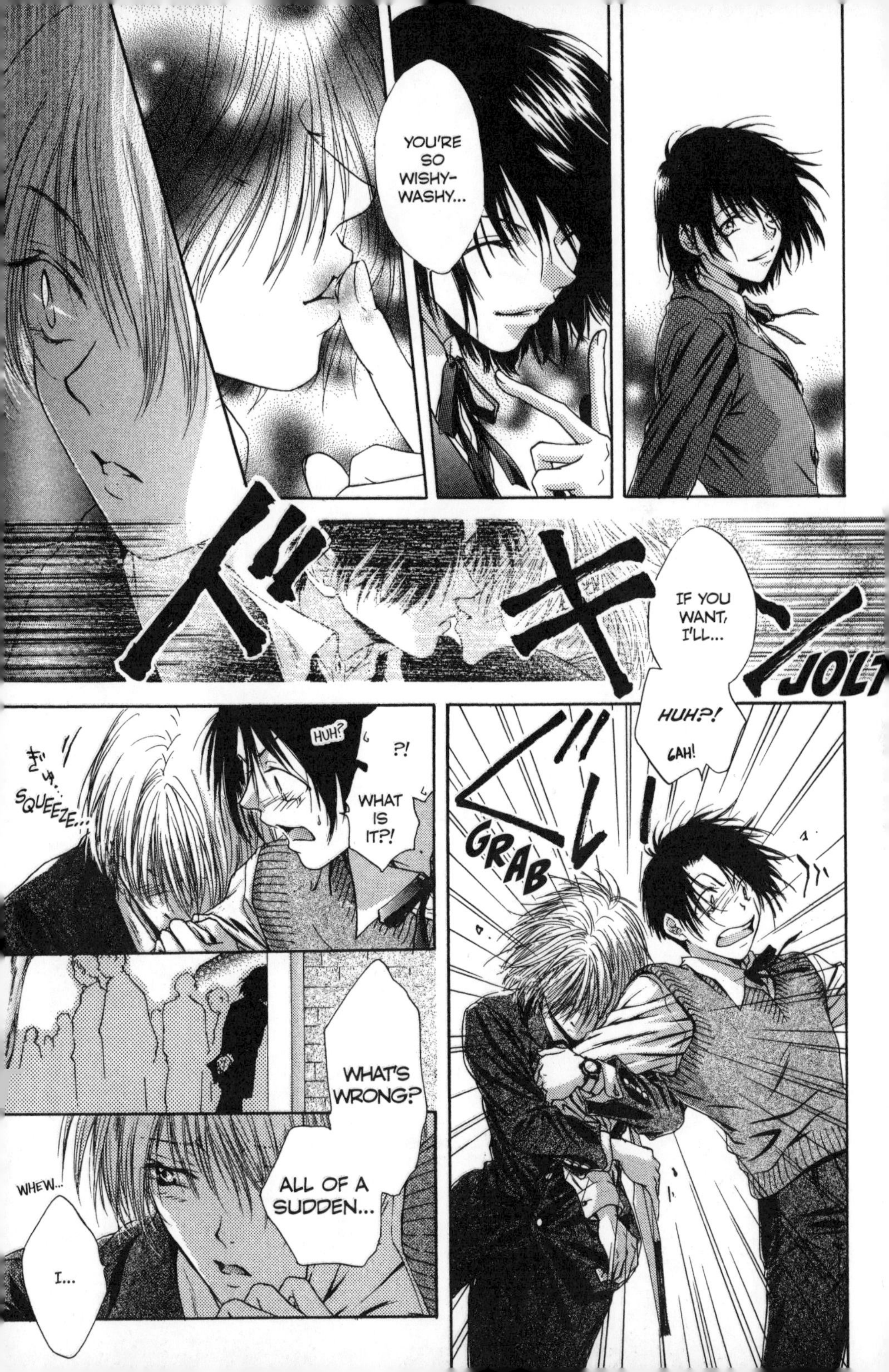

YOU'RE SO WISHY-WASHY...
IF YOU WANT, I'LL...
JOLT
HUH?!
GAH!
GRAB
HUH?
?!
WHAT IS IT?!
ぎゅ...
SQUEEZE...
WHAT'S WRONG?
ALL OF A SUDDEN...
WHEW...
I...

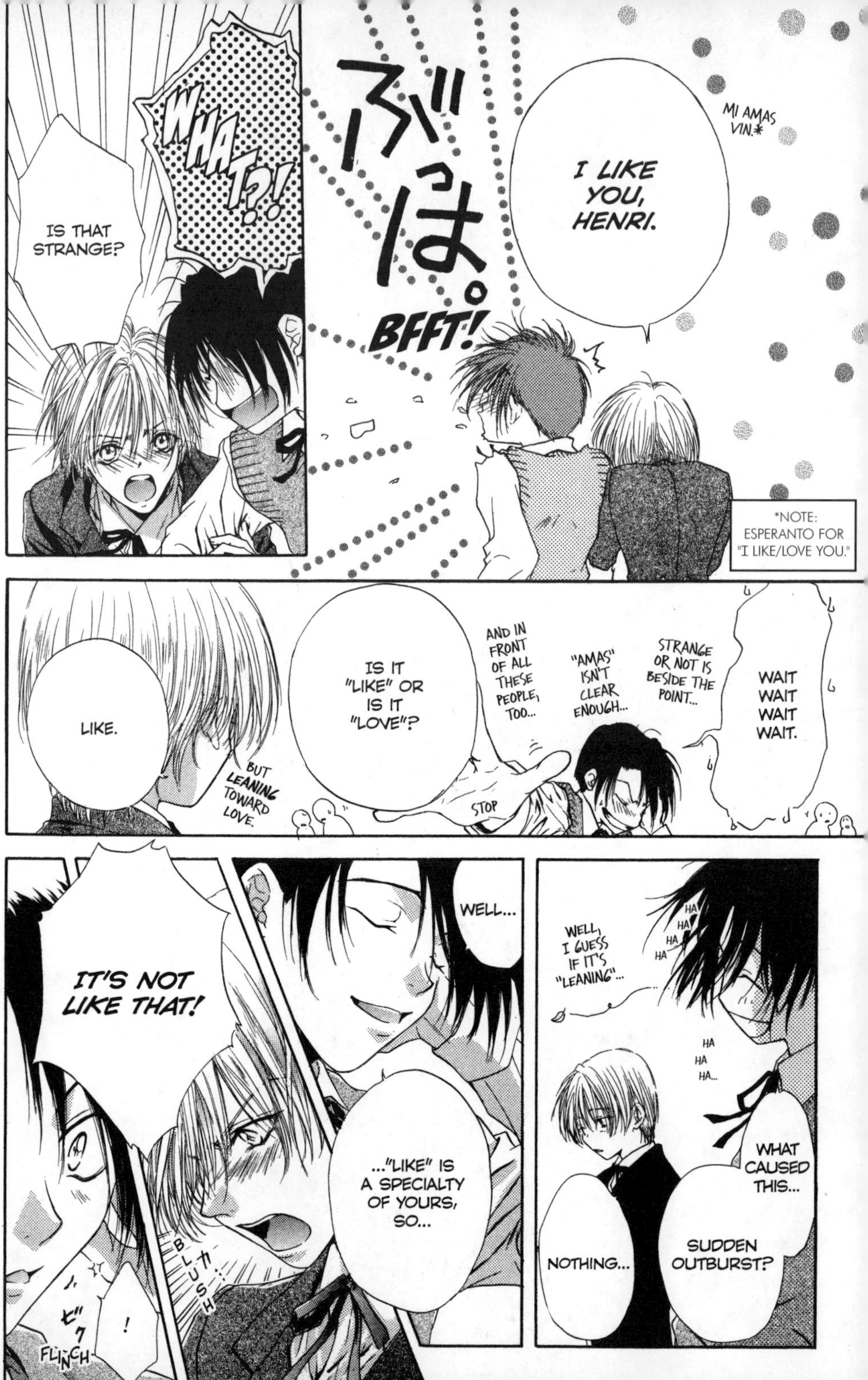

MI AMAS VIN.*
I LIKE YOU, HENRI.
ぶっは。
BFFT!
*NOTE: ESPERANTO FOR "I LIKE/LOVE YOU."
WHAT?!
IS THAT STRANGE?
WAIT WAIT WAIT WAIT.
STRANGE OR NOT IS BESIDE THE POINT...
"AMAS" ISN'T CLEAR ENOUGH...
AND IN FRONT OF ALL THESE PEOPLE, TOO...
STOP
IS IT "LIKE" OR IS IT "LOVE"?
LIKE.
BUT LEANING TOWARD LOVE.
HA HA HA HA
WELL, I GUESS IF IT'S "LEANING"...
HA HA HA...
WHAT CAUSED THIS...
SUDDEN OUTBURST?
NOTHING...
WELL...
..."LIKE" IS A SPECIALTY OF YOURS, SO...
カッ
BLUSH
IT'S NOT LIKE THAT!
!
ビクッ
FLINCH

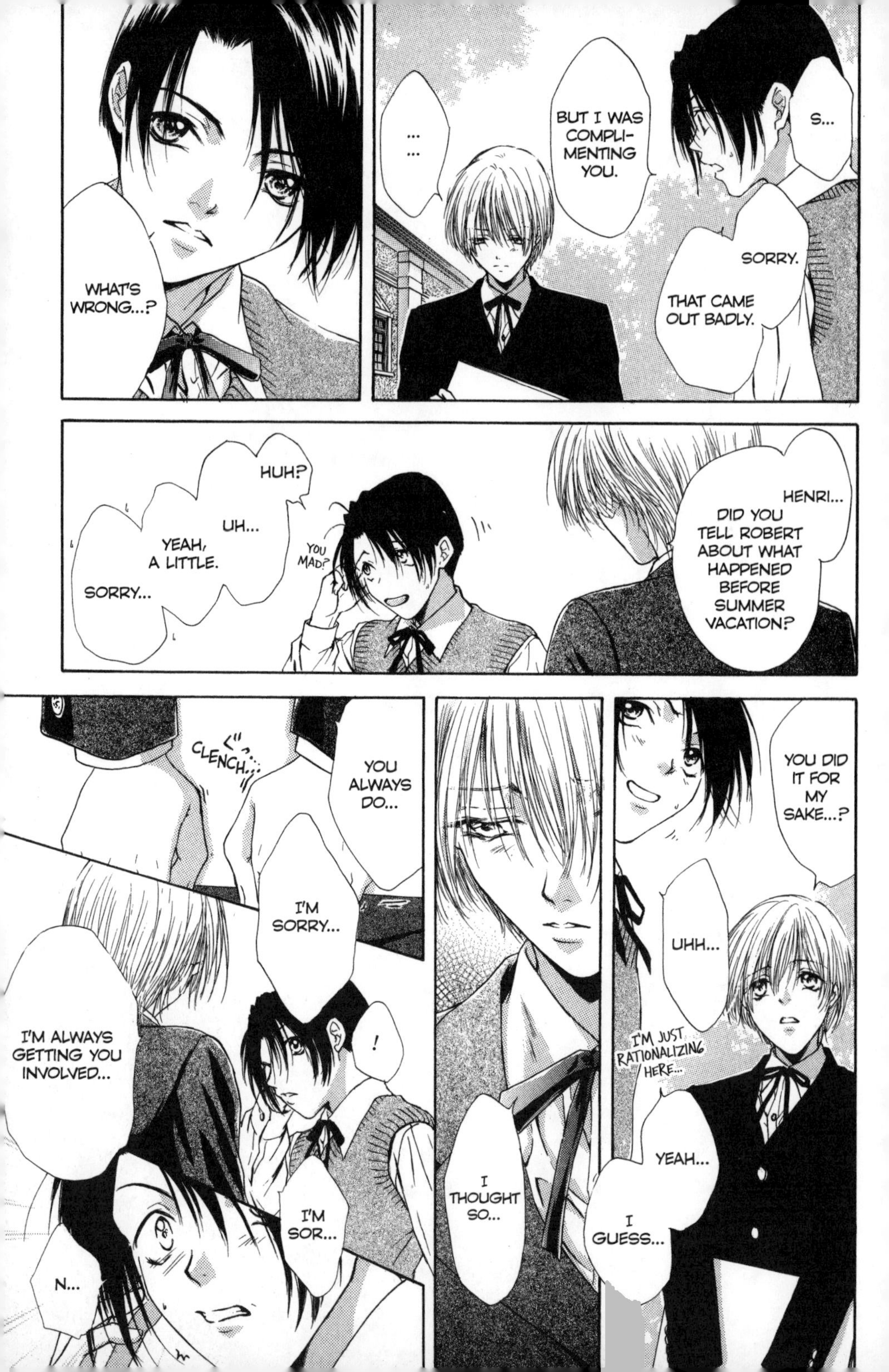
S...
SORRY.
THAT CAME OUT BADLY.
BUT I WAS COMPLI-MENTING YOU.
... ...
WHAT'S WRONG...?
HENRI... DID YOU TELL ROBERT ABOUT WHAT HAPPENED BEFORE SUMMER VACATION?
YOU MAD?
HUH?
UH... YEAH, A LITTLE.
SORRY...
YOU DID IT FOR MY SAKE...?
UHH...
I'M JUST RATIONALIZING HERE...
YEAH...
I GUESS...
I THOUGHT SO...
CLENCH...
YOU ALWAYS DO...
I'M SORRY...
!
I'M ALWAYS GETTING YOU INVOLVED...
I'M SOR...
N...

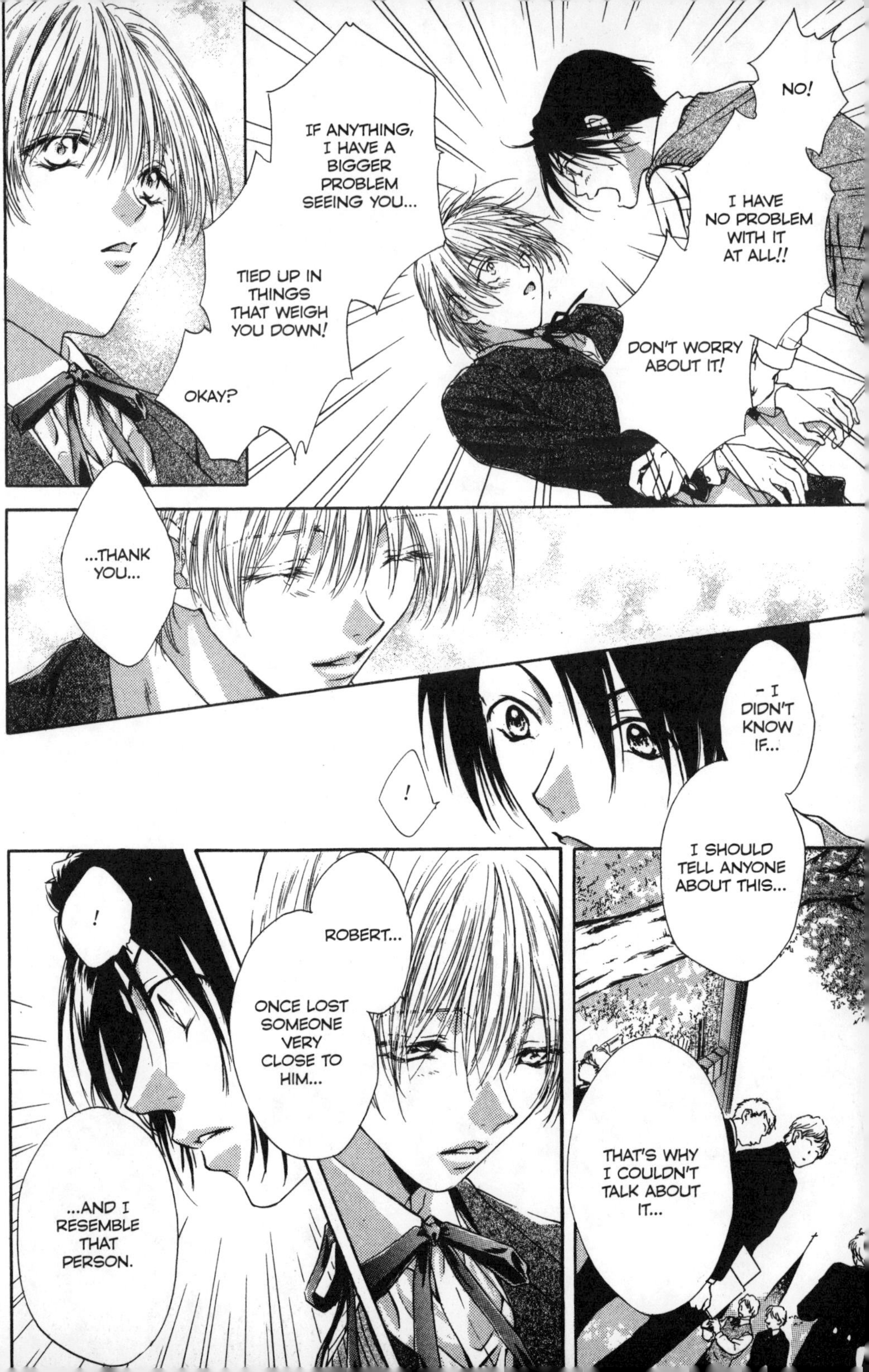
NO!
I HAVE NO PROBLEM WITH IT AT ALL!!
DON'T WORRY ABOUT IT!
IF ANYTHING, I HAVE A BIGGER PROBLEM SEEING YOU...
TIED UP IN THINGS THAT WEIGH YOU DOWN!
OKAY?
...THANK YOU...
!
- I DIDN'T KNOW IF...
I SHOULD TELL ANYONE ABOUT THIS...
THAT'S WHY I COULDN'T TALK ABOUT IT...
ROBERT...
ONCE LOST SOMEONE VERY CLOSE TO HIM...
!
...AND I RESEMBLE THAT PERSON.

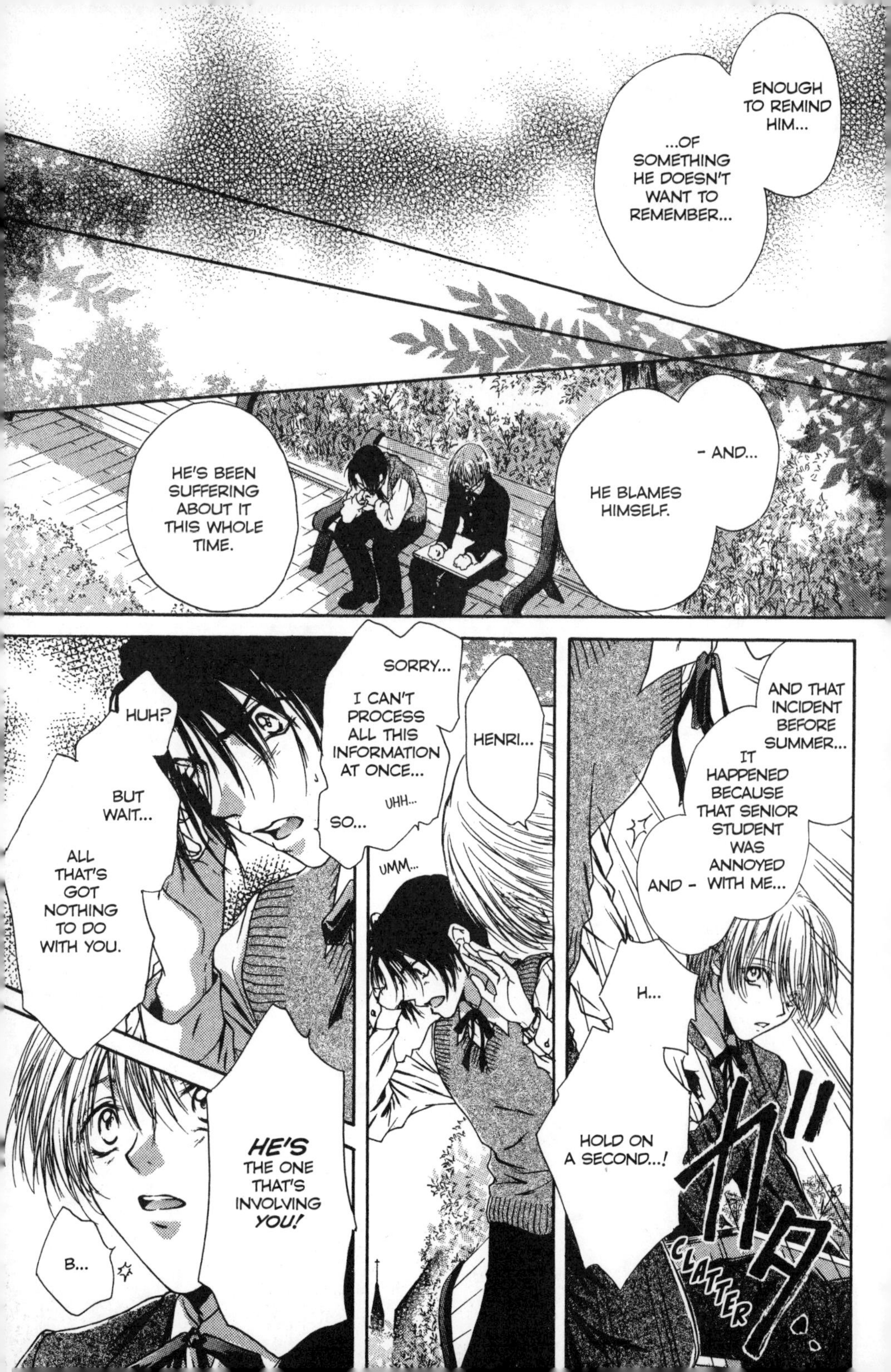
ENOUGH TO REMIND HIM...
...OF SOMETHING HE DOESN'T WANT TO REMEMBER...
- AND...
HE BLAMES HIMSELF.
HE'S BEEN SUFFERING ABOUT IT THIS WHOLE TIME.
AND THAT INCIDENT BEFORE SUMMER...
IT HAPPENED BECAUSE THAT SENIOR STUDENT WAS ANNOYED WITH ME...
AND -
H...
HOLD ON A SECOND...!
ガタ
CLATTER
HENRI...
SORRY...
I CAN'T PROCESS ALL THIS INFORMATION AT ONCE...
UHH...
SO...
UMM...
HUH?
BUT WAIT...
ALL THAT'S GOT NOTHING TO DO WITH YOU.
HE'S THE ONE THAT'S INVOLVING *YOU!*
B...

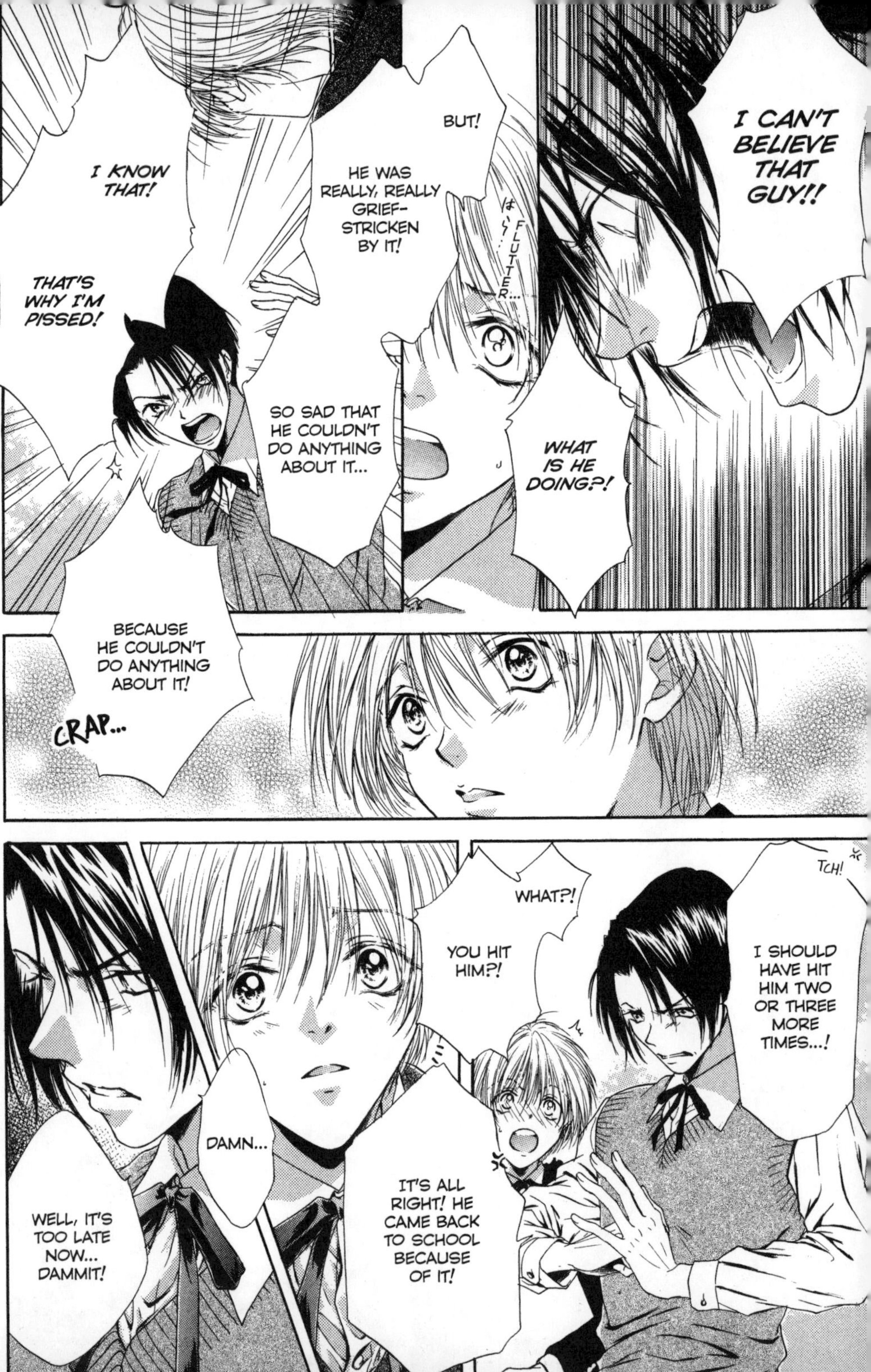
I CAN'T BELIEVE THAT GUY!!
WHAT IS HE DOING?!
BUT!
HE WAS REALLY, REALLY GRIEF-STRICKEN BY IT!
FLUTTER...
SO SAD THAT HE COULDN'T DO ANYTHING ABOUT IT...
I KNOW THAT!
THAT'S WHY I'M PISSED!
BECAUSE HE COULDN'T DO ANYTHING ABOUT IT!
CRAP...
TCH!
I SHOULD HAVE HIT HIM TWO OR THREE MORE TIMES...!
WHAT?!
YOU HIT HIM?!
IT'S ALL RIGHT! HE CAME BACK TO SCHOOL BECAUSE OF IT!
DAMN...
WELL, IT'S TOO LATE NOW... DAMMIT!

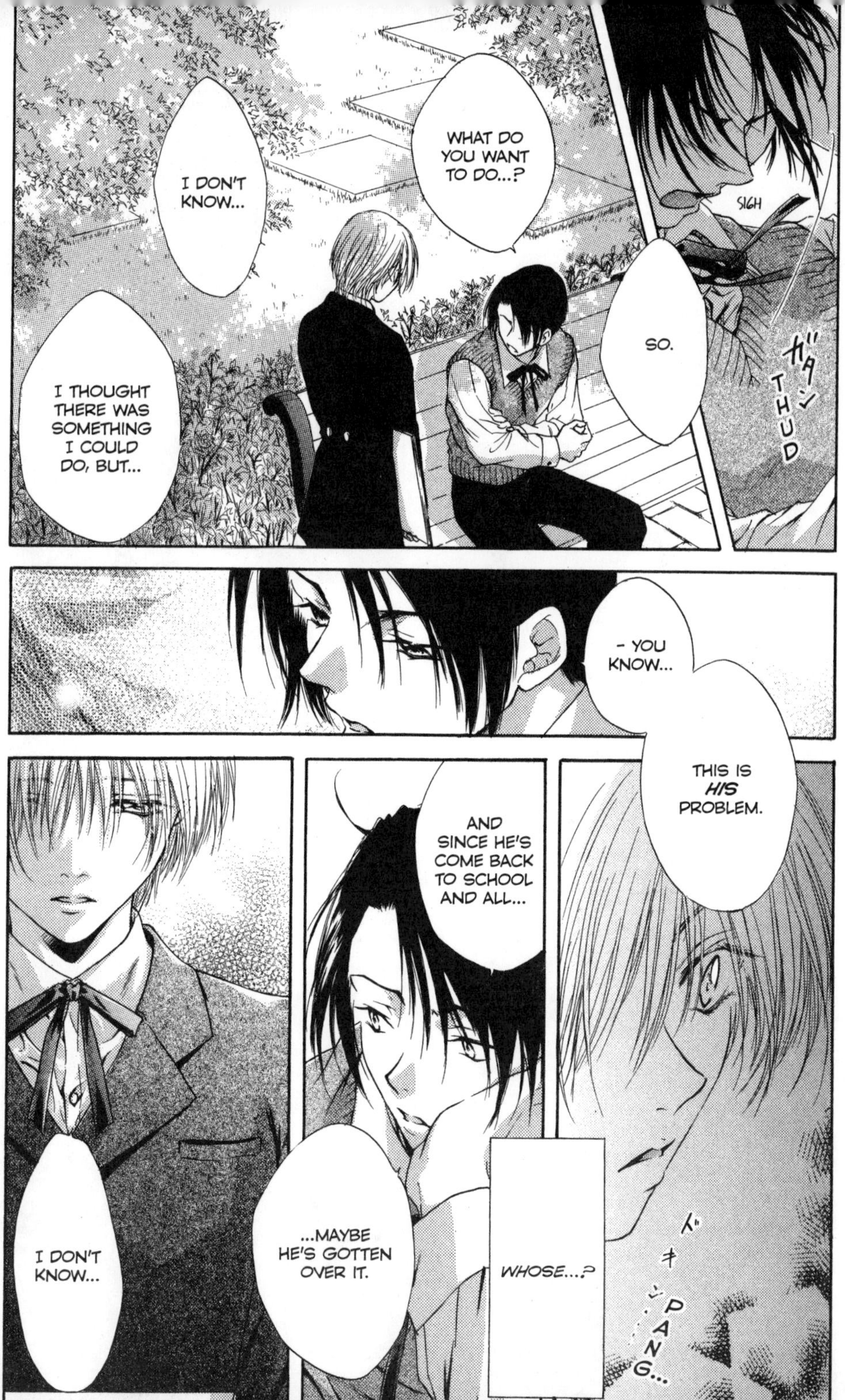
SIGH
ガタン
THUD
SO.
WHAT DO YOU WANT TO DO...?
I DON'T KNOW...
I THOUGHT THERE WAS SOMETHING I COULD DO, BUT...
- YOU KNOW...
THIS IS *HIS* PROBLEM.
WHOSE...?
ドキン
PANG...
AND SINCE HE'S COME BACK TO SCHOOL AND ALL...
...MAYBE HE'S GOTTEN OVER IT.
I DON'T KNOW...

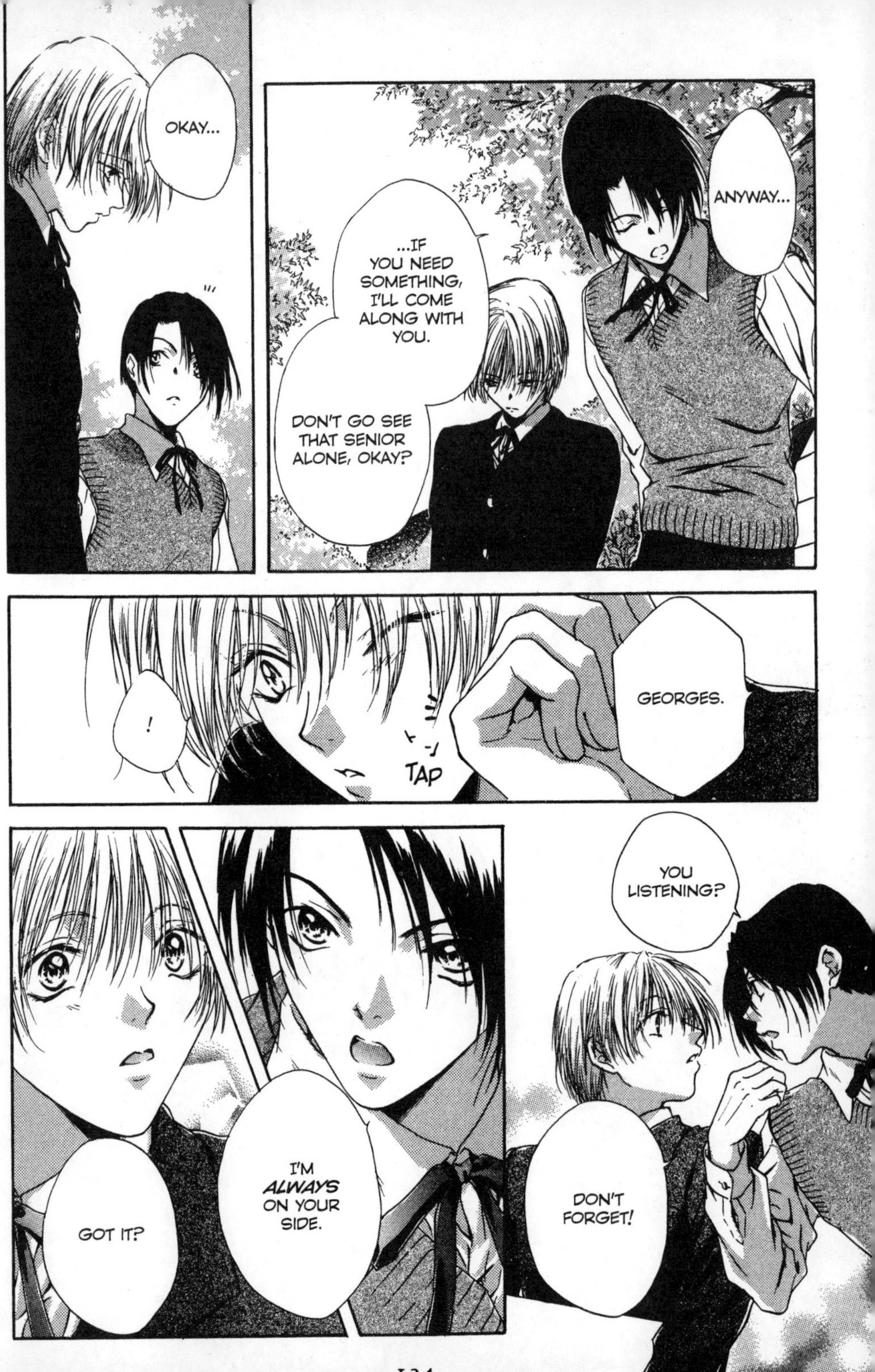
ANYWAY...
...IF YOU NEED SOMETHING, I'LL COME ALONG WITH YOU.
DON'T GO SEE THAT SENIOR ALONE, OKAY?
OKAY...
GEORGES.
TAP
!
YOU LISTENING?
DON'T FORGET!
I'M *ALWAYS* ON YOUR SIDE.
GOT IT?

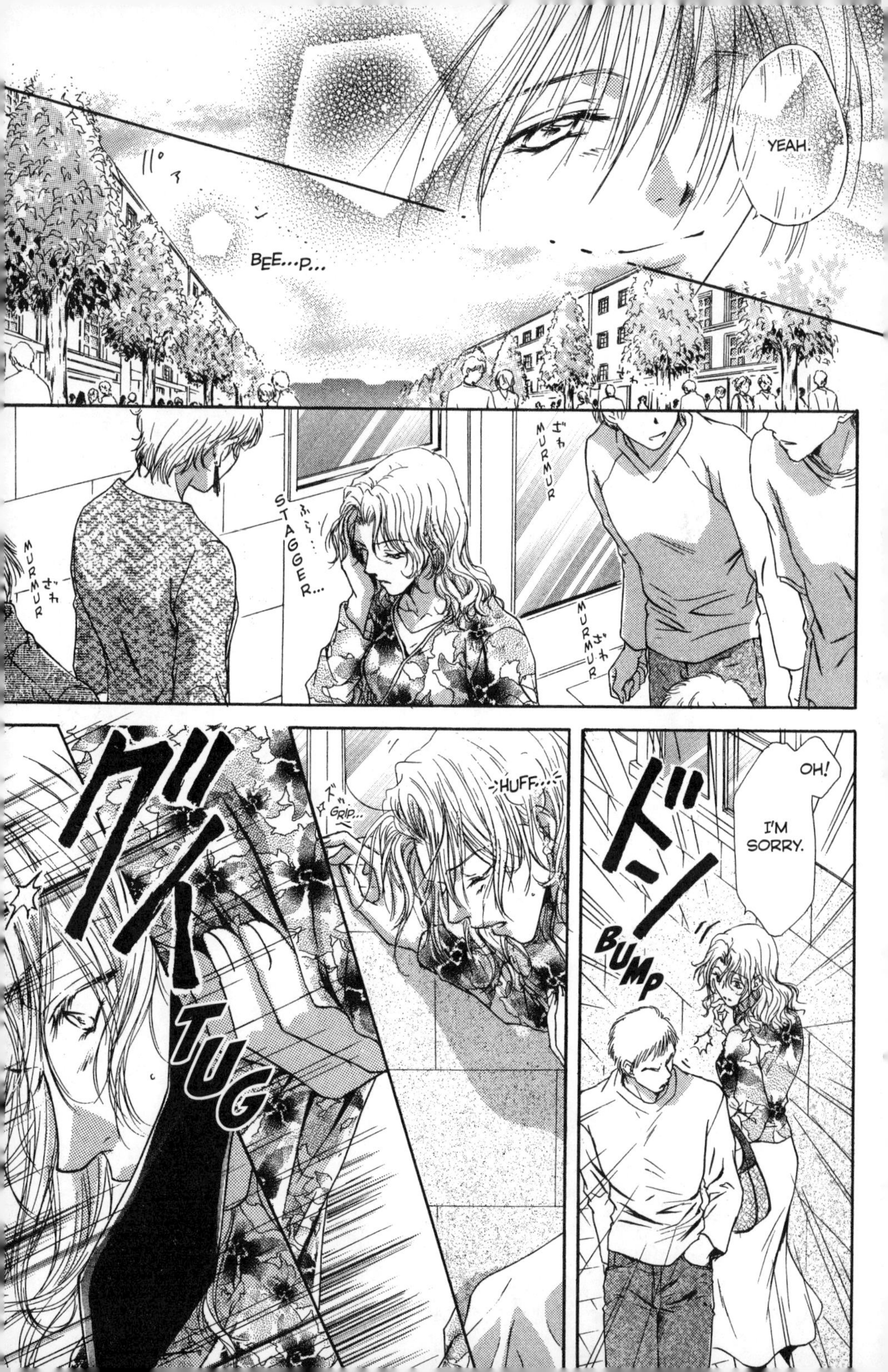

YEAH.
パァーン
BEE...P...
ざわ
MURMUR
ざわ
MURMUR
ふら…
STAGGER...
ざわ
MURMUR
ドン
BUMP
OH!
I'M SORRY.
HUFF...
GRIP...
グイ
TUG

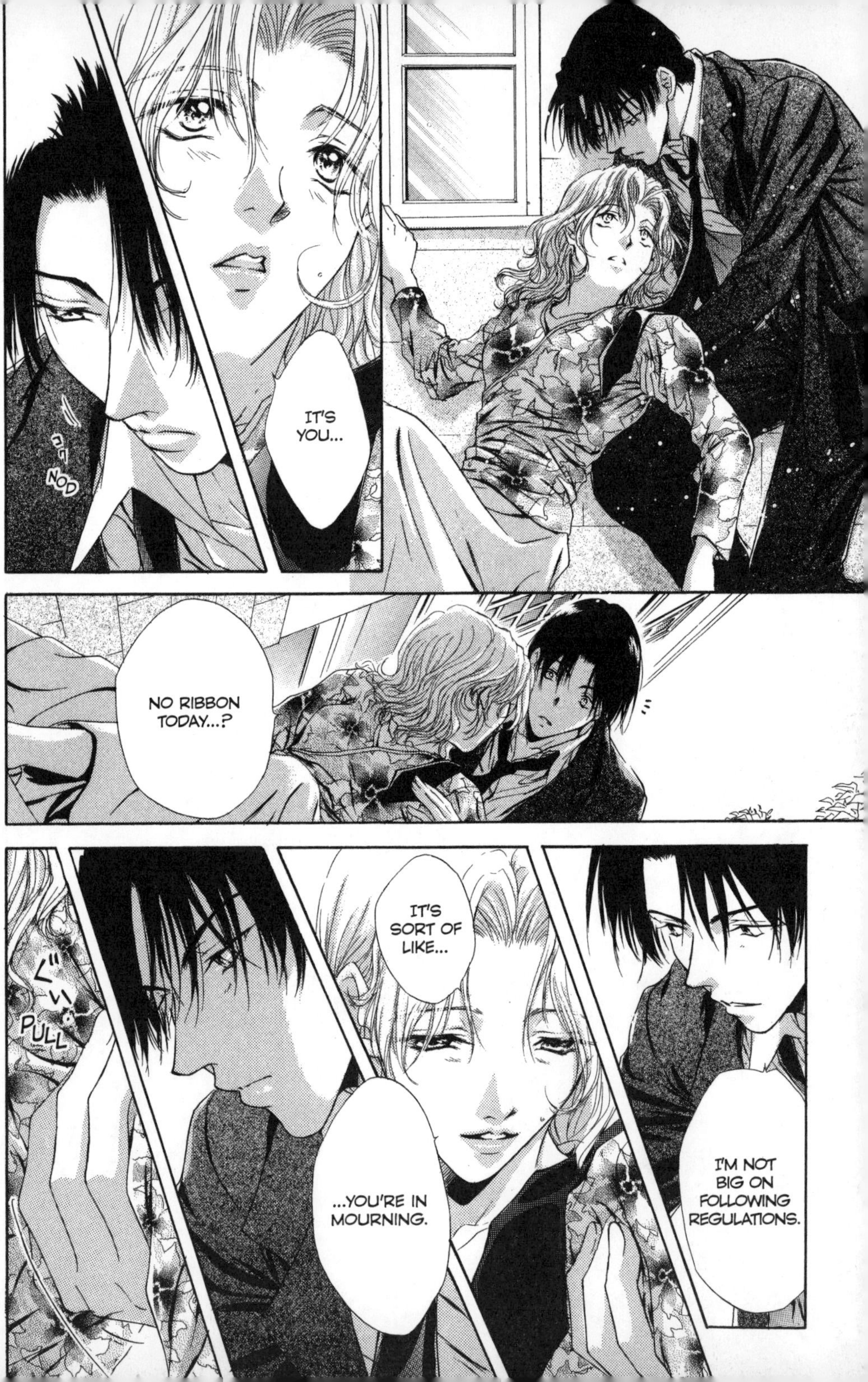

IT'S YOU...
コク NOD
NO RIBBON TODAY...?
!!
I'M NOT BIG ON FOLLOWING REGULATIONS.
IT'S SORT OF LIKE...
...YOU'RE IN MOURNING.
ぐい PULL

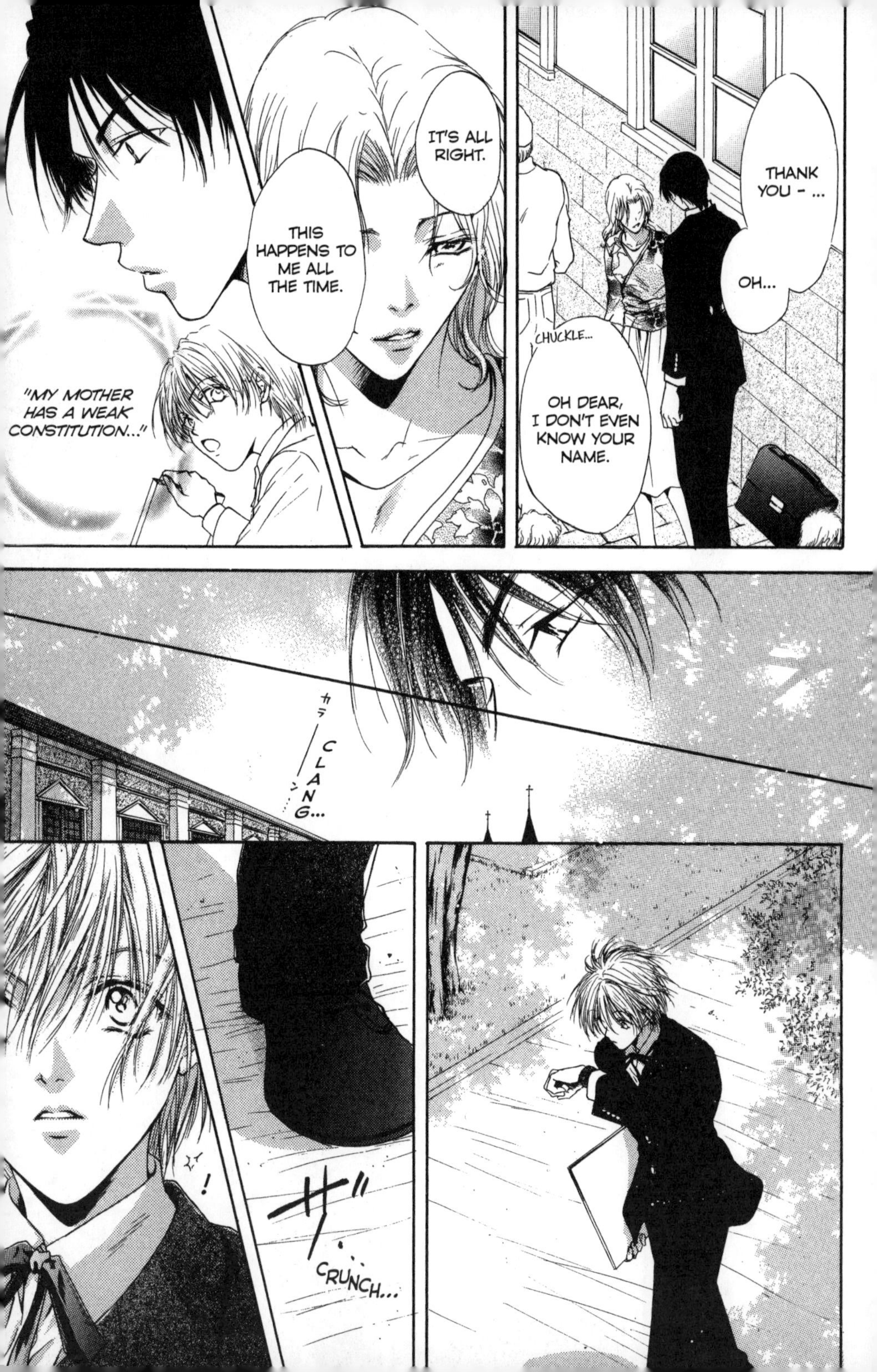
THANK YOU - ...
OH...
CHUCKLE...
OH DEAR, I DON'T EVEN KNOW YOUR NAME.
IT'S ALL RIGHT.
THIS HAPPENS TO ME ALL THE TIME.
"MY MOTHER HAS A WEAK CONSTITUTION..."
カラ―ン…
CLANG...
ザッ
CRUNCH...
!

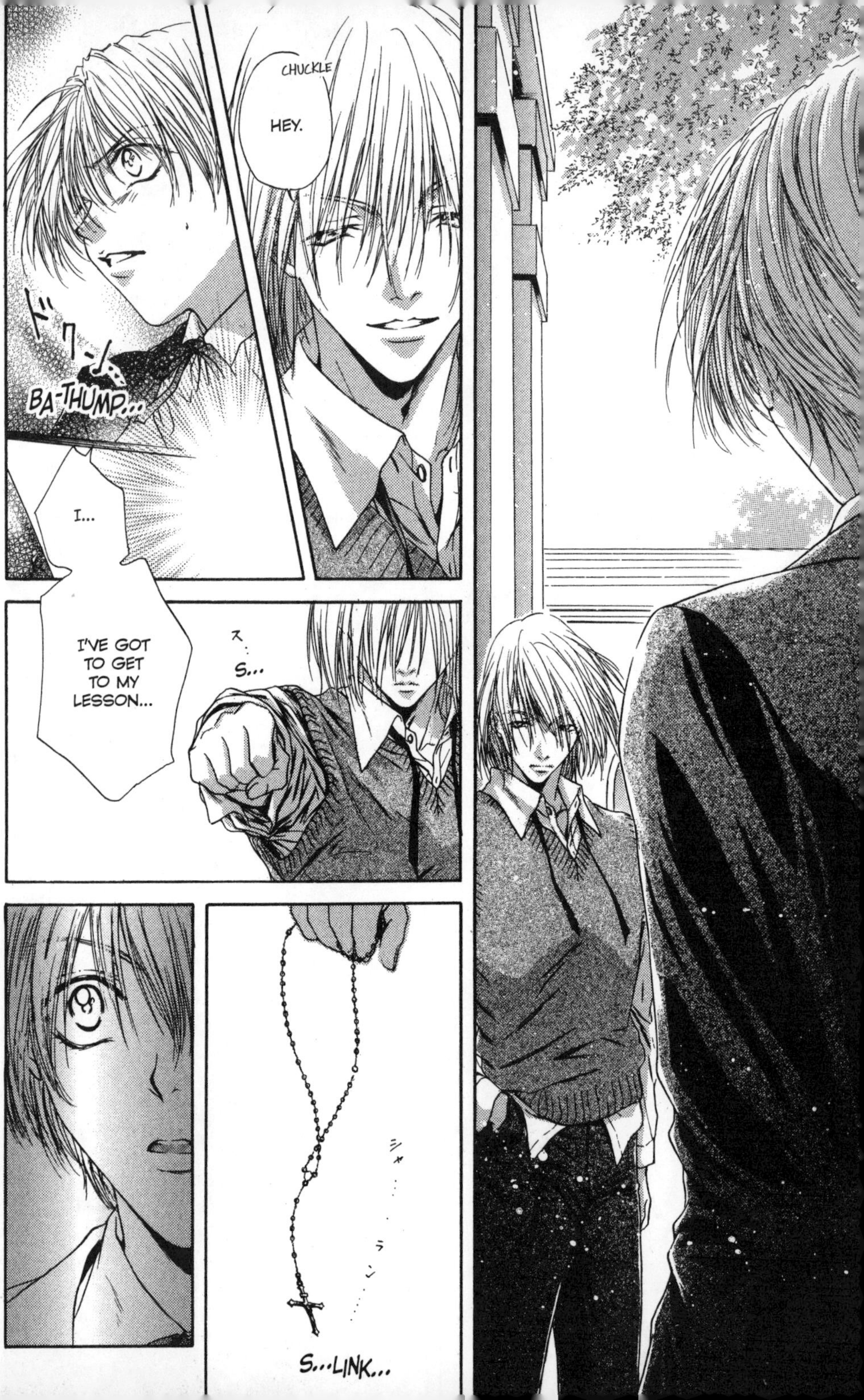
CHUCKLE
HEY.
BA-THUMP...
I...
I'VE GOT TO GET TO MY LESSON...
S...
S...LINK...

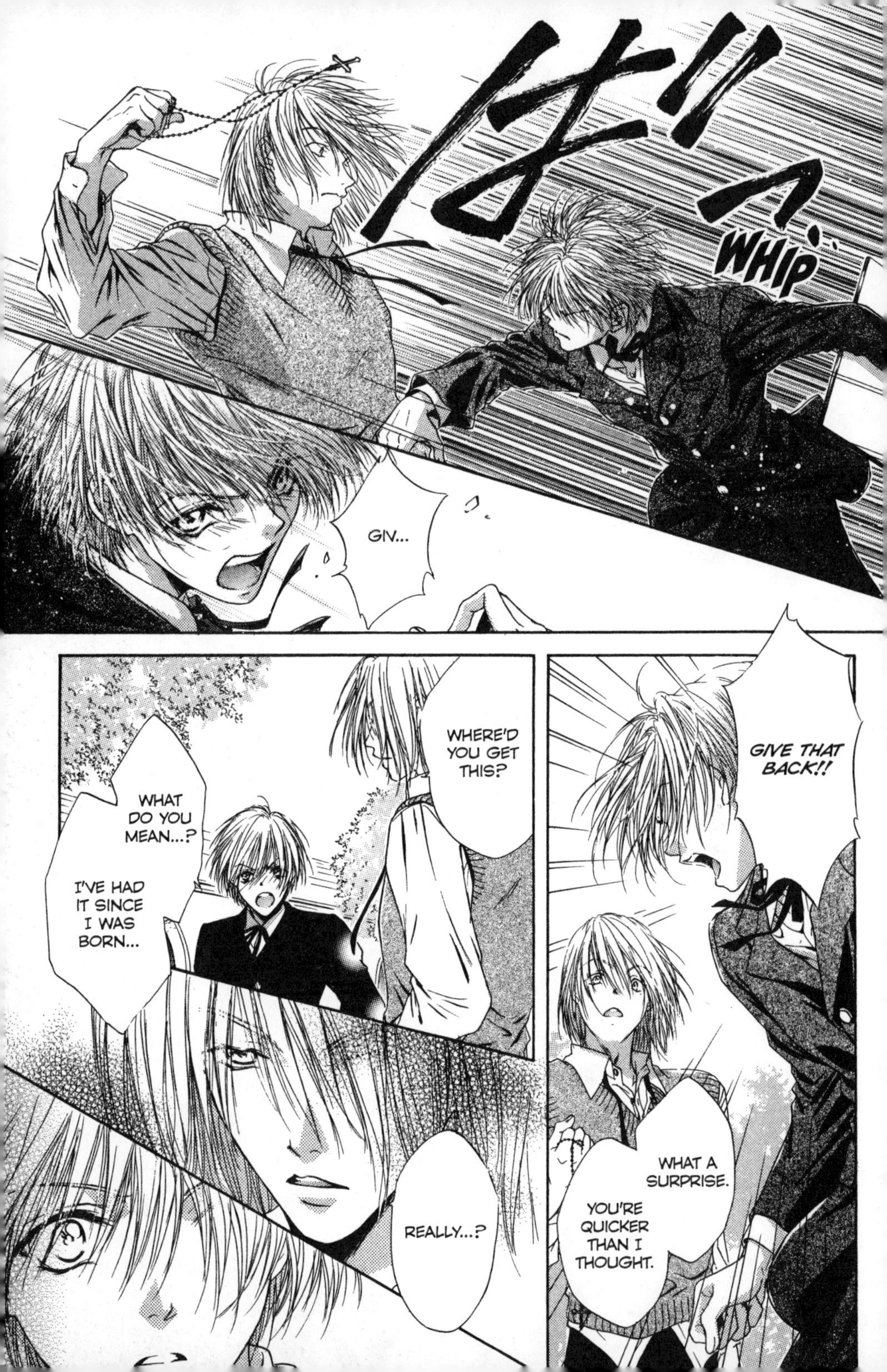
WHIP
GIV...
GIVE THAT BACK!!
WHAT A SURPRISE.
YOU'RE QUICKER THAN I THOUGHT.
WHERE'D YOU GET THIS?
WHAT DO YOU MEAN...?
I'VE HAD IT SINCE I WAS BORN...
REALLY...?

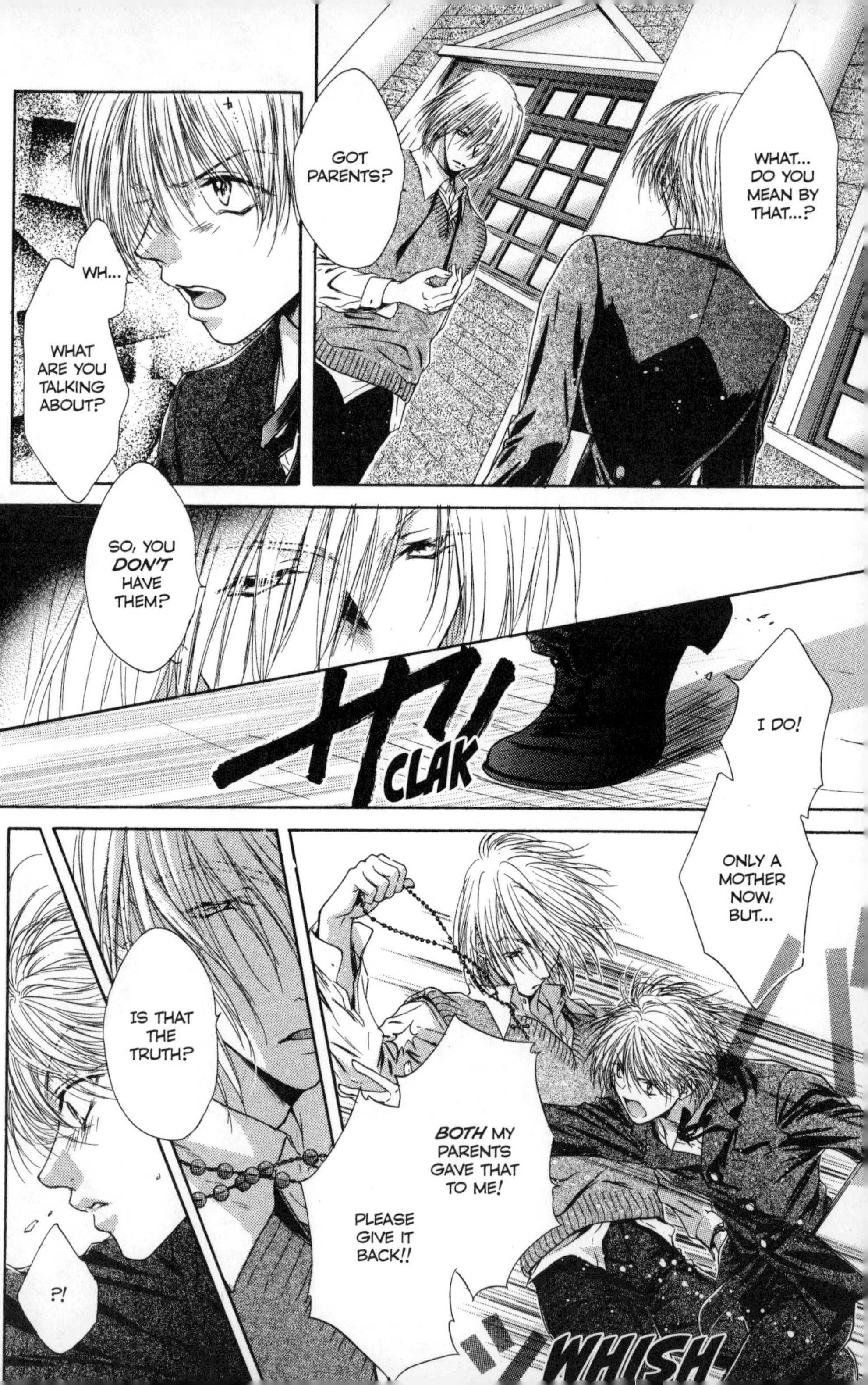
WHAT... DO YOU MEAN BY THAT...?
GOT PARENTS?
WH...
WHAT ARE YOU TALKING ABOUT?
SO, YOU *DON'T* HAVE THEM?
CLAK
I DO!
ONLY A MOTHER NOW, BUT...
BOTH MY PARENTS GAVE THAT TO ME!
PLEASE GIVE IT BACK!!
WHISH
IS THAT THE TRUTH?
?!

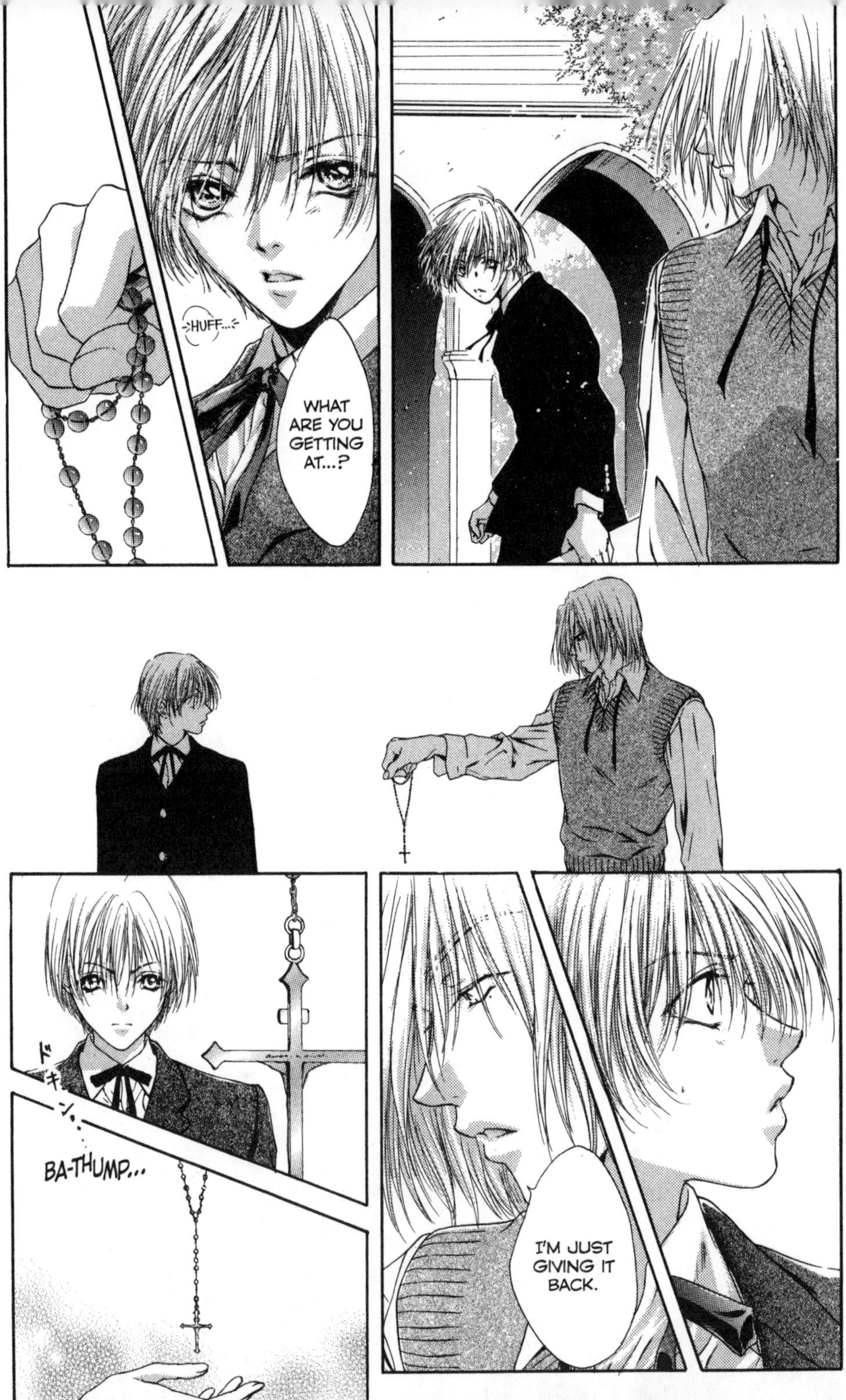
HUFF...
WHAT ARE YOU GETTING AT...?
I'M JUST GIVING IT BACK.
ドキン…
BA-THUMP...

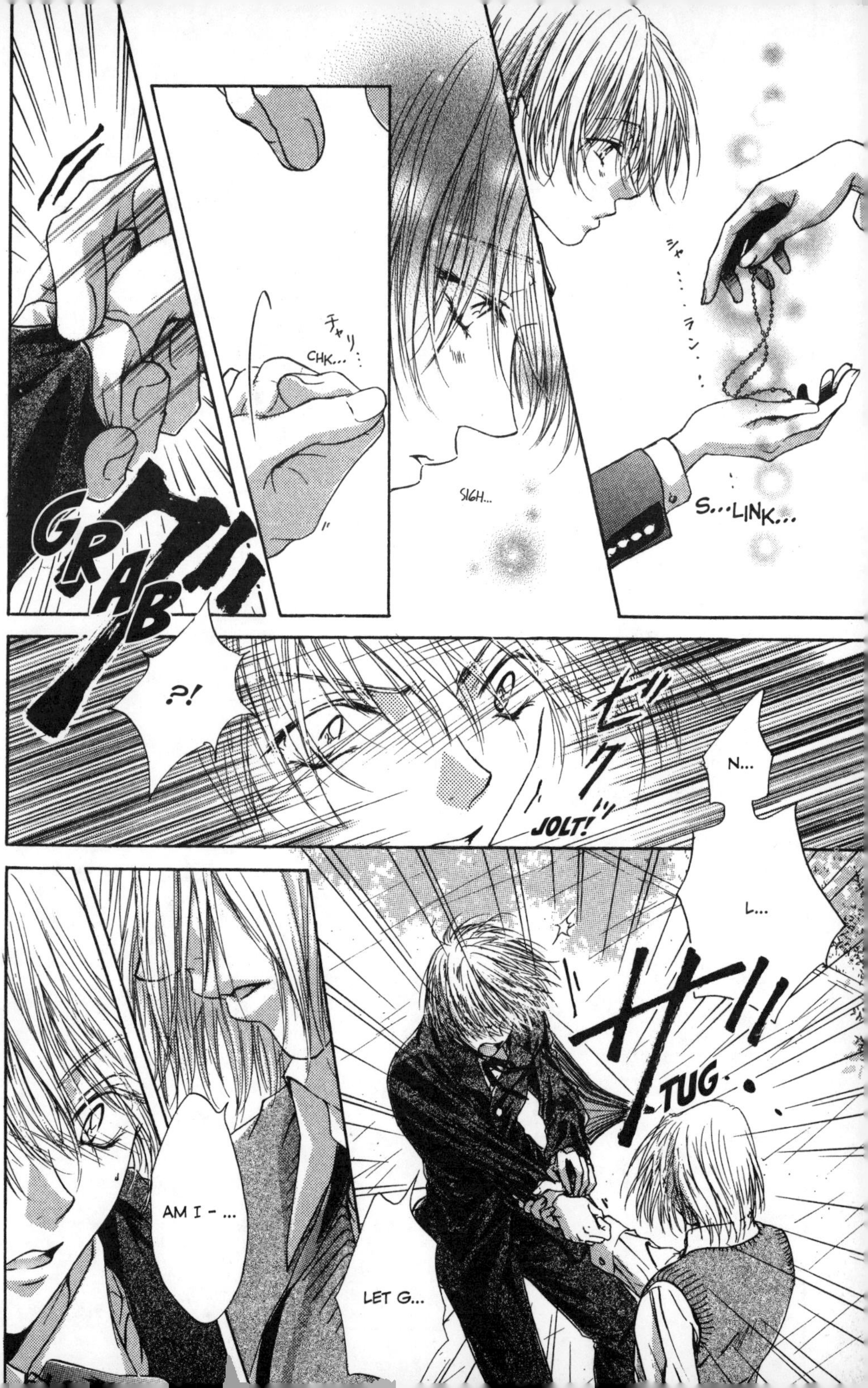

シャ……ラン……
S...LINK...
SIGH...
チャリ…
CHK...
GRAB!!
N...
ビクッ
JOLT!
?!
L...
TUG
LET G...
AM I - ...

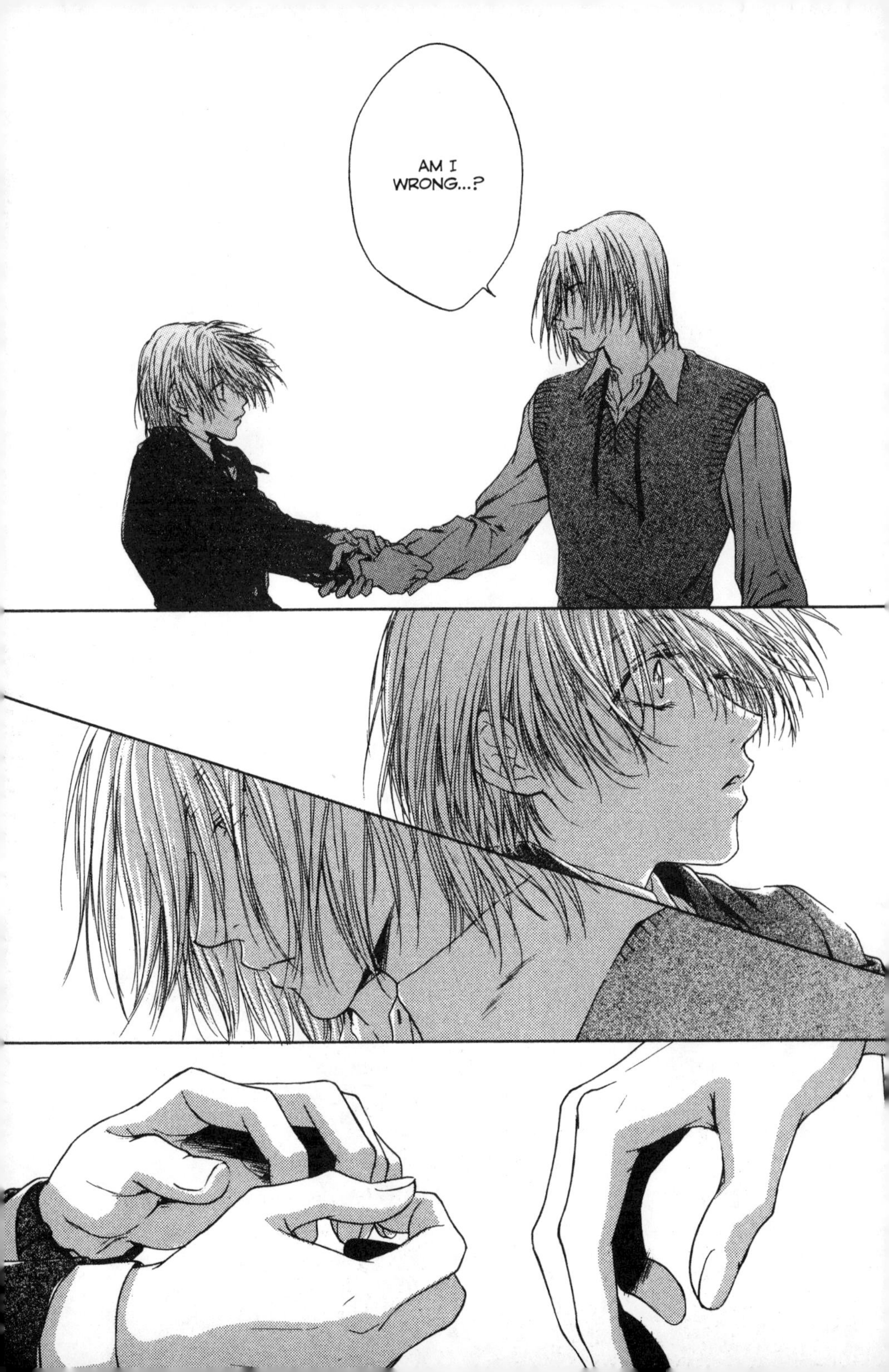
AM I WRONG...?

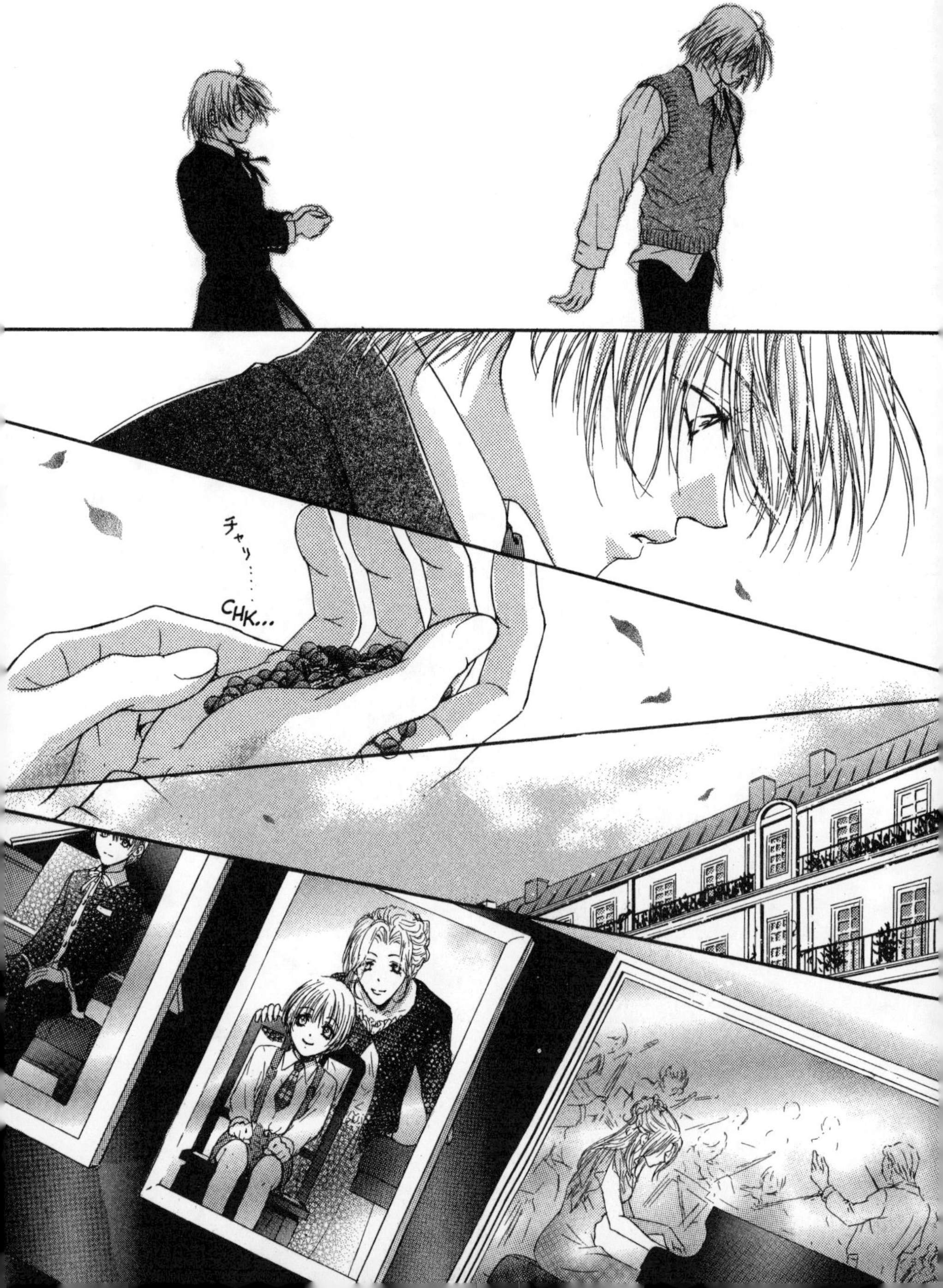
チャリ……
CHK...

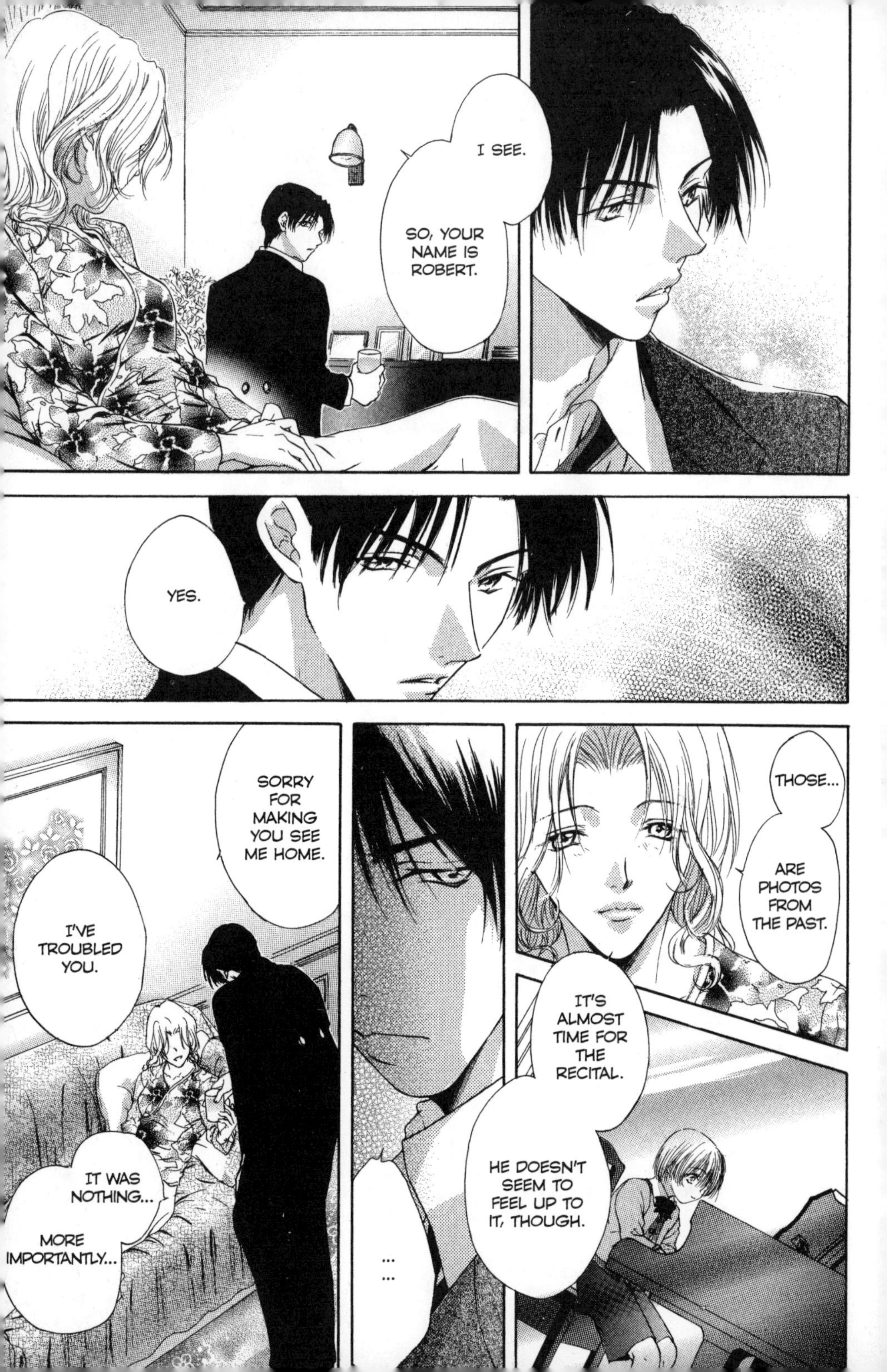
I SEE.
SO, YOUR NAME IS ROBERT.
YES.
SORRY FOR MAKING YOU SEE ME HOME.
I'VE TROUBLED YOU.
IT WAS NOTHING...
MORE IMPORTANTLY...
......
THOSE...
ARE PHOTOS FROM THE PAST.
IT'S ALMOST TIME FOR THE RECITAL.
HE DOESN'T SEEM TO FEEL UP TO IT, THOUGH.

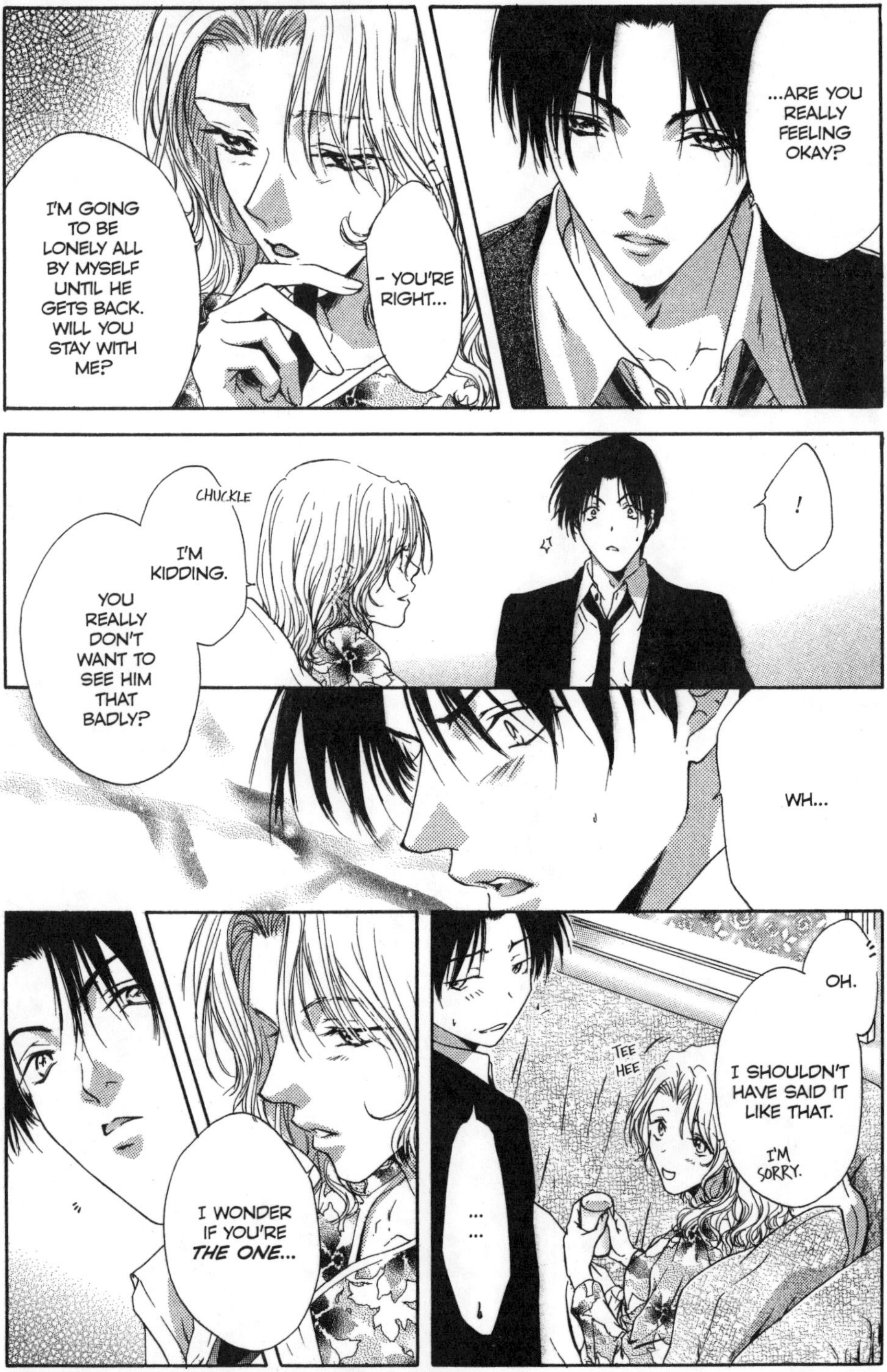
...ARE YOU REALLY FEELING OKAY?
- YOU'RE RIGHT...
I'M GOING TO BE LONELY ALL BY MYSELF UNTIL HE GETS BACK. WILL YOU STAY WITH ME?
!
CHUCKLE
I'M KIDDING.
YOU REALLY DON'T WANT TO SEE HIM THAT BADLY?
WH...
OH.
I SHOULDN'T HAVE SAID IT LIKE THAT.
I'M SORRY.
TEE HEE
... ...
I WONDER IF YOU'RE *THE ONE*...

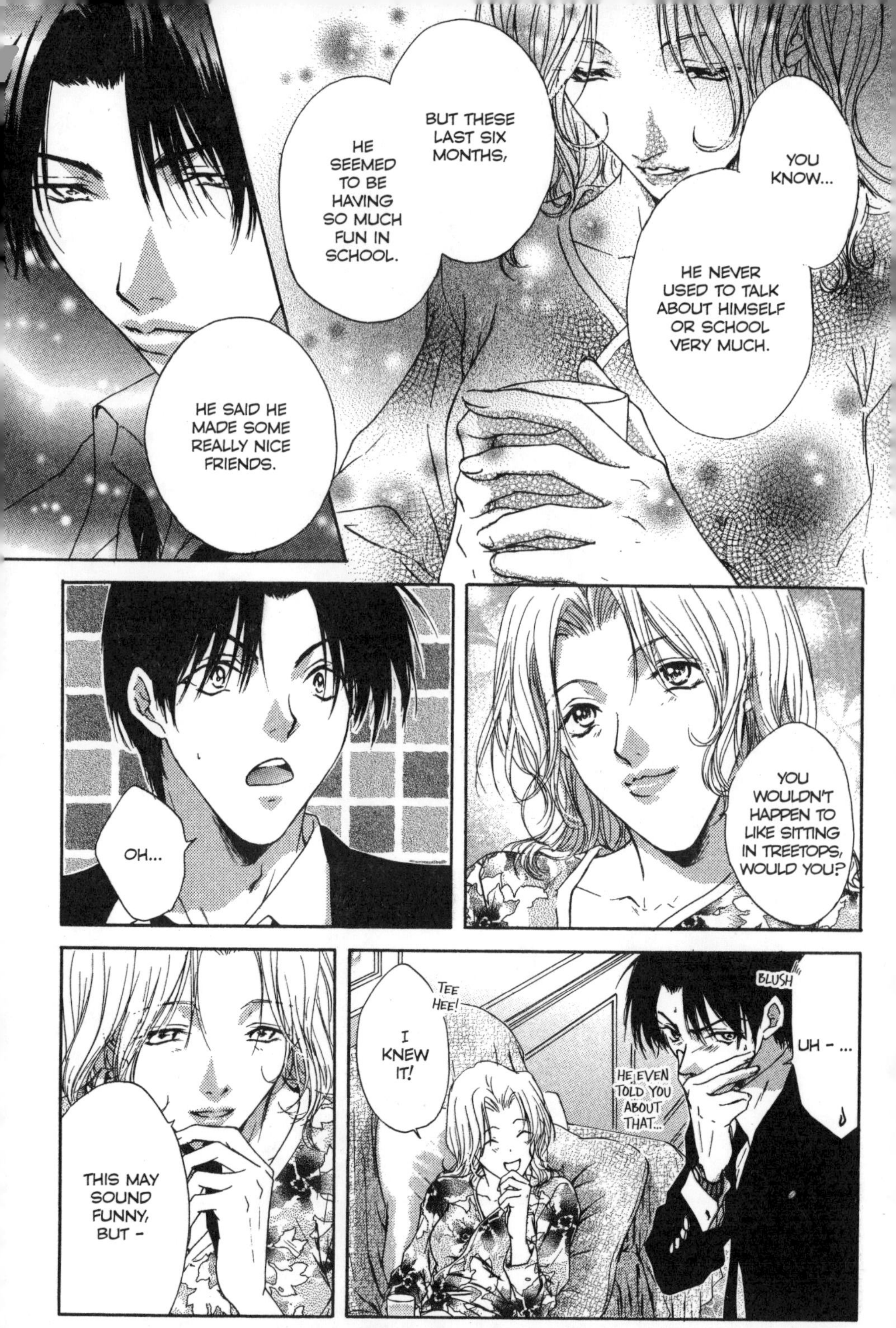
YOU KNOW...
HE NEVER USED TO TALK ABOUT HIMSELF OR SCHOOL VERY MUCH.
BUT THESE LAST SIX MONTHS,
HE SEEMED TO BE HAVING SO MUCH FUN IN SCHOOL.
HE SAID HE MADE SOME REALLY NICE FRIENDS.
YOU WOULDN'T HAPPEN TO LIKE SITTING IN TREETOPS, WOULD YOU?
OH...
BLUSH
UH - ...
HE EVEN TOLD YOU ABOUT THAT...
TEE HEE!
I KNEW IT!
THIS MAY SOUND FUNNY, BUT -

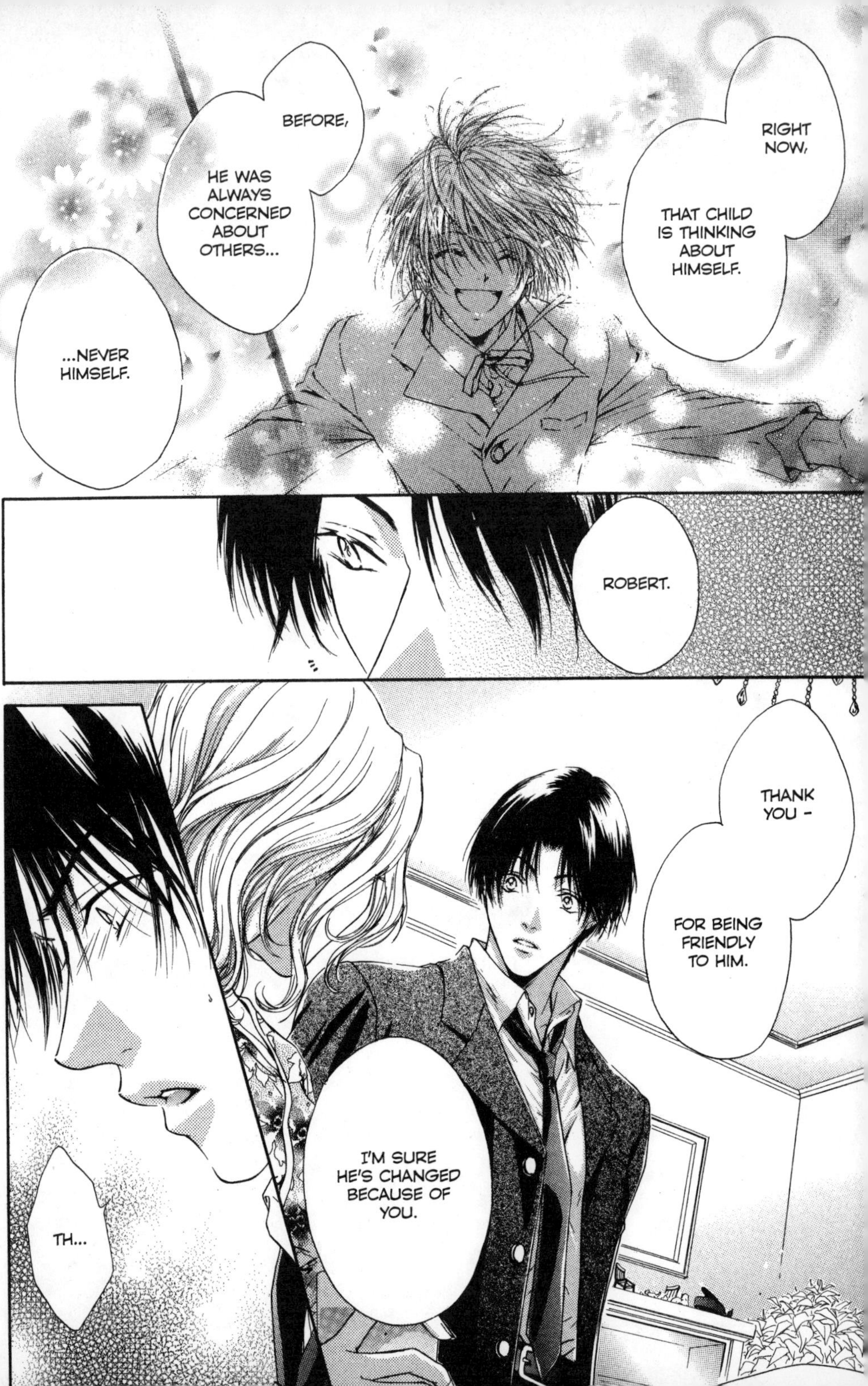
RIGHT NOW,
THAT CHILD IS THINKING ABOUT HIMSELF.
BEFORE,
HE WAS ALWAYS CONCERNED ABOUT OTHERS...
...NEVER HIMSELF.
ROBERT.
THANK YOU -
FOR BEING FRIENDLY TO HIM.
I'M SURE HE'S CHANGED BECAUSE OF YOU.
TH...

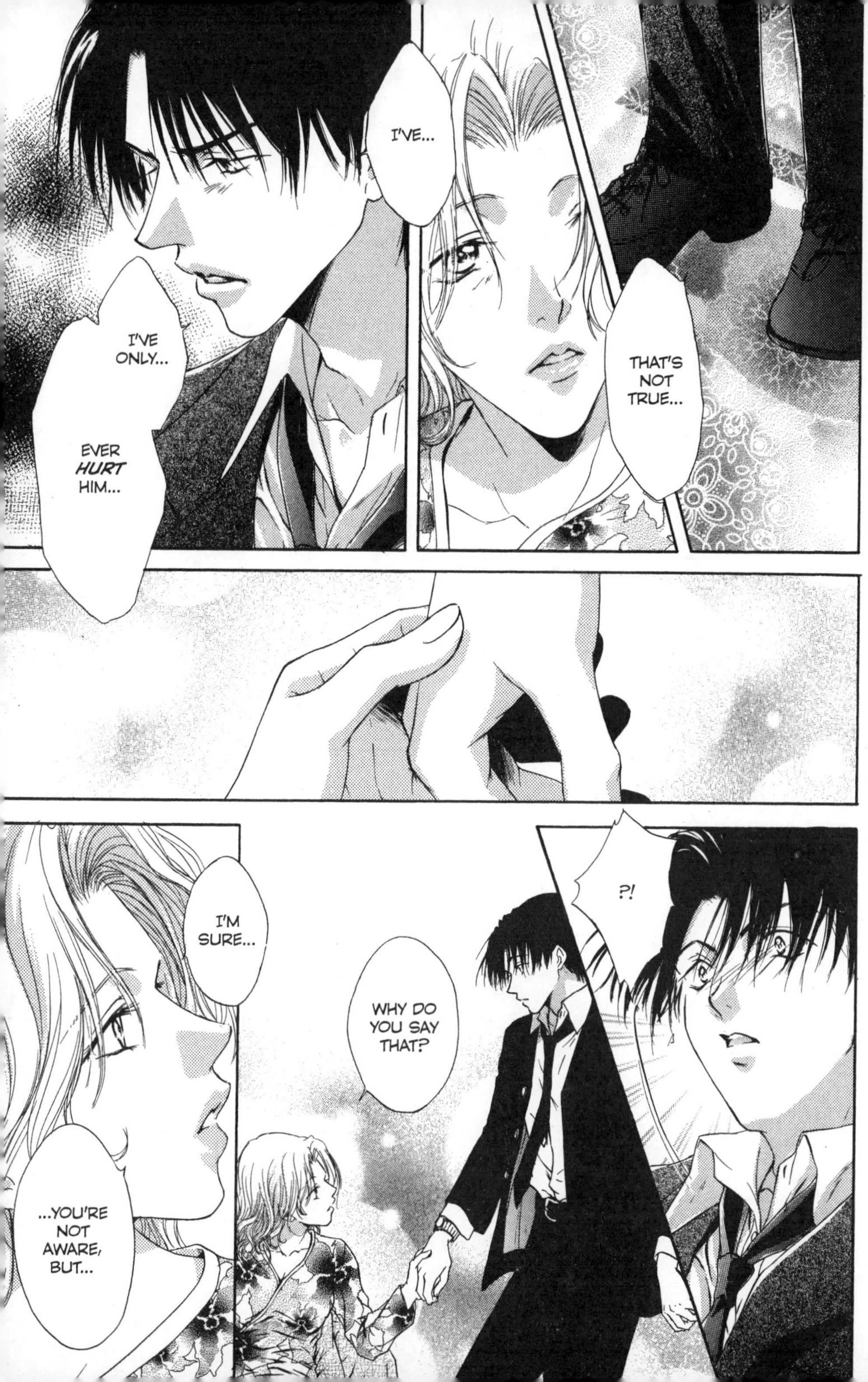
I'VE...
I'VE ONLY...
EVER *HURT* HIM...
THAT'S NOT TRUE...
?!
WHY DO YOU SAY THAT?
I'M SURE...
...YOU'RE NOT AWARE, BUT...

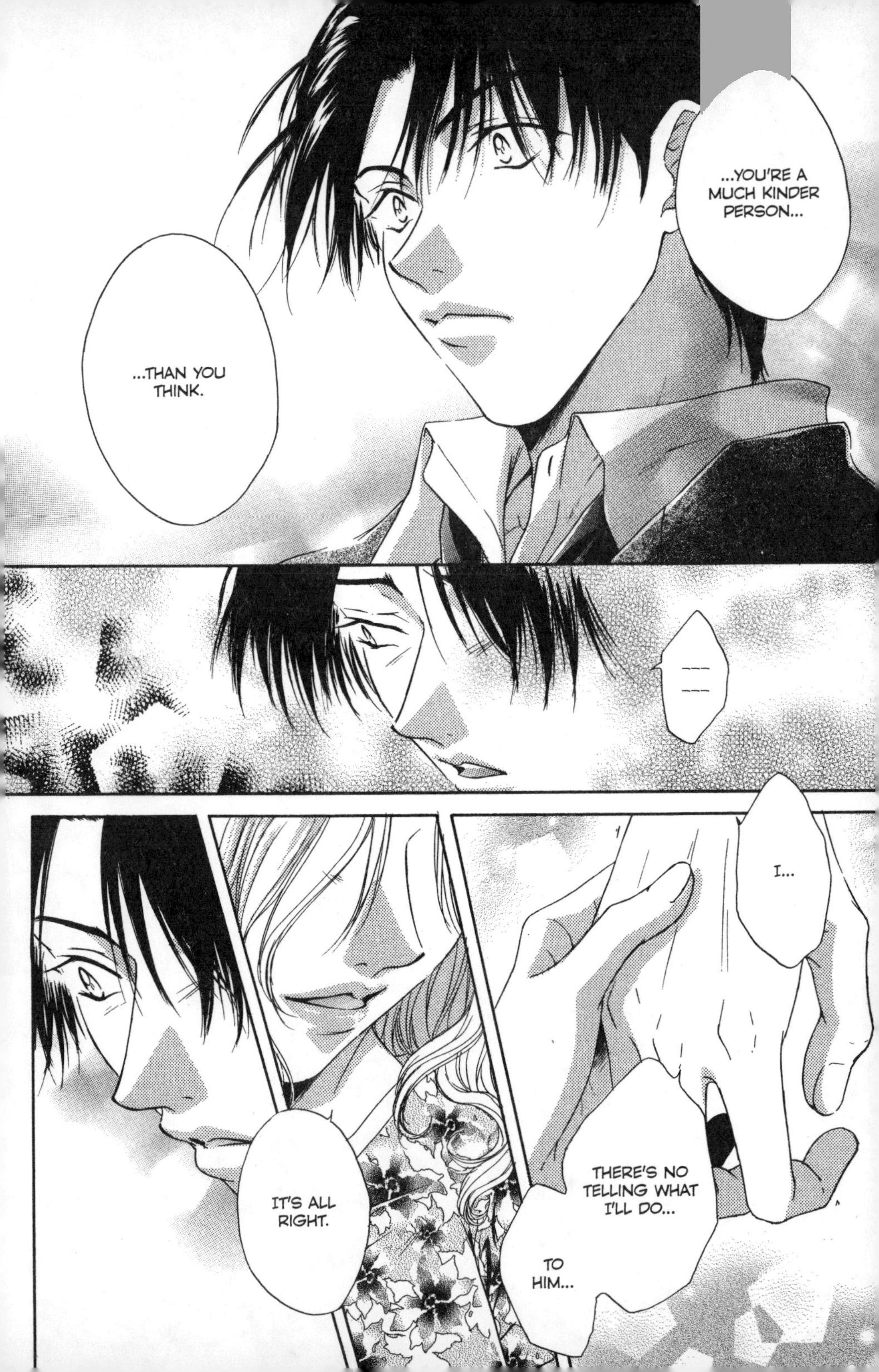
...YOU'RE A MUCH KINDER PERSON...
...THAN YOU THINK.
———
I...
THERE'S NO TELLING WHAT I'LL DO...
TO HIM...
IT'S ALL RIGHT.

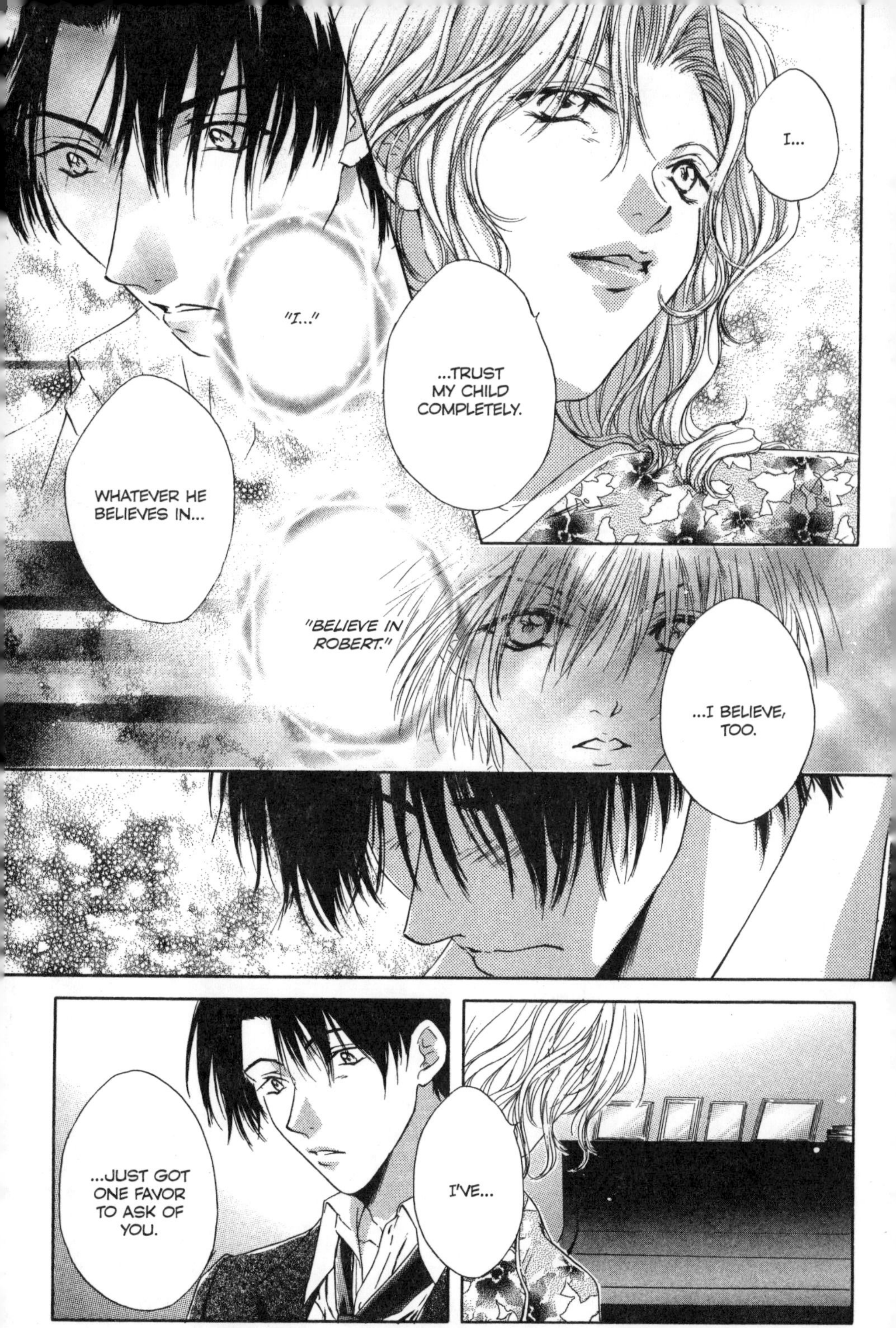

I...
...TRUST MY CHILD COMPLETELY.
"I..."
WHATEVER HE BELIEVES IN...
...I BELIEVE, TOO.
"BELIEVE IN ROBERT."
I'VE...
...JUST GOT ONE FAVOR TO ASK OF YOU.

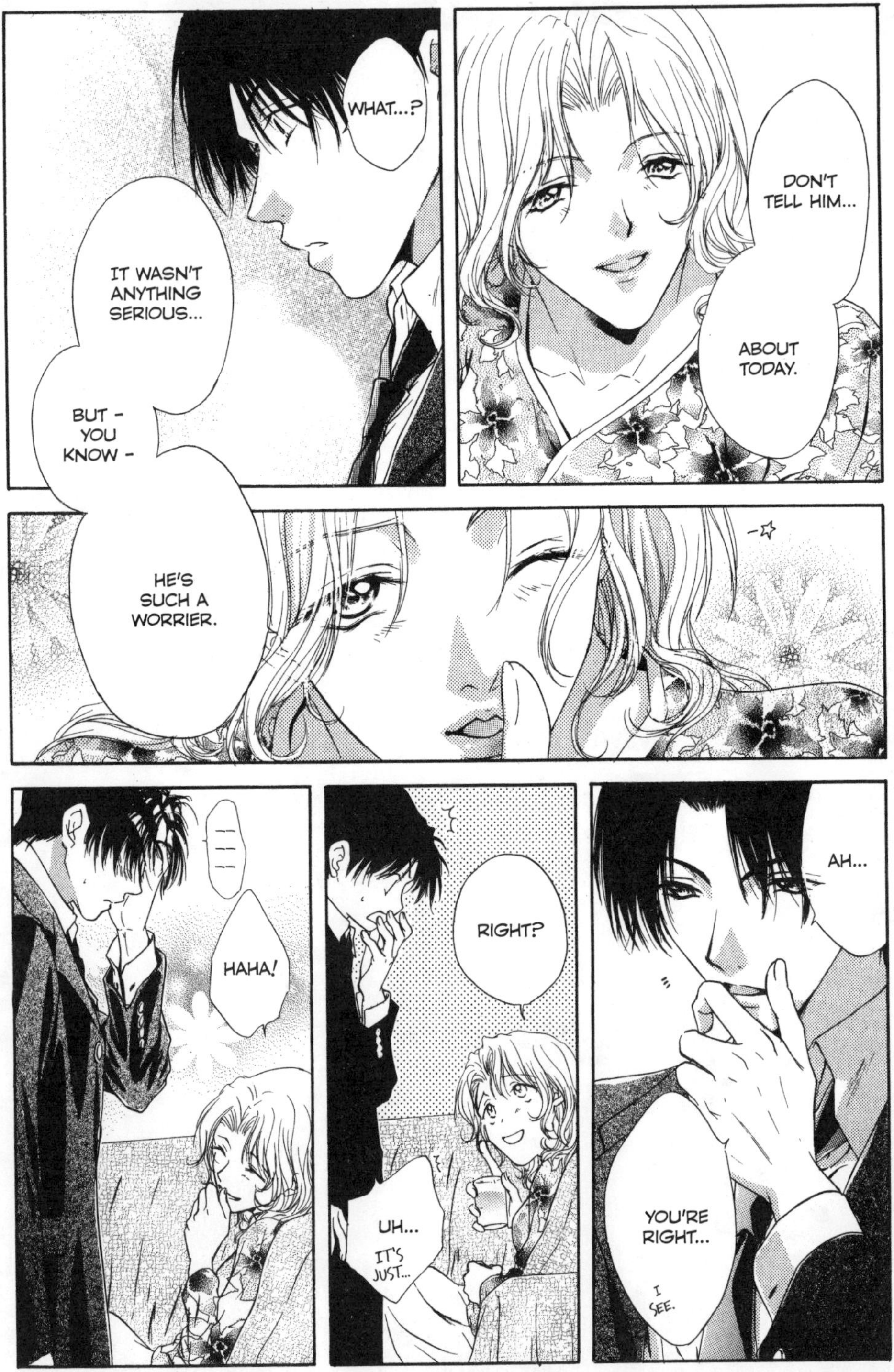
DON'T TELL HIM...
ABOUT TODAY.
WHAT...?
IT WASN'T ANYTHING SERIOUS...
BUT - YOU KNOW -
HE'S SUCH A WORRIER.
AH...
YOU'RE RIGHT...
I SEE.
RIGHT?
UH...
IT'S JUST...
———
HAHA!

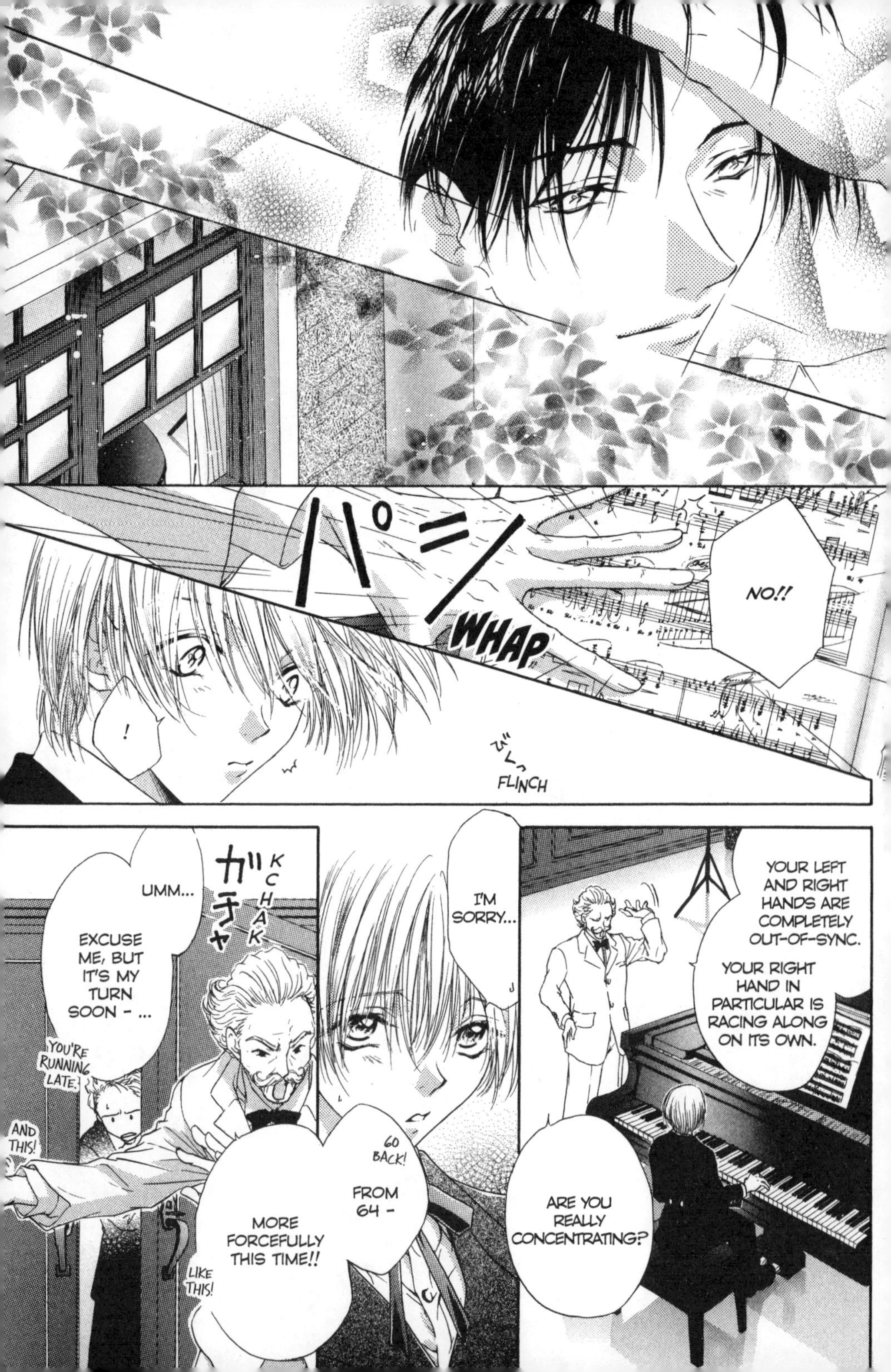

NO!!
パン
WHAP
びくっ
FLINCH
!
YOUR LEFT AND RIGHT HANDS ARE COMPLETELY OUT-OF-SYNC.
YOUR RIGHT HAND IN PARTICULAR IS RACING ALONG ON ITS OWN.
ARE YOU REALLY CONCENTRATING?
I'M SORRY...
ガチャ
KCHAK
UMM...
EXCUSE ME, BUT IT'S MY TURN SOON - ...
60 BACK!
FROM 64 -
MORE FORCEFULLY THIS TIME!!
YOU'RE RUNNING LATE.
AND THIS!
LIKE THIS!

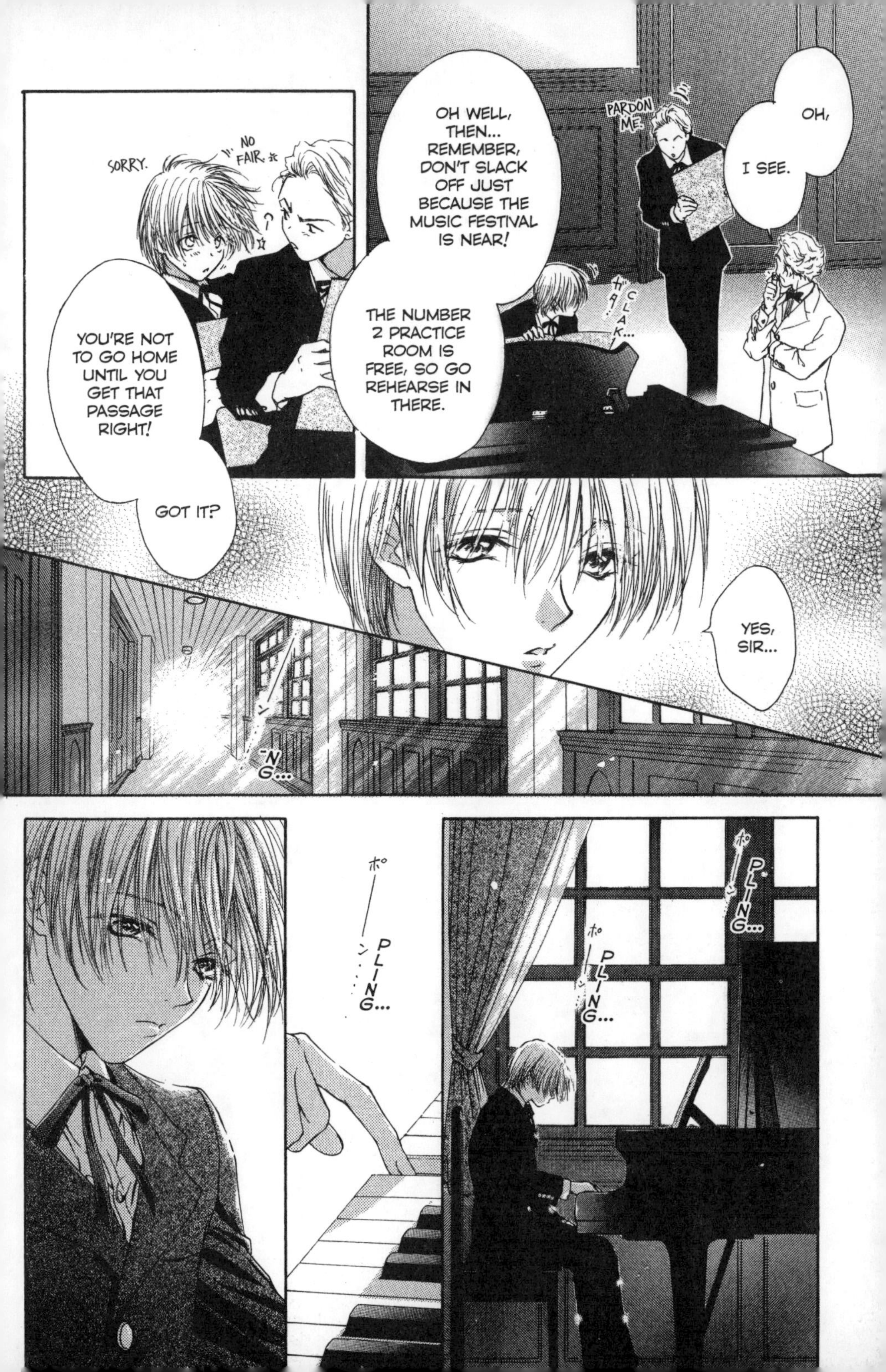
OH, I SEE.
PARDON ME.
CLAK...
OH WELL, THEN... REMEMBER, DON'T SLACK OFF JUST BECAUSE THE MUSIC FESTIVAL IS NEAR!
THE NUMBER 2 PRACTICE ROOM IS FREE, SO GO REHEARSE IN THERE.
NO FAIR.
SORRY.
YOU'RE NOT TO GO HOME UNTIL YOU GET THAT PASSAGE RIGHT!
GOT IT?
YES, SIR...
-NG G...
PLING...
PLING...
PLING...

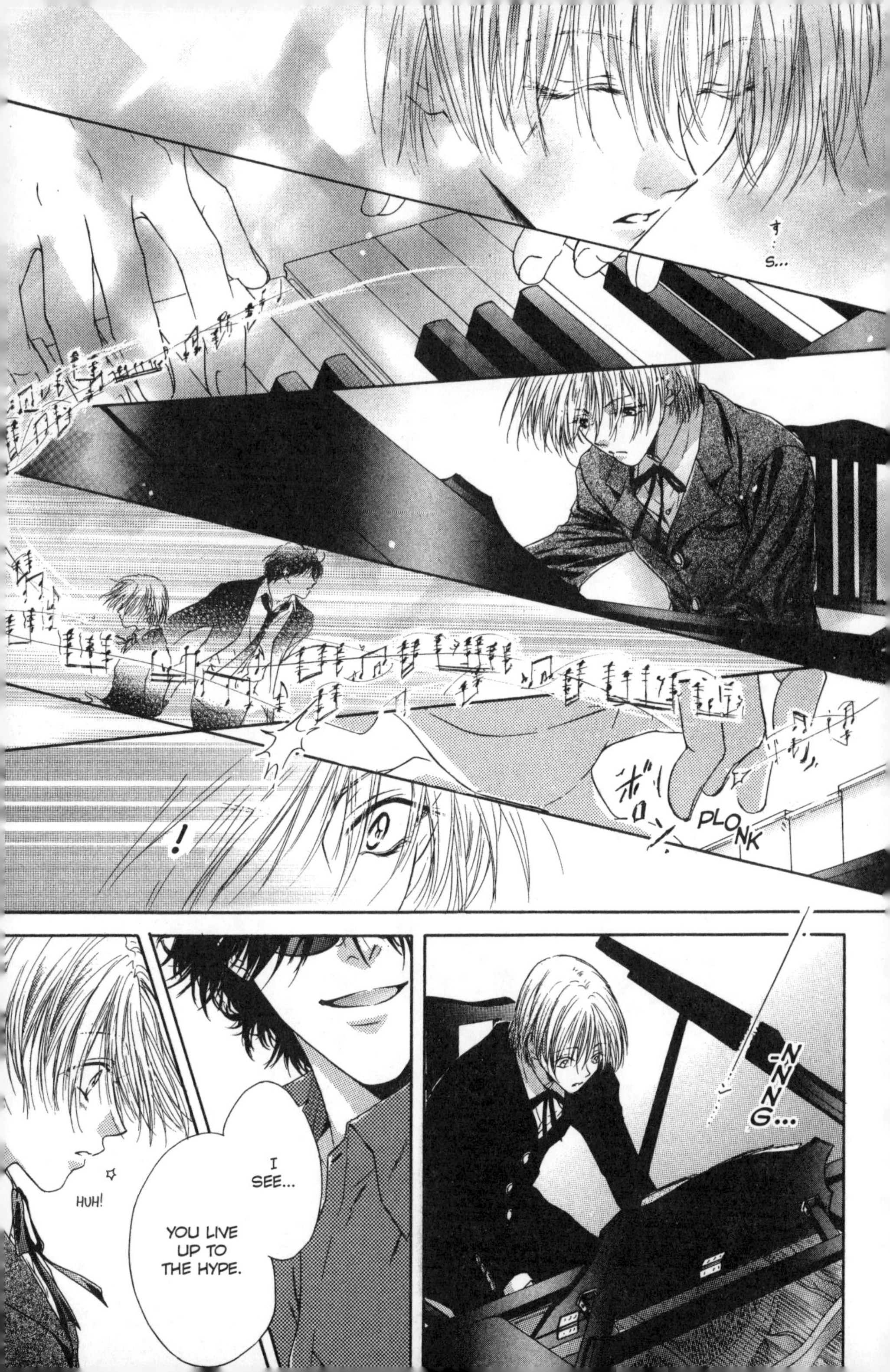

す
S...
ボロン
PLONK
!
-NNNG...
I SEE...
YOU LIVE UP TO THE HYPE.
HUH!

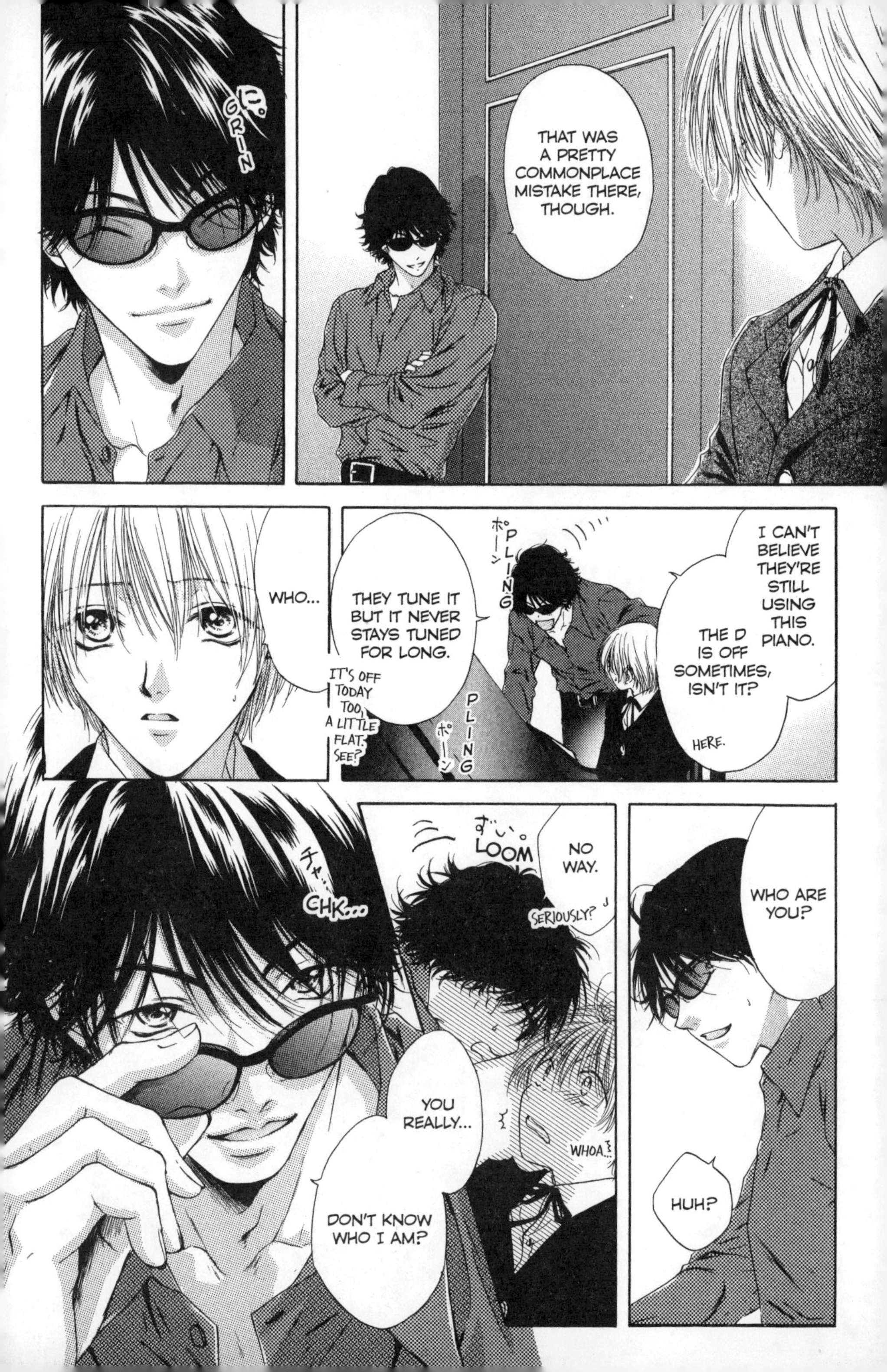
THAT WAS A PRETTY COMMONPLACE MISTAKE THERE, THOUGH.
に。 GRIN
I CAN'T BELIEVE THEY'RE STILL USING THIS PIANO.
THE D IS OFF SOMETIMES, ISN'T IT?
HERE.
ポーン PLING
THEY TUNE IT BUT IT NEVER STAYS TUNED FOR LONG.
IT'S OFF TODAY TOO, A LITTLE FLAT. SEE?
ポーン PLING
WHO...
WHO ARE YOU?
HUH?
NO WAY.
SERIOUSLY?
ずい。 LOOM
WHOA...
チャ… CHK...
YOU REALLY...
DON'T KNOW WHO I AM?

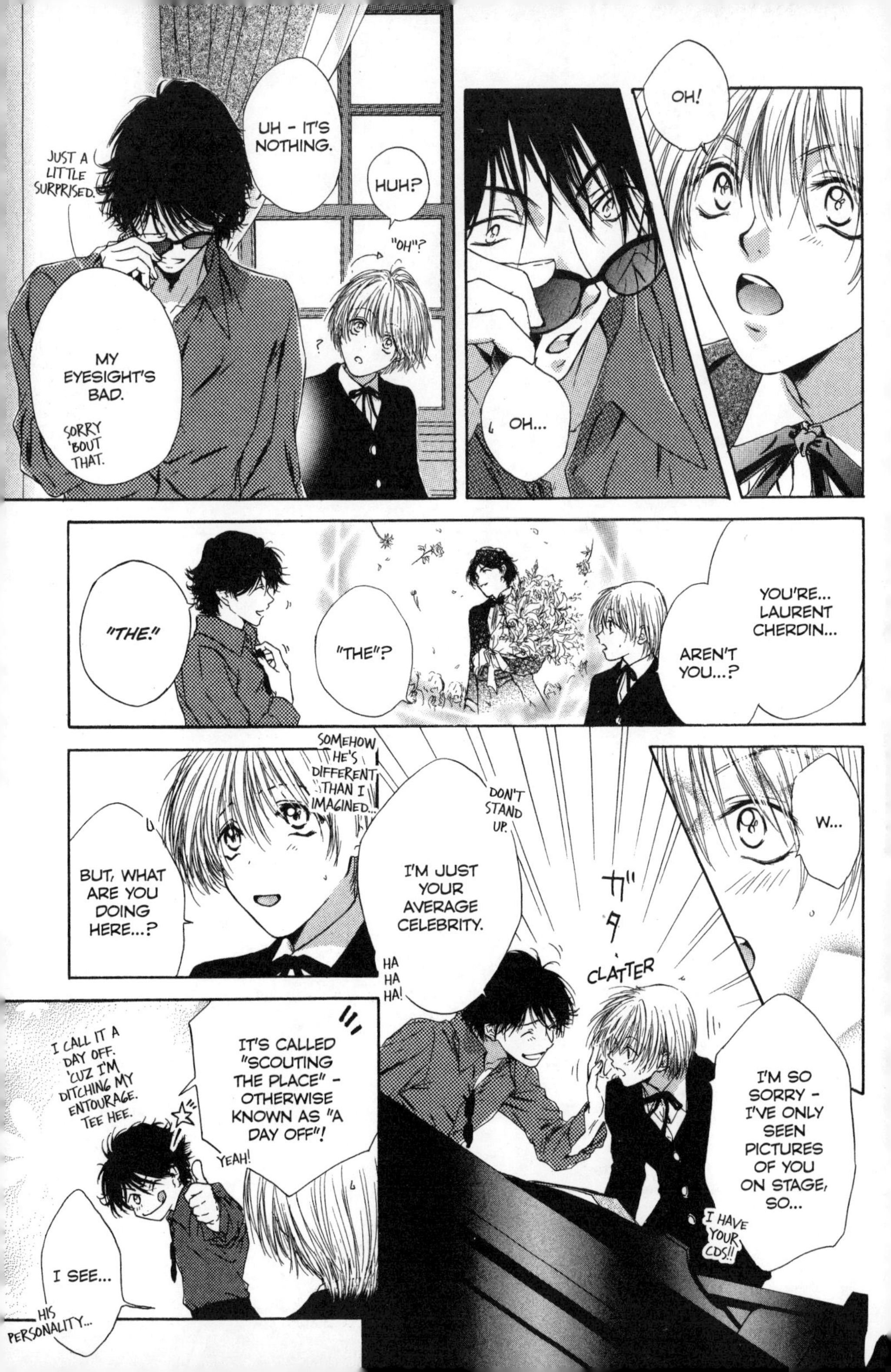

OH!
OH...
UH - IT'S NOTHING.
HUH?
"OH"?
JUST A LITTLE SURPRISED.
MY EYESIGHT'S BAD.
SORRY 'BOUT THAT.
YOU'RE... LAURENT CHERDIN...
AREN'T YOU...?
"THE"?
"THE."
W...
ガタ
CLATTER
I'M SO SORRY - I'VE ONLY SEEN PICTURES OF YOU ON STAGE, SO...
I HAVE YOUR CDS!!
DON'T STAND UP.
I'M JUST YOUR AVERAGE CELEBRITY.
HA HA HA!
SOMEHOW HE'S DIFFERENT THAN I IMAGINED...
BUT, WHAT ARE YOU DOING HERE...?
IT'S CALLED "SCOUTING THE PLACE" - OTHERWISE KNOWN AS "A DAY OFF"!
YEAH!
I CALL IT A DAY OFF. 'CUZ I'M DITCHING MY ENTOURAGE. TEE HEE.
I SEE...
HIS PERSONALITY...

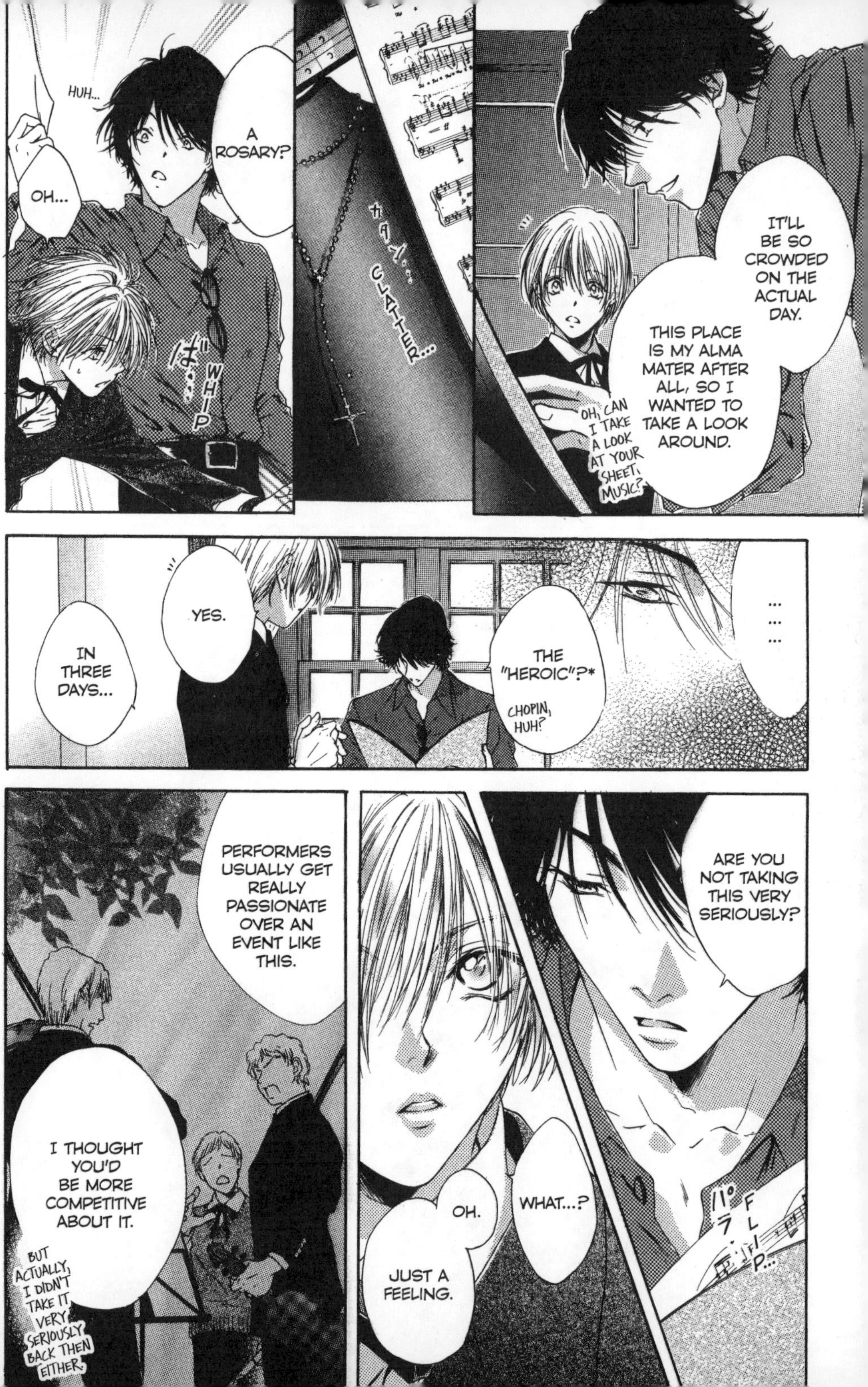
IT'LL BE SO CROWDED ON THE ACTUAL DAY.
THIS PLACE IS MY ALMA MATER AFTER ALL, SO I WANTED TO TAKE A LOOK AROUND.
OH, CAN I TAKE A LOOK AT YOUR SHEET MUSIC?
カタン…
CLATTER...
A ROSARY?
HUH...
OH...
ばっ
WHIP
...
...
...
THE "HEROIC"?*
CHOPIN, HUH?
YES.
IN THREE DAYS...
ARE YOU NOT TAKING THIS VERY SERIOUSLY?
パラ
FLIP...
WHAT...?
OH.
JUST A FEELING.
PERFORMERS USUALLY GET REALLY PASSIONATE OVER AN EVENT LIKE THIS.
I THOUGHT YOU'D BE MORE COMPETITIVE ABOUT IT.
BUT ACTUALLY, I DIDN'T TAKE IT VERY SERIOUSLY BACK THEN EITHER.

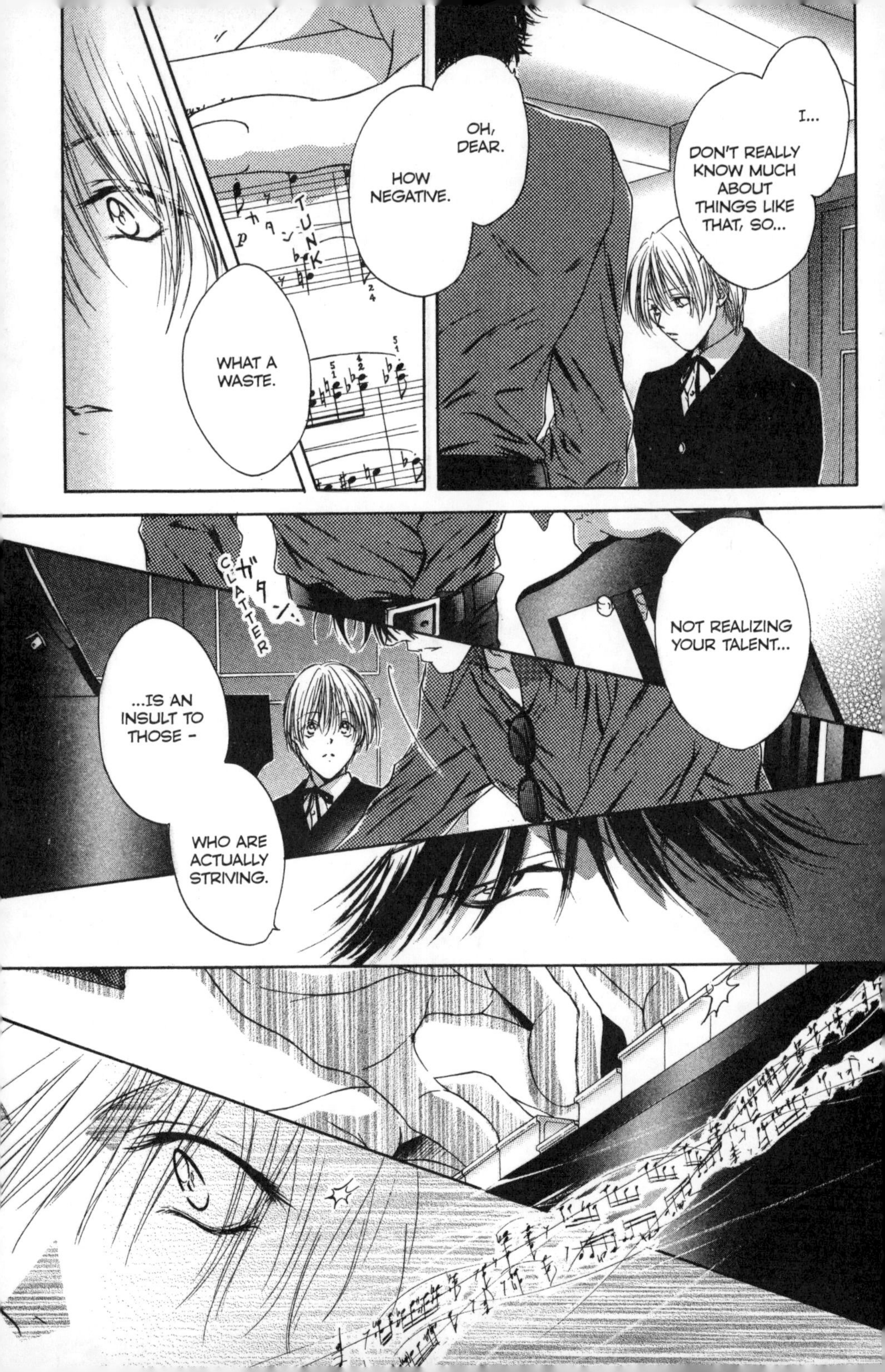
I...
DON'T REALLY KNOW MUCH ABOUT THINGS LIKE THAT, SO...
OH, DEAR.
HOW NEGATIVE.
TUNK
WHAT A WASTE.
NOT REALIZING YOUR TALENT...
CLATTER
...IS AN INSULT TO THOSE -
WHO ARE ACTUALLY STRIVING.

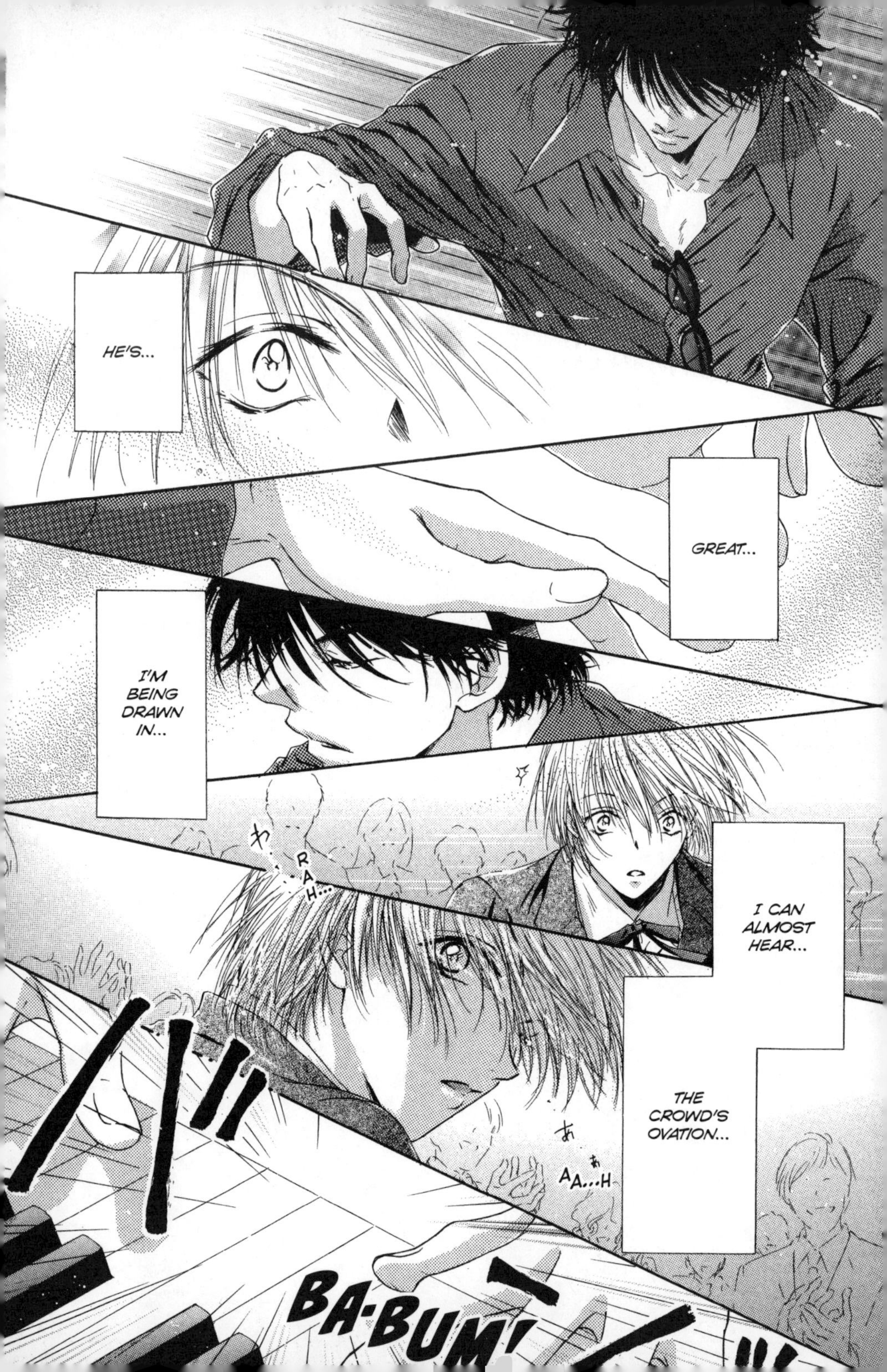
HE'S...
GREAT...
I'M BEING DRAWN IN...
I CAN ALMOST HEAR...
わ...RAH...
THE CROWD'S OVATION...
ああ AA...H
BA-BUM!

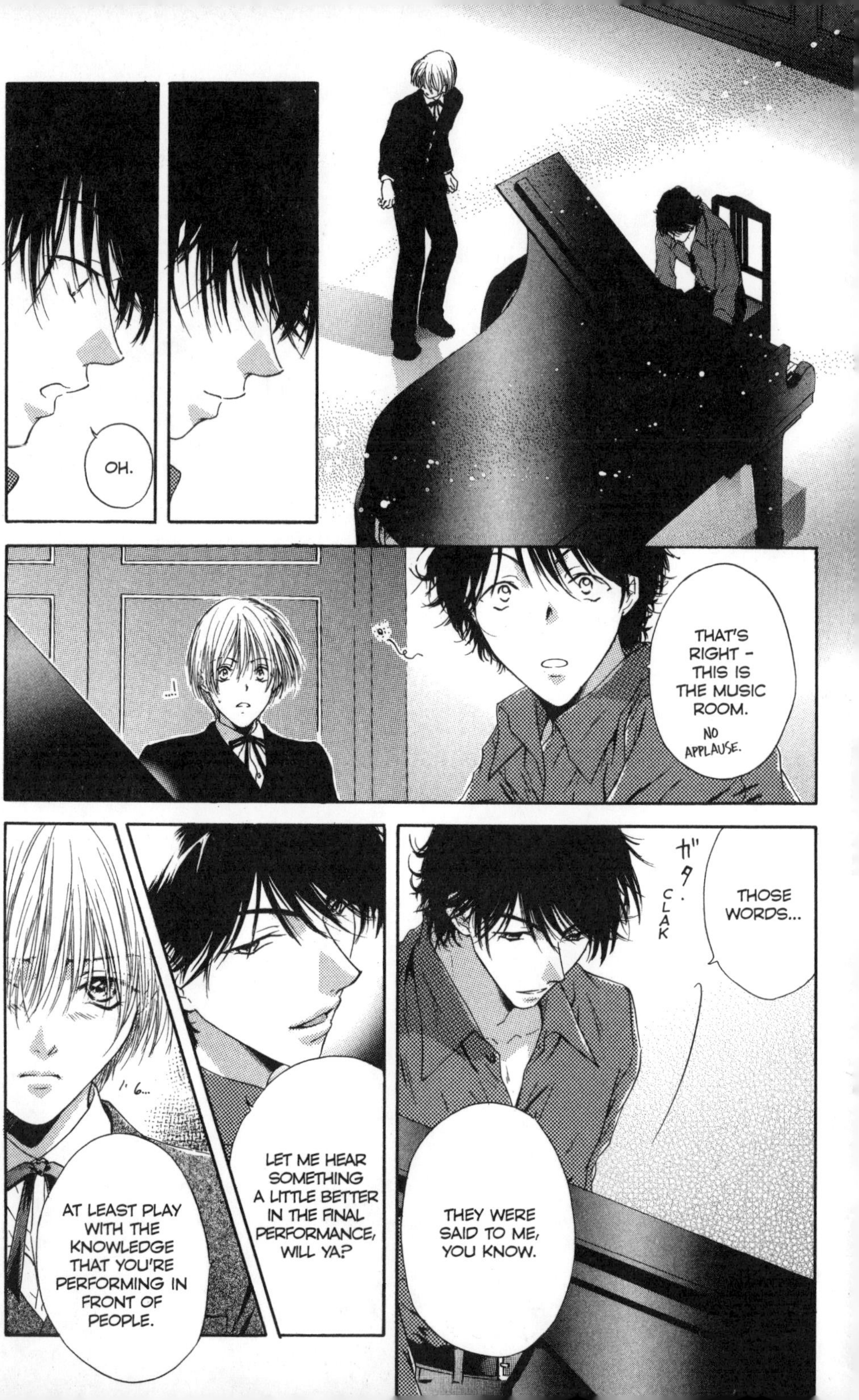
OH.
THAT'S RIGHT - THIS IS THE MUSIC ROOM.
NO APPLAUSE.
...!
THOSE WORDS...
ガタ.
CLAK
THEY WERE SAID TO ME, YOU KNOW.
LET ME HEAR SOMETHING A LITTLE BETTER IN THE FINAL PERFORMANCE, WILL YA?
AT LEAST PLAY WITH THE KNOWLEDGE THAT YOU'RE PERFORMING IN FRONT OF PEOPLE.

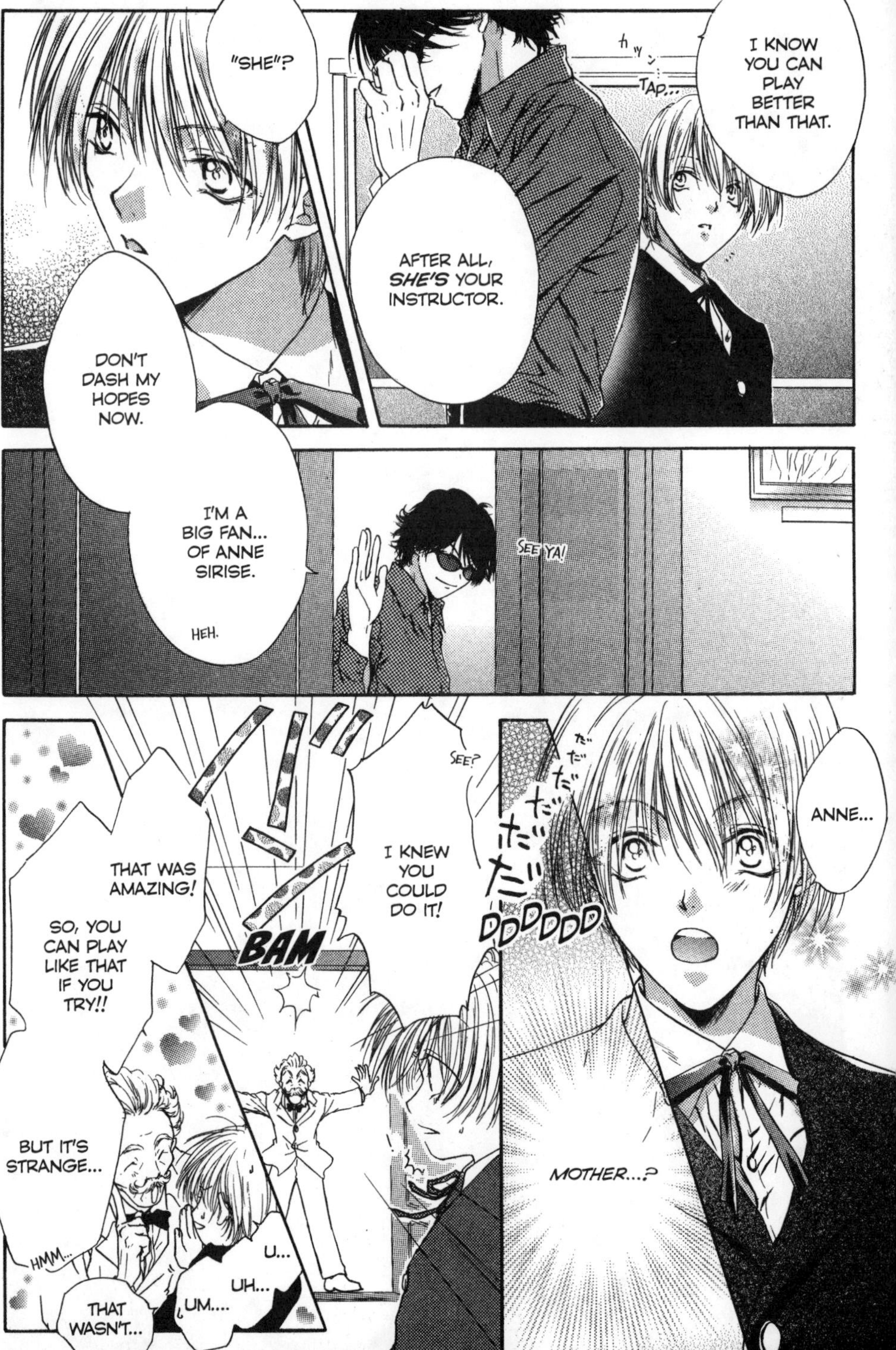

I KNOW YOU CAN PLAY BETTER THAN THAT.
カッン…
TAP...
AFTER ALL, SHE'S YOUR INSTRUCTOR.
"SHE"?
DON'T DASH MY HOPES NOW.
SEE YA!
I'M A BIG FAN... OF ANNE SIRISE.
HEH.
ANNE...
だだだだだ
DDDDDD
MOTHER...?
SEE?
I KNEW YOU COULD DO IT!
BAM
THAT WAS AMAZING!
SO, YOU CAN PLAY LIKE THAT IF YOU TRY!!
BUT IT'S STRANGE...
U...
UH...
UM....
HMM...
THAT WASN'T...

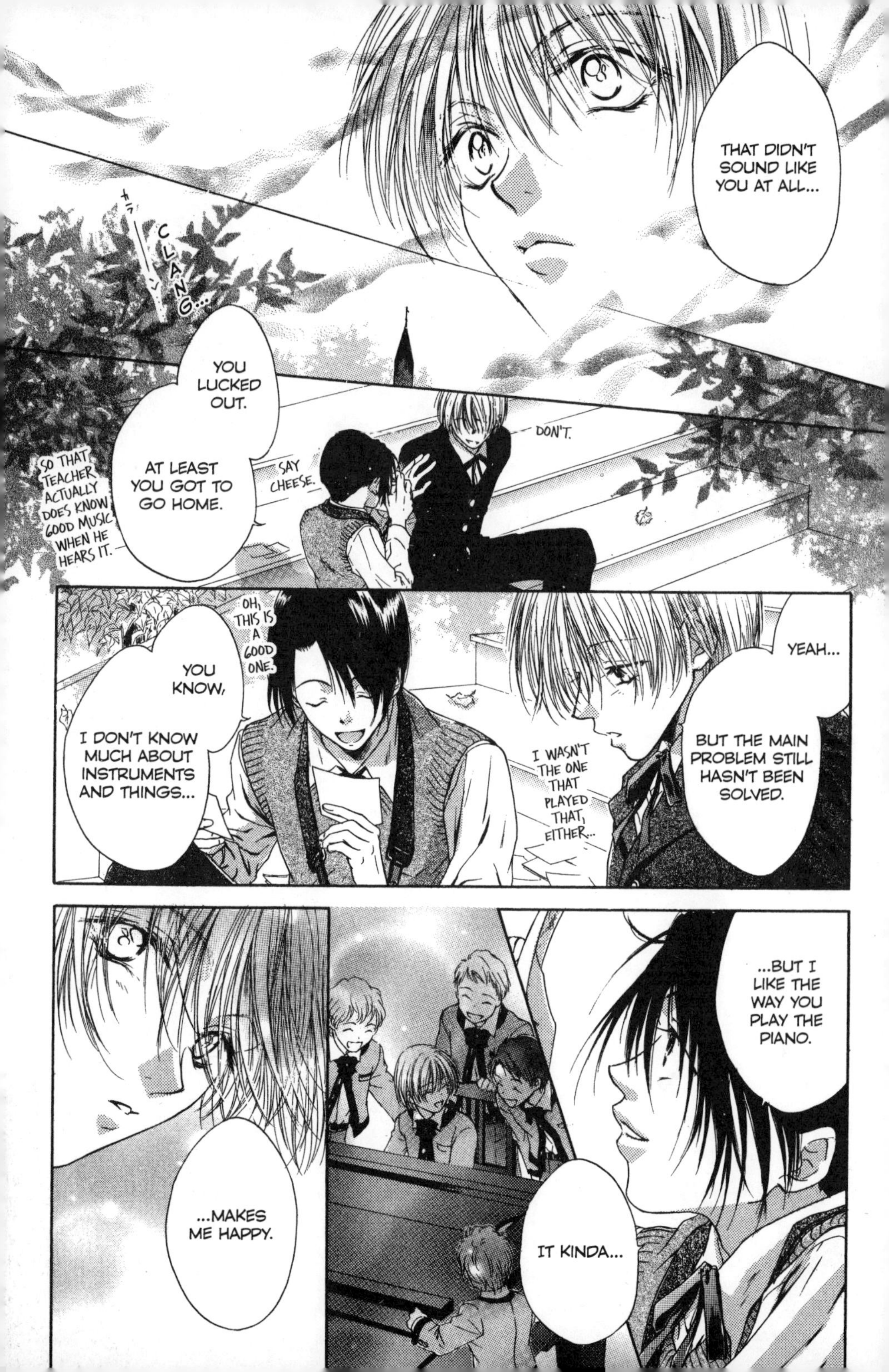
THAT DIDN'T SOUND LIKE YOU AT ALL...
CLANG...
DON'T.
SAY CHEESE.
YOU LUCKED OUT.
AT LEAST YOU GOT TO GO HOME.
SO THAT TEACHER ACTUALLY DOES KNOW GOOD MUSIC WHEN HE HEARS IT.
YEAH...
BUT THE MAIN PROBLEM STILL HASN'T BEEN SOLVED.
I WASN'T THE ONE THAT PLAYED THAT, EITHER...
OH, THIS IS A GOOD ONE.
YOU KNOW,
I DON'T KNOW MUCH ABOUT INSTRUMENTS AND THINGS...
...BUT I LIKE THE WAY YOU PLAY THE PIANO.
IT KINDA...
...MAKES ME HAPPY.

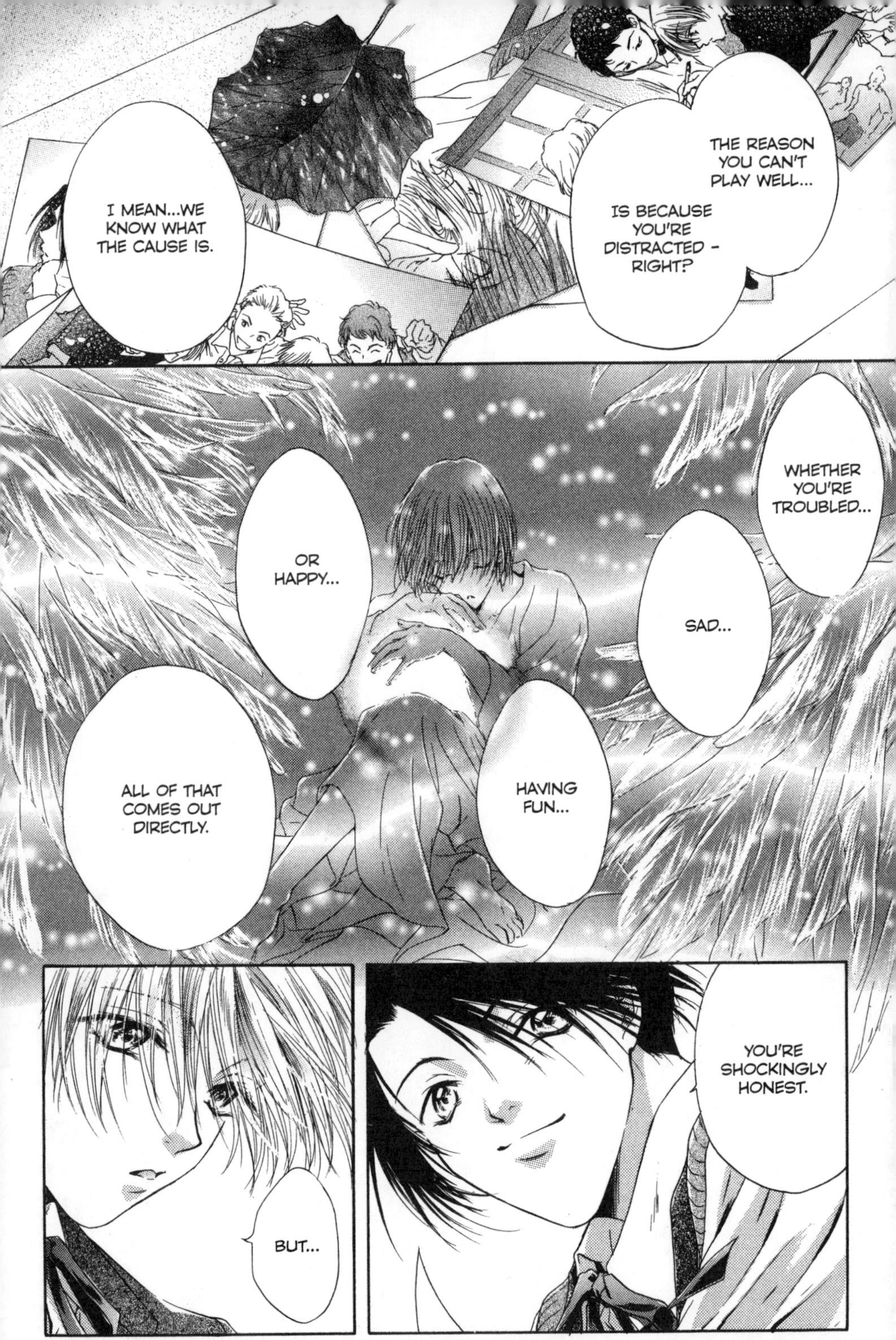
THE REASON YOU CAN'T PLAY WELL...
IS BECAUSE YOU'RE DISTRACTED - RIGHT?
I MEAN...WE KNOW WHAT THE CAUSE IS.
WHETHER YOU'RE TROUBLED...
SAD...
OR HAPPY...
HAVING FUN...
ALL OF THAT COMES OUT DIRECTLY.
YOU'RE SHOCKINGLY HONEST.
BUT...

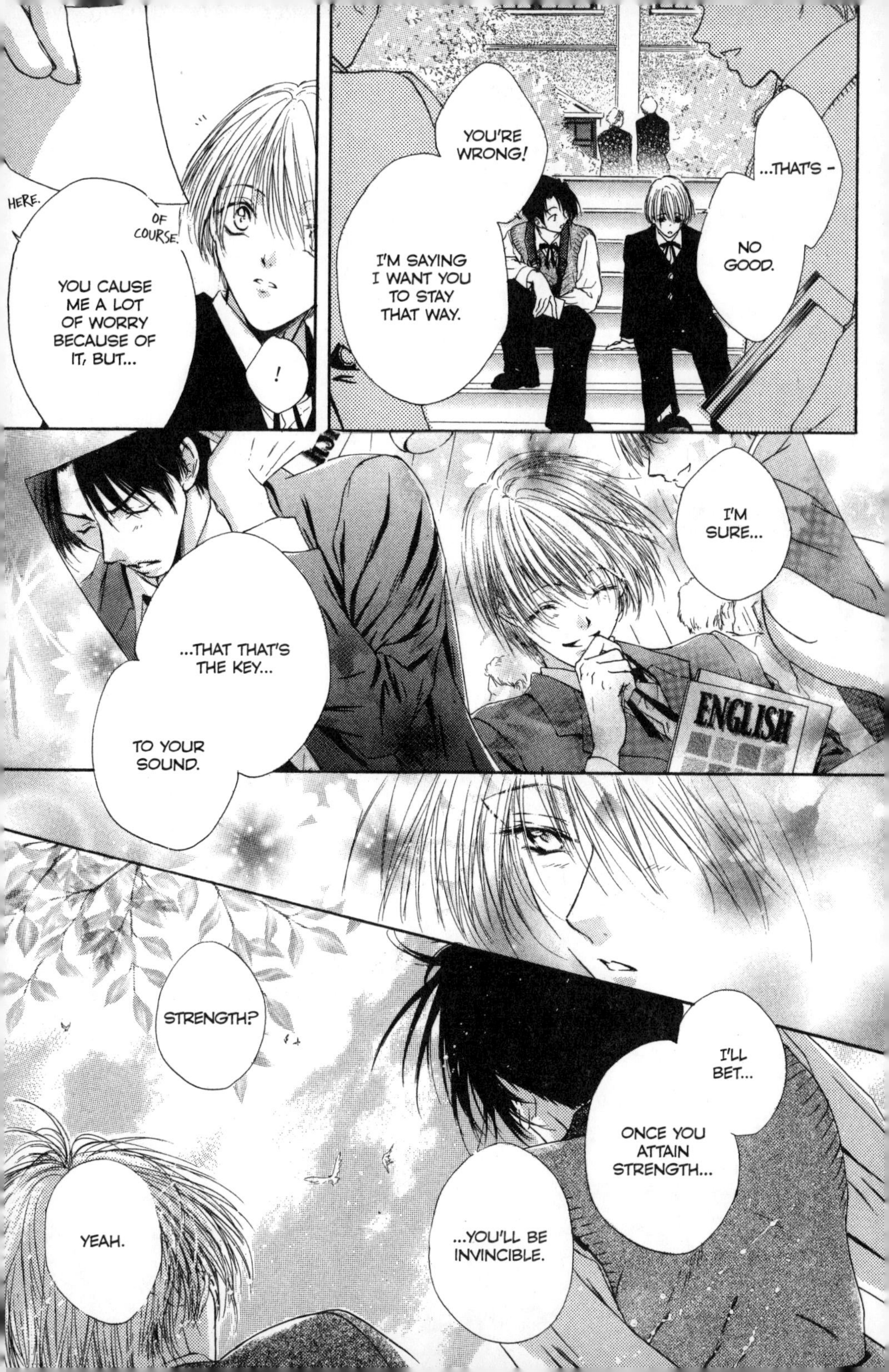
...THAT'S -
NO GOOD.
YOU'RE WRONG!
I'M SAYING I WANT YOU TO STAY THAT WAY.
OF COURSE.
HERE.
YOU CAUSE ME A LOT OF WORRY BECAUSE OF IT, BUT...
!
I'M SURE...
...THAT THAT'S THE KEY...
TO YOUR SOUND.
ENGLISH
I'LL BET...
ONCE YOU ATTAIN STRENGTH...
STRENGTH?
...YOU'LL BE INVINCIBLE.
YEAH.

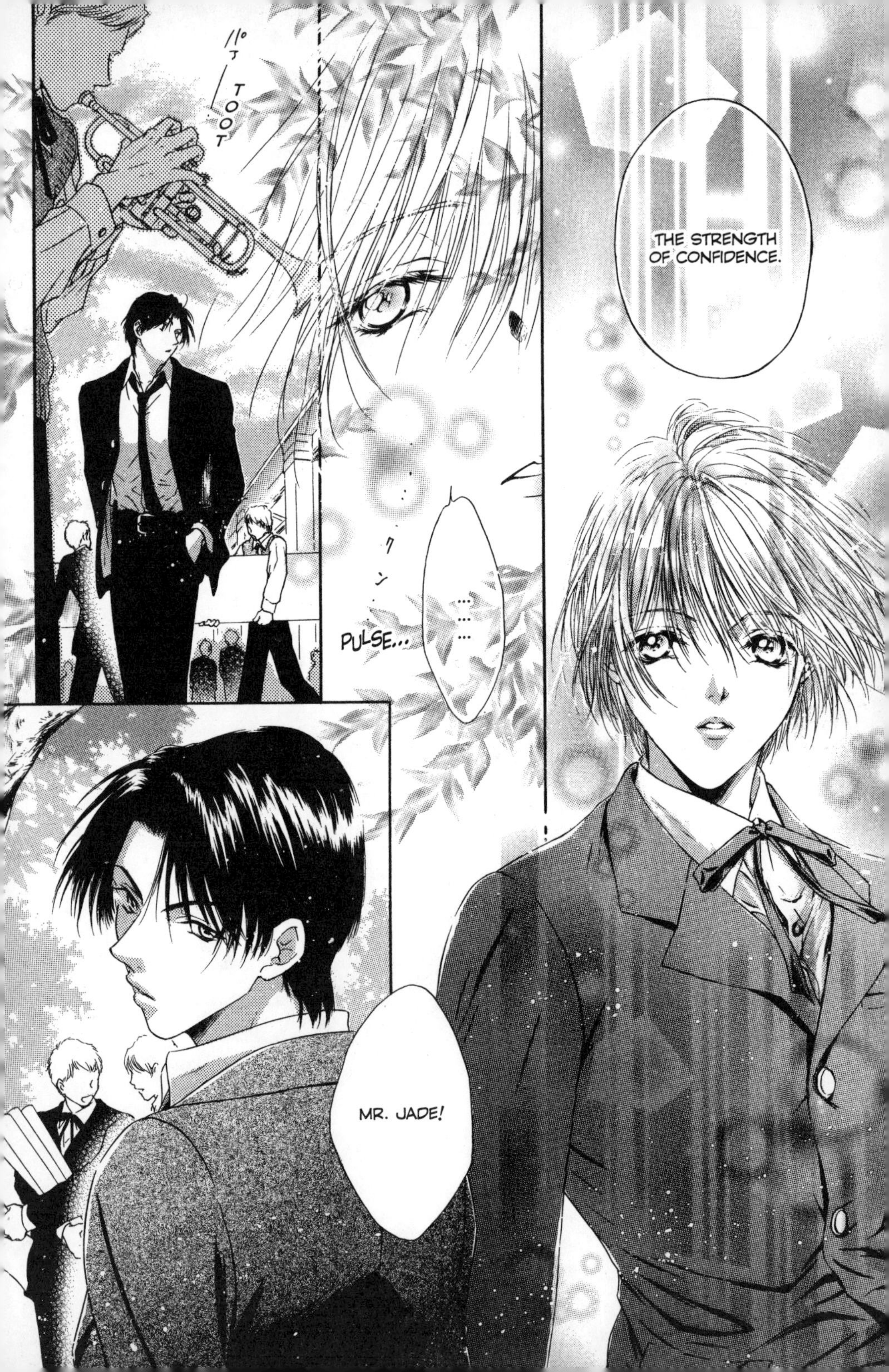
THE STRENGTH OF CONFIDENCE.
....
PULSE...
TOOT
MR. JADE!

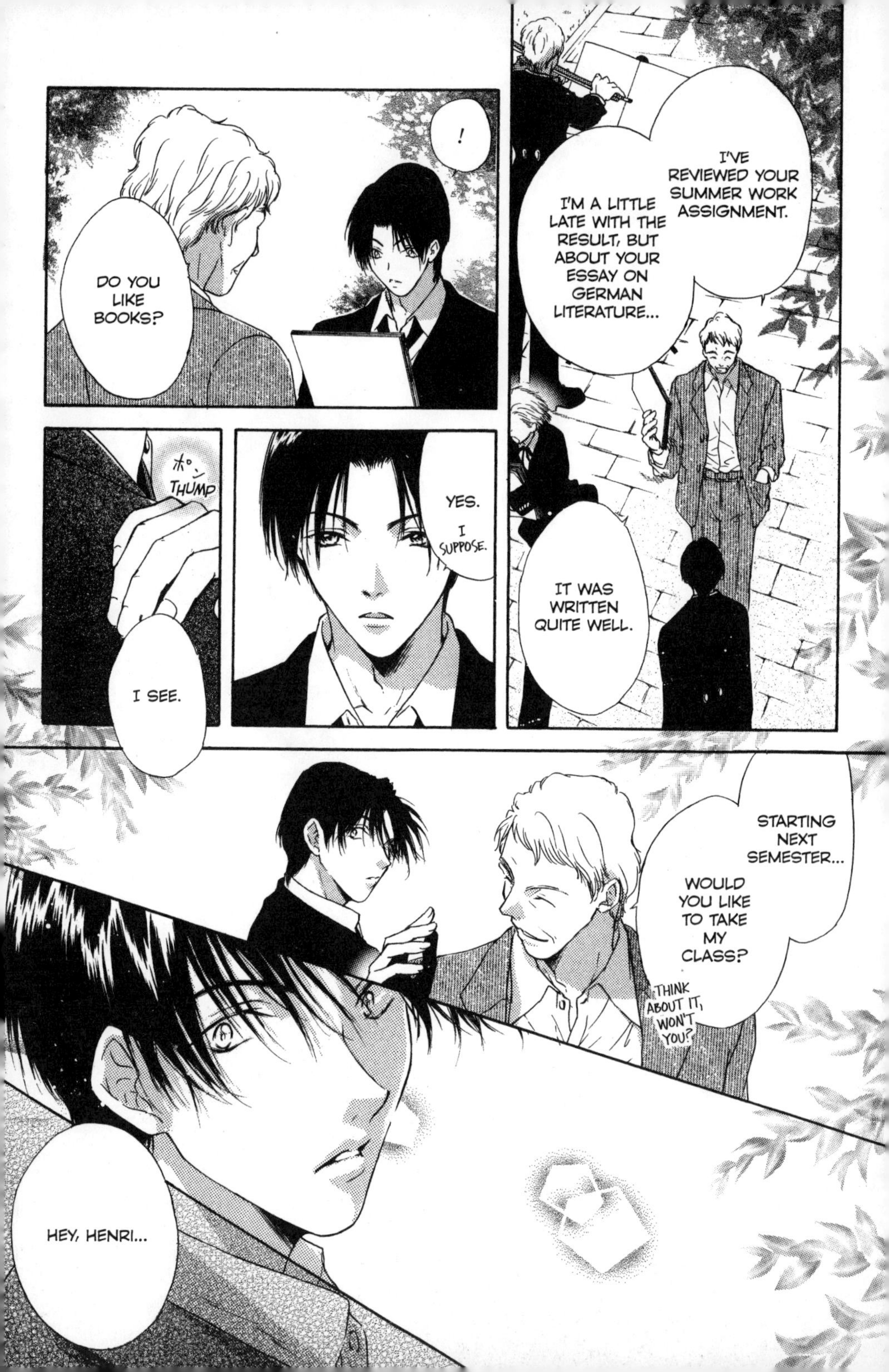
I'VE REVIEWED YOUR SUMMER WORK ASSIGNMENT.
I'M A LITTLE LATE WITH THE RESULT, BUT ABOUT YOUR ESSAY ON GERMAN LITERATURE...
IT WAS WRITTEN QUITE WELL.
!
DO YOU LIKE BOOKS?
YES.
I SUPPOSE.
ポン
THUMP
I SEE.
STARTING NEXT SEMESTER...
WOULD YOU LIKE TO TAKE MY CLASS?
THINK ABOUT IT, WON'T YOU?
HEY, HENRI...

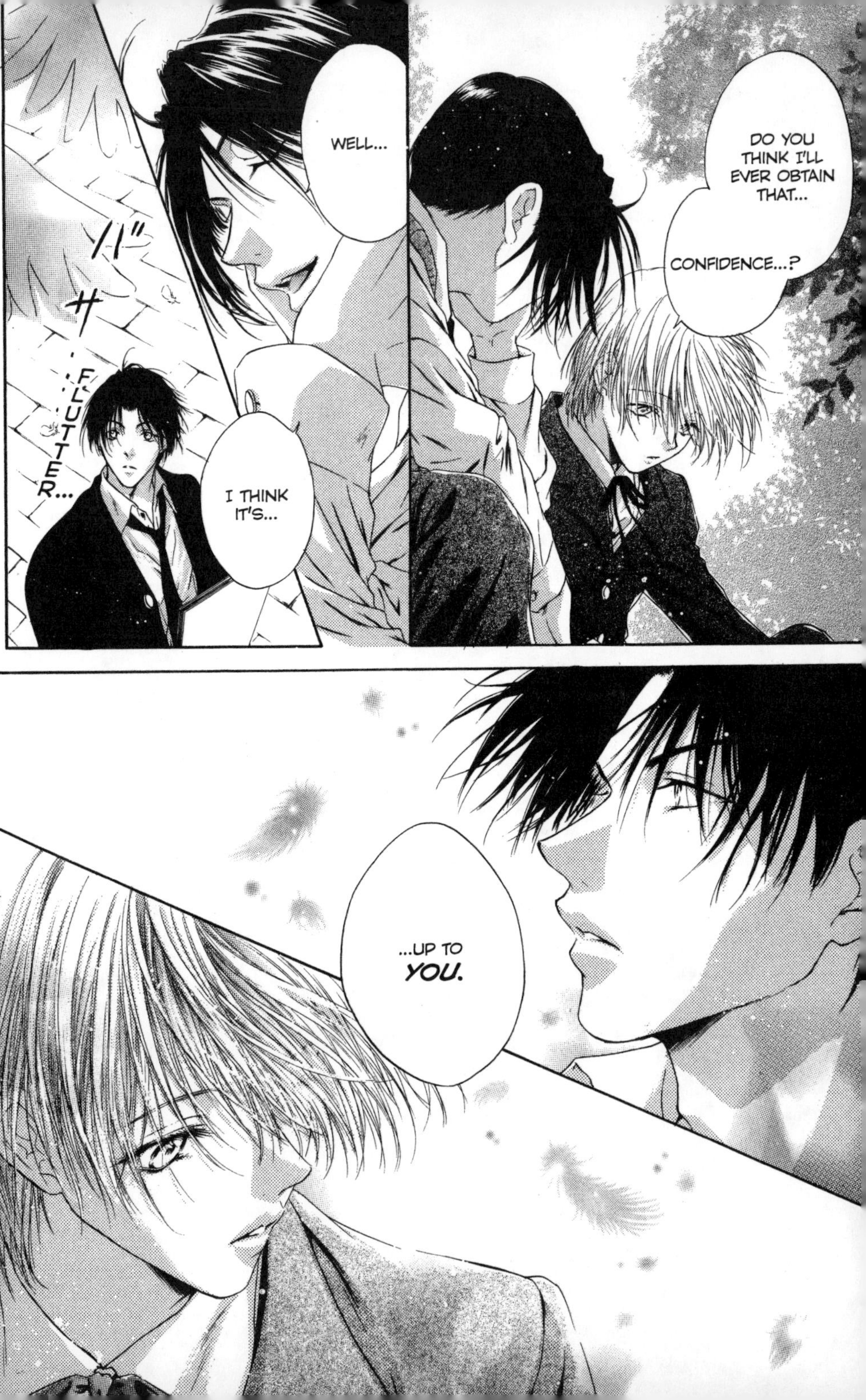
DO YOU THINK I'LL EVER OBTAIN THAT...
CONFIDENCE...?
WELL...
バサ・・
FLUTTER...
I THINK IT'S...
...UP TO *YOU.*

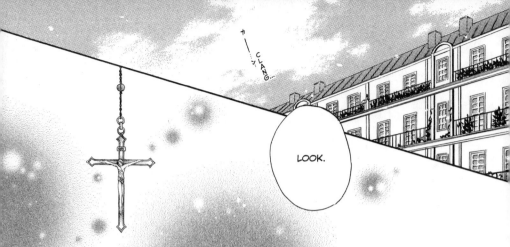

LOOK.

IT'S A PROTECTION OF-SORTS.

I'M SO GLAD.

YEAH.

YOU FOUND IT?

THE DAY AFTER TOMORROW IS THE MUSIC FESTIVAL.

TREAT IT WELL.

ARE YOU READY?

- I WILL.

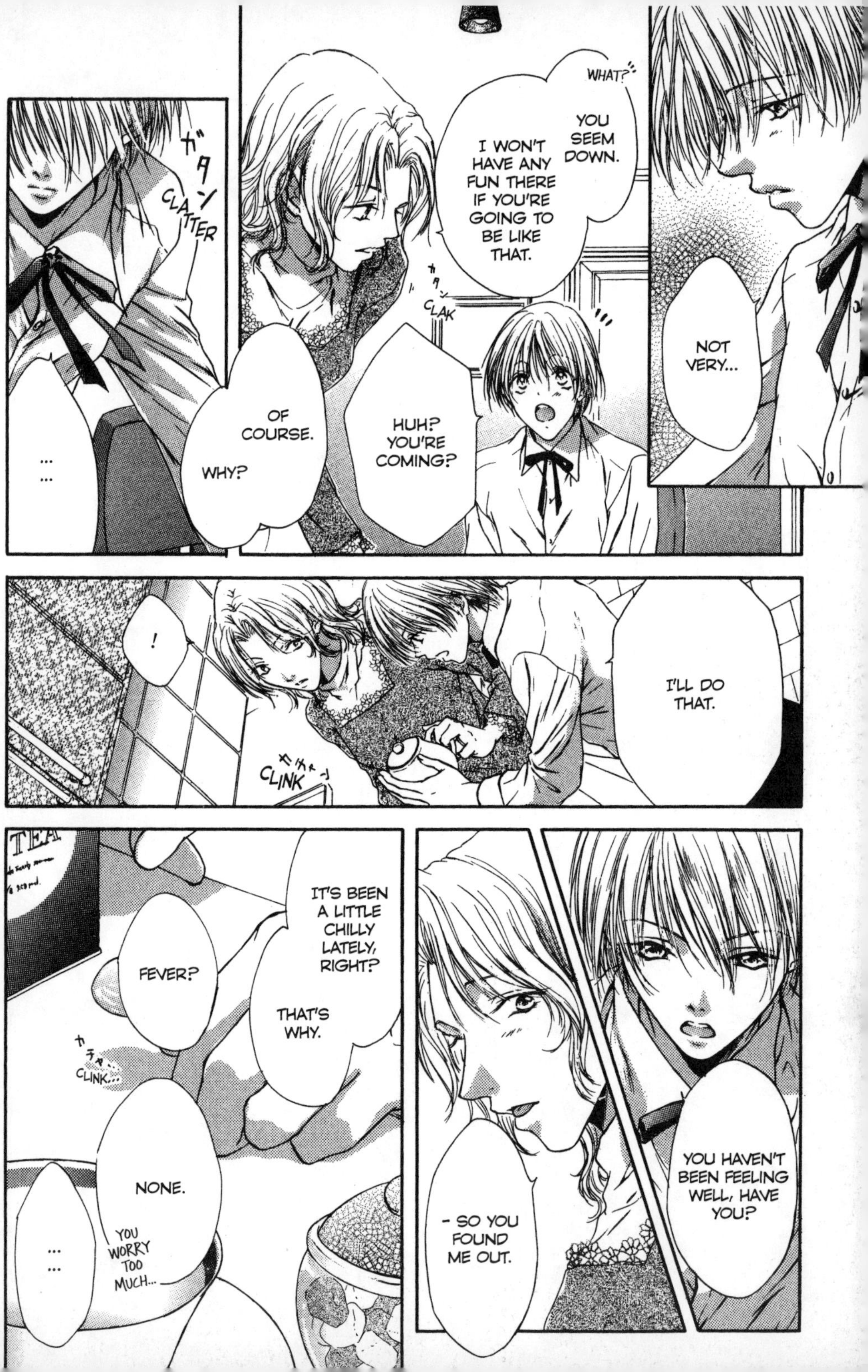
NOT VERY...
WHAT?
YOU SEEM DOWN.
I WON'T HAVE ANY FUN THERE IF YOU'RE GOING TO BE LIKE THAT.
CLAK
HUH? YOU'RE COMING?
OF COURSE.
WHY?
ガタン
CLATTER
... ...
I'LL DO THAT.
CLINK
!
YOU HAVEN'T BEEN FEELING WELL, HAVE YOU?
- SO YOU FOUND ME OUT.
IT'S BEEN A LITTLE CHILLY LATELY, RIGHT?
THAT'S WHY.
FEVER?
CLINK...
NONE.
YOU WORRY TOO MUCH...
... ...

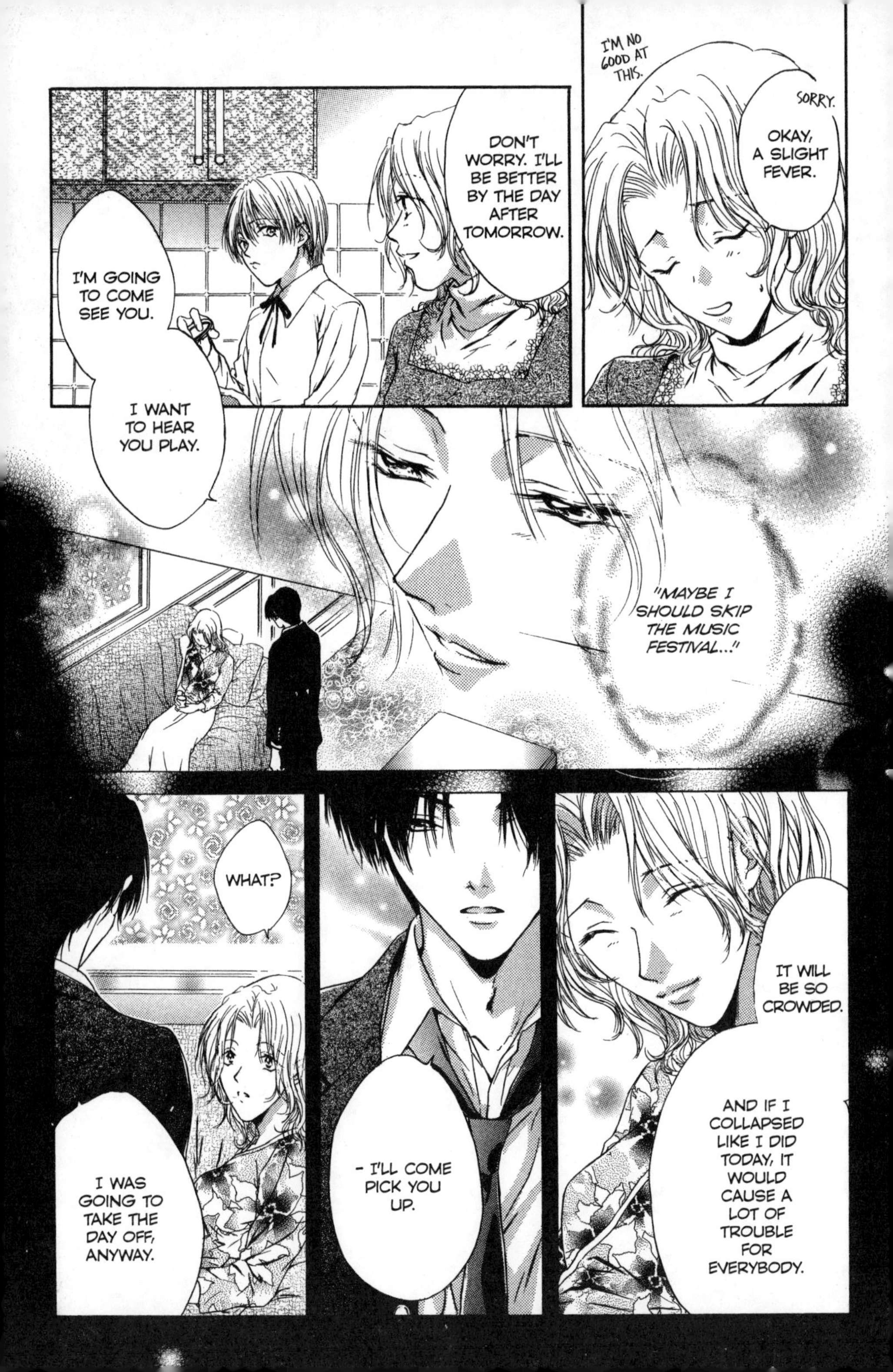
OKAY, A SLIGHT FEVER.
SORRY.
I'M NO GOOD AT THIS.
DON'T WORRY. I'LL BE BETTER BY THE DAY AFTER TOMORROW.
I'M GOING TO COME SEE YOU.
I WANT TO HEAR YOU PLAY.
"MAYBE I SHOULD SKIP THE MUSIC FESTIVAL..."
IT WILL BE SO CROWDED.
AND IF I COLLAPSED LIKE I DID TODAY, IT WOULD CAUSE A LOT OF TROUBLE FOR EVERYBODY.
- I'LL COME PICK YOU UP.
WHAT?
I WAS GOING TO TAKE THE DAY OFF, ANYWAY.

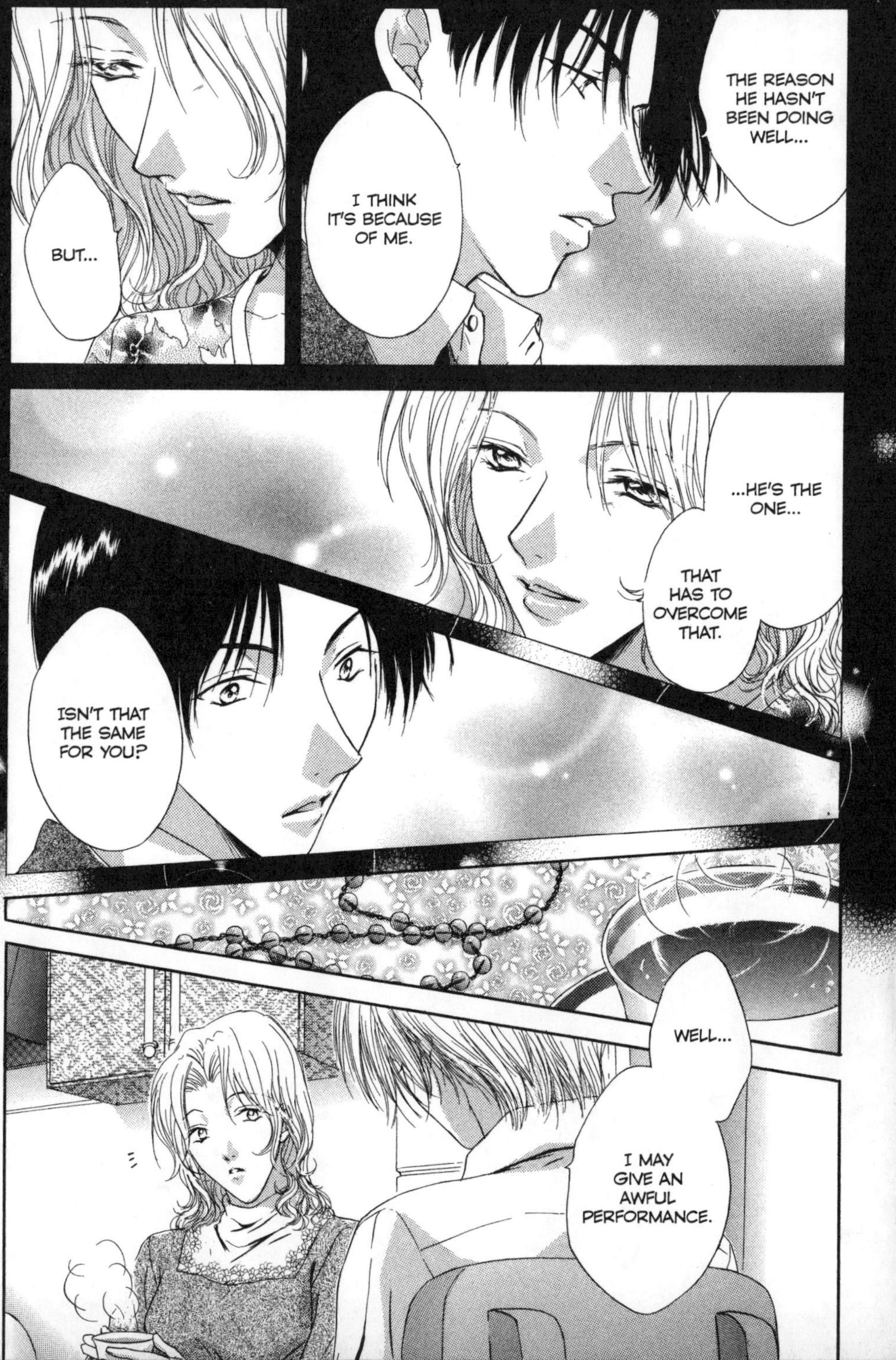
THE REASON HE HASN'T BEEN DOING WELL...
I THINK IT'S BECAUSE OF ME.
BUT...
...HE'S THE ONE...
THAT HAS TO OVERCOME THAT.
ISN'T THAT THE SAME FOR YOU?
WELL...
I MAY GIVE AN AWFUL PERFORMANCE.

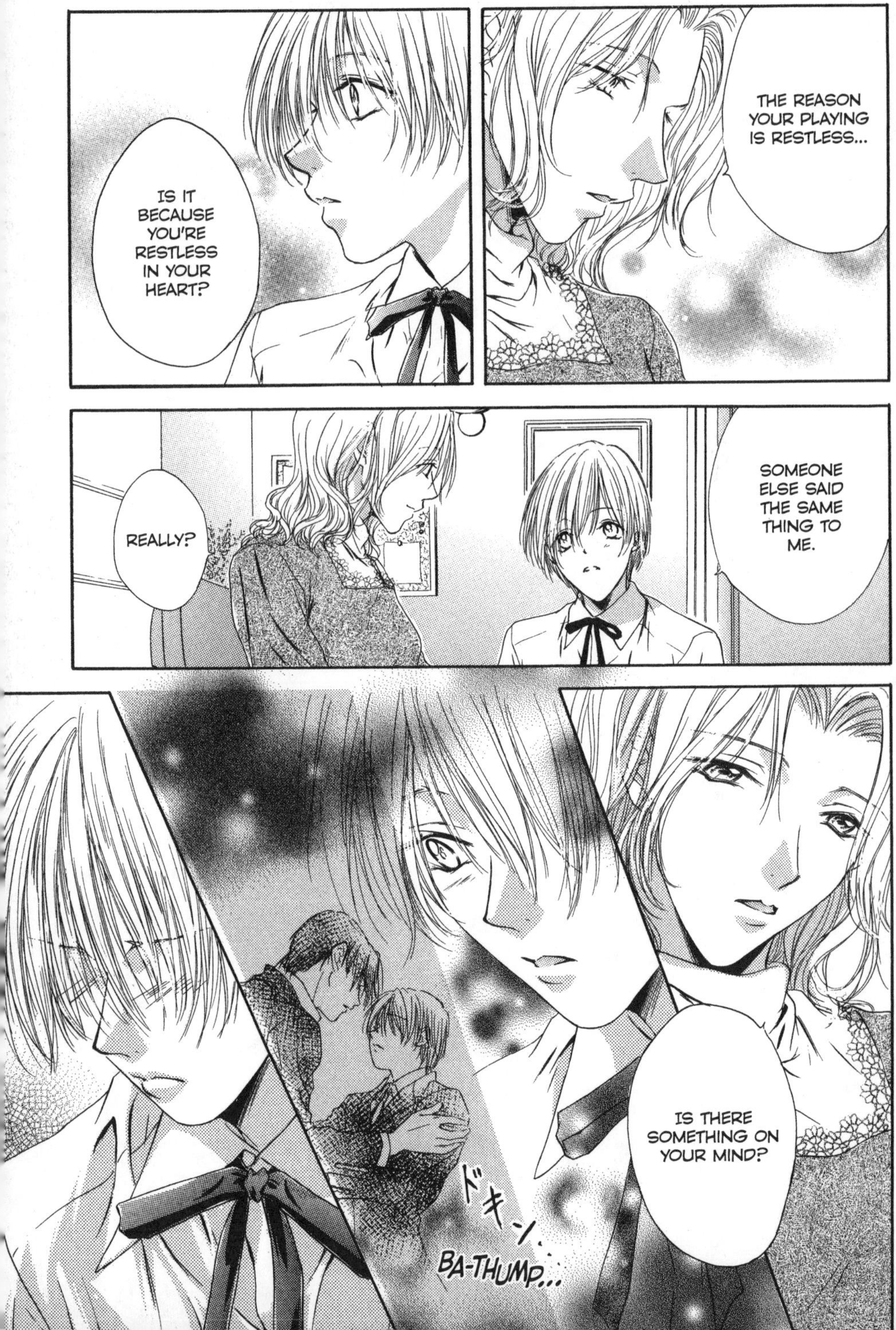
THE REASON YOUR PLAYING IS RESTLESS...
IS IT BECAUSE YOU'RE RESTLESS IN YOUR HEART?
SOMEONE ELSE SAID THE SAME THING TO ME.
REALLY?
IS THERE SOMETHING ON YOUR MIND?
ドキン…
BA-THUMP...

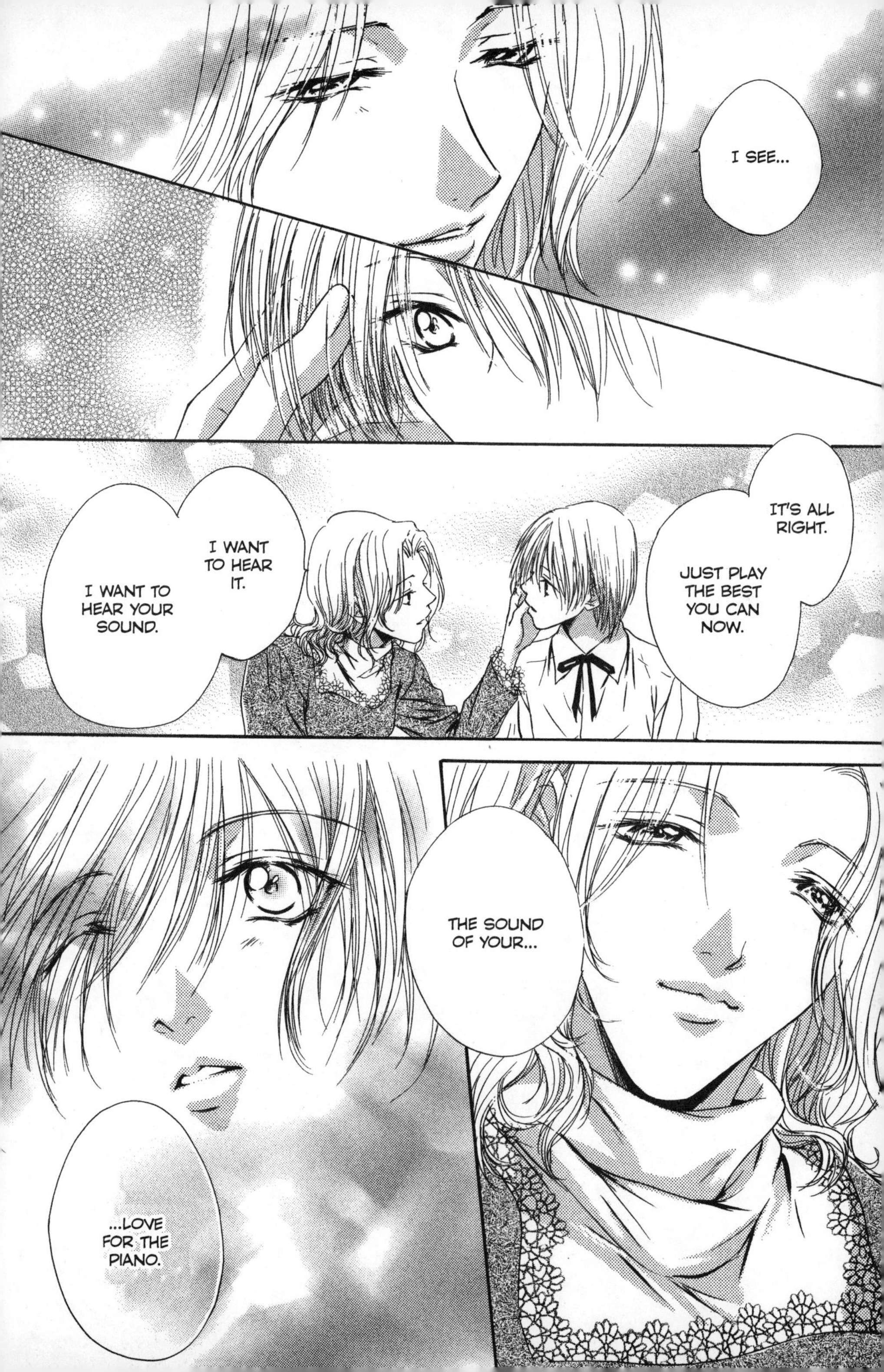
I SEE...
IT'S ALL RIGHT.
JUST PLAY THE BEST YOU CAN NOW.
I WANT TO HEAR IT.
I WANT TO HEAR YOUR SOUND.
THE SOUND OF YOUR...
...LOVE FOR THE PIANO.

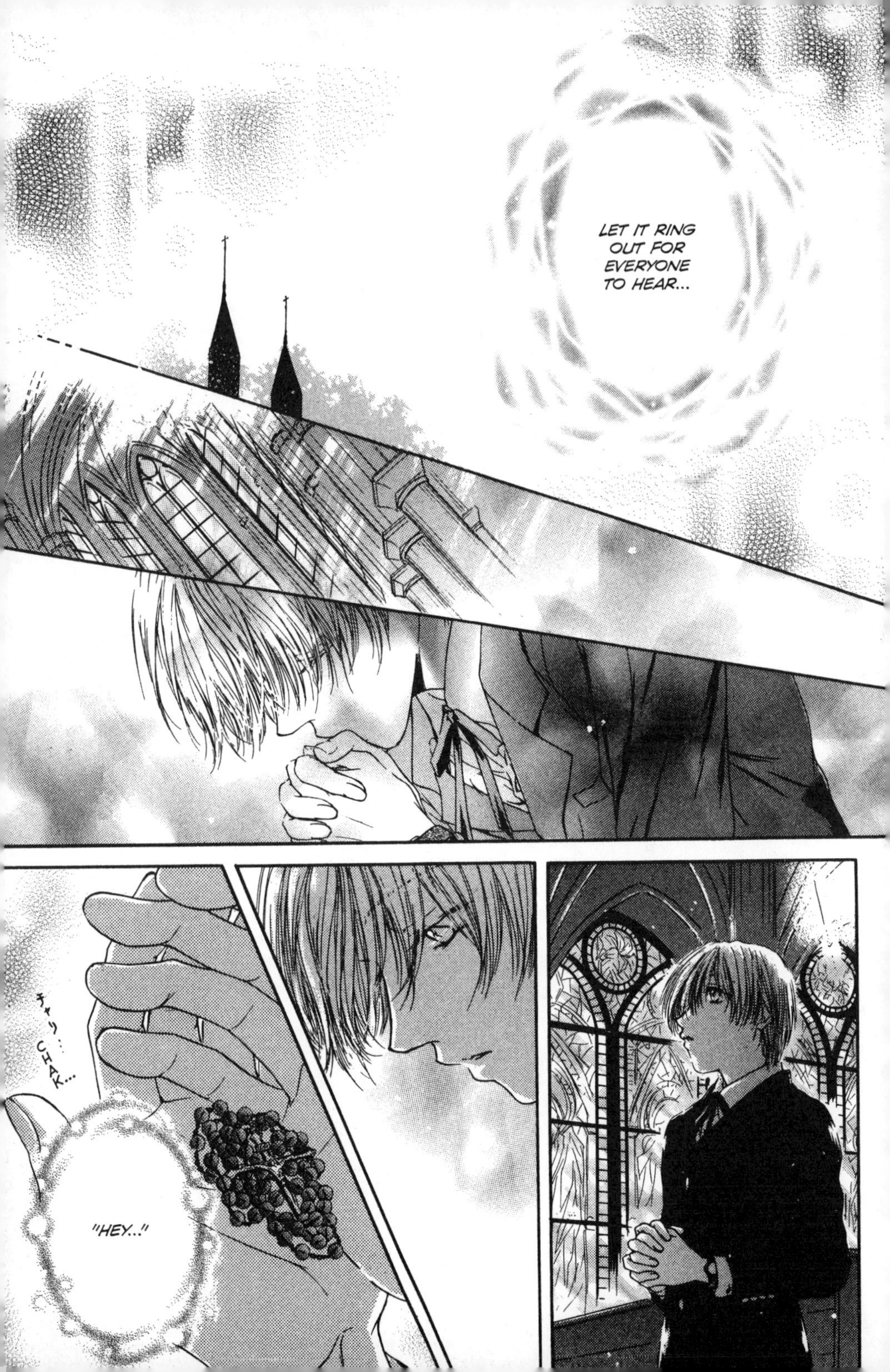
LET IT RING OUT FOR EVERYONE TO HEAR...
チャリ…
CHAK...
"HEY..."

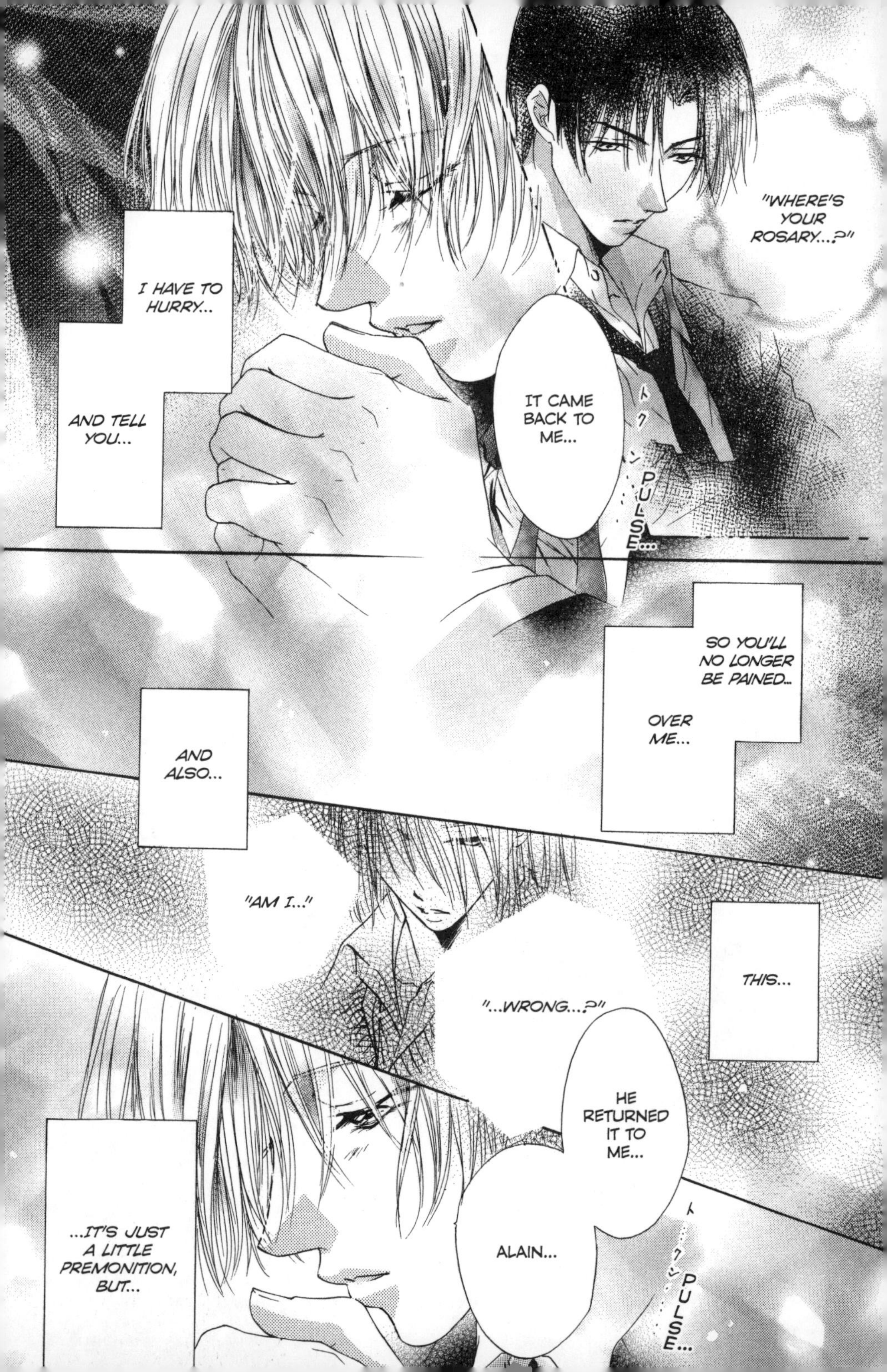
"WHERE'S YOUR ROSARY...?"
IT CAME BACK TO ME...
PULSE...
I HAVE TO HURRY...
AND TELL YOU...
SO YOU'LL NO LONGER BE PAINED...
OVER ME...
AND ALSO...
THIS...
"AM I..."
"...WRONG...?"
HE RETURNED IT TO ME...
ALAIN...
PULSE...
...IT'S JUST A LITTLE PREMONITION, BUT...

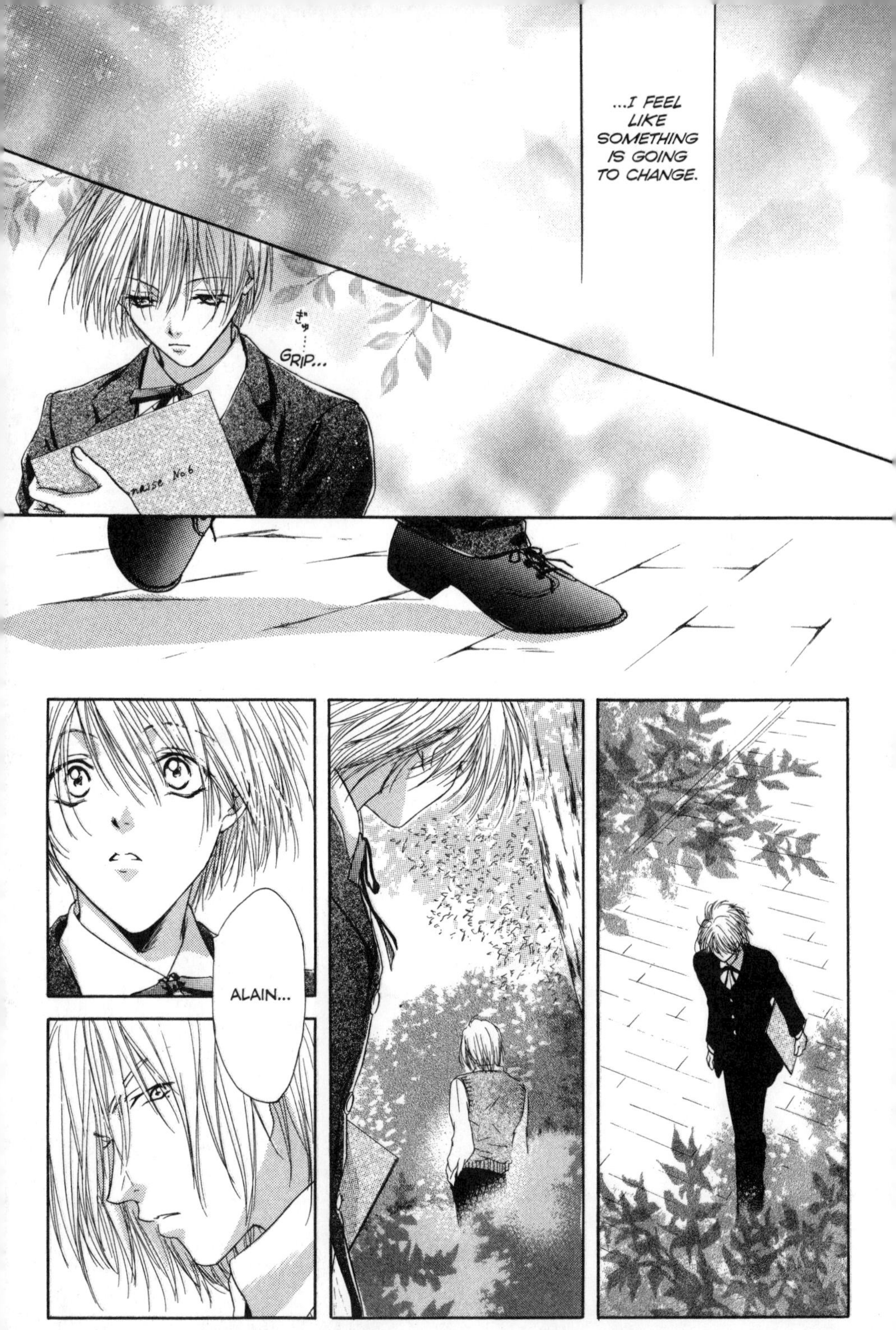
...I FEEL LIKE SOMETHING IS GOING TO CHANGE.
GRIP...
ALAIN...

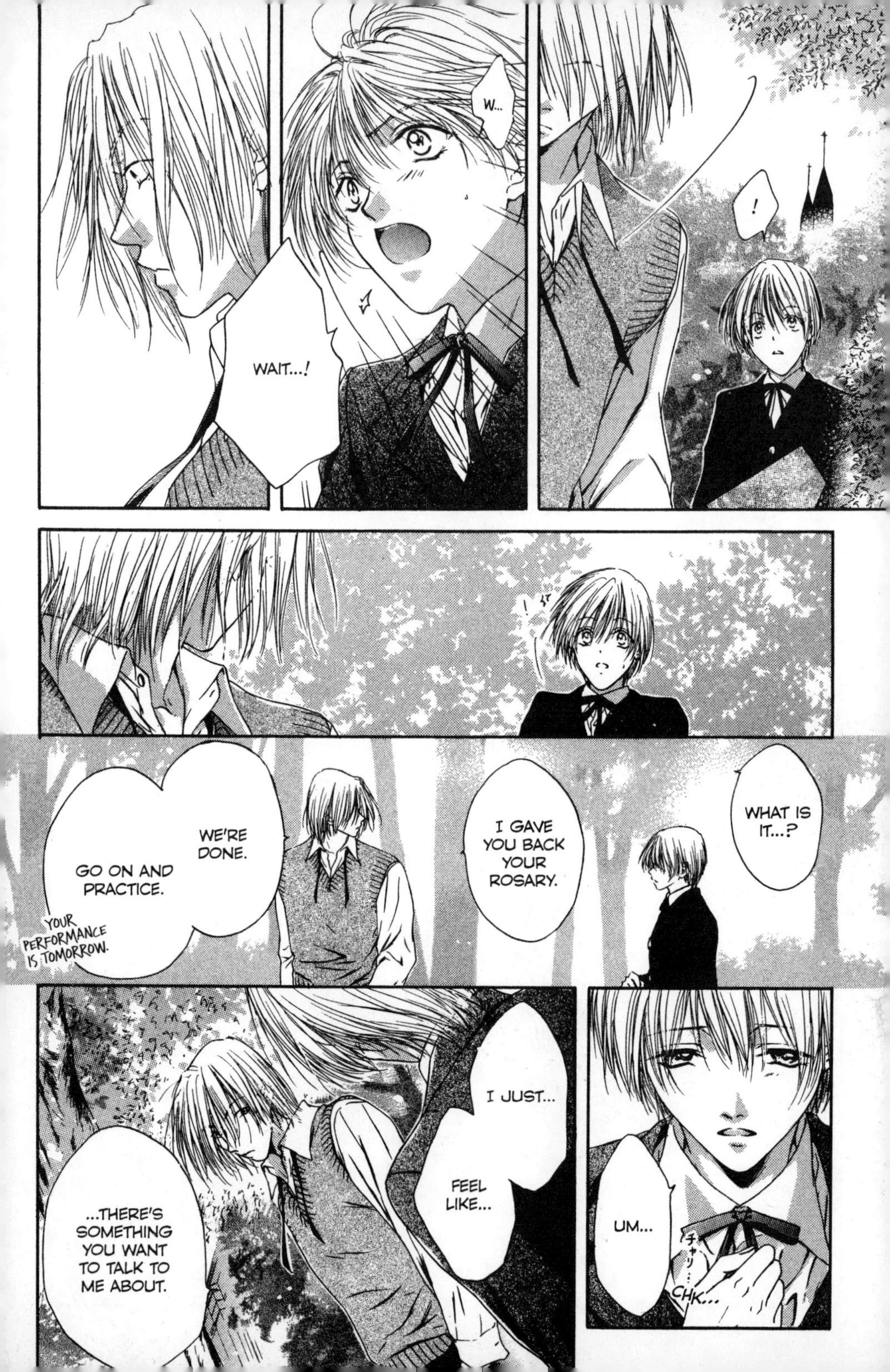
!
W...
WAIT...!
WHAT IS IT...?
I GAVE YOU BACK YOUR ROSARY.
WE'RE DONE.
GO ON AND PRACTICE.
YOUR PERFORMANCE IS TOMORROW.
UM...
チャリ…
CHK...
I JUST...
FEEL LIKE...
...THERE'S SOMETHING YOU WANT TO TALK TO ME ABOUT.

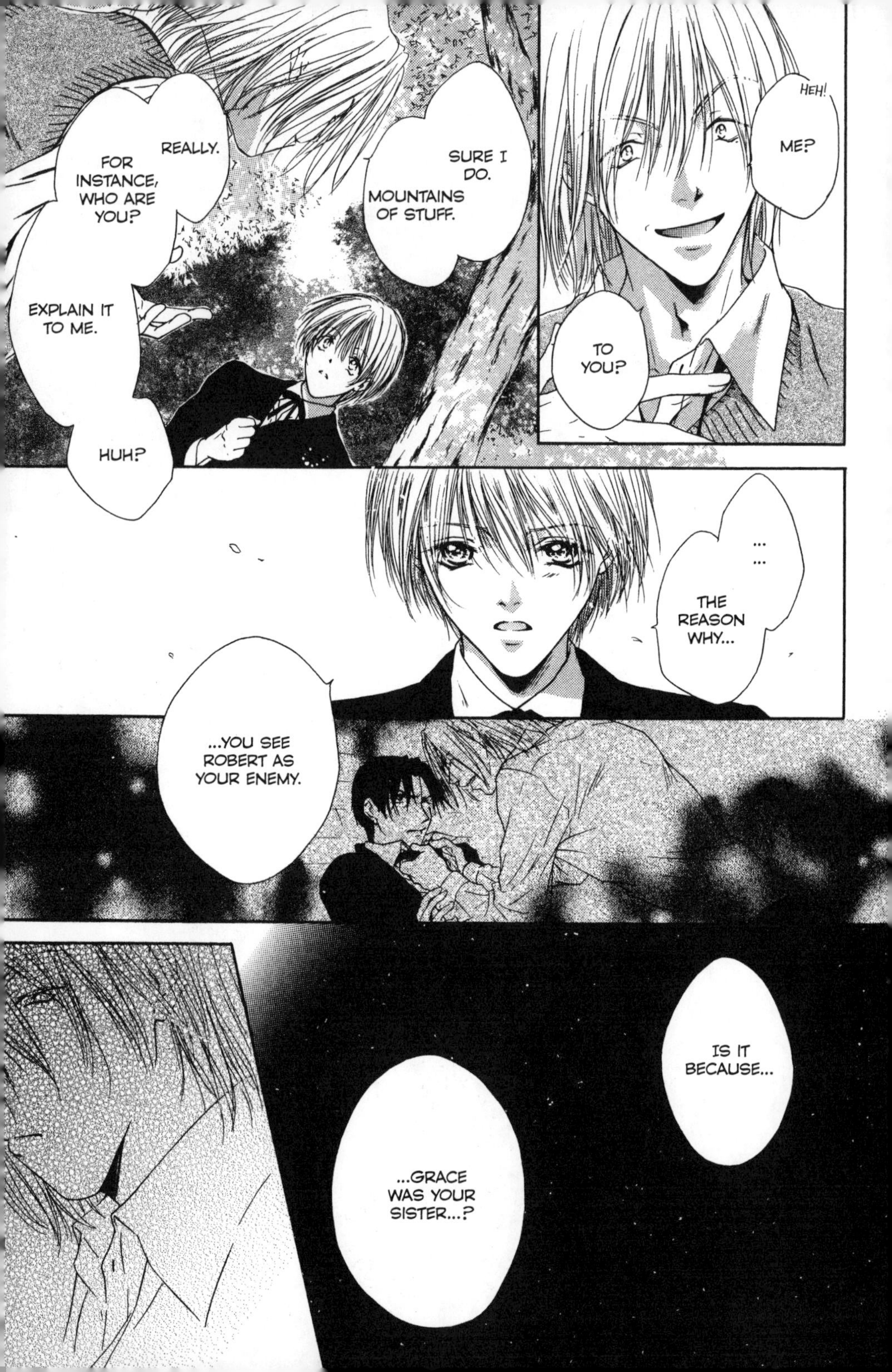
HEH!
ME?
TO YOU?
SURE I DO.
MOUNTAINS OF STUFF.
REALLY.
FOR INSTANCE, WHO ARE YOU?
EXPLAIN IT TO ME.
HUH?
...
...
THE REASON WHY...
...YOU SEE ROBERT AS YOUR ENEMY.
IS IT BECAUSE...
...GRACE WAS YOUR SISTER...?

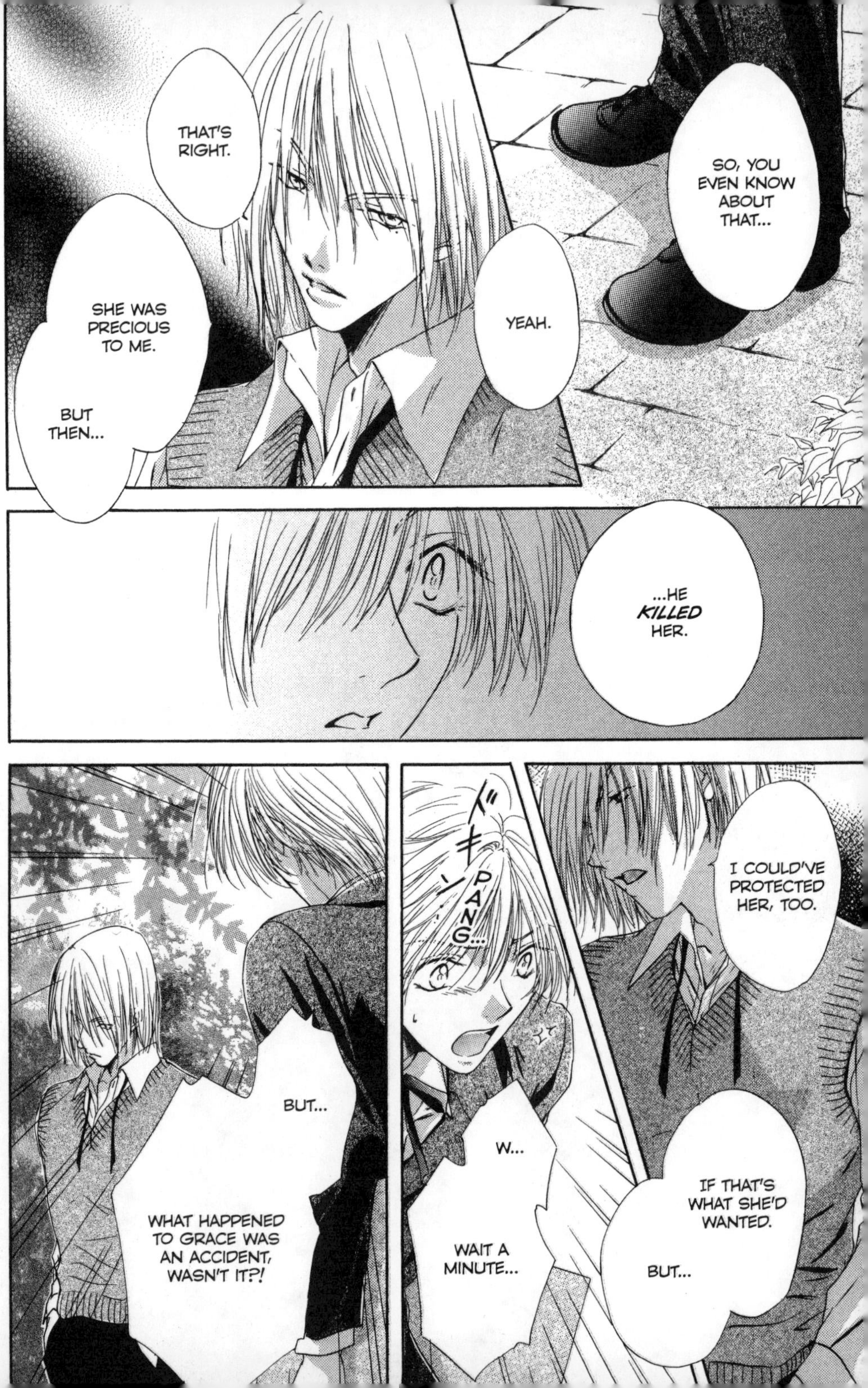
SO, YOU EVEN KNOW ABOUT THAT...
YEAH.
THAT'S RIGHT.
SHE WAS PRECIOUS TO ME.
BUT THEN...
...HE *KILLED* HER.
I COULD'VE PROTECTED HER, TOO.
ドキン
PANG...
IF THAT'S WHAT SHE'D WANTED.
BUT...
W...
WAIT A MINUTE...
BUT...
WHAT HAPPENED TO GRACE WAS AN ACCIDENT, WASN'T IT?!

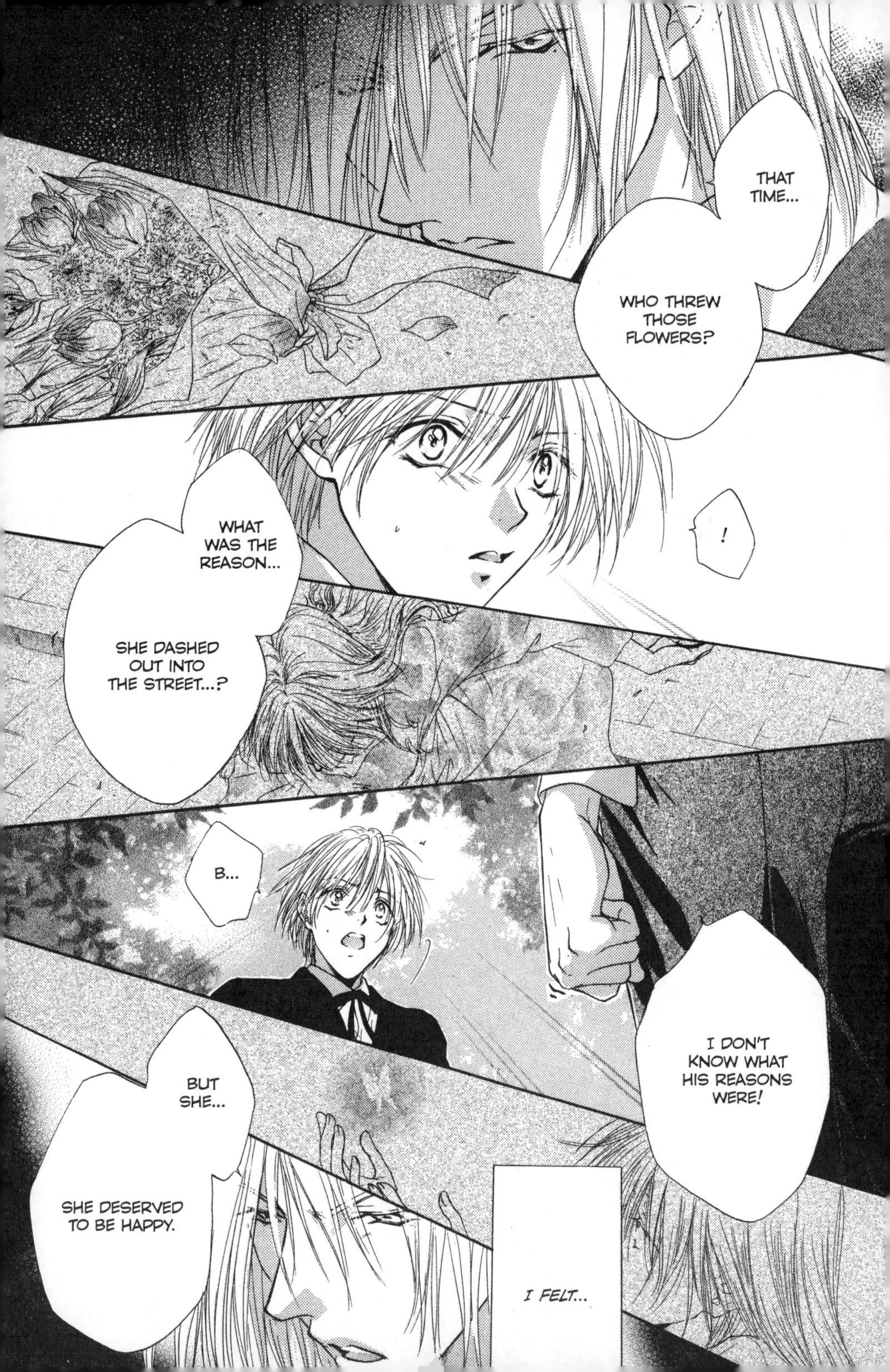
THAT TIME...
WHO THREW THOSE FLOWERS?
!
WHAT WAS THE REASON...
SHE DASHED OUT INTO THE STREET...?
B...
I DON'T KNOW WHAT HIS REASONS WERE!
BUT SHE...
SHE DESERVED TO BE HAPPY.
I FELT...

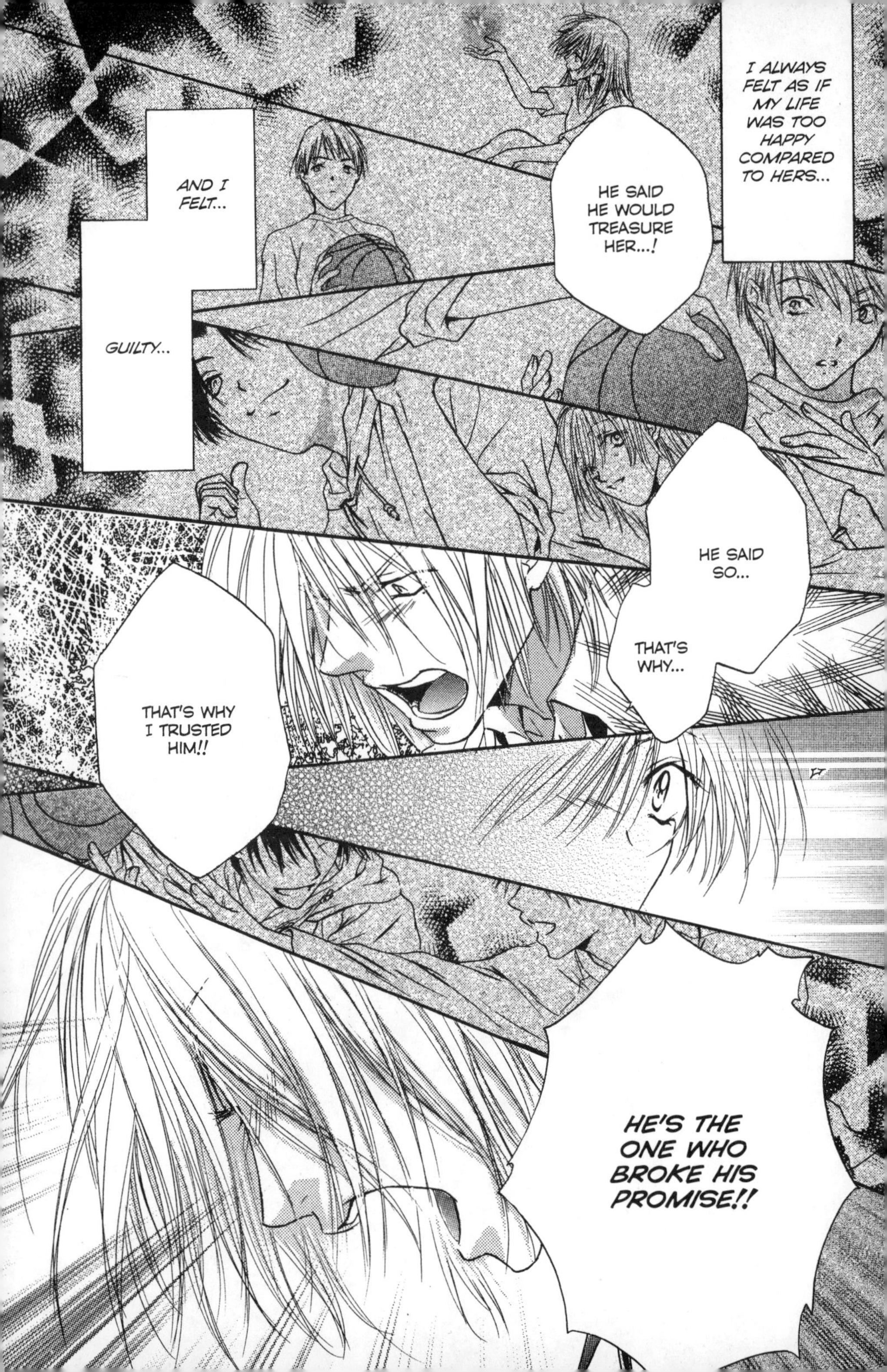
I ALWAYS FELT AS IF MY LIFE WAS TOO HAPPY COMPARED TO HERS...
HE SAID HE WOULD TREASURE HER...!
AND I FELT...
GUILTY...
HE SAID SO...
THAT'S WHY...
THAT'S WHY I TRUSTED HIM!!
HE'S THE ONE WHO BROKE HIS PROMISE!!

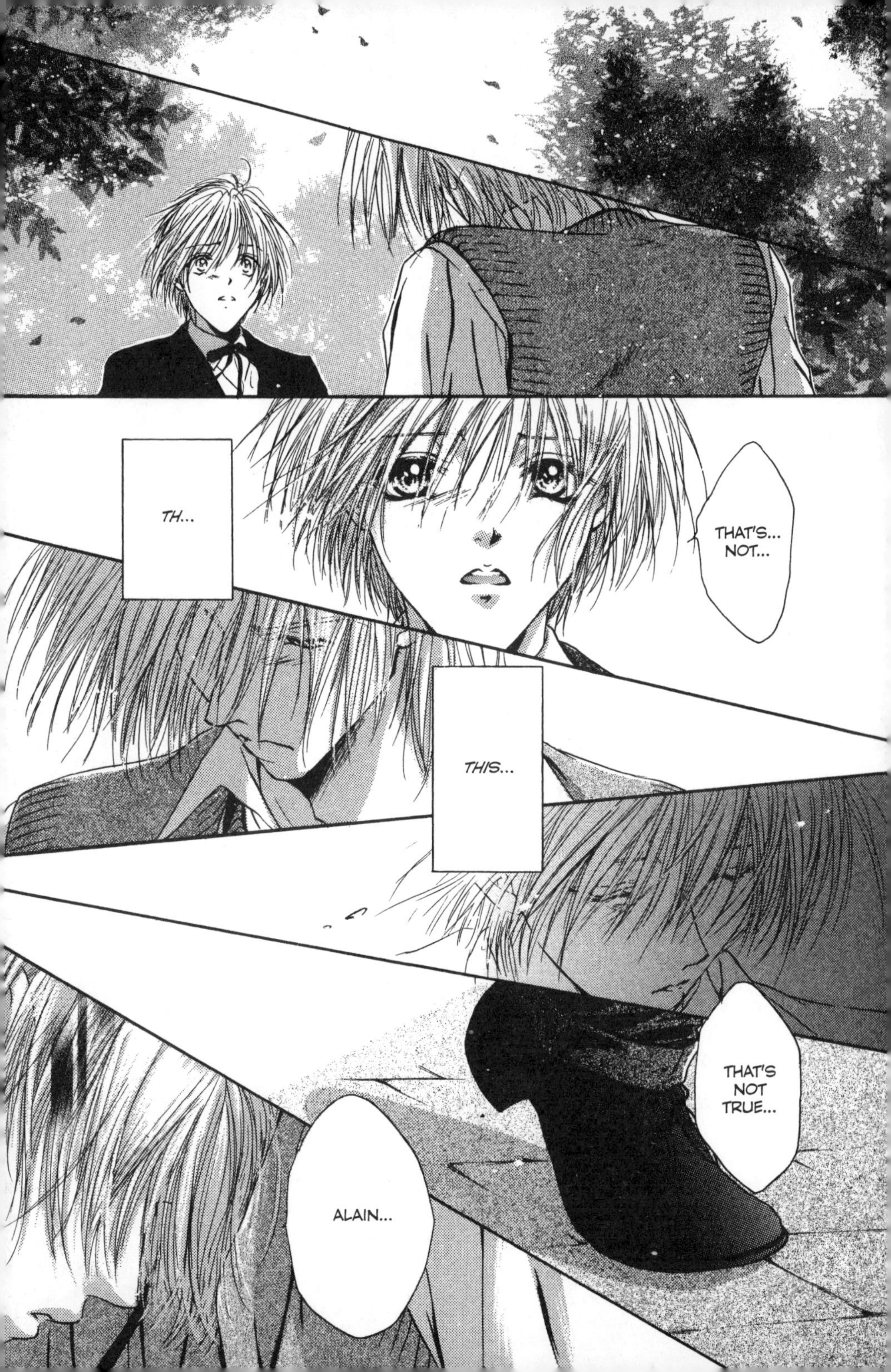
THAT'S... NOT...
TH...
THIS...
THAT'S NOT TRUE...
ALAIN...

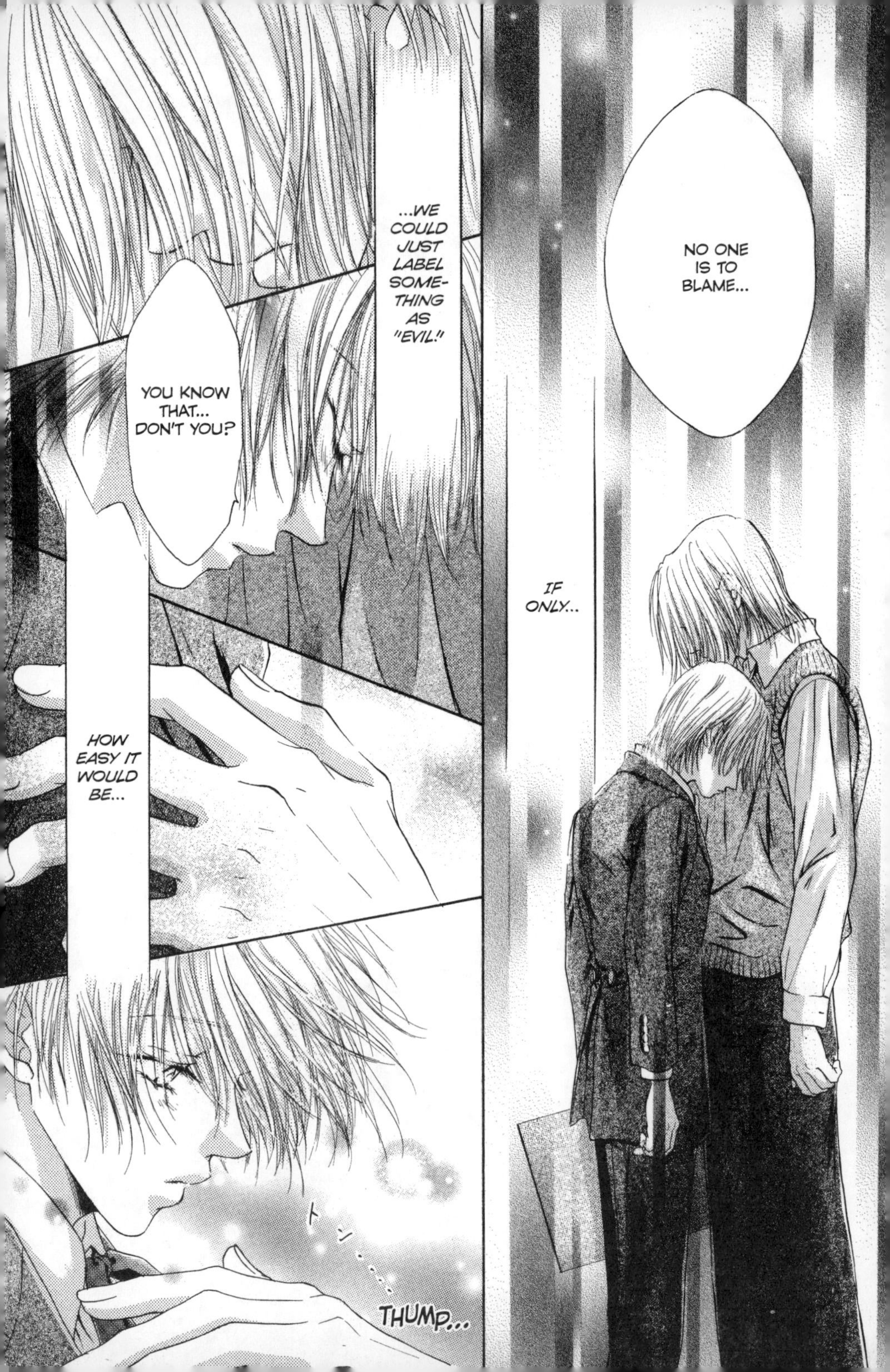
NO ONE IS TO BLAME...
IF ONLY...
...WE COULD JUST LABEL SOME-THING AS "EVIL."
YOU KNOW THAT... DON'T YOU?
HOW EASY IT WOULD BE...
トン…
THUMP...

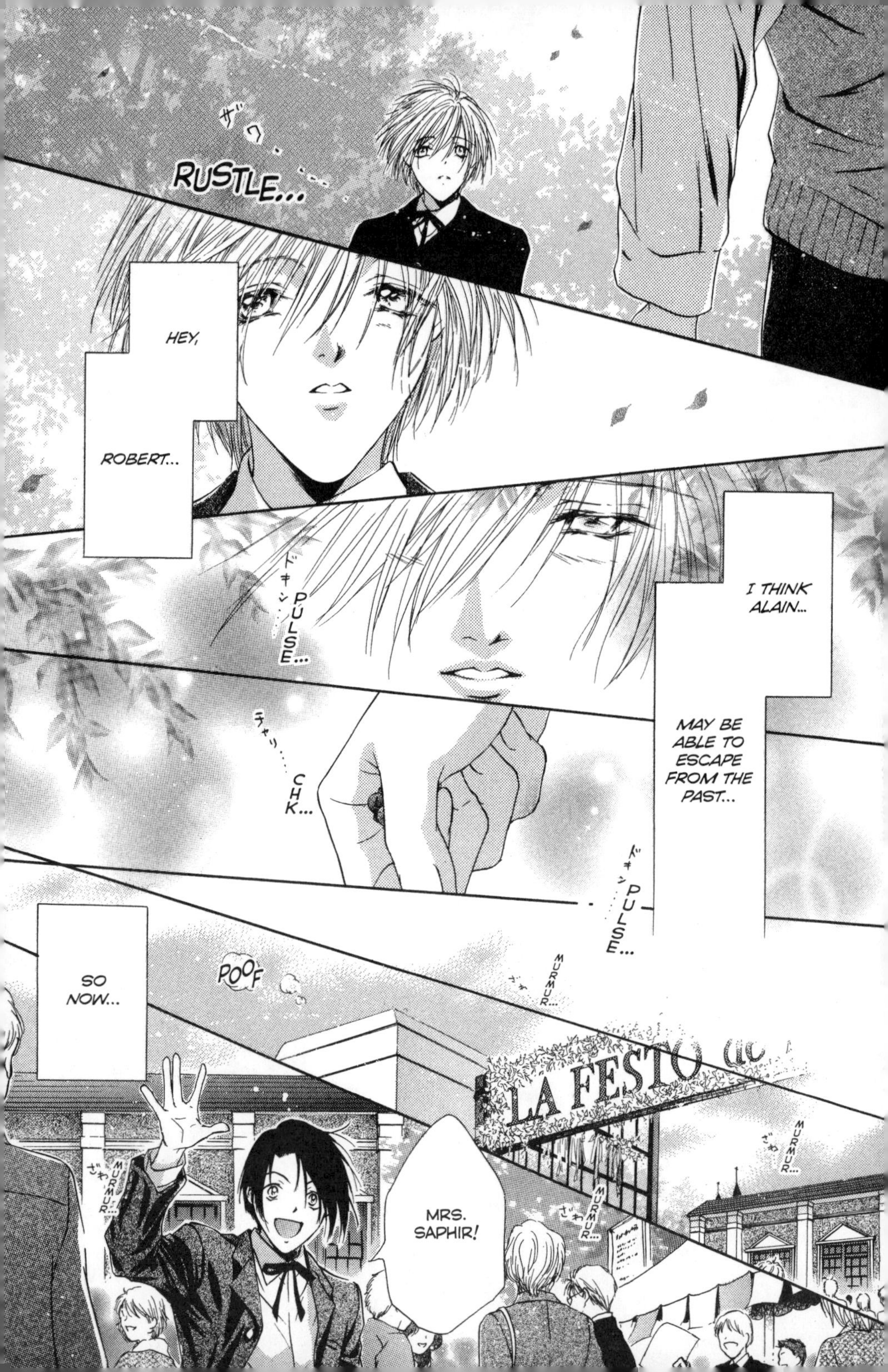

ザワ...
RUSTLE...
HEY,
ROBERT...
I THINK ALAIN...
ドキン
PULSE...
MAY BE ABLE TO ESCAPE FROM THE PAST...
ドキン
PULSE...
チャリ...
CHK...
ざわ
MURMUR...
POOF
SO NOW...
LA FESTO
ざわ
MURMUR...
ざわ
MURMUR...
MRS. SAPHIR!
ざわ
MURMUR...

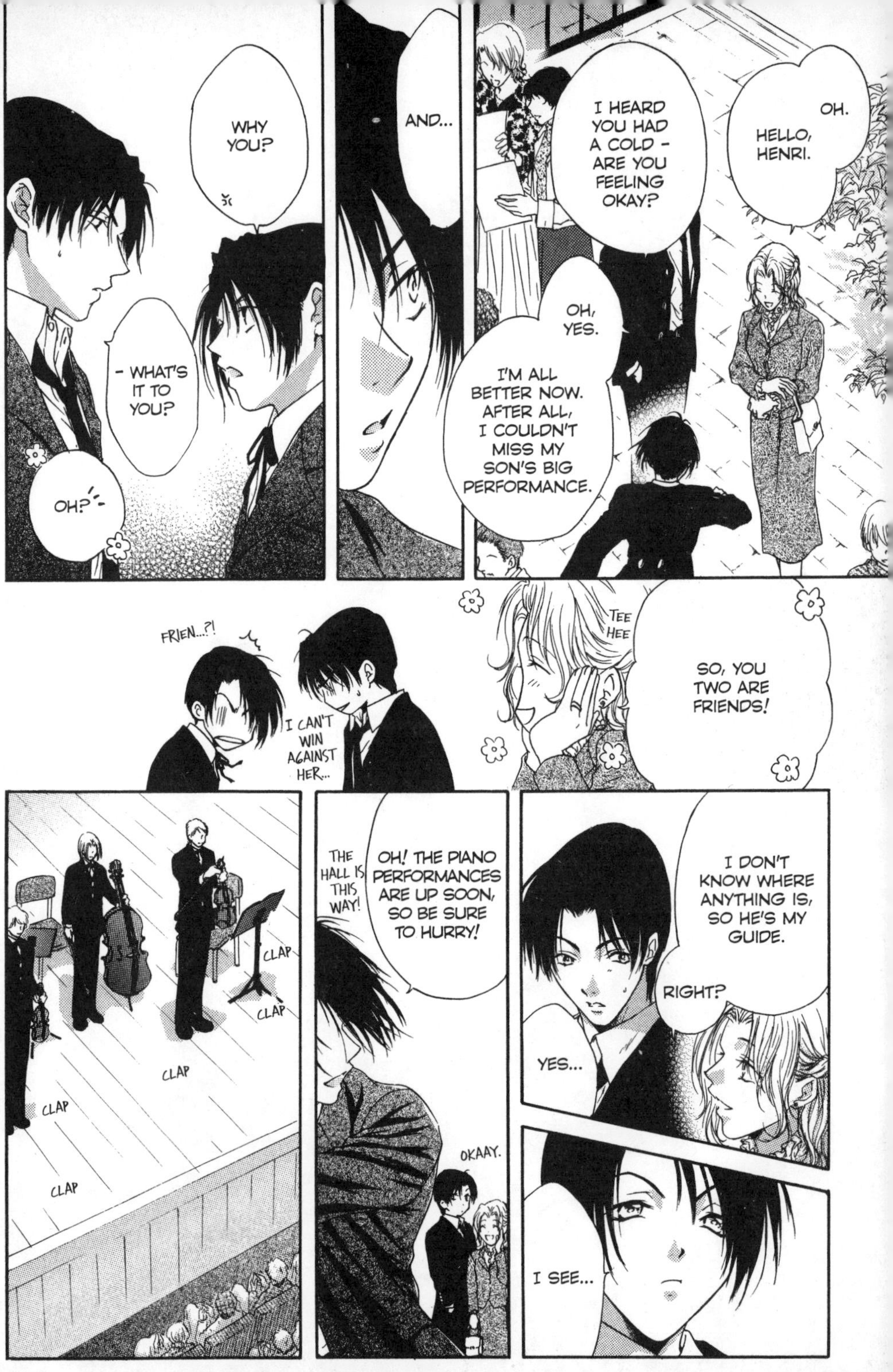
OH.
HELLO, HENRI.
I HEARD YOU HAD A COLD - ARE YOU FEELING OKAY?
OH, YES.
I'M ALL BETTER NOW. AFTER ALL, I COULDN'T MISS MY SON'S BIG PERFORMANCE.
AND...
WHY YOU?
- WHAT'S IT TO YOU?
OH?
TEE HEE
SO, YOU TWO ARE FRIENDS!
FRIEN...?!
I CAN'T WIN AGAINST HER...
I DON'T KNOW WHERE ANYTHING IS, SO HE'S MY GUIDE.
RIGHT?
YES...
I SEE...
OH! THE PIANO PERFORMANCES ARE UP SOON, SO BE SURE TO HURRY!
THE HALL IS THIS WAY!
OKAAY.
CLAP
CLAP
CLAP
CLAP
CLAP

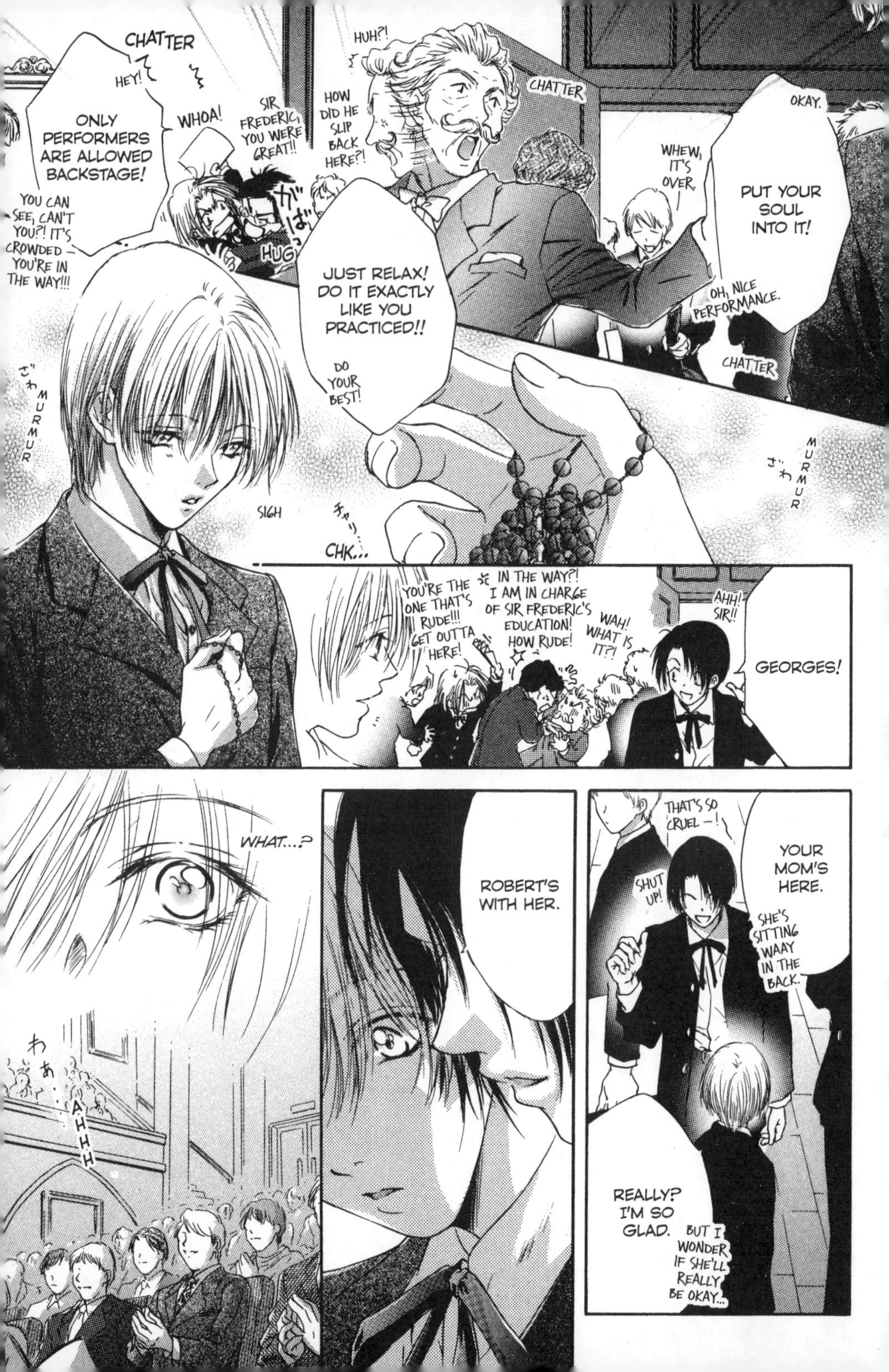
OKAY.
PUT YOUR SOUL INTO IT!
WHEW, IT'S OVER.
CHATTER
HUH?!
HOW DID HE SLIP BACK HERE?!
SIR FREDERIC, YOU WERE GREAT!!
HUG
WHOA!
CHATTER
HEY!
ONLY PERFORMERS ARE ALLOWED BACKSTAGE!
YOU CAN SEE, CAN'T YOU?! IT'S CROWDED — YOU'RE IN THE WAY!!!
OH, NICE PERFORMANCE.
CHATTER
JUST RELAX! DO IT EXACTLY LIKE YOU PRACTICED!!
DO YOUR BEST!
ざわ MURMUR
チャリ… CHK...
SIGH
ざわ MURMUR
AHH! SIR!!
GEORGES!
WAH! WHAT IS IT?!
IN THE WAY?! I AM IN CHARGE OF SIR FREDERIC'S EDUCATION! HOW RUDE!
YOU'RE THE ONE THAT'S RUDE!!! GET OUTTA HERE!
THAT'S SO CRUEL —!
YOUR MOM'S HERE.
SHUT UP!
SHE'S SITTING WAAY IN THE BACK.
REALLY? I'M SO GLAD.
BUT I WONDER IF SHE'LL REALLY BE OKAY...
ROBERT'S WITH HER.
WHAT...?
わあ… AHHH

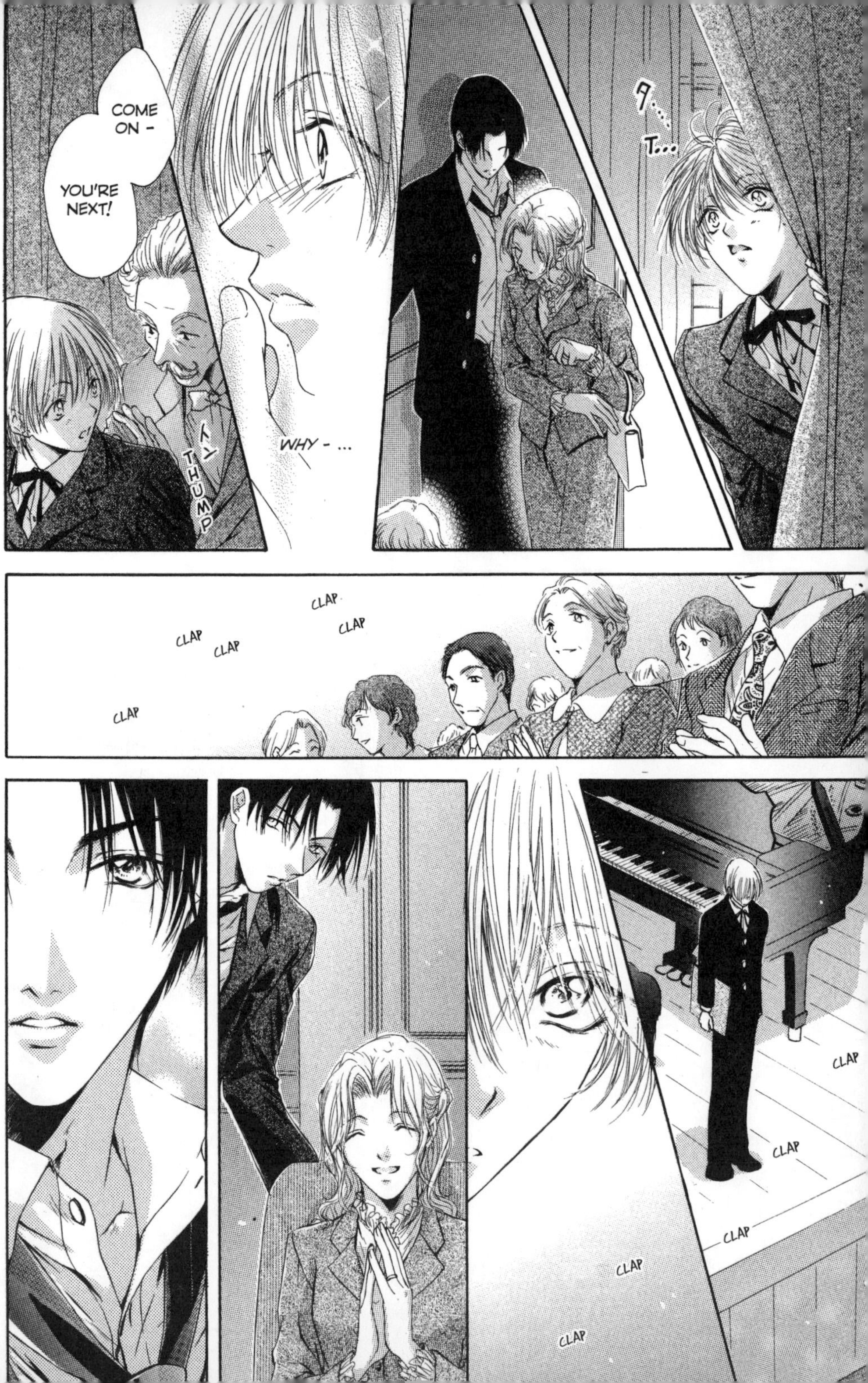

T...
WHY - ...
COME ON -
YOU'RE NEXT!
THUMP
CLAP
CLAP
CLAP
CLAP
CLAP
CLAP
CLAP
CLAP
CLAP
CLAP

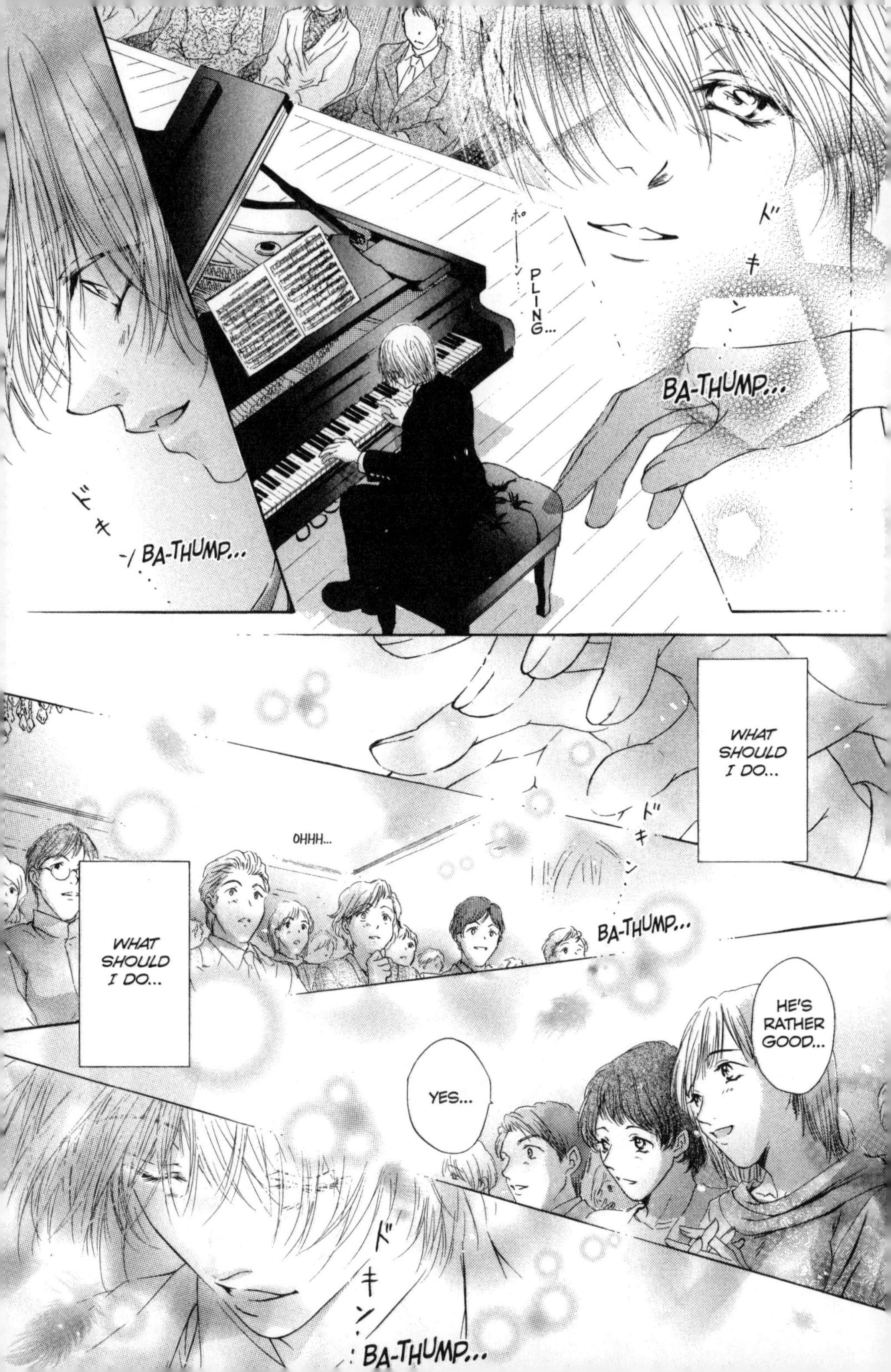

ドキン…
BA-THUMP...
ポーン…
PLING...
ドキ…
BA-THUMP...
WHAT SHOULD I DO...
ドキン…
BA-THUMP...
OHHH...
WHAT SHOULD I DO...
HE'S RATHER GOOD...
YES...
ドキン…
BA-THUMP...

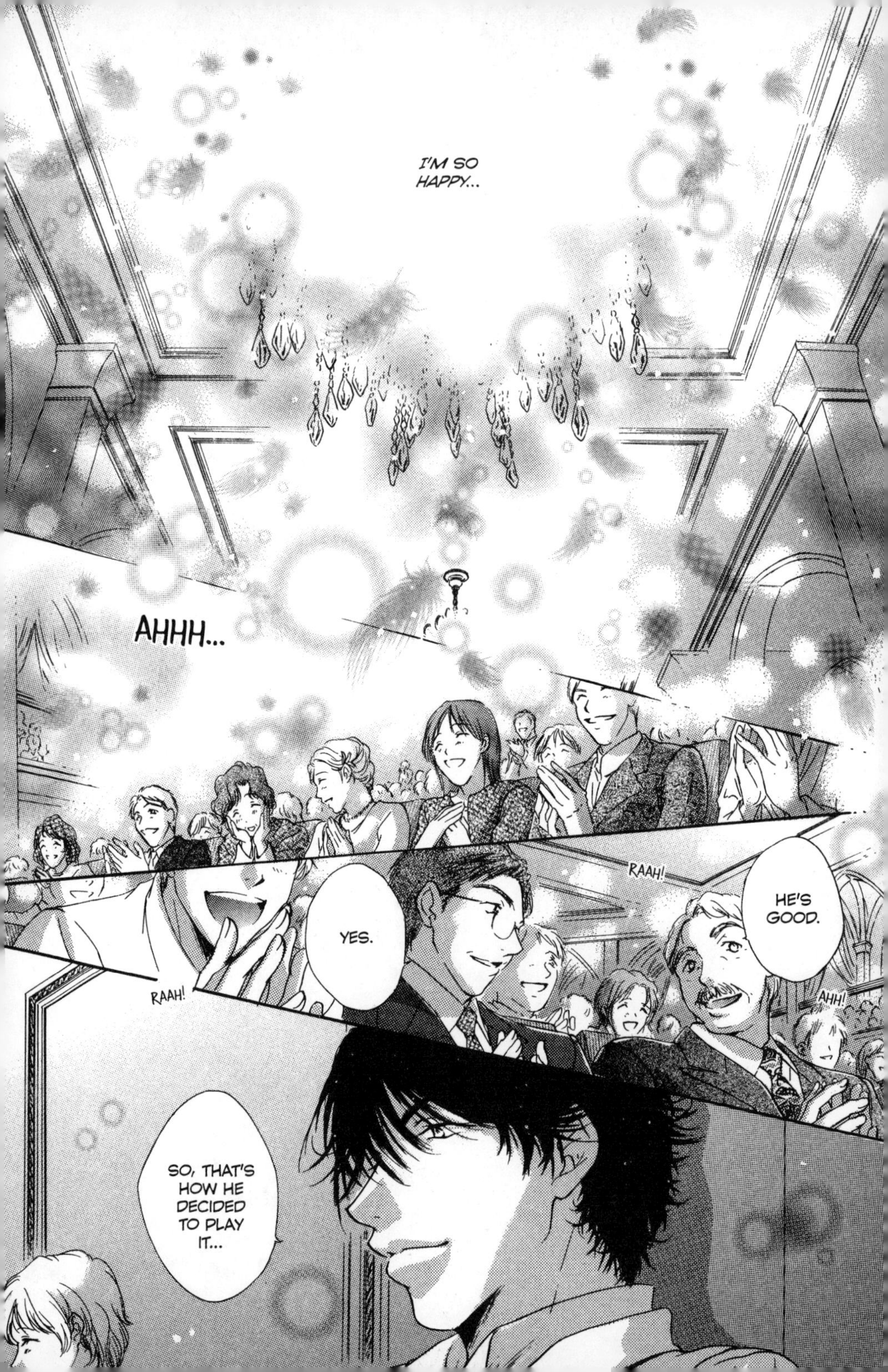
I'M SO HAPPY...
AHHH...
RAAH!
HE'S GOOD.
AHH!
YES.
RAAH!
SO, THAT'S HOW HE DECIDED TO PLAY IT...

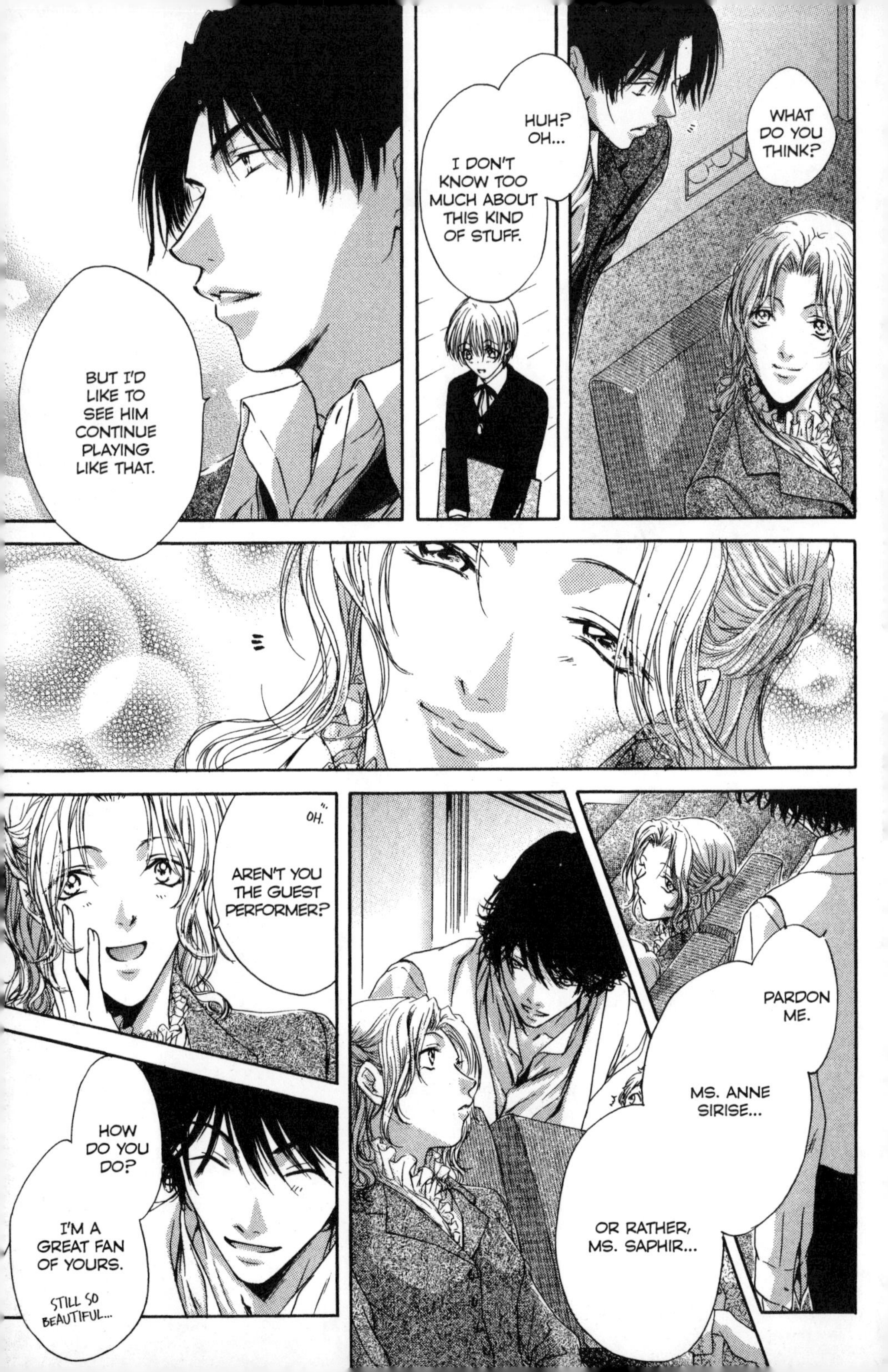
WHAT DO YOU THINK?
HUH? OH...
I DON'T KNOW TOO MUCH ABOUT THIS KIND OF STUFF.
BUT I'D LIKE TO SEE HIM CONTINUE PLAYING LIKE THAT.
PARDON ME.
MS. ANNE SIRISE...
OR RATHER, MS. SAPHIR...
"OH."
AREN'T YOU THE GUEST PERFORMER?
HOW DO YOU DO?
I'M A GREAT FAN OF YOURS.
STILL SO BEAUTIFUL...

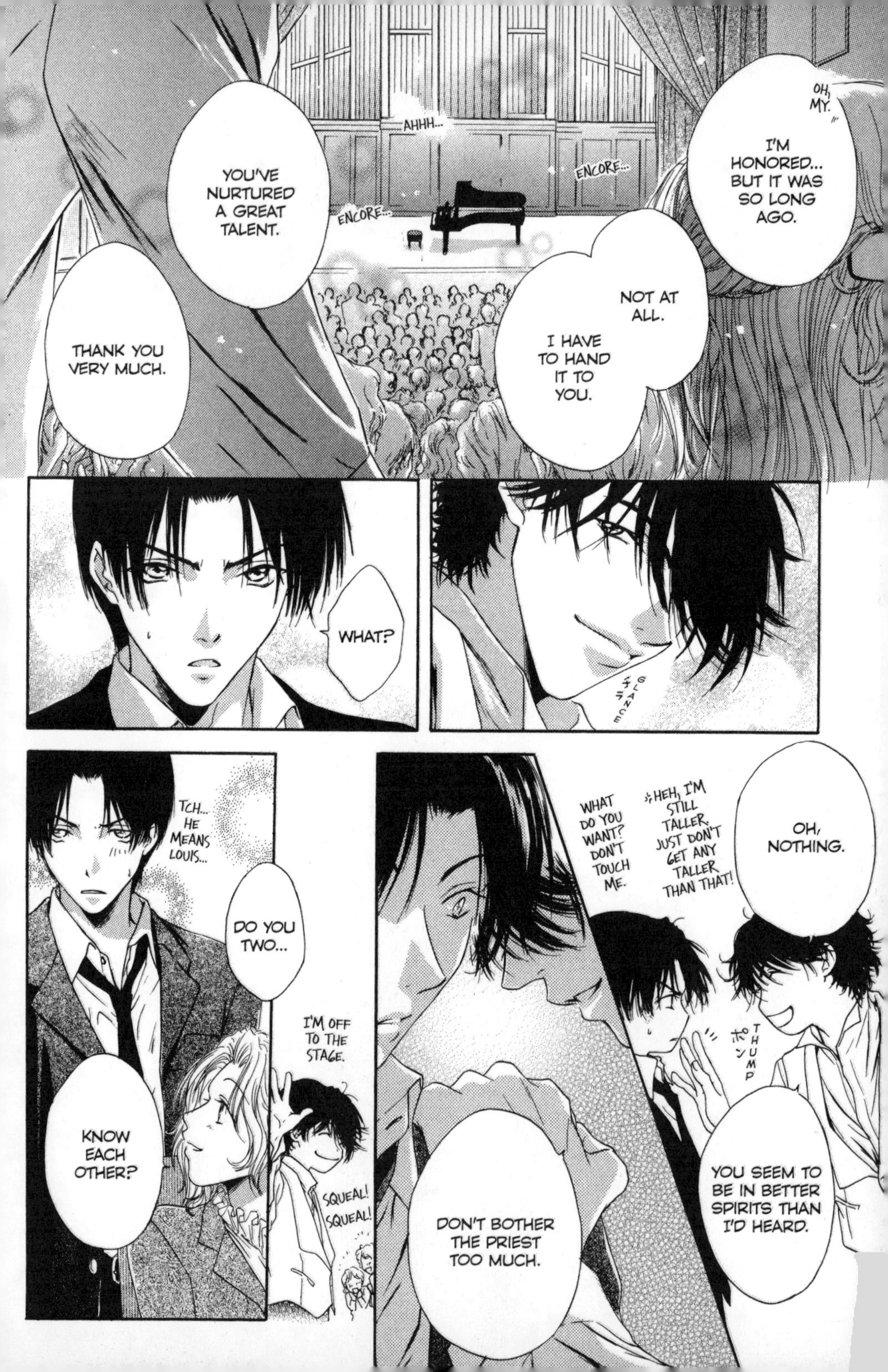
OH, MY.
I'M HONORED... BUT IT WAS SO LONG AGO.
ENCORE...
AHHH...
NOT AT ALL.
I HAVE TO HAND IT TO YOU.
YOU'VE NURTURED A GREAT TALENT.
ENCORE...
THANK YOU VERY MUCH.
GLANCE
WHAT?
OH, NOTHING.
HEH, I'M STILL TALLER. JUST DON'T GET ANY TALLER THAN THAT!
WHAT DO YOU WANT? DON'T TOUCH ME.
THUMP
YOU SEEM TO BE IN BETTER SPIRITS THAN I'D HEARD.
DON'T BOTHER THE PRIEST TOO MUCH.
TCH... HE MEANS LOUIS...
DO YOU TWO...
I'M OFF TO THE STAGE.
KNOW EACH OTHER?
SQUEAL! SQUEAL!

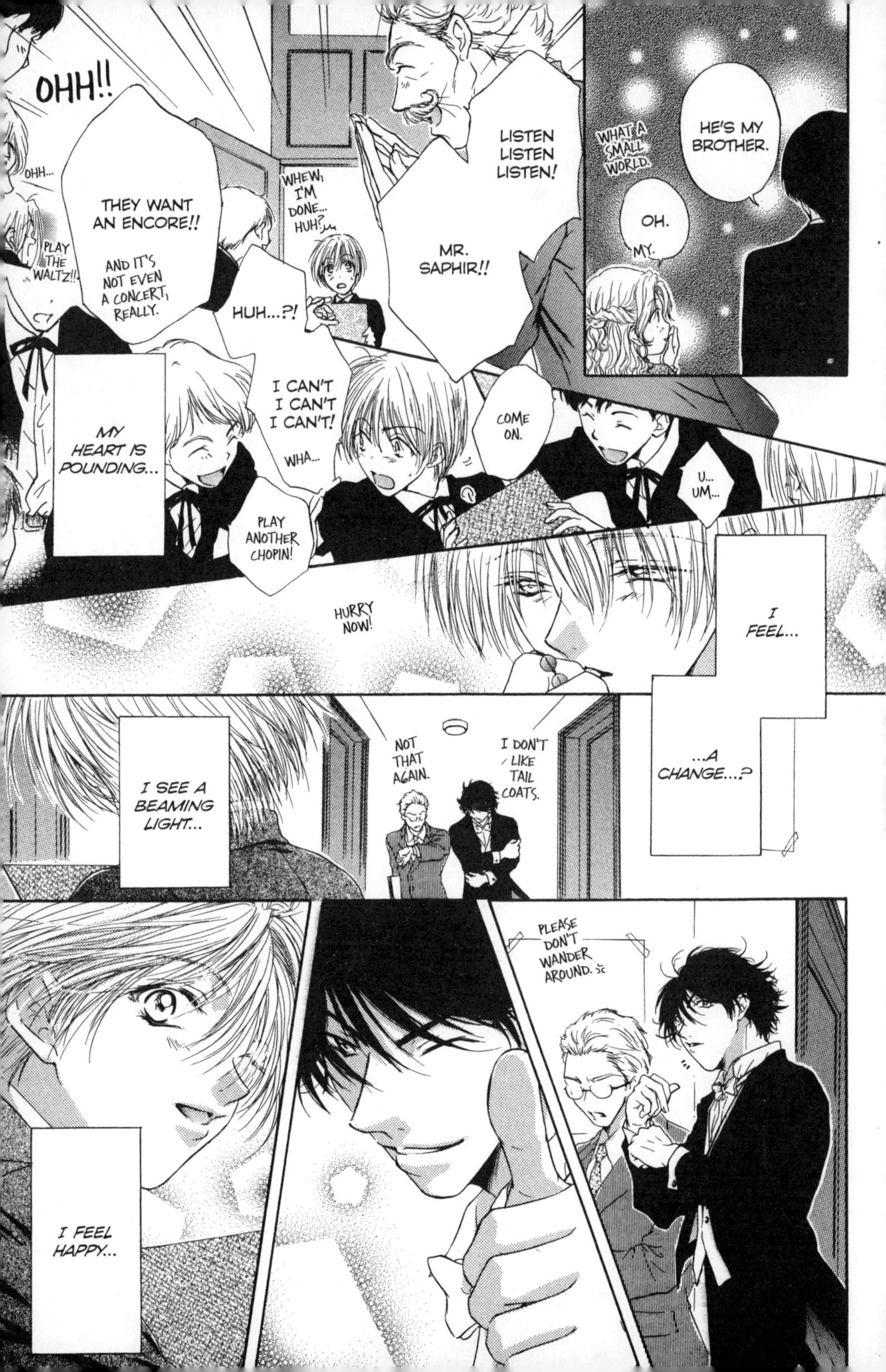

WHAT A SMALL WORLD.
HE'S MY BROTHER.
OH.
MY.
LISTEN LISTEN LISTEN!
MR. SAPHIR!!
WHEW, I'M DONE... HUH?
HUH...?!
THEY WANT AN ENCORE!!
AND IT'S NOT EVEN A CONCERT, REALLY.
OHH!!
OHH...
PLAY THE WALTZ!!
U... UM...
COME ON.
I CAN'T I CAN'T I CAN'T!
WHA...
PLAY ANOTHER CHOPIN!
MY HEART IS POUNDING...
I FEEL...
HURRY NOW!
...A CHANGE...?
I DON'T LIKE TAIL COATS.
NOT THAT AGAIN.
I SEE A BEAMING LIGHT...
PLEASE DON'T WANDER AROUND.
I FEEL HAPPY...

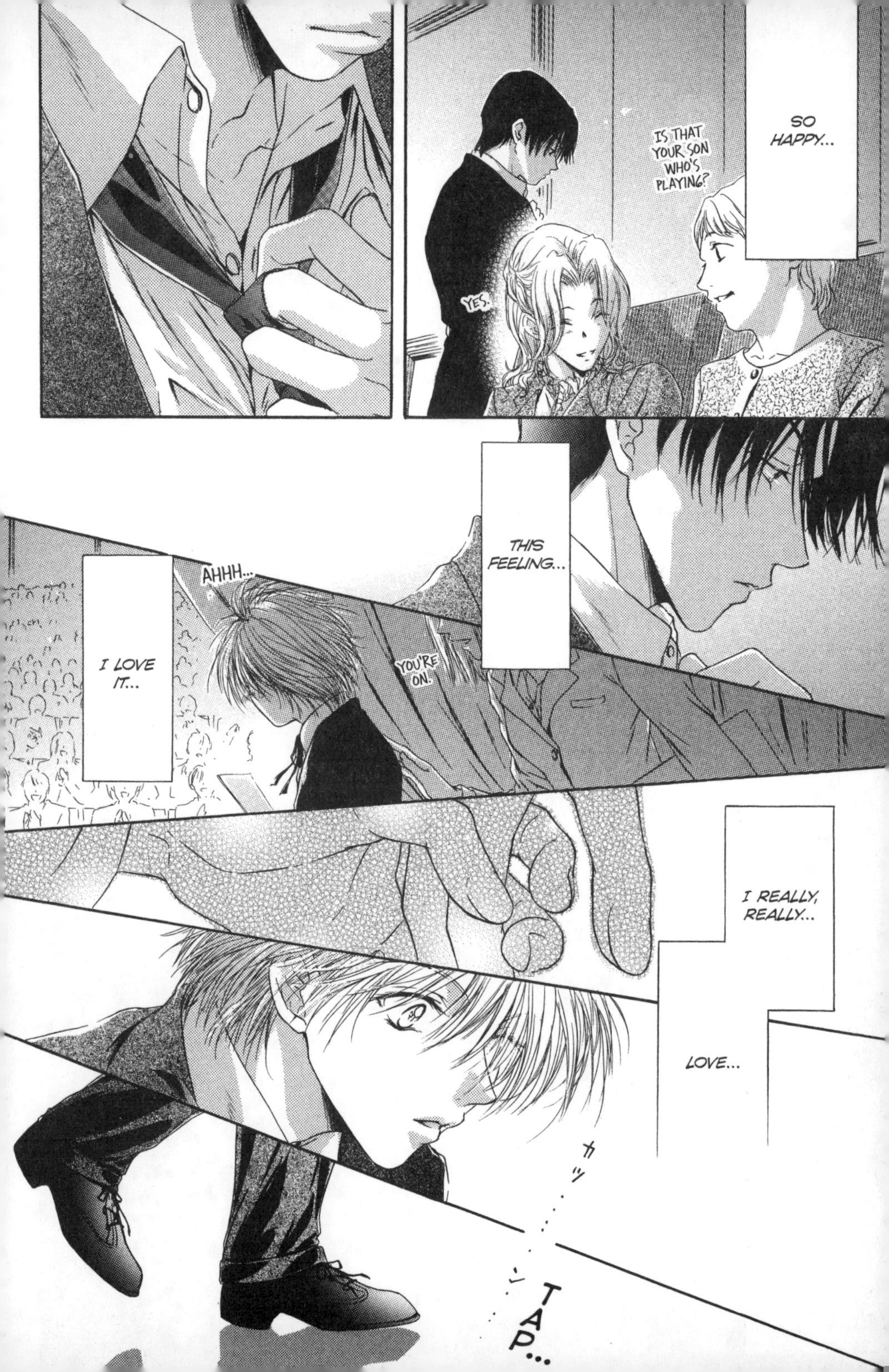
SO HAPPY...
IS THAT YOUR SON WHO'S PLAYING?
YES.
THIS FEELING...
I LOVE IT...
AHHH...
YOU'RE ON.
I REALLY, REALLY...
LOVE...
カッ
ン
TAP...

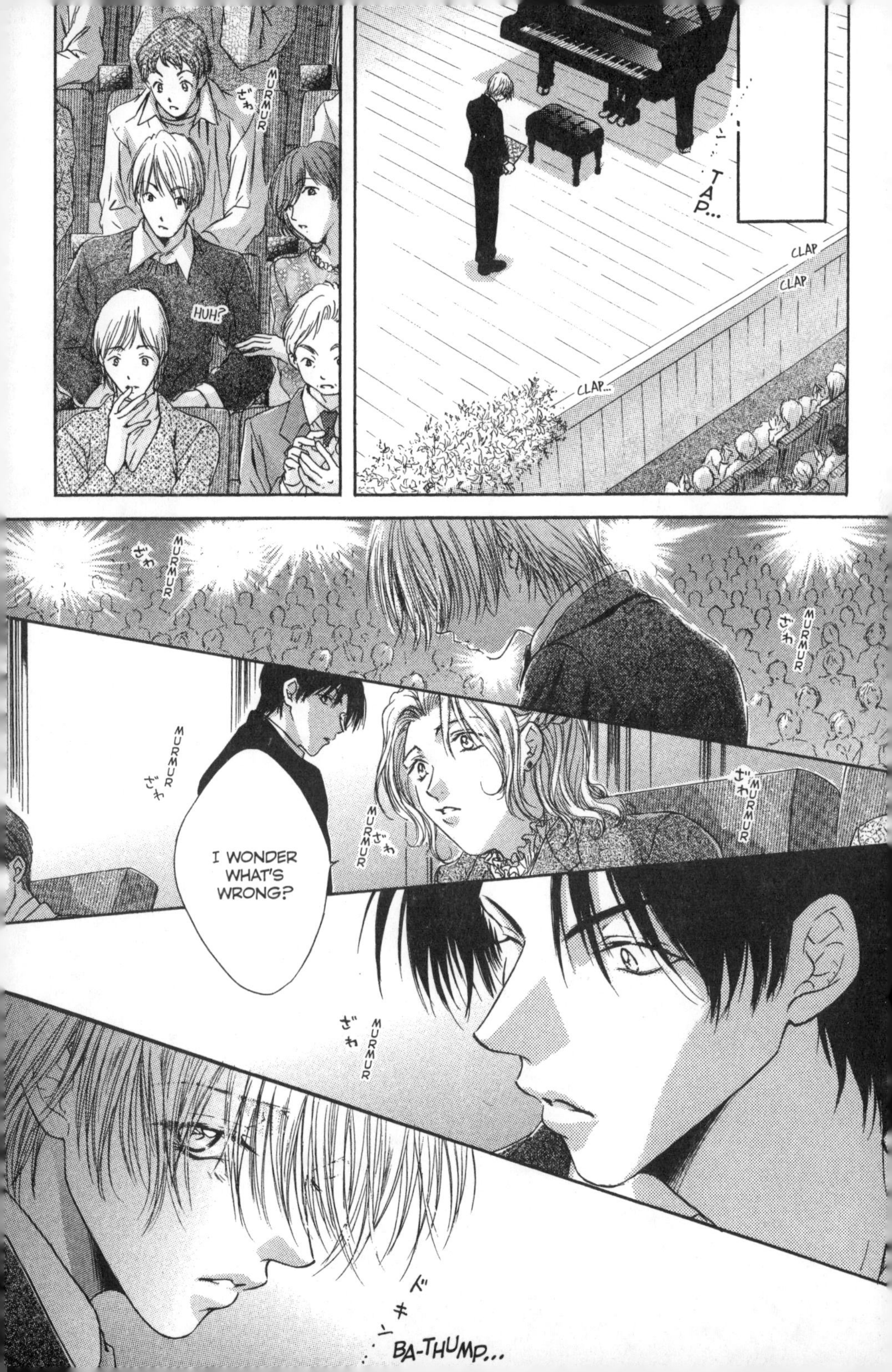
TAP...
CLAP
CLAP
CLAP...
MURMUR ざわ
HUH?
MURMUR ざわ
MURMUR ざわ
MURMUR ざわ
MURMUR ざわ
MURMUR ざわ
I WONDER WHAT'S WRONG?
MURMUR ざわ
ドキン
BA-THUMP...

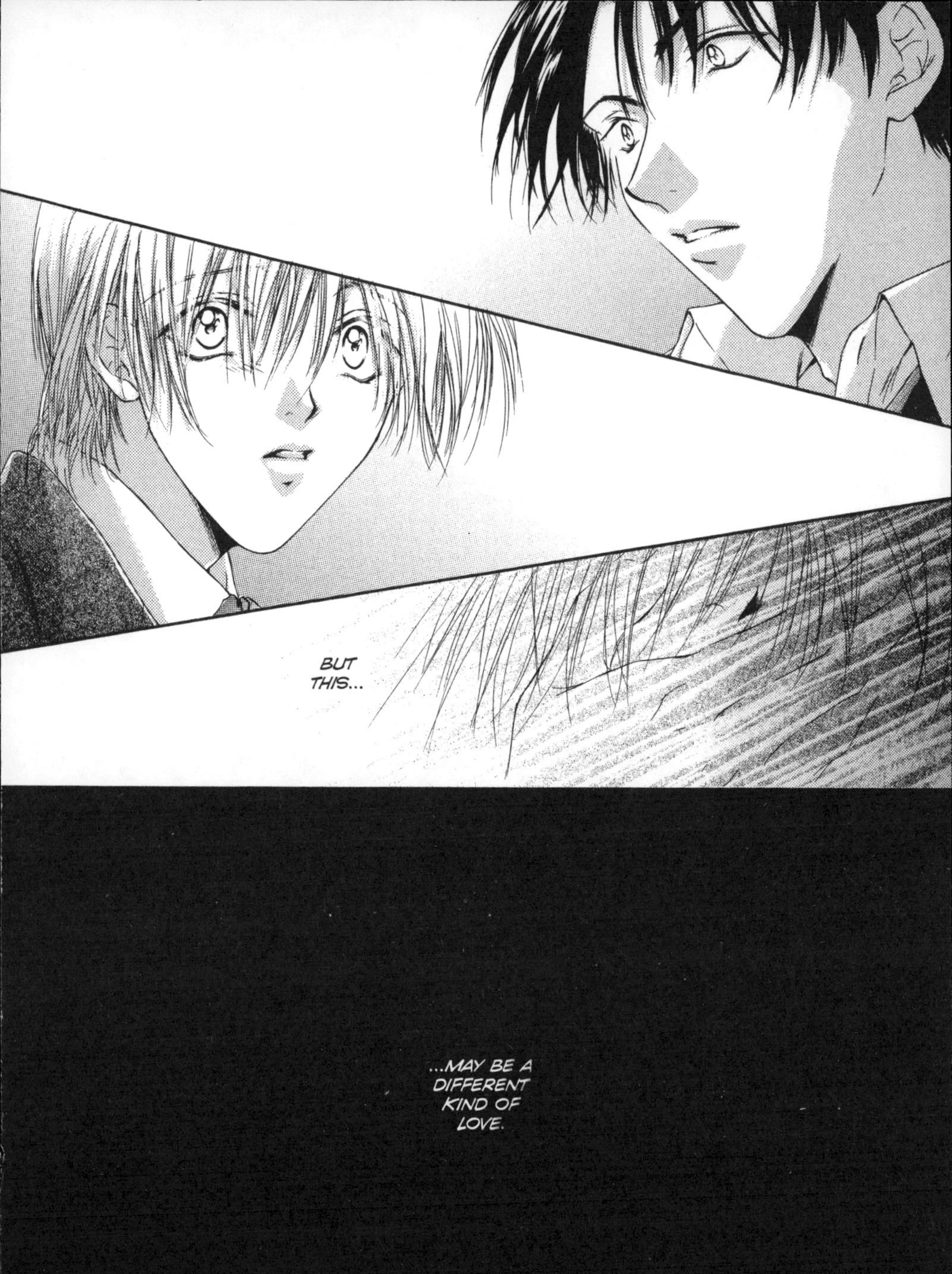
BUT THIS...
...MAY BE A DIFFERENT KIND OF LOVE.

FIVE

PROMENADE

HELLO.
THIS IS CHIGUSA KAWAI. AND THIS IS "LA ESPERANCA", VOLUME 5. YET AGAIN, A LONG TIME HAS PASSED SINCE VOLUME 4. I'M SORRY...AND YET, EVEN AS I WRITE THIS AFTERWORD, I'M NOT MAKING ANY PROGRESS ON THE ORIGINAL ARTWORK I HAVE TO DRAW FOR THESE GRAPHIC NOVEL COMPILATIONS... I'M A LITTLE WORRIED WHETHER IT'LL BE OUT BY THIS FALL... (BECAUSE, TENTATIVELY, THE SEASON IN WHICH THE EXTRA STORY IS SET IS AUTUMN. THE COVER WILL BE AUTUMN-ISH, TOO...) THE MAIN FOCUS OF THIS VOLUME IS THE ROSARY AND MOURNING. (I MAY ELABORATE ON THAT A BIT MORE, BUT...) IF YOU ENJOY IT, I'LL BE VERY HAPPY.
THE CHARACTER INTRODUCTIONS ARE SPARSE THIS TIME BECAUSE THERE WEREN'T MANY GUEST APPEARANCES... THE ONLY MAJOR ONE IS BIG BRO LAURENT. SO FOR THE REST, HERE'S A SMALL GLIMPSE AT THE VARIOUS SIDE CHARACTERS.

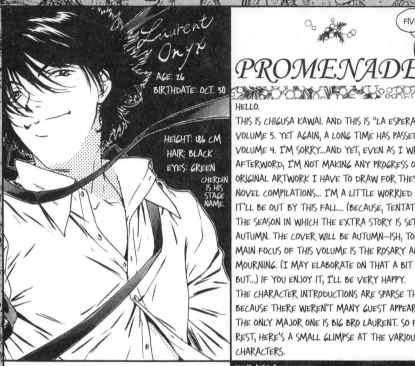

Laurent Onyx
AGE: 26
BIRTHDATE: OCT. 30
HEIGHT: 186 CM
HAIR: BLACK
EYES: GREEN
CHERDIN IS HIS STAGE NAME.

HE IS ALSO A MUSIC PAL OF GEORGIE'S.
ONE-QUARTER JAPANESE.
SOMETIMES TALKS AND ACTS FUNNY.
PLAYS THE CLARINET.
HE PLAYS THE VIOLIN. HE DOESN'T HAVE A NAME. THIS IS THE ONLY PICTURE OF HIM WITHOUT A GOOFY FACE...
Ed
(Edmond)

CHAPTER 10 – "AVE MARIA" PTS. 1, 2 + 3

→ JUST BEFORE DEADLINE, THE MANUSCRIPT FOR PT. 1 MET WITH A HORRIBLE FATE AS MY BABY NIECE WET HERSELF ON TOP OF IT.

AAAH!
W'ZZZ
I SERIOUSLY CRIED.
I KNOW - I SHOULDN'T HAVE BEEN WORKING WITH HER THERE LIKE THAT...
ROLL
ROLL
WAAH!
POOR THING...

IN PT. 2, I RAN OVER ROBERT'S FACE WITH MY CHAIR. PT. 3 WAS...SOMEHOW SPARED.
THIS CHAPTER MET WITH A LOT OF MISFORTUNE...AND JOSH RETURNS! HE'S BACK TO STIR THINGS UP. TO READ MORE ABOUT HIM, BE SURE TO CHECK OUT VOLUME 2!

CHAPTER 11 – "THE WATCH"

→ THIS IS MOSTLY A SIDE-STORY, FEATURING ALAIN. A LOT OF PEOPLE TOLD ME THEIR IMAGE OF HIM CHANGED GREATLY AFTER THIS. HEH HEH. IT'S A STORY OF ONE DAY IN HIS LIFE, FROM MORNING TO EVENING. THEN THERE'S FREDDY WITH HIS CELLO CASE. (LAUGH) PLEASE DON'T YELL, "USE A SHOULDER STRAP!" AT HIM. HE'S JUST VERY PROTECTIVE OF HIS CELLO. (ACTUALLY, I ONLY DREW HIM LIKE THAT BECAUSE HE LOOKED SO CUTE.)

CHAPTER 12 – "THE ANGEL'S POLONAISE" PTS. 1, 2 & 3

→ AN UNUSUALLY LONG CHAPTER TITLE. A STORY ABOUT THE SCHOOL FAIR AND MUSIC FESTIVAL. THE MUSIC GEORGES PLAYS IN THE RECITAL IS A SUPER DIFFICULT PIECE OF CHOPIN'S, CALLED THE "HEROIC" POLONAISE (NO.6 IN A-FLAT MAJOR, OP.53). IT'S A FAMOUS PIECE, VERY ELEGANT AND BEAUTIFUL, SO I'M SURE EVERYONE'S HEARD IT AT LEAST ONCE. AND OH, THAT'S RIGHT – HENRI'S INTO PHOTOGRAPHY, SO HE'S ACTUALLY A CAMERA NUT. ALSO, BIG BROTHER LAURENT FINALLY MAKES HIS APPEARANCE. THE ONYX FAMILY'S THREE SIBLINGS – CLEARED! ACTUALLY, AT FIRST I HAD PLANNED FOR HIM TO APPEAR WITHOUT ANY DIALOG, BUT IT TURNED OUT TO BE IMPOSSIBLE...HIS CHARACTER WAS JUST TOO OVERPOWERING. BY THE WAY, NONE OF THE THREE ARE RELATED BY BLOOD. ROBERT IS SLIGHTLY BIASED IN HIS VIEW OF THE TWO BROTHERS...I'D LIKE TO DRAW UP THAT STORY SOME DAY, TOO. OR SOMETHING. (THIS IS OFF-TOPIC, BUT IT'S LAURENT'S CD THAT JOSH IS LOOKING AT IN THE CHIBI-CHARACTERS ILLUSTRATION IN VOLUME 4. HE BOUGHT IT 'CUZ HE LIKED THE COVER.)

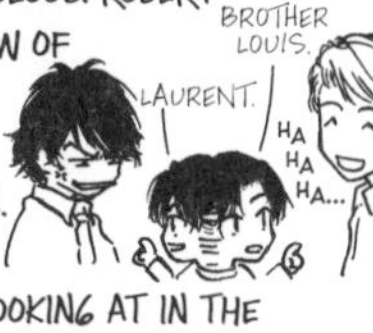
BROTHER LOUIS.
LAURENT.
HA HA HA HA...

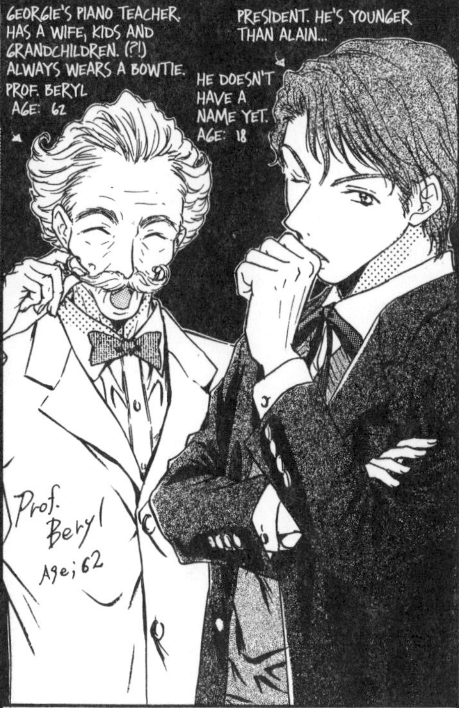
PRESIDENT. HE'S YOUNGER THAN ALAIN...
HE DOESN'T HAVE A NAME YET. AGE: 18
GEORGIE'S PIANO TEACHER. HAS A WIFE, KIDS AND GRANDCHILDREN. (?!) ALWAYS WEARS A BOWTIE.
PROF. BERYL AGE: 62
Prof. Beryl Age; 62

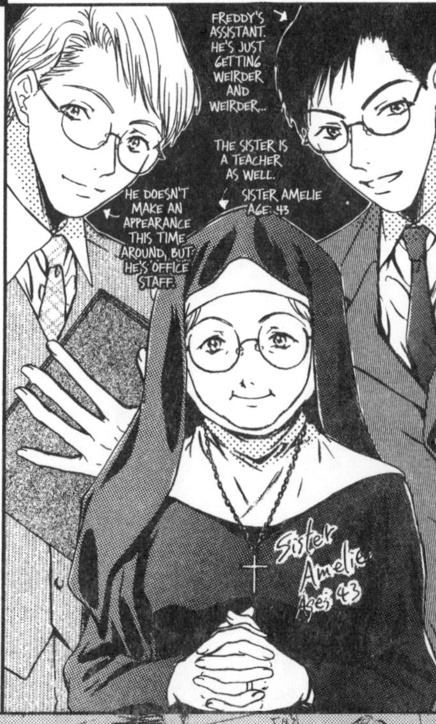
FREDDY'S ASSISTANT. HE'S JUST GETTING WEIRDER AND WEIRDER...
HE DOESN'T MAKE AN APPEARANCE THIS TIME AROUND, BUT HE'S OFFICE STAFF.
THE SISTER IS A TEACHER AS WELL.
SISTER AMELIE AGE: 43
Sister Amelie Age; 43

WHEN "THE ANGEL'S POLONAISE" RAN IN THE MAGAZINE, MUSICAL TERMS WERE WRITTEN AS SUB-SUBTITLES ON THE TITLE PAGE. (THEY'VE BEEN REMOVED FOR THIS GRAPHIC NOVEL COMPILATION, THOUGH.) THEY INDICATED THE THREE PASSAGES OF MUSIC THAT GEORGES EXPERIENCES – THAT WAS THE IMAGE I HAD.

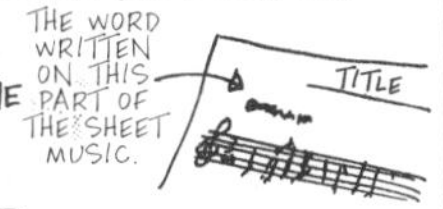
THE WORD WRITTEN ON THIS PART OF THE SHEET MUSIC.
TITLE

PART 1 RAUSCHEND (STIRRINGLY), PART 2 SCIOLTAMENTE (FREELY, WITH ABANDON), PART 3 TENERAMENTE (TENDERLY, WITH LOVE) ARE THE MEANINGS. BUT FOR ALL THAT, THE ENDING ISN'T QUITE PEACEFUL, THOUGH...HA HA HA. NO, I WANT THEM TO END UP HAPPY. REALLY. BECAUSE THEY'RE MY CHILDREN. BUT I GUESS I'LL HAVE THEM TOUGH IT OUT A LITTLE BIT MORE. OKAY?

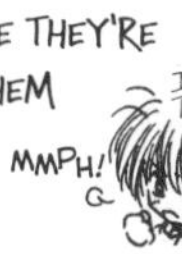
I'LL TRY!
MMPH!
YEAAH!!

WELL THEN, THANK YOU VERY MUCH FOR READING. SEE YOU AGAIN.
'04 SUMMER
IT'S SO HOT!!

Chigusa Kawai
CHIGUSA KAWAI

SPECIAL THANKS TO OCHI-SAMA.

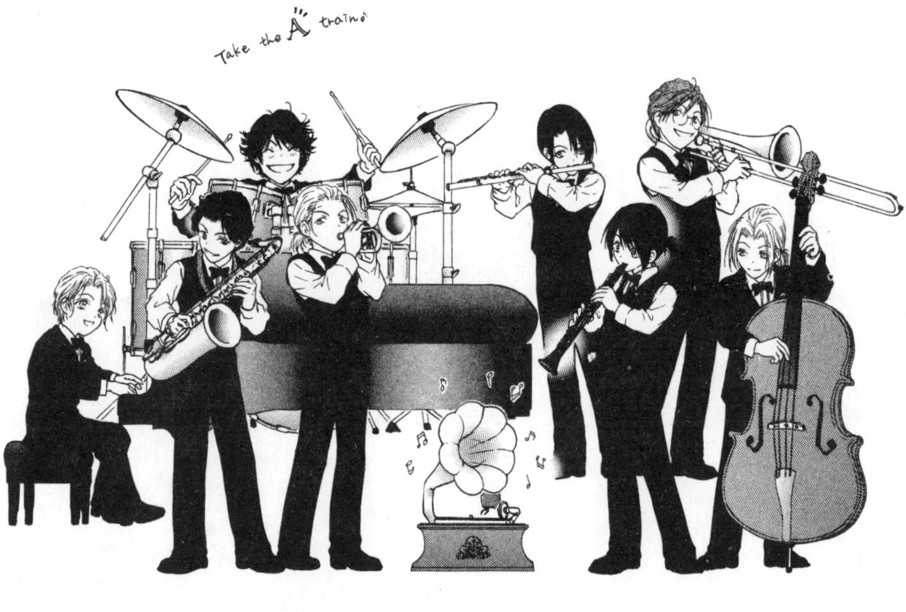
Take the A train

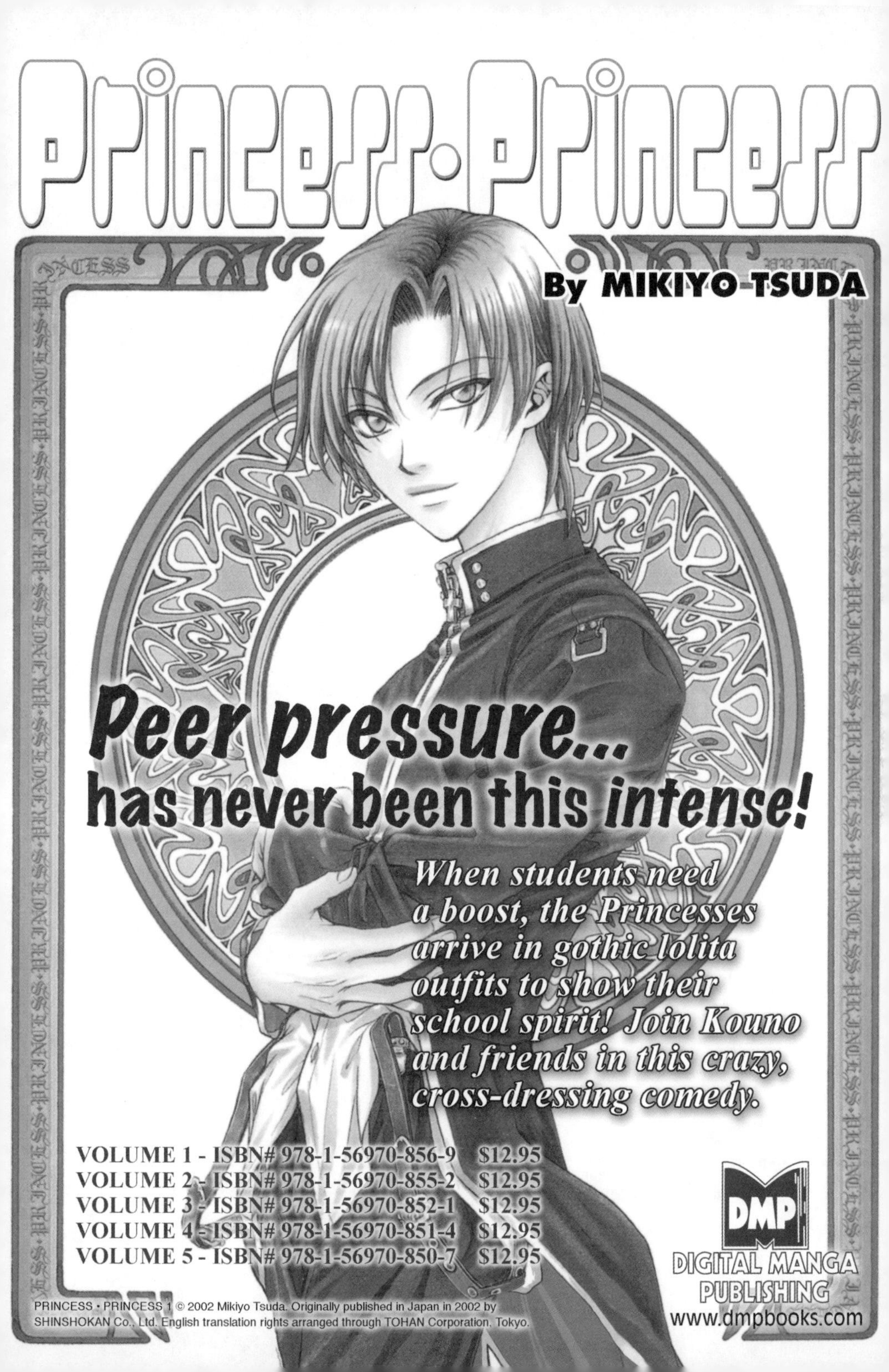
Princess · Princess
By MIKIYO TSUDA
Peer pressure...
has never been this intense!
When students need a boost, the Princesses arrive in gothic lolita outfits to show their school spirit! Join Kouno and friends in this crazy, cross-dressing comedy.
VOLUME 1 - ISBN# 978-1-56970-856-9 $12.95
VOLUME 2 - ISBN# 978-1-56970-855-2 $12.95
VOLUME 3 - ISBN# 978-1-56970-852-1 $12.95
VOLUME 4 - ISBN# 978-1-56970-851-4 $12.95
VOLUME 5 - ISBN# 978-1-56970-850-7 $12.95
DMP
DIGITAL MANGA PUBLISHING
www.dmpbooks.com
PRINCESS • PRINCESS 1 © 2002 Mikiyo Tsuda. Originally published in Japan in 2002 by SHINSHOKAN Co., Ltd. English translation rights arranged through TOHAN Corporation, Tokyo.

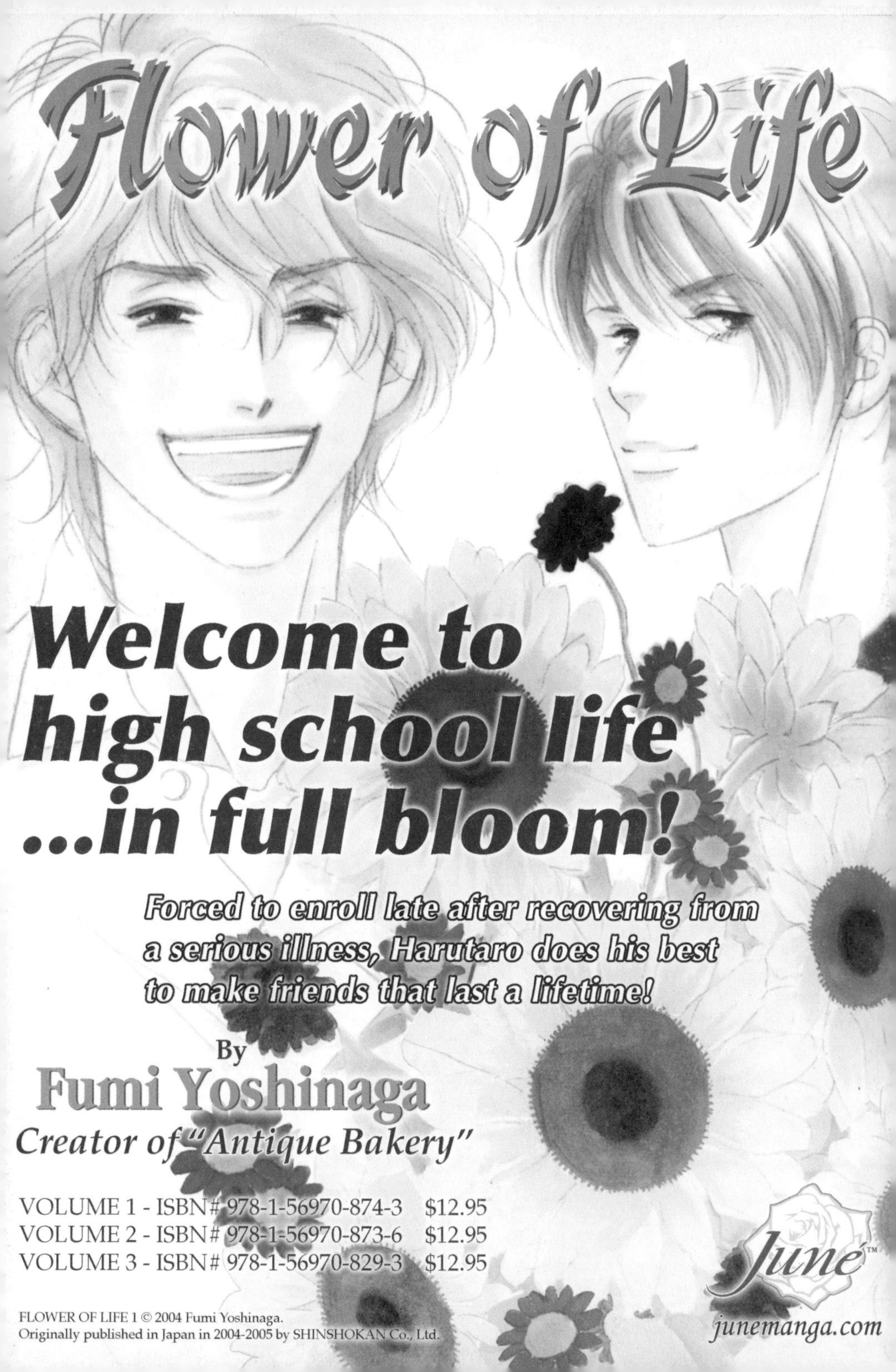
Flower of Life
Welcome to high school life ...in full bloom!
Forced to enroll late after recovering from a serious illness, Harutaro does his best to make friends that last a lifetime!
By
Fumi Yoshinaga
Creator of "Antique Bakery"
VOLUME 1 - ISBN# 978-1-56970-874-3 $12.95
VOLUME 2 - ISBN# 978-1-56970-873-6 $12.95
VOLUME 3 - ISBN# 978-1-56970-829-3 $12.95
June™
junemanga.com
FLOWER OF LIFE 1 © 2004 Fumi Yoshinaga.
Originally published in Japan in 2004-2005 by SHINSHOKAN Co., Ltd.

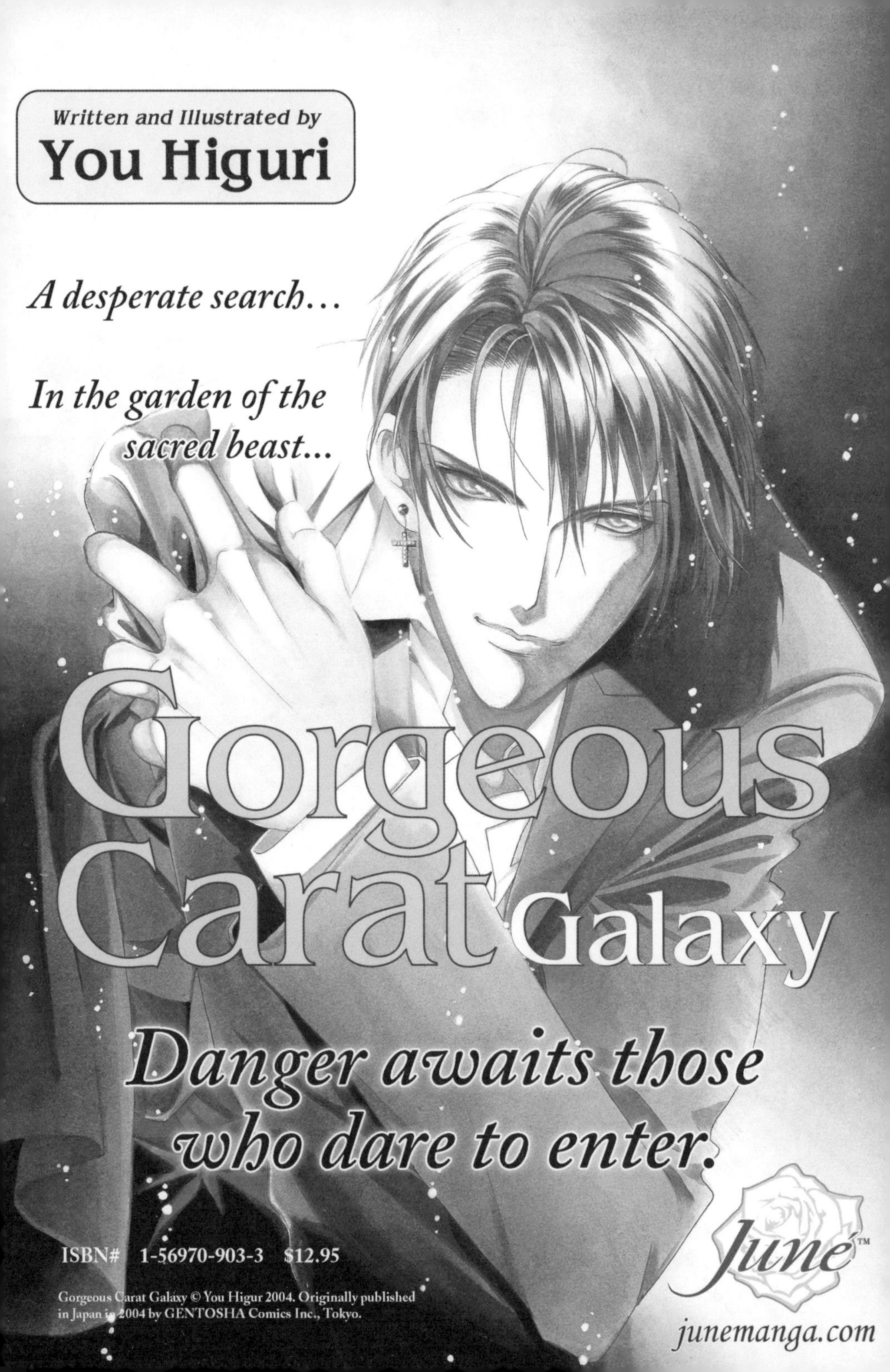
Written and Illustrated by
You Higuri
A desperate search…
In the garden of the sacred beast…
Gorgeous Carat Galaxy
Danger awaits those who dare to enter.
ISBN# 1-56970-903-3 $12.95
Gorgeous Carat Galaxy © You Higur 2004. Originally published in Japan in 2004 by GENTOSHA Comics Inc., Tokyo.
June™
junemanga.com

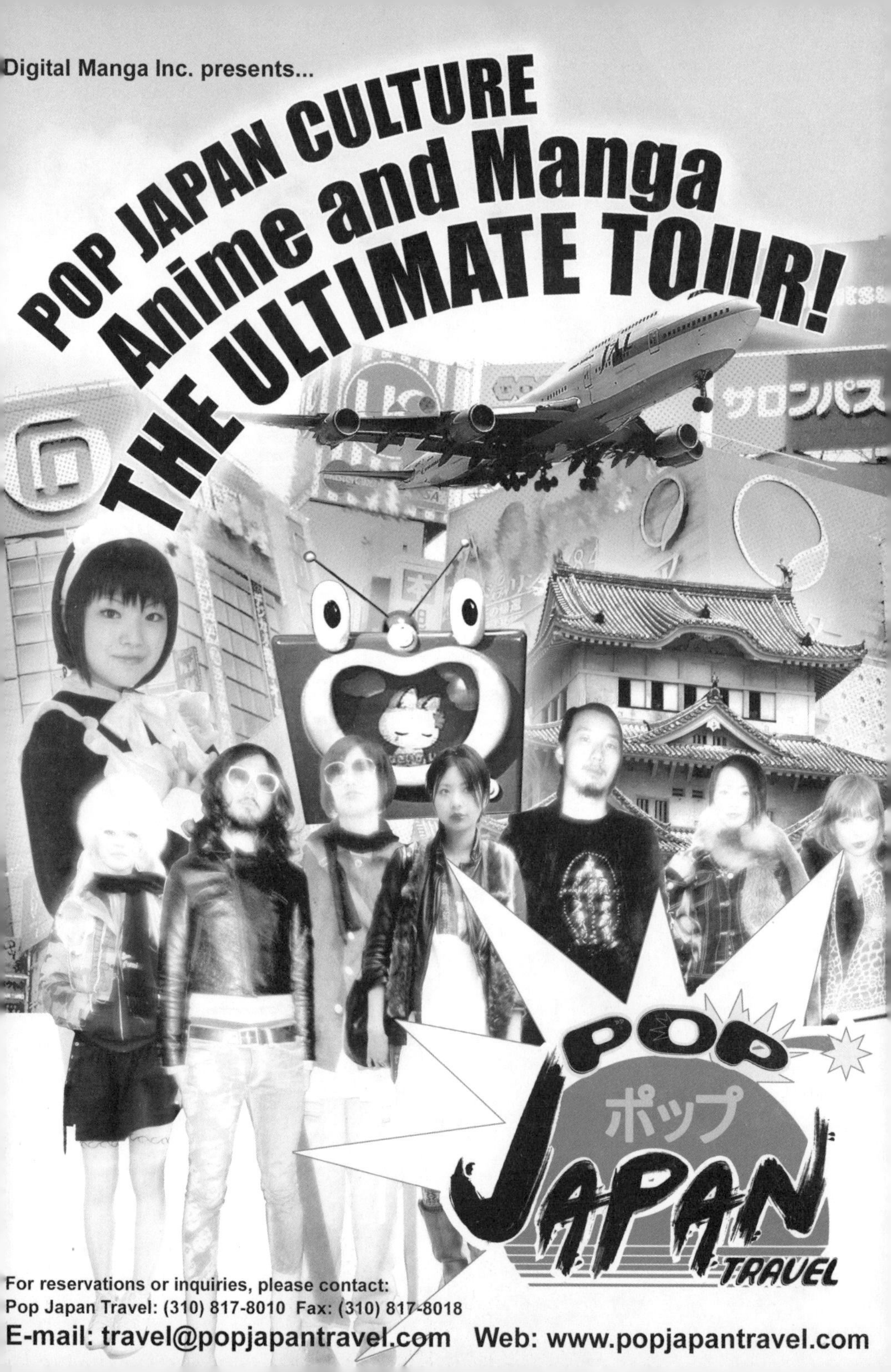
Digital Manga Inc. presents...
POP JAPAN CULTURE
Anime and Manga
THE ULTIMATE TOUR!
サロンパス
POP
ポップ
JAPAN
TRAVEL
For reservations or inquiries, please contact:
Pop Japan Travel: (310) 817-8010 Fax: (310) 817-8018
E-mail: travel@popjapantravel.com Web: www.popjapantravel.com

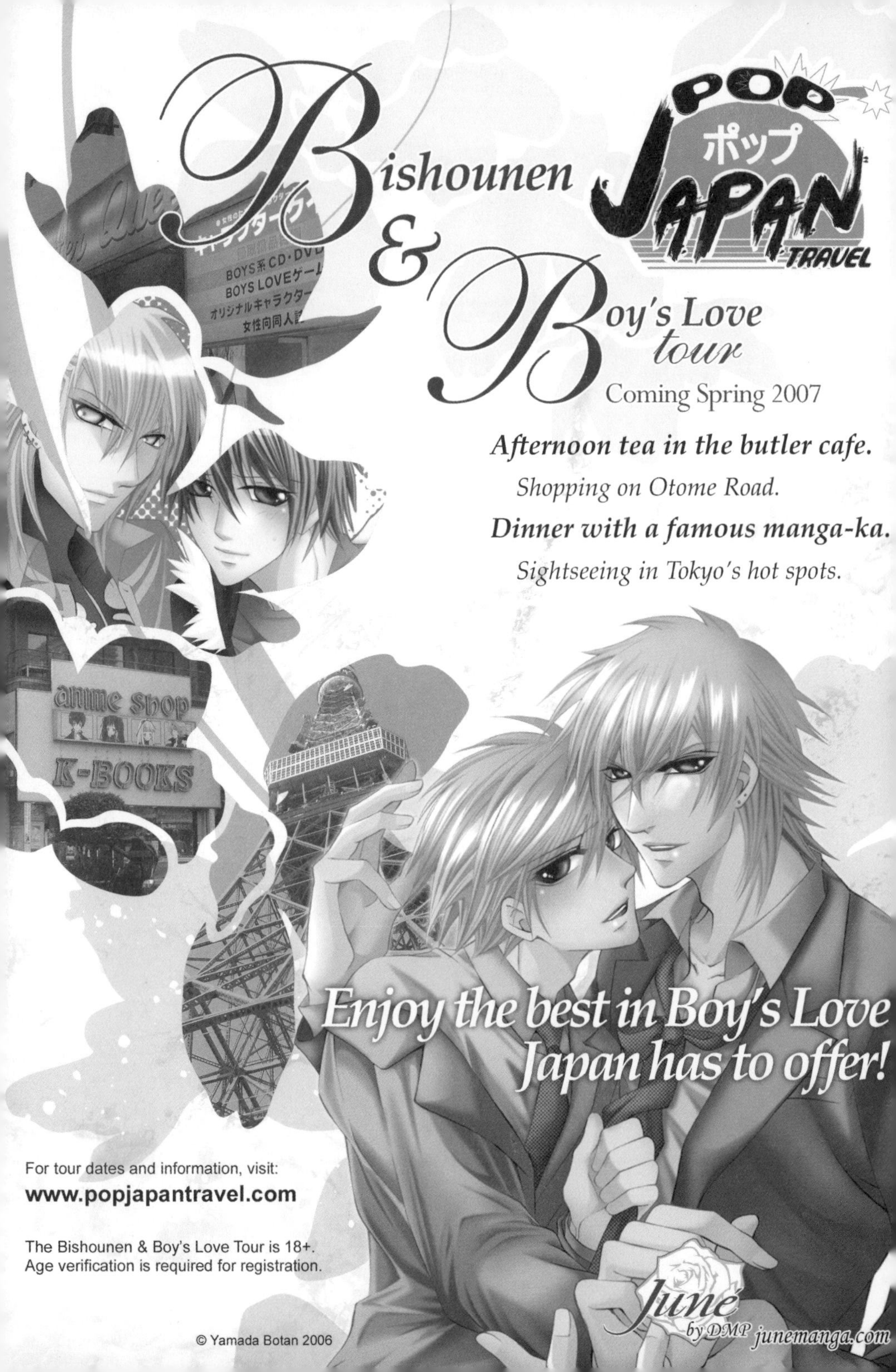

Bishounen & Boy's Love tour
POP ポップ JAPAN TRAVEL
Coming Spring 2007
Afternoon tea in the butler cafe.
Shopping on Otome Road.
Dinner with a famous manga-ka.
Sightseeing in Tokyo's hot spots.
anime shop
K-BOOKS
Enjoy the best in Boy's Love Japan has to offer!
For tour dates and information, visit:
www.popjapantravel.com
The Bishounen & Boy's Love Tour is 18+.
Age verification is required for registration.
Juné by DMP junemanga.com
© Yamada Botan 2006

STOP

This is the back of the book! Start from the other side.

***NATIVE MANGA* readers read manga from *right to left*.**

1
2
1
3
2
3
5
4
4
6
5
8
7
6

*If you run into our **Native Manga** logo on any of our books... you'll know that this manga is published in it's true original native Japanese right to left reading format, as it was intended. Turn to the other side of the book and start reading from right to left, top to bottom.*

Follow the diagram to see how its done.
Surf's Up!

NATIVE MANGA
READ RIGHT TO LEFT